CAMBRIDGE LATIN AMERICAN STUDIES

GENERAL EDITOR
MALCOLM DEAS

ADVISORY COMMITTEE
WERNER BAER   MARVIN BERNSTEIN
RAFAEL SEGOVIA

34

FROM DESSALINES TO DUVALIER

From Dessalines to Duvalier

Race, Colour and National Independence in Haiti

DAVID NICHOLLS

CAMBRIDGE UNIVERSITY PRESS

CAMBRIDGE

LONDON   NEW YORK   NEW ROCHELLE
MELBOURNE   SYDNEY

Published by the Press Syndicate of the University of Cambridge
The Pitt Building, Trumpington Street, Cambridge CB2 1RP
32 East 57th Street, New York, NY 10022, USA
296 Beaconsfield Parade, Middle Park, Melbourne 3206, Australia

First published 1979

Printed in the United States of America
Typeset by Ward Partnership, Widdington, Essex
Printed and bound by Vail-Ballou Press, Inc., Binghamton, New York

Library of Congress Cataloguing in Publication Data

Nicholls, David, 1936–

From Dessalines to Duvalier.

(Cambridge Latin American studies; no. 34)

Bibliography: p.

Includes index.

1. Haiti – History. 2. Haiti – Race relations.
3. Haiti – politics and government. I. Title.
II. Series.
F1921.N58   972.94'06   78-27271
ISBN 0 521 22177 3

In memory of Mam
who loved people and books
and taught me to

Contents

Preface

The present volume is the result of ten years' work on Haitian history and politics. It deals with the role played by ideas of race and colour in the period of national independence. These are not, of course, the only significant variables and there is a danger in singling them out. When I returned to England after having spent several weeks at the house of a Haitian friend, I wrote to tell him that I had left behind my toothbrush and one or two other items. In his reply he told me that I had also left my *lunettes bicouleures* with which I view the Haitian past. I will undoubtedly be criticised by some for having worn these glasses during the writing of this book and for having in consequence presented an unbalanced picture. It has been central to my thesis that divisions closely connected with colour have been one of the principal reasons why Haiti has failed to maintain an effective independence. It is not the only reason, but I hope I have shown in the body of the book that colour has played a major role in Haitian politics from Dessalines to Duvalier. With respect to the idea of race the same might be said, and I believe that the claims I make about the importance of race, particularly in the nineteenth century, are substantiated in the following chapters.

I wish to thank a number of institutions for financial assistance: I am grateful to Alister MacIntyre and the Institute of Social and Economic Research (Jamaica), to Hugh Tinker and the Institute of Race Relations (London), to Kenneth Kirkwood and the Race Relations Unit (Oxford) and to the Rector and Fellows of Exeter College, Oxford. Also I wish to thank Roger Gaillard, Hervé Boyer, Roger Désir, Jules Blanchet and other Haitian friends who have helped me to understand something of their country. I should particularly mention Leslie Manigat, whose ideas I do not always share, but who is invariably imaginative and stimulating in person and in print. Thanks are also due to Henock Trouillot, director of the Archives Nationales in Port-au-Prince, for his unintended kindness in refusing to allow me access to the archives. If he had, I would probably have been faced with such daunting practical problems that this book might never have been finished. The book has benefited from the criticisms and suggestions of Malcolm Cross, David Geggus, Walker Connor and Malcolm Deas, the editor of this series. I should also thank the librarians of the institutions mentioned in the bibliographical note, notably Frère Lucien of St Louis de Gonzague, to whose vigilance and dedication generations of scholars are indebted. I am grateful to Bess Leach for having typed and retyped a considerable part of the MS.

Littlemore   *David Nicholls*

Chapter 2 is based on Nicholls, 'Race, couleur et indépendance en Haïti', *Revue d'Histoire Moderne et Contemporaine*, April–June 1978, and part of chapter 3 is based on Nicholls, 'A work of combat: mulatto historians and the Haitian past, 1847–1867', *Journal of Interamerican Studies*, February 1974.

Note on terminology

The name *Ayti* is used to refer to the whole island in pre-Columbian times. *Hispaniola* (*Española*) is the name given to the whole island by the Spanish. *Saint Domingue* refers to the French colony existing on the western third of the island from 1697 to 1803. *Santo Domingo* is the name given to the eastern part of the island during the period of Spanish colonial rule (1697–1821 and 1861–5). *Santo Domingo* is also the name of the capital of the eastern part of the island, but it should be clear from the context which entity is being referred to; the city was called *Ciudad Trujillo* from 1936 to 1961. *Haiti* is the independent republic consisting substantially of the former French colony of Saint Domingue, but also including the eastern part of the island from 1822 to 1844. *The Dominican Republic* is the independent state consisting substantially of the former Spanish colony, existing from 1844 to 1861 and from 1865 to the present.

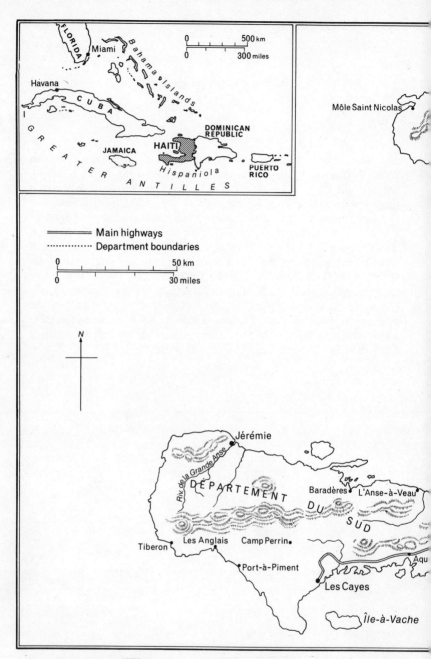

Note: The number of departments and their boundaries have changed frequently. The map shows the position in 1956. The constitution of 1957 created four additional departments.

1. Introduction

Ideas of race, colour and national independence have played a central role in the history of Haiti. Independence was declared and maintained by men who saw Haiti as a symbol of redemption for the whole African race. Independence, however, has continually been threatened by deep divisions in the population, closely connected to colour distinctions. No one who is at all familiar with the history of Haiti can fail to see how hostility between blacks and mulattoes has frequently opened the way to foreign intervention in the affairs of the country. How is it that racial pride should have been among the principal causes of Haitian independence, while colour prejudice should have been one of the chief factors undermining this independence? If this colour prejudice developed out of the racialism of colonial Saint Domingue, how is it that one idea has acted upon Haitians as a centripetal force, while the effect of the other has been centrifugal?

It is thus crucial to the argument of the present book that a distinction be maintained between ideas of race and colour.[1] The term 'race' will be used to refer to a set of persons who regard themselves and are generally regarded as being connected in some significant way by extrafamilial common descent. It is therefore a concept which is not essentially 'objective' in its reference;[2] it depends rather upon people's beliefs and assumptions that the race to which they see themselves belonging is genetically distinct from other races in some important way. The importance may stem from the fact that *others* ascribe importance to common descent and justify discrimination on this ground, or it may stem from members of the race themselves believing that they differ significantly from other races. In the Caribbean white racialism has tended to be of this second kind with respect to those whom Europeans regard as belonging to the African or black race. As we shall see, in colonial Saint Domingue most whites regarded all those who had any non-white 'blood', going back seven generations, as belonging to the black race, whatever their colour, and as sharing in the acquired or innate inferiority of that race. Non-whites were thus lumped together for certain purposes and were discriminated against in a number of ways. The racialism or racial consciousness of the non-whites was, however, of the first kind distinguished above: almost all black and coloured Haitians accepted the fact that they belonged to the black or

1

African race – that biologically they shared a common descent. They denied the *objective* significance of this fact, and vehemently argued that the various human races were equal and differed in no important respect. Yet they fully recognised the fact that others saw significance in racial differences and their racial consciousness stemmed from this recognition and from a determination to combat theories of racial inequality; they wished to demonstrate the capacity of members of the black race to achieve progress and to build a civilised community, according to European standards, which they accepted as being of universal application. Race was throughout the nineteenth century a uniting factor among Haitians.

African racialism in Haiti, and in the Caribbean generally, can, however, be seen to have undergone a transformation in the twentieth century. Many Haitian intellectuals in the period of the United States occupation of Haiti (1915–34) began to assert an inherent and significant difference between the races. Their racialism became that of the second type distinguished above. These men, most of them black, though there were also some mulattoes among them, asserted that members of the black race shared a common psychology (acquired or innate), that their social mores were different from those of whites, that they should therefore cease to accept European standards and should develop a specifically African way of living. This *négritude* doctrine was fiercely resisted by other Haitians, mostly among the mulatto elite, and race became a divisive factor in Haiti, generally reinforcing the colour divisions.

In this work the term 'colour' will refer to phenotypical or somatic characteristics, specifically to skin colour, type of hair, nose and lips. I shall frequently speak of two colour groups, blacks and mulattoes. Although this classification has a basis in objective phenotypical differences, anyone who knows the Caribbean will be aware that from this purely objective standpoint there is a category of persons in the middle, whom it is difficult to place. Nor is it simply a question of a continuum from black to near-white, for there are many persons, for example, who have dark skin but whose facial features are of a European type.[3] I use the terms 'black' (*noir*) and 'mulatto' (*mulâtre* or *jaune* in French) partly because Haitians themselves frequently use them, and they see them as constituting a significant distinction.[4] Those of indeterminate appearance are often sorted out according to their family background or economic status; as the Brazilians say, 'money lightens'. There are indeed occasions on which Haitians themselves cannot agree on whether to call a man black or mulatto. Léon Laleau recalls a discussion with President Sténio Vincent on whether a particular Haitian was black; eventually the president clinched the argument: 'Of course he was black, he looked just like President T. S. Sam.'

I

Racial unity

The declaration of independence at Gonaïves on 1 January 1804 had for Haitians and for foreign observers, friendly and hostile, a significance which was far greater than the immediate consequences of the event would warrant. Certainly Saint Domingue had been at the time of the French revolution one of the most profitable colonies in the world and had played an important part in the economic life of eighteenth-century France; the loss of such a colony was bound to have economic and political consequences for the metropolitan power. The defeat of the French army in 1803 put an effective end to Napoleon's ambition to create a new world empire in the Caribbean; in November of that year the French sold Louisiana to the United States. But the significance of Haitian independence was greater than this. A rebellion of the free coloured population, united to a successful slave revolt, had overthrown a white government. Haitian independence presented a radical challenge to colonialism, to slavery and to the associated ideology of white racialism. The situation was different from that in the North American colonies or in the mainland colonies of South America, where elements of the white colonial elite had led the struggle for independence. In Saint Domingue the whites, with the exception of a few Poles and Germans, fought against the revolutionary movement with all the weapons in their power. The Haitian war of independence was also, therefore, a civil war between the white residents, backed by Napoleon's army, and the mass of the population. By its very nature the war thus implied something of a *social* revolution, in a way in which the other independence movements of the hemisphere did not. The transfer of power to a new elite was the very least which victory would ensure; under Dessalines there was even the possibility of effective mass participation in the politics of the country.

Lord Acton claimed that revolutionary movements prior to the Belgian and Greek struggles of the nineteenth century resisted governments 'because they misgoverned, not because they were of a different race'.[5] Basing himself on Acton's analysis, a recent writer has suggested that 'only after 1831 does one encounter movements that were *totally* unambiguous in their linkage of ethnicity and politics'.[6] As we shall see, the very basis of the Haitian claim to independence was racial identity. The independence movement of 1803—4 was as unambiguously ethno-national as any later movement. The revolution in its early stages was certainly a protest against oppression; national independence was not the first object of the mulattoes and blacks. Toussaint's hostility to the mulattoes — his emphasis upon colour division rather than on racial unity – was not unconnected with his refusal to break with France. 'While Toussaint Louverture exists', he told Colonel Vincent, 'the colony of Saint Domingue will not become the property of the mulattoes, it will always remain an integral part of the French Republic.'[7] It was the invasion of Leclerc's army that led blacks and mulattoes once more to see themselves as belonging to a single race and as sharing a common destiny. Independence movements based upon ethnic identity have become a familiar feature of our world; anti-colonial struggles based specifically upon racial identity (rather than on other ethnic factors) have been particularly evident in the period since the end of the second world war. It may be instructive to see the Haitian experience as providing a model of post-colonial politics.

Haiti was, then, a symbol of anti-colonialism and of racial equality. Britain, Spain and other European powers with colonies in the Caribbean were apprehensive about the existence of a free black state in the region. The British hardly needed reminding by the French prime minister Villèle in 1825 that 'recognition of a Black Empire founded upon insurrection and upon the Massacre of the White Population would have a most pernicious moral Effect'.[8] European philanthropists, for their part, saw Haiti as a test case for black self-government. While supporters of slavery painted a grim picture of Haiti, citing the problems which faced the country as conclusive evidence against the wisdom of emancipation in the British colonies, philanthropists frequently under-emphasised the less pleasant aspects of life in the country. For both groups the question was an ideological one, and few Europeans could be found who took a dispassionate view of the Haitian situation.

The black and coloured population of the Caribbean colonies looked to Haiti as a 'sign of redemption'. In declaring independence Dessalines and his fellow generals had implicitly asserted the principle of racial equality. 'Through Haiti we take possession of the world', cried an anonymous writer in the *Revue des Colonies*, edited by the Martiniquan mulatto, C. A. Bissette.[9] More than a century later a fellow countryman, Aimé Césaire, mayor of Fort de France, wrote: 'Saint Domingue is the first country in our modern times to have set concretely, and offered to the thought of men – in all its racial, economic and social complexity – the great problem that the twentieth century is attempting to solve: the colonial problem.'[10] The success of the Haitians provided inspiration for negroes throughout the Caribbean during the nineteenth century; the example of their struggle against French colonialism was, according to Governor Eyre of Jamaica, 'constantly before the peasants of this country'.[11] North American blacks also looked to Haiti in the nineteenth century as a potential centre of black resistance to colonialism, slavery and oppression. James Theodore Holly believed that the emigration of negroes from the United States to Haiti would benefit 'the Negro race throughout the world', while the African Methodist Episcopal Church stated that one of the objects of its mission in Haiti was to 'aid in making the Haytian nationality and government strong, powerful and commanding among the civilized nations of the earth'.[12] Early Haitian history has inspired many imaginative writers from the 'third world', including Alejo Carpentier, Edouard Glissant and Césaire himself.[13]

This present book will, however, primarily be concerned not with foreign views of Haiti, but with how Haitians have seen themselves, and how they have understood the problems which faced them. I shall argue that Haitian writers, mulatto and black, bourgeois and middle-class, conservative and Marxist, were practically unanimous in portraying Haiti as a symbol of African regeneration and of racial equality. Mulatto intellectuals from the elite, like Beaubrun Ardouin, who in appearance could well have been taken for Europeans, proudly regarded themselves as Africans — as members of the black race. From the earliest days of independence until the present we shall note how Haitians have seen their country as the first fruit of a movement towards the freedom of black people; in matters of citizenship and property the laws of the country clearly reflected this vision. In the first constitution of the country, Haitians of whatever colour (including those Germans and Poles who had been given Haitian nationality) were designated 'black', and citizenship was open to all persons of African or Indian descent; whites were prevented from owning land, and the very term *blanc* in Haitian *créole* connotes a foreigner.[14] Even into the Duvalier era, Haitians have continued to take a special interest in the affairs of the black race throughout the world; as President Geffrard had ordered a special requiem mass at the death of John Brown in 1859, so Duvalier declared several days of national mourning after the assassination of Martin Luther King more than a hundred years later.

Haitians in the nineteenth century saw their country not merely as a symbol of black regeneration, but as an effective proof of racial equality. The black and coloured population of Saint Domingue had, on its own initiative and without positive assistance from outside, cast off the yoke of slavery and colonialism and had declared independence. J. C. Dorsainvil urged his fellow countrymen to investigate and to understand the reasons for the Haitian insistence on 'the idea of the conservation of this independence'. Frederick Douglass, the former slave who became United States minister to Haiti, remarked on the significance of independence for the Haitian people: 'There is perhaps no one point upon which the people of Hayti are more sensitive, superstitious and united, than upon any question touching the cession of any part of their territory to any foreign power.'[15] Full autonomy was regarded as being of vital importance; cultural, economic and political progress had to be achieved in order to demonstrate to the world that race does not constitute a significant difference among human beings. Legitimate pride in the achievements of the past has, however, occasionally led to an arrogant posture of superiority on the part of Haitians towards blacks of other nations. In his book *L'Afrique dans la poésie haïtienne*, Maurice Lubin has written in this vein of Haitians taking the road to Africa, 'carrying with them a little of their knowledge and competence for the benefit of the newly independent states.'[16] These African states have not always welcomed such patronising visitors.

In the field of foreign relations the racial factor has also played an important role. On the one hand Haiti has allied itself, at least symbolically, with Ethiopia and Liberia and later with the newly independent states of Africa, while on the other hand the policy of neighbouring states in the hemisphere towards the black republic has undoubtedly been influenced by racial prejudice. The United States' refusal to recognise Haitian independence until 1862 was largely determined by such prejudice, as was the failure to invite Haiti to the Panama conference of 1825. Relations between Haiti and the Dominican Republic from 1844 until the present day have, in particular, been affected by the racial issue, which has at times been raised in a quite specific manner by Dominican politicians.

As the following chapters show, an important change took place in Haitian ideas about race during the period under consideration. De Vastey and Milscent in the early years, also Janvier and Firmin later in the nineteenth century, rebutted European theories of racial inequality, insisting that there is no significant difference between the races. In the period of the United States occupation, from 1915 to 1934, however, intellectuals involved in the ethnological movement elaborated a conception of *négritude* that entailed a belief in the distinctive character of black people, which was said by some writers to be derived from biological factors. Also significant at this time was a new appreciation of Africa and of things African by a number of Haitian writers. While in the nineteenth century contemporary Africa was generally regarded by literate Haitians as a barbarous continent in need of civilisation, the ethnological movement, and the literary revival associated with it, led to a romantic admiration for the simple, unsophisticated and pure life of Africa, which was contrasted with the decadence of Europe. There was too a re-evaluation of African customs and traditions in Haiti and particularly of the Voodoo religion. The change in emphasis is well illustrated in two poems, both entitled 'Le Lambi' (the conch-shell, used by the slaves of Saint Domingue as a call to battle). The first poem, written by Jean Joseph Vilaire at the end of the nineteenth century, has no mention of Africa, but is a glorification of Haitian history; the author sees two spirits in the shell, the soul of the ocean and the soul of the heroes of independence. Claude

Fabry, however, writing in the 1930s, sees in the *lambi* first of all 'the soul of the hirsute African', and he hears the call to return to the African bush and to dance, 'ignorant, free and nude'.[17] Only very occasionally are there to be found in the writings of nineteenth-century Haitians favourable references to the Africa of their day. There are hints of this in Félix Darfour, himself born in Africa, in Beauvais Lespinasse, and even in Justin Lhérisson, who in 'Nostalgie' wrote:

Dans les sombres forêts de l'Afrique sauvage
Où, gigantesque, croît le Baobab sacré,
J'ai vécu libre, heureux, sans ces fers d'esclavage
Que le Blanc a forgés pour le noir exécré.

In the period leading up to the United States invasion occasional writers can be found who refer sympathetically to the Voodoo religion, but the Pan-African movement, led by Bénito Sylvain, while defending the interests of colonised Africans and attacking the excesses of imperialism, saw little of value in contemporary African culture.

Colour conflicts

Although the conception of Haiti as a symbol and proof of black dignity was powerful in strengthening the will to national independence, there were deep divisions among Haitians, going back to colonial times, which were to facilitate a gradual erosion of effective independence during the nineteenth century, culminating in the United States occupation. As we shall see in the second part of the present chapter, there was, during the colonial period and into the revolutionary period, considerable suspicion and hostility between the free coloured population (known as *affranchis*) and the slaves. The vast majority of the slaves were black, while the most powerful and most vocal of the *affranchis* were mulattoes. The *affranchis* were often wealthy landowners, who had a common economic interest with the whites, and who at significant stages of the revolutionary struggle allied themselves to the colonists against the slaves. After independence these predominantly mulatto *anciens libres* retained the ownership of their lands and some of them even acquired more land from their white fathers, who, before fleeing the country, transferred property to their illegitimate offspring. Thus, although the whole elite class of colonial times was eliminated with independence, a new elite of predominantly mulatto landowners was ready to take its place. This group, however, had to contend with a rival black elite some of whom had belonged to the *affranchi* caste during the colonial period, but most of whom derived their power from positions which they occupied in the revolutionary army. The black party, led first by Dessalines, then by Christophe, was determined to combat mulatto dominance. The black elite was particularly strong in the North, and in the rural areas, while the mulattoes were more powerful in the cities of the South and West, where they engaged in commerce, which they soon found to be more lucrative and less hard work than farming. A geographical factor is thus evident in the party conflicts in Haiti, strengthening the economic and colour divisions by reinforcing them.

Much of Haiti's political history in the nineteenth century is to be seen as a struggle between a mulatto, city-based, commercial elite, and a black, rural and military elite. Each party, however, needed members of the other colour in order to demonstrate that it was really a national party; in addition the mulattoes invariably required support from some black generals and often found it advisable to act behind the mask of a black puppet president, while the blacks, when in power, relied upon mulattoes to fill bureaucratic posts and to ensure a minimum of support from the business community. Nevertheless the hostility between the two groups was frequently such that each would prefer to invite foreign intervention in the affairs of Haiti than to allow its rivals to gain power. Again and again we find Haitian politicians requesting foreign military aid in exchange for offers to cede territory for a naval base, or for commercial favours. In the early part of the nineteenth century it was the British and French who were most keen to acquire privileges in Haiti; later on in the century these were gradually replaced by the United States and Germany. One British diplomat observed in 1843, with respect to 'the ill concealed hatred' between blacks and mulattoes, 'The leading men here acknowledge that the independence of the country is at stake upon this question.'[18]

I have suggested that politics in Haiti from 1804 to 1915 was largely concerned with a struggle for power between two elite groups, desig-nated principally by colour; I have also indicated that these colour divisions developed out of the 'caste' distinctions of colonial Saint Domingue. It might at first appear to be the case that the two parties struggling for power in the nineteenth century were (in Coleridgean terms) the party of permanence, with its landed interest, and the party of progress, with its commercial and manufacturing interest; and that these parties were struggling for domination of the machinery of state and of what Coleridge called 'the National Church' or 'the clerisy'. This national church is roughly the equivalent of what political sociol-ogists today call the agencies of political socialisation, such as school, press, church and cultural organisations.[19] Perhaps the same point might be made in more fashionable jargon, by maintaining that the black party represented the feudal aristocracy, while the mulattoes were the new bourgeoisie arising to challenge the dominance of the aristocracy.[20] Neither of these accounts is, however, satisfactory. In the first place many of the leading politicians in what I have called the mulatto party were landowners of considerable proportions, as well as being business-men. Secondly the supporters of the mulatto party can scarcely be called a bourgeoisie in any developed sense, as there was little manu-facturing industry in the country, and the commerce in which they engaged consisted largely in the export of primary products. Thirdly it would be wrong, as we shall see, to describe the situation in colonial or post-colonial Haiti as feudal. Fourthly on critical issues of economic policy the line of confrontation cut across the party divisions. It is necessary, as O. C. Cox has insisted, to distinguish between political classes on the one hand and social classes or sub-classes on the other.[21] A political class is a coherent group or collection of groups whose members recognise a common interest or a common objective which they hope to realise by concerted action. Social classes or sub-classes, for their part, are not social groups; they are not organised social entities, but are theoretical constructions of social scientists. 'Social class two' does not in any sense exist as a group, but as part of a clas-sificatory system devised by social scientists and used by bureaucrats. Similarly 'the working class' does not exist as a group, when it is con-ceived of merely as the totality of those individuals whose income is derived mostly from wages rather than from investment or from rent. While it may properly be said that members of social classes have similar interests, it is only when they become conscious of these interests and begin to organise themselves that they become political classes with common interests, which in turn manifest themselves as political parties in certain contexts. A class 'in itself' then becomes a class 'for itself', as Marx put it in one of his earlier writings.[22] Thus a lack of consciousness, or a false consciousness, may result in political parties cutting across social classes and sub-classes, or even in whole social classes being unrepresented in the political struggle. As Marx observed with respect to the politics of ancient Rome, the class struggle took place between two sections of a privileged minority, with 'the great, productive mass of the population' forming 'the purely passive pedestal for these combatants'.[23]

In nineteenth-century Haiti the two main parties which were con-tending for power, distinguished broadly by colour, did not, then, represent the interests of two distinct social classes, but are more prop-erly to be seen as representing two factions of a single class. For most of the time the great mass of rural workers and small peasants was politically inactive, though at crucial stages peasant groups did inter-vene either on the initiative of one of the political parties, or under the effective leadership of a man from their own class. These sporadic actions frequently served to bring down governments or to rectify particular grievances but rarely had any significant effect upon the general policy pursued by the succeeding regime. They are thus to be seen as rebellions rather than as revolutionary movements. Important in these uprisings was a class of independent peasants large enough to be self-supporting and to make small loans to their neighbours, but small enough to be excluded from the ruling elite groups. These peasants also maintained links with the small towns and regional capitals. It was from this social class that the *piquets* and *cacos* bands were organised and manned from the time of Jean-Jacques Acaau to the rising against the American occupation under Charlemagne Péralte.

In the period of the United States occupation there is to be seen a growth in the small black urban middle class, which began at this time to play an important role in political affairs. The government of Sténio Vincent (1930–41) found it useful to cultivate this class, and the fall of his successor Elie Lescot in 1946 can partly be attributed to his studied neglect of the black middle class, who were almost all excluded from office and cut off from state patronage during the period of his presidency. As we shall see in chapter 6, the victory of Dumarsais Estimé in the elections of 1946 is to be understood as a partial victory for this black middle class, which also provided much of the support for François Duvalier in 1956–7. In 1946 the urban working class began to play a significant role in the struggle for political power, under their populist leader Daniel Fignolé, whose Mouvement Ouvrier Paysan represented an attempt by black middle-class politicians to unite urban proletariat, rural workers and small peasants in a single party. This party soon split over whether to continue to support Estimé's government; it came together once more in opposition to Paul Magloire (1950–6), but was rent asunder during the election campaigns of 1956–7, owing to the bitter rivalry between Fignolé and Duvalier.

The power struggles in the period since 1946 can be understood only in the light of the changing class structure in the country, and of a growing consciousness among sections of the middle and working classes. Nevertheless any attempt to account for political developments in the period solely in terms of social class would be misconceived. The colour factor, together with strong regional loyalties, complicates the picture. Furthermore we need to be on our guard against assuming that class divisions in post-colonial and economically dependent countries are the same as those in metropolitan countries. As Sidney Mintz has written: 'any uncritical transfer of analytic categories developed to describe western European history to cases of the Caribbean kind may vitiate the analysis itself.'[24]

The struggle for supremacy between black and mulatto groups in nineteenth-century Haiti is reflected in the development of competing ideologies. On the one hand mulatto writers insisted that government should be in the hands of the most competent and qualified section of the population. Many of them imported liberal and democratic ideas from Europe and were in favour of a system of representative government. Yet some of them believed that the franchise should be restricted to a relatively small section of the population. They frequently attacked militarism in politics, for large parts of the army were controlled by blacks. The mulattoes of the nineteenth century were generally pro-French and Catholic in cultural and religious matters, strongly supporting the 1860 Concordat with the Vatican. Mulatto historians developed a whole legend of the past, according to which the real heroes of Haitian independence were the mulatto leaders Ogé, Chavannes and Rigaud, and the true pattern of statesmanship is to be seen in Alexandre Pétion. The black leaders were portrayed as either wicked or ignorant, and the legend was clearly designed to reinforce the subjugation of the masses and the hegemony of the mulatto elite. Mulatto writers normally avoided direct reference to the colour question, or when they did mention colour it was usually in the context of a claim that no significant colour differences existed in Haiti and that the only distinctions recognised were those based on ability and integrity. Some mulatto ideologists, however, argued that a mixing of the races strengthens a people.

The black aspirants to power, on the other hand, pictured themselves as the champions of the poor black rural workers and small peasants, maintaining that political power should be in the hands of the more numerous part of the population. They frequently argued in favour of an authoritarian, populist government which would realise the hopes of the masses in the face of intrigue by mulatto politicians, and they defended the political role of the army, which was one of the few channels along which a non-elite black Haitian could rise to a position of power. Associated with this *noiriste* ideology was a whole black legend of the Haitian past, according to which the heroes were Toussaint, Dessalines, Christophe, Goman, Acaau, and later Salnave, Salomon and Antoine Simon. Yet it should be stressed that mulatto and black intellectuals of the nineteenth century agreed that in cultural matters the European pattern of civilisation was the one which Haiti should follow. Although they pointed to the fact that western civilisation had begun with the blacks of northern Africa, this was used as evidence for the fundamental equality of the races, rather than as a basis upon which to build an ideology of *négritude*. Until the period of the United States invasion there is hardly to be found a trace of that ideology which claims that black people are different from Europeans and that Haitians, who belong to the black race, should look to contemporary Africa as the pattern to be followed. Black writers of the nineteenth century were quite as insistent as their mulatto fellow countrymen that African 'superstitions', particularly the Voodoo religion, should be eliminated, and black heads of state, especially in the

early period, persecuted the cult. It was only with the ethnological movement, led by Jean Price Mars, J. C. Dorsainvil and Arthur Holly, that
African traditions in Haiti received sympathetic attention. The younger
disciples of these men, including Carl Brouard, Louis Diaquoi and
François Duvalier, developed ideas of *négritude*, and incorporated them
into the *noiriste* ideology which they had inherited from black writers
of the previous century. Recent publicists who suggest that Salomon
and the National Party were pro-African in any cultural sense – that
they were the precursors of *négritude* – are not only wrong, but are
frequently themselves attempting to reinforce a legendary view of the
past.[25]

Another fact that should perhaps be emphasised is that in general
mulatto writers and politicians were no less and no more patriotic
than were their black counterparts. One of the principal differences of
opinion among Haitians of the nineteenth century was on whether
foreign citizens should be allowed to own land in Haiti and whether
foreign capital should be attracted into the country. The confrontation
on these issues seems to have cut across the division between black and
mulatto.[26] Again, while Boyer, Geffrard, Saget, Dartiguenave, Borno,
Vincent and Lescot can be accused of having pursued policies detri-
mental to the political autonomy of Haiti, the same charge might also
be brought against black presidents like Salomon, Nord Alexis, Simon,
Guillaume Sam, Estimé, Magloire and Duvalier. Leslie Manigat has
recently asserted that in the early period the black leaders took a
stronger position against foreign intervention than did the mulattoes.[27]
Yet with respect to Pétion and Christophe this thesis needs modification.
The former's support for Bolívar and his maintenance of the Dessalinian
prohibition of foreign ownership contrasts sharply with Christophe's
position as outlined in chapter 2. The conclusion of this chapter is not,
however, that Pétion was a more intransigent nationalist than Christophe,
but that in certain respects each leader opened the way for foreign
intervention in Haiti's domestic affairs. Certainly since the declaration
of independence it has been necessary for Haitian leaders to balance
one power against another, invoking the limited intervention of one
power to counteract the influence of another, but it is not good enough
to denounce one set of leaders for selling out to foreigners while praising
the others for astute diplomacy when they behaved in precisely the
same manner. On contemplating the record of presidents since the
assassination of Dessalines in 1806 the Haitian patriot will echo the
words of the Psalmist: 'there is none that doeth good, no, not one'!

I have suggested that the conflict between black and mulatto ideologists in Haiti can be seen in terms of a struggle for hegemony. By this
is meant a battle for control and dominance not only in the arena of
political institutions, but in the explicitly ideological sphere and in the

field of 'political culture' in general. Most governments are able to exist only because of a whole collection of beliefs and assumptions often unconsciously held by the mass of the population. To call this collection of assumptions a 'value consensus' is misleading because it suggests that there is a single integrated set of beliefs which is shared by all or most of the population. Recent empirical enquiry leads us to doubt whether such a value consensus exists even in the case of what might be thought to be relatively homogeneous countries.[28] Nevertheless, for a government to remain in power for any length of time it is essential that it is accorded some kind of legitimacy by a large proportion of the population. The struggle for dominance in the cultural field has a direct effect in the sphere of practical politics; much of the present study will illustrate this contention.

An island divided

Race, then, for the Haitians constituted the basis of their claim to independence; the situation in the eastern part of the island provides an interesting contrast. After having been defeated in the west in 1803, a section of the French army under General Louis Ferrand established itself in Santo Domingo where it remained until 1809. The eastern part of the island then became a part of the Spanish empire once more until 1821, a period known as La España Boba. On the invitation of some Dominicans Boyer marched into the eastern part of the island, which became a part of Haiti until 1844, when it became independent once more. In 1861 Santana submitted to the Spanish crown, but independence was restored in 1865. Although the anti-Haitianism of the east had a strong racial content, the Dominicans had little conception of a peculiar ethnic factor which united themselves. They were part of Hispanic America and cannot during the nineteenth century be said to have formed a nation distinct from Puerto Rico and Cuba. These Spanish-speaking islands constituted a single cultural community with a similar economic structure, and it is wrong to speak of Dominican independence in terms of the emergence of a 'nation-state', as Gérard Pierre-Charles does.[29] Pedro F. Bonó, writing in 1895, pointed to the fact that the Dominican Republic was founded on the idea of *el cosmopolitanismo* in contrast to the Haitian basis of *el exclusivismo de una sola raza*. A few paragraphs earlier Bonó lamented the lack among Dominicans of that 'cohesion indispensable to every group which desires to be unflinchingly independent'.[30] Yet Bonó does not appear to recognise the fact that the absence of a conscious racial basis is connected to the lack of national feeling. Perhaps cosmopolitanism combined with anti-Haitianism was an insufficient basis for a national spirit to emerge. The willingness of Dominicans to return to the Spanish empire in 1861, and later negotiations with the United States for a protectorate, which appears to have had considerable popular support, suggest that the centripetal tendencies (which were always at work in Haiti, based upon racial consciousness) were very much weaker in the Dominican Republic. There was consequently less determination to combat European and United States encroachments upon national independence. The traditional resistance in Haiti to foreign ownership of land, as we have seen, also had a racial basis; together with the structure of land tenure this enabled Haitians, during and since the occupation period, to curb United States economic penetration more successfully than their eastern neighbours.

While the absence of a racial basis to nationalism in the Dominican Republic has meant that the centripetal factor has been less powerful than in Haiti, it should also be noted that in general colour divisions have played a less significant role in Dominican politics than in the politics of the black republic. This is not to say that political conflicts have not been deep and bitter in the east, nor that these divisions have never led to foreign intervention, but that there are not the same hard and persistent colour bifurcations in the political life of the country. If the centripetal tendencies resulting from ethnic (racial) identity are weaker in the east, so are the centrifugal tendencies consequent upon ethnic (colour) dichotomy.

Time present and time past

A historical essay is an attempt to understand and to explain the past, including the quite recent past, in terms which are comprehensible to the present. The writing of history begins with material from the present; all we have are the records of the past, memorials, documents and memories. The writing of history is a constructive activity which consists not in gathering together past 'facts', but in attempting a coherent explanation of the records of the past. Facts are not the starting point of the enquiry, they are part of its conclusion. Furthermore a historical essay begins with a problem or with a series of questions which require answers. The present essay is concerned to explain the role played by ideas of race, colour and independence in Haitian history. My interest in Haiti began in 1967 as an endeavour to understand how the Duvalier regime came to power, how it retained power and in particular what were the sources of its 'legitimacy' – how did it project itself to the Haitian people? The accounts of Haiti which I had come across (with the possible exception of a brief essay by Sidney Mintz and some occasional writings by Leslie Manigat) not only failed to answer these questions, but hardly thought it necessary to ask them. Since that time the situation has not improved markedly, and novelists have vied with journalists and academics in presenting Haiti and its government as a bizarre phenomenon totally defying explanation. One recent book on Haiti finds it necessary to 'explain' the politics of the country in terms of supposed deficiencies in the child-rearing habits of the Haitian people and to the 'paranoia in the majority of Haitians'. Duvalier's own policy and behaviour are similarly ascribed to psychological abnormality.[31] In my own work on Haiti, what began as an attempt to understand and explain contemporary politics soon turned into an investigation into the past, and new questions needed to be answered.

The present essay is a history of ideas; its underlying hypothesis is that the ideas and beliefs of Haitians, which must be seen largely as the products of their history, have influenced their actions, and that the story of the country cannot therefore properly be told without a knowledge of these ideas. For us to comprehend what was said and believed in the past it may be necessary to employ concepts which were not themselves used by those whose ideas we are studying. This is the case for two reasons. In the first place, as I have already insisted, history involves explaining the past *to the present*, and this must be done in language which can be understood in the present. Secondly it is frequently the case that the meaning of what was said and done in the past is clearer to us than it was to those who were themselves involved. The significance, for example, of what came to be called 'the storming of the Bastille' was hardly understood by those who took part in it. The same clearly might be said of those blacks and mulattoes of Saint Domingue who rose up against their colonial masters. As we, who are familiar with the struggles of the Algerians and the Vietnamese, look back to the Haitian experience, things emerge as significant which would have been ignored by earlier historians. It is for this reason that we might properly use terms like 'black power', 'third world' and 'neo-colonialism' about Haiti of the nineteenth century.[32] They are indeed terms invented in our own time, and yet they may have a proper application to an earlier state of affairs when it is seen from the standpoint of the present. It is an untenable positivism which forbids the use of such 'anachronisms'. Again, a text from the past frequently tells us more than its author intended; in our quest for understanding we are therefore by no means restricted to an investigation of the author's intentions, nor to an uncritical repetition of the concepts which he himself used.

Certainly, as Bradley insisted, it is only by analogy from present experience that we are able to make sense of the past; also we must surely relate past events to the present, for the present is the outcome of the past and therefore part of its meaning; but this is not to say that we study the past in order to guide us in shaping the future, as Ernst Troeltsch concluded.[33] There is a valuable distinction between a 'historical' study of the past 'for its own sake' — that is, one undertaken in such a way as to help us to understand the past — and a 'practical' study of the past calculated to assist us in changing or maintaining some aspect of the present. An account of the past which makes no attempt to understand the past but which is explicitly designed to influence the future is not then historical. Karl Kautsky wrote:

While the Marxist view of history guards us from the danger of measuring the past with the standard of the present and sharpens our appreciation of each epoch and each nation, it also frees us from the other danger, that of attempting to adapt our presentation of the past to the immediate practical interest we are defending in the present.[34]

Unfortunately there are many occasions on which this view of history has not had the liberating effects described.

The writing of history is a purposive activity, but it frequently has consequences which are unintended. Even though the author may intend to write about the past without wishing to influence the future, this cannot be. All that takes place in the present will in some way affect the future. Might it not therefore be better to recognise the fact and to write an account of the past which will have an impact on the future in a way which the author regards as beneficial, either by forwarding 'the revolution' or by maintaining the status quo? If all history is ideological in its effects, it might as well be explicitly and benevolently so. At this point two considerations might properly be borne in mind. In the first place a healthy humility and a sense of humour ought to reassure the historian that the effects of his writing on the course of events will probably be relatively insignificant. Secondly a coherent and comprehensible account of the past can do no ultimate harm to a cause which claims to be forwarding what is right and true. A present concern which is not based upon righteousness and truth has no valid claim to consideration. 'Nowhere have the people ever benefited', writes Eugene Genovese, 'from the efforts of those intellectuals who have beneficently lied to them, ostensibly for their own good and in order to provide them with the beliefs necessary to shore up their courage and sustain them in battle.'[35]

The aim of the present study is neither to edify nor to instruct, but this does not mean that it can make pretensions to be 'value free'. The writing of history involves making judgments. It is necessary to distinguish between the significant and the trivial, and what an author or a generation considers to be significant depends upon their specific experiences as interpreted and understood by themselves. Again we do not find it necessary to explain what we judge to be true and reasonable in the same way that false beliefs and irrational actions are accounted for. The mere fact that a belief is true is normally thought to be a sufficient explanation for its being accepted, though there are undoubtedly other causal factors at work in its acceptance. A belief which appears to us to be false requires a peculiar sort of explanation which lays emphasis upon the non-rational causes which lead men to accept it. It is thus necessary to avoid on the one hand a positivism which assumes that there are historical 'facts' simply waiting to be discovered, and on the other a rigid structuralism which suggests that the evidence can be forced into any shape which is determined by the preconceptions of the historian. Certainly some preliminary framework is necessary in order to make sense of the evidence at all. But the documents must then be allowed to 'speak for themselves' in such a way as to lead the historian to modify his framework where the evidence calls for it. We might use the term 'co-relation' to describe this dynamic process of understanding.

If the object of this essay is to explain the past, is this not equivalent to a justification of it? Hegel seemed to think so. He saw his essay on the German constitution as promoting a calmer outlook and a generally conservative approach. 'For it is not what is that makes us irascible and resentful', he wrote, 'but the fact that it is not as it ought to be. But if we recognize that it is as it must be . . . then we also recognize that it is as it ought to be.'[36] Hegel here went beyond the legitimate bounds of the historian when he wrote of things being as they *must* be; they are as they are, and they are as they are partly because men did as they did. The historian's job is to make these actions intelligible, not to pronounce them inevitable. Nevertheless, in general, Hegel's warning against dealing with a hypothetical past is salutary, and if heeded would help social scientists to avoid much of the nonsense which they are often found talking. Consider, for example, the question, addressed to a Turkish peasant, about what he would do if he were president of Turkey. 'My God! How can you ask such a thing?' was the bewildered man's reply. 'How can I . . . I cannot . . . president of Turkey . . . master of the whole world . . . ' Riesman goes on to say that many peasants, when asked where they would like to live if they could not live in their native village, replied that they would rather die. 'They could not conceive of living anywhere else, any more than of being somebody else.'[37] Commenting on this extraordinary episode, W. A. Mullins writes: 'Clearly the peasant views himself as being politically impotent . . . He is simply not historically aware.'[38] A rational consideration of what these questions imply, however, should leave the reader in little doubt as to which of the parties in this encounter was historically unaware. There is no story of what might have been alongside the story of what was.

If it is true that to understand and explain the past it is necessary for the historian to appeal to some analogous experience in the present, this is not to say that he must himself be actively involved in some contemporary battle, to which his historical writing is thought to

contribute. Karl Popper refers to *The Open Society and its Enemies*
as 'my war effort', and this is perhaps why it is such a bad book.[39]
A certain detachment is called for in the historian. It is sometimes
suggested that the only people who can write about black history are
those who have shared 'the black experience'. This is frequently used
as a substitute for careful criticism of a book which the speaker dis-
likes. It does not merit extended consideration, and only merits mention
at all because it is a statement often made in the contemporary Caribbean. That there is no single black experience should be obvious, and if
the social background of many of those on whose lips the phrase
occurs is anything to go by, it would appear that living in a comfortable
detached house in one of the cooler suburbs, being waited on by
servants, and commuting to the campus in one of the family cars is at
least part of what is meant by 'the black experience'! And yet some
kind of active involvement in life is a necessary condition of historical
understanding. 'It seems ridiculous to me', wrote Rousseau, 'to attempt
to study the world as a mere observer. He who wishes only to observe
will observe nothing . . . We observe the actions of others only to the
extent to which we ourselves act.'[40]

One further point which is implied in what has already been said is
that the historian writes from the standpoint of the present, within
the horizons of the present, and that he cannot claim that his work,
however good, can be the last word. The moving horizon of the present
opens up new landscapes from the vantage points of which the past will
certainly appear different from the way it appears to us. The meaning
of past events will change, and present criteria of what constitutes a
satisfactory explanation will also shift. Fresh understanding, interpretation and explanation will therefore be required. Only at the eschaton
will historians be given the golden handshake.

The present work is concerned, then, with the role of ideas of race,
colour and independence in Haitian politics, and it inevitably raises
the general issue of the relationship between ideology and politics. It
will be clear from what follows that I do not believe that an ideology
is always to be thought of as a mere 'derivation', to use the language of
Pareto — that it is a mere product of political activity and of economic
interest, having no real importance in determining the course of history.
Ideologies are indeed to be understood and explained partly as the
rationalisation of the interests of particular social groups, but this does
not mean that they are nothing but camouflage cynically erected in
order to divert attention from the real issues. How a social group sees
the world is undoubtedly affected by its place in that world and by its
economic or other interests. The way in which that group acts is, however, partly determined by its perception of its interests and by its
understanding of the world that faces it. The following chapters illus-

trate how ideologies emerge out of concrete historical conflicts and confrontations, and how, having come into being, they play an active part in affecting the course of events.

II

It was in December 1492 that the Indians of the island of Ayti (as they called it) discovered Columbus strolling with some of his men on their beaches. With this discovery began a new era in the life of the island, named Hispaniola by Columbus. During the sixteenth and seventeenth centuries the island was colonised by the Spanish and, very early on, black slaves were introduced from Africa. The native Indians soon died out, were killed, or inter-married, and little that was distinctive remained in the colony from the pre-Columbian period.[41] The northwestern part of the island was a centre from which French buccaneers set out to harass the Spanish galleons and, with the decline in Spanish power, France managed to acquire the western third of the island under the treaty of Ryswick in 1697. Within a few years large numbers of French settlers were beginning to arrive in the new colony of Saint Domingue. Plantations of indigo, sugar, cotton and coffee were rapidly developed on the basis of slave labour and French capital; an economy of dependence on the metropolis was established from which the country has not even to this day succeeded in shaking itself free, though the mode of dependence and the metropolis in question have changed. As O. C. Cox has insisted, it is a mistake to regard the colonial economies of the New World as instances of feudalism on the European model; they were, in his words, 'the beginning of an entirely different economic enterprise – the dawn of colonial capitalism'.[42] By the mid eighteenth century Saint Domingue was a flourishing colony with a rapidly growing population, which continued to increase up to the time of the French revolution. By 1789 there were approximately 790 sugar plantations, 2,000 coffee plantations, 700 cotton cultivators and over 3,000 small producers of indigo. Sugar exports to Europe from Saint Domingue were almost equal to the total exported from the British colonies, and she was the world's principal coffee grower. The population was composed of roughly 450,000 slaves, 40,000 whites and something over 30,000 free coloureds (or *affranchis*).[43] The life of the colony was dependent upon imports from France, though the metropolitan government found it increasingly difficult to enforce the prohibition of foreign trade.

The pattern of settlement and of economic development was significantly different in the three departments of the colony. The North was the first region to be developed seriously and it was here that most of the large and flourishing plantations were to be found. Although

the northern region comprised less than one-quarter of the area of the
colony, it contained two-fifths of the white population and well over
one-third of the slaves. The *affranchis* were less influential in this region
than they were in the West and the South. The southern region was
the last to be developed, owing partly to its mountainous terrain which
made large plantations less economical than in the northern and Artibonite plains. The six and a half thousand *affranchis* of the South
owned much of the land and were more powerful than their numbers
would suggest. As we shall see, the regional factor became significant
in the revolutionary period, when André Rigaud made his headquarters
there; since that time the South has remained the stronghold of the
mulattoes, and it was from this region that Louis Déjoie, Duvalier's
principal opponent in 1957, received much of his support. The mountainous nature of the terrain had made land communications difficult
and had encouraged the development of sea links. The major towns of
the colony were all on the coast, and it was through these ports that
the agricultural products of each region were exported. Throughout
the nineteenth century a lively system of coastal communication was
maintained between these towns, which managed, however, to retain
a distinctive civic life and style. During the United States occupation
the road system, centring on the capital, was improved and this had the
effect of destroying coastal traffic, and of draining life from these
towns. The subsequent decay of the road system has not, however,
resulted in a significant revival of civic life in the provinces.

Class, colour and caste

The social divisions of the colony, which were closely related to its
economic structure, were complicated, but some knowledge of their
nature is essential for an understanding of the revolutionary and post-
colonial conflicts and confrontations. There were three castes, or
status groups, in colonial Saint Domingue, whose respective positions
were defined by law and custom. Individuals were born into one of
them and mobility was difficult to achieve. The first caste was composed of the *blancs*, the white colonial inhabitants; then there were
the *affranchis*, or free coloureds, who under the *Code Noir* of 1685
should have enjoyed equal rights with the whites, but who in practice
were the victims of serious social and legal disabilities;[44] finally there
were the slaves. The caste lines were not absolutely rigid, for manu-
mission allowed a slave to pass into the category of *affranchi*; also it
was known for very light-skinned *affranchis* to pass for white. Among
this latter group was probably Moreau de Saint Méry, the politician
and historian, who became a leading apologist of the *grands blancs*
during the revolutionary period.[45]

The colour divisions in colonial Saint Domingue largely, but not wholly, reinforced caste or status divisions. The first caste was practically co-extensive with white colour. The *affranchis* were mostly of mixed race, known generally as mulattoes, *gens de couleur* or *jaunes*, while the vast majority of the slaves were black. It is, however, important to stress that a proportion of the *affranchis* was black, while some slaves were mulatto.

Social class divisions generally reinforced the colour and status divisions noted above, but again the coincidence is not complete. While the colonial administrators were all white, a small section of the class of large landowners and merchants was mulatto. A middle class of smaller landowners, independent craftsmen and employees was composed of *petits blancs*, mulattoes and a few blacks. Finally manual work in the fields and domestic work was performed by the slaves; most of the mulatto slaves, however, were to be found in domestic rather than in field work. It will be clear that while the members of the *affranchi* caste were the victims of racial prejudice and discrimination, many of them had similar economic interests to the whites.[46]

The whites

The whites were firmly in control of the affairs of the colony until 1789. The government was essentially in the hands of the governor general — always a military officer — and the intendant, who was particularly concerned with public administration, finance and justice in the colony. Both these officials were appointed by and were responsible to the royal government in France, and when they agreed on any matter their power was practically unlimited. Of the governor general, Bryan Edwards wrote, 'He was, in truth, an absolute prince, whose will, generally speaking, constituted law.' The power of the two officials extended to the furthest corner of the colony and to the minutest detail of life; it was not supplemented or limited by an effective system of local government, nor were there, according to Ardouin, the checks of public opinion and custom which were to be found in France itself.[47] The colonial assembly set up after the revolution of 1789, in which the large landowners and merchants alone were represented, had little power, and its only hope of exercising real influence lay in its ability to bring pressure upon the ministry through its agents in Paris. The three regions into which the colony was divided, the North, the South and the West, each had a hierarchy of officials responsible to the centre. As may well be imagined, the *grands blancs* were frequently at odds with the colonial officials. Many of the latter, however, under social pressure from their fellow whites, gave up the humanitarian or liberal views which they had brought with them from France. Governor de Fénelon of Martinique, for example, explained in a letter to the French government in 1764 how he had changed his opinions on slavery: 'The safety of the whites requires that the negroes be maintained in the most profound ignorance. I have come to believe firmly that it is necessary to drive the negroes like beasts.'[48] British administrators in India during the nineteenth century, like Henry Maine and Fitzjames Stephen, as well as Jacques Soustelle in twentieth-century Algeria, underwent a similar change as a result of colonial experience.

It was generally assumed, not only in France but also among the colonists, that the main purpose of a colony was to enrich the mother country by providing a market for its surplus products, a home for its surplus population and a source of cheap raw materials. As Gaston Martin observed, 'Everything in the colony has to be seen as a function of the metropolis; everything has to be made for the metropolis or by the metropolis.'[49] For the merchants of Nantes and Bordeaux this meant maintaining the closed commercial relationship between France and Saint Domingue, and in particular the forbidding of imports from Britain and from the United States. The colonial planters, for their part, while recognising that the colony existed in order to enrich the metropolis, argued that this could be achieved by allowing a measure of free trade. In 1794 the Chambre d'Agriculture of Cap Français considered and approved a *Mémoire* which clearly recognised that colonies were 'canals which serve to augment industry and national activity', and Hilliard d'Auberteuil, a spokesman of the white colonists, stated, 'the end for which colonies are established is to procure new markets for the superfluous merchandise of the metropolis in exchange for other useful products'.[50] Charles Esmangart, who is later to appear on the stage as one of the commissioners sent by Louis XVIII to effect a reconciliation with Haiti, maintained a similar position.[51] The colonists, however, argued that a degree of free trade was not incompatible with metropolitan prosperity, and that a supply of cheap slaves (who were sold at half the Saint Domingue price in the British colonies at the end of the eighteenth century) would increase the prosperity of France as well as of her West Indian colonies.

Resentment of metropolitan domination among the planters and merchants of Saint Domingue led during the eighteenth century to demands for an increased autonomy and even for the independence of the colony. Saint Domingue, they argued, had not been conquered, nor bought, nor had it submitted to France. The relationship was a free one which might be broken off if it became too irksome for the population.[52] The *petits blancs* and *affranchis* were, however, less keen on the idea of independence, knowing that it would mean un-bridled domination by the colonial aristocracy.

Life in the colony, was, for the rich whites, pleasant and even 'civilised'. In contrast to the situation in the British colonies of the Caribbean, most of the plantation owners lived for at least a part of the year in the colony, though they frequently made their homes in

Port-au-Prince or in Cap Français (later Cap Haïtien).[53] Theatres brought some of the latest plays from France and the influence of the Enlightenment was propagated through intellectual societies, like the Cercle des Philadelphes of Cap Français, and through the Masonic lodges which were a familiar feature of colonial Saint Domingue. The colony was, according to Dr Arthaud, 'inhabited for many years by men of reflection, who are today interested in the arts and the sciences'. In 1784, together with a number of *grands blancs*, he founded the Cercle. Practically all those involved were enthusiastic Freemasons, who maintained contact with lodges in France and with such leading American Masons as Benjamin Franklin. Although they expressed progressive views, the members of the Cercle were among the principal defenders of slavery.[54] Many of the *grands blancs* nevertheless cherished the hope of returning to live in France having made their fortune in the Antilles.[55]

The slaves

The vast majority of the population of Saint Domingue were slaves brought from Africa or born of slave parents in the colonies. Most of them worked on large sugar plantations under harsh and degrading conditions. Under article 22 of the *Code Noir* slaves were to be given weekly rations of salt beef or fish and also ground provision, but the decree was largely ignored in the colony. The code itself, prescribing as it did conditions for the treatment of slaves, was rejected by many of the *grands blancs* as 'a violation of the rights of property'.[56] The field slaves were forced to work all day and part of the night, with a two-hour break in the middle of the day for a meal. On Sundays they were frequently allowed to cultivate small gardens from which they were expected to feed themselves and their dependants.[57] There is little evidence to suggest that the treatment of slaves in Catholic Saint Domingue was substantially less severe than it was in the British colonies, though an anonymous writer, resident in Jamaica, claimed that 'the mild and kind treatment' of negroes in the French colonies was due to the influence of the Catholic religion.[58] Very few contemporary visitors, however, were impressed by the mildness and kindness of the slave owners of Saint Domingue, and Bryan Edwards, a careful and experienced observer of Caribbean life, denied any significant difference between the two systems in this respect.[59] The slaves retained elements of the culture which they had known in Africa, and in particular the Voodoo religion, which was widely practised in the plantations. It was an amalgam of the various religious beliefs and practices of West Africa, which even incorporated certain Christian symbols.

There was a significant distinction between those slaves who had been born in the Caribbean, the *negs créoles*, and those born in Africa,

the *negs bossals*. The former had become influenced by European
ways of life and thought, while the *bossals* retained most of their
African customs and it was probably they who in general controlled
the Voodoo cult. During the revolutionary period this distinction was,
as we shall see, to take on political importance.

Large numbers of slaves had from time to time fled from the plantations and had set up free communities in the mountainous interior
of the island. They were known as *marrons*, deriving from the Spanish
cimarrón.[60] There has been considerable controversy in recent years
about the cause of *marronage* in Saint Domingue, and also about the
role played by these outlaws during the revolutionary period. Yvan
Debbasch has argued that 'the will to liberty' was not one of the
principal causes of *marronage* and that various other psychic and social
factors influenced the decision of slaves to flee the plantations.[61]
Marronage, though it constituted an implicit challenge to the system of
slavery, was not an explicitly revolutionary movement, and its leaders
were thus frequently willing to accept amnesty or to negotiate with the
government for recognition, on the condition that they would not
further disturb the colonial system.[62] Debbasch suggests, therefore,
that *marronage* was not a major contributory factor to the revolution
of 1791, and that those who see in the *marrons* the revolutionary forefathers of Toussaint Louverture are guilty of writing an 'histoire
partiale'.[63] Although it is true that many of the *marrons* fled after
robbery or because of ill-treatment from their masters, there are cases
that may be specified in which these causes are absent. 'Good masters',
observes Gabriel Debien, 'often had more *marrons* than very severe
masters.'[64] It is certainly not, in the circumstances, unreasonable to
suggest with Fouchard that a love of liberty was one of the principal
causes of *marronage*. Debien is nevertheless critical of a tendency among
Haitian historians to see in *marronage* the principal origin of the rising
of 1791.[65]

The affranchis

A strict caste-like distinction was maintained between the whites of all
classes on the one hand and the free coloured population or *affranchis*
on the other. Throughout the eighteenth century the *affranchis* were
increasingly the object of discriminatory regulations. Certain professions
were closed to them, their clothing was to some extent prescribed
and harsher legal penalties were applied to them than to the whites.[66]
The majority of the *affranchi* caste was, as we have noted, mulatto,
though there was a proportion of free blacks. The actual number of
free blacks is a matter of some disagreement. Moreau de Saint Méry
estimated that one-third of the *affranchis* were black, while Julien

Raimond, a mulatto apologist writing from Paris, claimed that 'there are not more than 1500 of them in all'.[67] Although the colour and caste lines did not therefore entirely coincide we can say that colour was a fairly reliable *badge* of status. Also observant critics of the social situation in the colony noticed that colour prejudice was so powerful that in many respects mulatto slaves regarded themselves and were generally regarded as superior to free blacks, 'à cause de leur rapprochement du Blanc par leur nuance, et par leurs mœurs'.[68] One visitor to the island, Baron de Wimpffen, claimed that colour was a more significant factor than status; he therefore included mulatto slaves with *affranchis* in his second category, and free blacks ('who are proprietors of land, and by no means numerous') with slaves.[69] In a celebrated sentence he made his point: 'It is by your skin, however branded it may be, and not by your parchment, however worm-eaten, that your pretensions to gentility are adjusted'.[70] A similar prejudice existed in the British colonies: in Jamaica free blacks were segregated from free mulattoes in the militia, and in St Vincent mulatto slaves were not normally employed in the fields.[71]

Racialism, related to colour prejudice, was an abiding feature of colonial life. Non-whites were categorised by Moreau de Saint Méry into ten classes according to the number of 'parts' black and 'parts' white in their genetic composition, going back seven generations:

noir	0–7 parts white
sacatra	8–23 parts white
griffe	24–39 parts white
marabou	40–48 parts white
mulâtre	49–70 parts white
quarteron	71–100 parts white
métif (or *métis*)	101–112 parts white
mamelouc	113–120 parts white
quarteronné	121–124 parts white
sang-mêlé	125–127 parts white [72]

It is interesting to note that the nearer the person approached white the finer the distinction which was made. Moreau de Saint Méry clearly placed emphasis upon the racial composition of the various classes, though he also discussed their phenotypical features. Daniel Bell is quite wrong when he suggests that 'race, in terms of "blood", is a nineteenth century concept', and that earlier racial theories were concerned with physical characteristics.[73] It was widely believed, or at least asserted, that slavery had imprinted a 'stain' upon the black man which had been passed on to his successors, even when these were of mixed blood and born free. In his 'Discours préliminaire' to the *Cahiers de doléances* presented by the whites of Saint Domingue to the States General of 1789, the Comte de Reynaud declared: 'The free coloured people, whatever be the distance from their origins, always retain the stain of slavery and are declared incapable of all public functions.'[74] Hilliard d'Auberteuil, clearly influenced by the eighteenth-century belief of the *philosophes* in the natural goodness of man, stated that in becoming slaves the negroes 'contracted an infinity of vices' which they had not known in their natural state.[75] It was, he insisted, in the interests of the colonists to 'cover the black race with such disdain that whoever descends from it, to the sixth generation, should be covered by an indelible stain'.[76] It was even held that marriage to a coloured person imparted the 'stain' to the white partner. When the Marquis de Laage, an officer in the army of Saint Domingue, married a coloured woman in Bordeaux, he was forbidden to return to his post, since, as the minister of the navy told the governor general, 'these sorts of alliance leave with the whites an indelible stain'.[77] Only by maintaining a belief in the racial inferiority of the African could the system of slavery be perpetuated, and this, so the whites argued, involved discriminatory measures against the *affranchis*. Furthermore the racial prejudice of the whites led to colour prejudice on the part of the mulattoes; as we have noted, a mulatto slave was generally regarded as being superior to a free black. In his bitter controversy with Julien Raimond, Moreau de Saint Méry pointed out that 'the mulatto *affranchi* despised the black *affranchi*'.[78]

Despite the indignities to which the *affranchis* were compelled to submit, they managed to prosper, and by the time of the French revolution they possibly owned as much as one-third of the land and one-quarter of the slaves in the colony. This suggests that, bearing in mind the difference in numbers, the average *affranchi* was as rich as the average white.[79] One of the spokesmen of this group in fact claimed that the proportions were even larger, and that half the land was in the hands of the free coloured population.[80] The stability of the colonial system depended to a considerable extent upon the *affranchis* believing that they had a fundamental interest in maintaining, in its substance, the economic system which prevailed in the colony, and the social relations which went with it. It was, for example, the mulatto *affranchis* who pursued the fugitive slaves. Governor de Fayet, as early as 1733, stated that the colony depended upon the military service of these mulatto *affranchis*, and that it was they alone who could destroy the *marrons*. Moreau de Saint Méry suggested that they were performing a similar role up to the time of the revolution.[81] The ambivalent position of the *affranchis* in colonial Saint Domingue, having economic interests similar to the whites and yet being the victims of discrimination and persecution, explains the role which they were to play in the revolutionary years.

From what has already been said it will be clear that I do not regard as sound the recent claim by Jean Fouchard that the *affranchi* caste contained more blacks than mulattoes. In his interesting study *Marrons de la liberté*, Fouchard draws attention to the undoubted fact that there were in the colony a number of slaves who had left their plantations, but who had settled in the towns; although they were legally slaves they were *de facto* free, often with the tacit consent of their former masters.[82] They were known as 'reputé affranchis sans l'être', and were 'de toutes nuances'.[83] Although it is important to distinguish this class from the *marrons* proper, they had interests which were different from the *affranchis* proper and should not be assimilated to them. The latter were strongly in favour of a strict enforcement of the provisions of the *Code Noir*, while many of the former were content with the status quo. Furthermore it is probable that a large proportion of the *affranchis sans l'être* were in fact mulattoes; and, knowing the colour prejudice which existed at the time, it is likely that those among this group who managed to find acceptance among the *affranchis* would have been mulattoes.[84] As will become clear as our study progresses, Fouchard, a spokesman of the mulatto elite in contemporary Haiti, has reasons for denying the *noiriste* assertion that caste and colour were effectively coincident in colonial Saint Domingue.[85]

The revolution

I have attempted to give an impression of life in colonial Saint Domingue in the eighteenth century. It is inevitably a static picture of the anatomy of the colony, for a dynamic account of colonial life would require much more space than is available here. The justification for giving such a picture is that, although significant developments were taking place below the surface, there was a certain stability which led most inhabitants to assume that the way of life in the colony would not change drastically. Modifications they realised there must be, but any major redistribution of power was not envisaged. Hilliard d'Auberteuil spoke for most of the free population when he denied the possibility of a slave rebellion owing to the lack of communication between slaves of different plantations; 'What have we to fear from the slaves?' he complacently remarked in 1777.[86]

It was undoubtedly the revolutionary movement in France itself which initiated a period of rapid change in Saint Domingue, where tensions had been building up for many years. Revolutionary ideas spread to the colony and many of the *grands blancs* saw this as a good opportunity to press their claims to greater autonomy for the territory. At the same time some of the less privileged whites and many of the *affranchis* saw in the revolutionary movement a chance to reassert their own interests against those of the colonial aristocracy. The *affranchis* in particular were insistent that the Declaration of the Rights of Man should apply to the colony and that their claims to equal status with the whites should be acknowledged. To this end a mulatto, Vincent Ogé, with encouragement from the Amis des Noirs in Paris,[87] returned to Saint Domingue determined to secure equal rights for the *affranchis*. By mid-1790 the colony was in considerable confusion, with whites divided against whites and with militant demands being made on behalf of the free coloureds. Ogé, together with Jean-Baptiste Chavannes and other mulatto leaders, after an appeal to arms, was arrested and executed, an action which bitterly alienated the *affranchis*. It is important to note that Ogé and his fellow *affranchis* were not immediately concerned to abolish slavery, but merely to assert their own rights. As we have noted, the free coloureds of Saint Domingue owned perhaps as many as one-quarter of the slaves in the colony. The spokesmen of this caste, Julien Raimond and C. S. Milscent, drew attention to the common economic interests which the whites shared with the *affranchis*. Furthermore the number of slaves was so large that the whites needed the free coloureds to help maintain order. Raimond pointed out that there had been less trouble from the slaves in the South and West where the *affranchis* were still armed than in the North where they had been disarmed.[88] Milscent defended slavery and argued that the colonial economy would be unworkable without it. Yet he wished to dissociate slavery from theories of racial inferiority, which he claimed to be scientifically untenable. He criticised those who held that the slave would obey his master only so long as he believed in his own inferiority.[89]

With the outbreak of the slave rebellion in August 1791 the whites soon came to appreciate the arguments of the *affranchis* that there was a common interest binding together these castes. The revolt spread rapidly through the northern province and then to the rest of the colony. Properties were burned and sacked, whites were slaughtered and the confusion was general. The whites and *affranchis*, discovering their common interest, came together in various parts of the country in the name of 'the preservation of property'.[90]

It is impossible here to trace in detail the story of the revolution: of the relationship between events in the colony and developments in Paris, of the British and Spanish invasions of Saint Domingue, of the successive commissions sent by the French government, of the skilful leadership of Toussaint Louverture. The story has been well told by C. L. R. James in his celebrated book *The Black Jacobins*.[91] Here I can only point to some features of the revolutionary period as they relate to the theme of the present book.

Anciens *and* nouveaux libres

Slavery was abolished in Saint Domingue in August 1793, and the commissioners sent by the republican government attempted to gain the support of the former slaves against the Spanish and the British forces. Toussaint, who had been a slave on the Bréda plantation, had emerged as leader of the blacks.[92] He had at one point gone over to the Spanish, but in mid-1794 he switched his support to the republican French. Other black leaders, including Jean François and Biassou, remained with the Spanish, but this did not seriously weaken the arm of Toussaint. Saint Domingue was temporarily secured for the French; but which group would control the course of events in the colony itself? The *affranchis*, or *anciens libres*, were determined that it should be themselves, and from 1796 to 1801 there was an extended struggle between *anciens* and *nouveaux libres* for hegemony, with the French authorities powerless to determine the outcome. A premature attempt by the predominantly mulatto *anciens libres* to seize power under Villate in 1796 initiated the struggle, which culminated in the war of the South between the armies of Toussaint and those of André Rigaud, who had succeeded to the leadership of the *anciens libres*. The causes of the conflict were many; the classes represented by the two leaders had different economic and political interests; also there was the personal rivalry between Toussaint and Rigaud and the ever-present colour issue. Colour was certainly not the principal cause of the conflict, and black leaders like Pierre Michel and Barthelmi allied themselves with Rigaud. Nevertheless Toussaint denounced the mulatto general for his colour prejudice. The social structure of the colony was such that these personal and colour factors were able to play an important role in influencing the course of events.

Toussaint emerged from the war of the South as undisputed master of Saint Domingue, and in the constitution of 1801 he was proclaimed governor general. Already he had opened negotiations with Britain and with the United States, and commercial agreements had been reached, as between sovereign states. The policy pursued by the black general included the liberation of colonial trade, the effective political autonomy of Saint Domingue, legal liberty for the slaves, a revival of the plantation system and a new deal for those whites who were willing to accept his leadership and policies. He was indeed the Kenyatta of the Caribbean, and his conciliatory policy towards foreign interests is frequently compared favourably with the more radical policies of Dessalines by latter-day apologists of neo-colonialism.[93] Napoleon was, however, unprepared to accept the autonomy of Saint Domingue; he set out to reimpose strict metropolitan control and to subdue these 'gilded Africans'. An army of 5,000 men landed at Cap Français under Napoleon's brother-in-law Leclerc, who had been instructed to suppress the liberation movement by exploiting the divisions between blacks and mulattoes, and eventually to reintroduce slavery. First he met with resistance from Toussaint and his fellow black generals, but later, with reinforcements having arrived from France, and with support from the mulatto generals Rigaud and Pétion, he was able to convince the blacks that co-operation was the only course of action open to them. Rigaud was then arrested and deported to France; Toussaint was tricked into captivity and shipped to France where he died shortly afterwards in the fort of Joux in the Jura. At this point the only resistance to the French came from peasant irregulars. Soon, however, mulatto and black generals began to desert the French army with their men; they agreed to accept the leadership of Jean Jacques Dessalines and the final stage of the liberation struggle began in November 1802. The French armies were unable to control the situation, which was exacerbated by the rapid spread of yellow fever. By November 1803 the blacks and mulattoes were the undisputed masters of Saint Domingue.

From revolution to independence

Why was Saint Domingue the scene of the only successful slave rebellion in the Caribbean? Certainly the disarray of the colonial masters was one of the factors which must be taken into account. The revolution in Paris had manifested deep divisions among Frenchmen both in France and in the colonies, and it undoubtedly provided the occasion for the Haitian revolutionary wars. Nevertheless there were a number of developments in the colony itself which together constituted a revolutionary situation. Martinique and Guadeloupe, for example, remained securely under European control. One important factor was the rapid growth of the *affranchi* caste in Saint Domingue, and the crucial role which they played in the colonial regime. 'This class of people', wrote Laborie, 'has been remarked to encrease, with a degree of rapidity far exceeding that of any kind of population in the West Indies.'[94] Their numbers had probably more than doubled, possibly quadrupled, in the fifteen years prior to 1789.[95] In the neighbouring Spanish colony of Santo Domingo their proportion of the population was indeed much greater, but the crucial difference between the two colonies was the size of the slave population; where there were over 450,000 slaves in Saint Domingue, there were only about 15,000 slaves in the Spanish two-thirds of the island.[96] In Jamaica the population structure was different again, with a huge slave population as in Saint Domingue, but with the whites outnumbering the *affranchis* by nearly six to one. The population of Saint Domingue was such that the colonial system could be maintained in normal circumstances only with the co-operation of the free coloured population. The alternative mode of keeping order was by stationing a large French army in the colony; but the very size of Saint Domingue put it in a category quite different from that of the other French colonies in the region, where a relatively small force could keep control. This method was, of course, the one which Napoleon tried in 1802, but the international situation made it impossible for him to maintain the army at a sufficiently high level. Appeals for reinforcements by Leclerc and then by Rochambeau, his successor, could not be met, and the colony was lost to France for ever.

Divisions among the whites, the population structure, the international situation: these are all factors which must be taken in account when attempting to explain the course of events leading up to Haitian independence. To conclude from this that the black slave population played a merely passive role in the revolution would be seriously to misconceive the situation. Perhaps we may excuse the anthropologist Leyburn for a somewhat naive approach to the past, when he suggests that 'it was not the resentment of slaves against their masters which caused the final explosion; the slaves were tinder used by others to keep the conflagration burning'.[97] Less innocent, however, is T. O. Ott in his explicitly historical work, *The Haitian Revolution*. The author clearly sees that 'there was no monolithic cause of the slave rebellion', yet he commits himself to the extraordinary view that the whites and mulattoes 'handed them [the slaves] the colony by default', and 'forced them' into a course of action which they would not otherwise have adopted.[98] Do we conclude from the fact that the German army was more efficient than the Russian army in 1917, that the Russian peasants were discontented and so on, that Lenin was handed the country by default? Could any serious historian suggest that because Batista's government was corrupt, because the urban middle and working classes in Cuba were restless because the Communist Party was ineffective, Fidel Castro and the guerrillas of the Sierra Maestra played a merely passive role in the Cuban revolution and were 'forced' into the action which they took? Certainly the slave rebellion and the subsequent activity of the blacks must be seen in their historical context; the movement succeeded because of its structural relationship to the global situation. But this is not to say that the slaves were merely passive. Perhaps there is to be detected in the work of these scholars a trace of the belief that blacks are incapable of initiating anything. Ott betrays where his own sympathies lie when he refers to the failure of the *grands blancs* to unite with the *affranchis* as 'one of the greatest tragedies of the revolution'.[99]

From the standpoint of our present essay there are some further questions which need to be posed, even if they cannot be answered conclusively. What role did Voodoo play in the slave rebellion? The religion certainly provided an institution through which the African past of the slaves was perpetuated and also an instrument of solidarity and communication during the colonial period. Earlier slave revolts, such as the one led by Mackandal in the mid eighteenth century, were inspired by Voodoo, as was the ceremony in the Bois Caiman presided over by Boukmann, an *houngan* (Voodoo priest), on the eve of the slave rising. In the prayer traditionally ascribed to him, he called upon *Bon Dieu*, who knows the wickedness of the whites, to inspire his black disciples, and to strengthen them in their struggle.[100] In their letter to Governor General Blanchelande, the rebellious blacks of the Camp de Galiffet wrote, 'God, who fights for the innocent, is our guide; he will never desert us; therefore this is our motto: "Vanquish or die".'[101] If religion is opium, then it should be emphasised that opium is not always a sedative, but may become a source of inspiration and a prelude to action. The *créole* blacks, however, led by Toussaint, Dessalines and Christophe, attempted to suppress the Voodoo cult, for it was a powerful institution from the leadership of which they were effectively excluded.

Another hotly contested issue is whether Toussaint or Rigaud was the real prophet of Haitian independence. On the one hand, as we shall see, mulatto historians have frequently denounced the black leader as a collaborator with the whites who preferred maintaining the country under French sovereignty to sharing power with the mulattoes in an independent state. Black historians, on the other hand, see Rigaud as an instrument, used by the French in order to sow the seeds of discord among Haitians. There is truth in both accusations, though neither contains the whole truth. Toussaint was content for Saint Domingue to remain under the French flag, but he was willing to accept this situation only as long as it was he who was the effective ruler in the colony. Rigaud for his part was willing to side with the French only so long as it served what he believed to be the interests of the class to which he belonged. Both leaders needed to work within the situation which faced them, making temporary alliances for the sake of expediency. To accept at face value everything that either man said, particularly when they were asserting their loyalty to France, would be a mistake only less grave than to deny that each man put the interests of his particular class and colour above the cause of national independence; in this respect they were the first in a long line of Haitian leaders.

2. Fathers of national independence

1804-1825

On 1 January 1804 the independence of Haiti was formally proclaimed by Jean Jacques Dessalines and the victorious black and coloured generals.[1] The 1801 compromise which had been reached by Toussaint, according to which the country had enjoyed full internal self-government while still being part of French territory, had failed to secure liberty for the people. Napoleon had sent a formidable army under Leclerc to reimpose strict metropolitan control, to reintroduce slavery and to take away political power from these 'gilded Africans', as the French leader called them. This move at first met with resistance from Toussaint and his fellow generals, but one by one they made their peace with the superior forces. Toussaint was deported, and the remaining generals were obliged to collaborate with the invading army of Leclerc. For a time, open resistance to the French forces came only from bands of irregulars. Dessalines, however, while he was fighting against these irregulars, was also probably giving them secret assistance. In mid-October 1802 Pétion rebelled against the French and he was followed immediately by Christophe and others. The last stage of the struggle for independence had begun. Blacks and mulattoes were convinced that at this stage of the battle it was the whites who were their common enemy, and that they must at all costs be defeated. Complete independence became the goal of the black and mulatto generals fighting under the leadership of Dessalines.

Haiti's early years, from the declaration of independence to the recognition of independence by the former metropolitan power, can conveniently be divided into three periods, associated with the names of four leaders. The first three years, under the domination of Dessalines, set the pattern in many important respects for the future development of the country. The black general adopted the title of emperor during the first year of independence, but was assassinated in October 1806. After a few months of uncertainty Haiti split into a southern republic (comprising the departments of the South and West) and a northern state. Leadership of the former was in the hands of Alexandre Pétion, while the northern state was controlled by Henry Christophe, who in 1811 became King Henry I. Christophe retained the black and red imperial flag while Pétion returned to the blue and red horizontally-placed colours which constituted the first flag of independent Haiti.[2] Further complications were introduced into the situation by the fact that the region of La Grand'Anse in the South was controlled by the former *marron* Goman, who formed an alliance with Christophe and who was made Comte de Jérémie.[3] Then in 1810 André Rigaud returned to Haiti and led the South into an independent republic, distinct from Pétion's state. After some months, however, he died and General J.-M. Borgella brought the erring province back into union with the West. Pétion was proclaimed president for life in 1816 and nominated as his successor General Jean-Pierre Boyer, who assumed office on his death in 1818. King Henry committed suicide in 1820 and the country was once more united. The third period, then, begins in 1820 with Boyer as president of a united Haiti; in 1822 at the invitation of some of the leaders of the Spanish-speaking eastern part of the island Boyer marched into Santo Domingo and ruled the whole of Hispaniola until he was removed from office in 1843. Haitian independence was accepted by France in 1825. This chapter will be particularly concerned with the way in which Haiti emerged as a symbol of black liberation in the eyes of Haitians themselves, and in the eyes of foreign observers, hostile and sympathetic alike. We shall note the way in which this racial factor influenced Haitian thinking in the fields of foreign relations, laws of citizenship, laws governing the foreign ownership of property, and in the relationship between plantation and subsistence agriculture. We shall, however, observe the somewhat ambivalent attitude adopted by Haitians in this early period towards Africa and things African. It will also become clear that colour distinctions — going back to the racialism of colonial days — were perpetuated into the era of independence and, being largely coincident with economic class distinctions, became increasingly significant in the politics of the country, particularly during the presidency of Boyer.

It is difficult to estimate the size of the population in these years immediately after the declaration of independence, though the total in 1825 was considerably greater than the population in 1789 in spite of the loss of life during the revolutionary period and the emigration of many whites. Other residents attempted to leave the country and two ordinances issued in October 1804 were designed to prevent them from leaving by ship. Exports, particularly of sugar, declined in these years; in the South and West, and to a lesser extent in the North, the *nouveaux libres* left the plantations to work on small plots of land which they secured from the government or on which they squatted. On this land they grew crops for local consumption and coffee for export. Foreign merchants living in the coastal cities soon secured control of the import and export sector of the economy, though a number of mulatto Haitians also engaged in foreign commerce. Dessalines had prescribed no official religion, but in the constitutions of the northern state and of the southern republic after 1806 the Roman Catholic religion was declared the religion of the country, though toleration was granted to other faiths. Methodist missionaries were active in Port-au-Prince under Pétion, and some Anglican priests were engaged in educational work under Christophe. Nevertheless the popular religion of the Haitian people was then, as it is now, Voodoo. Government was conducted by military officers assisted by civilian ministers, and was, despite the republican constitution of 1806, dictatorial in substance, as we shall see.

I

Dessalines and black liberation

With the departure of the French armies and the declaration of independence a number of pressing problems faced the government. There was, in the first place, the question of the relationship, diplomatic and commercial, between Haiti and the other powers of the region, particularly Britain, Spain and the United States. A successful slave revolt had occurred, an alliance had been forged between the free coloured population and the former slaves, and the colonial power had been defeated. These events had serious implications for the other slave colonies of the region. The abolition of slavery was written into the first constitution of Haiti, and lay at the very basis of the national liberation struggle. Dessalines himself recognised the significance of the step which Haitians had taken, and the possible consequence which this had for other French colonies. He looked over the sea to Martinique, where slavery still existed. 'Unfortunate Martiniquans', he declared, 'I am not able to fly to your assistance and break your chains. Alas, an invincible obstacle separates us . . . But perhaps a spark from the fire which we have kindled will spring forth in your soul . . .'[4] Dessalines also made explicit claims to the Spanish part of the island, which he invaded in 1805:

Having decided to recognise as borders only those traced by nature and the seas, convinced that as long as a single enemy still breathes on this territory there remains something for me to do in order to hold with dignity the post to which you have appointed me . . . I have resolved to regain possession of the integral part of my dominions and to destroy even to the last vestiges the European idol.[5]

With statements like these, there can have been little doubt in the minds of the colonising powers that Haiti represented a potential threat to their position.

The first constitution of Haiti proclaimed that all Haitians no matter what their shade of skin were to be called 'black'; this included even those German and Polish groups in Saint Domingue who had fought with the liberation movement and had become citizens. Perhaps this is the first time that the term 'black' has been used in an ideological sense.[6] Furthermore, the constitution stated that no white man, whatever his nationality, should set foot in Haiti as a master or property owner, and that he was unable to acquire property in the future (art. 12). Just as colonial Saint Domingue had been based upon a system of white superiority, so Haiti became a symbol of black power.

The first draft of the declaration of independence had been drawn up by an educated mulatto, Charéron, who formulated a long and reasoned defence of the step which was being taken towards independence. After it had been read out, Boisrond Tonnerre, also a mulatto, who had been drinking heavily, stammered, 'All that which has been formulated is not in accordance with our real feelings; to draw up the Act of Independence, we need the skin of a white man for parchment, his skull for a writing desk, his blood for ink, and a bayonet for pen.' Dessalines replied in Haitian *créole*, 'C'est ça, Mouqué, c'est ça, même mon vlé! C'est sang blanc, mon besoin.' ('That is right, sir, that is right, that is my wish. I need white blood.') It was Boisrond Tonnerre who produced the final text of the declaration.[7]

Foreign relations

Dessalines found it necessary to reassure nations other than France and Spain that the newly independent state posed no threat to the security of their colonies. In his first proclamation as head of state, he warned Haitians against a spirit of proselytism which might lead them to interfere with their neighbours, and thus to endanger the independence of their own country. Haitians ought not to concern themselves with the internal affairs of the neighbouring islands. 'Peace to our neighbours, but anathema to the name of France' was the slogan with which he summed up the policy of Haiti. The constitution of May 1805 confirmed this assurance to foreign powers: 'The emperor will not undertake any enterprise with a view to making conquests or to troubling the peace and the internal regime of foreign colonies.'[8]

Yet despite these assurances on the part of Dessalines, the mere existence of an independent black state which had achieved liberation by a violent struggle against a white colonial administration posed a threat to other nations. 'The existence of a negro people in arms', wrote Talleyrand to General Louis Turreau in Washington, 'occupying a country which it has soiled by the most criminal acts, is a horrible spectacle for all white nations.'[9] Haiti came to be regarded by foreigners as well as by Haitians themselves as the symbol of black dignity and of human equality. The existence of Haiti gave hope to the slave population of the New World and thus constituted a warning and a possible threat to the European colonial powers, and to the slave-owners of the United

States. For these reasons Dessalines and later heads of state laid emphasis upon the principle of non-intervention, and attempted in their foreign policy to play off one power against another so as to forestall the possibility of a united assault on the black state.

The law of Haiti forbade foreign ownership of property, but the new government fully realised the importance of foreign trade, and encouraged the overtures which were being made by Britain and the United States. George Nugent, the governor of Jamaica, opened negotiations with Dessalines in 1803, seeking a commercial agreement. The Americans were also keen on developing trade with Haiti, and during the first two years of independence the United States was Haiti's most important trading partner. An anonymous Haitian writer, in a contribution to the official *Gazette*, warned against the danger of American imperialism. Owing to its proximity, as well as to the frequent visits of its citizens to the ports of the Empire and to 'the pretentions to which these might give birth,' the United States might in future be a greater threat to Haitian independence than would the countries of Europe.[10] Owing, however, to pressure from the French government, whose diplomatic support the Americans needed in their dispute with Spain over the details of the Louisiana purchase, the United States government placed an embargo upon commerce with Haiti in February 1806.[11]

When it was suggested to Dessalines that his fierce policy towards the former French colonists would jeopardise his trade relations with other white countries, the emperor replied:

Such a man does not know the whites. Hang a white man below one of the pans in the scales of the customs house, and put a sack of coffee in the other pan; the other whites will buy the coffee without paying attention to the body of their fellow white.[12]

The imperial constitution proclaimed commerce to be, after agriculture, a principal source of wealth, and guaranteed protection to foreign merchants. Yet commerce was closely controlled by the government. In November 1805 the government — 'wishing to assure exclusively to Haitian speculators the benefits resulting from the exploitation of salt', and 'desiring to favour the prosperity of this branch of internal commerce' — forbade the importation of this commodity. Other goods could be imported by licensed merchants only. By a decree of 2 September 1806 Dessalines imposed a 10-per-cent tax on all imported goods and, in an attempt to raise further revenue, set a tax on exports of coffee and other goods.[13] This policy was attacked by the group which assassinated the emperor in October 1806.

Property and the colour question

In internal affairs Dessalines was also faced with serious problems. Independence had been won as the result of the tenuous alliance

between the *anciens libres* and the *nouveaux libres*. We have already
seen that these groups were largely (though not entirely) identifiable
in terms of colour distinctions. Most of the leading *anciens libres*
were mulattoes and the vast majority of the former slaves were black.
The *anciens libres* were property owners, and had retained their property
through the revolutionary period. What is more, some of them had
received property from their white fathers who had fled the country,
and others had illegally seized vacant properties, particularly in the
South. With the abolition of slavery in 1793 the legal distinction
between these two groups had been done away with, but as the country
moved towards independence these two economic classes, which were
largely identifiable by colour differences, faced one another. We have
also noted that these economic and colour distinctions were reinforced
by regional factors, so that the mulattoes were strongest in the South
and West, while the blacks dominated the political and military forces
in the Artibonite and North. It was Dessalines's ambition to eliminate
colour prejudice from the life of the country, and this was reflected
in the constitutional article already quoted, which referred to all
Haitians as black; he offered the hand of his daughter to Pétion as a
token of his determination to break down colour lines. Yet the economic disparity between the two groups had to be faced. In a well-
known statement Dessalines referred to the unjust situation whereby
the *anciens libres* retained all the private property of the country, while
the former slaves remained without land. Why should the sons of the
white colonists have property and those whose fathers are in Africa
have none? 'The sons of the colonists', he declared, 'have taken advantage of my poor blacks. Be on your guard, negroes and mulattoes, we
have all fought against the whites; the properties which we have conquered by the spilling of our blood belong to us all; I intend that they
be divided with equity.'[14] Whether Dessalines intended to divide the
land into small properties and distribute them to the people, or whether
he meant to extend state ownership with blacks enjoying equality with
mulattoes, is not entirely clear. What was clear to his hearers was the
emperor's intention of confiscating some of the recently acquired land
from the *anciens libres*, and this is certainly one of the reasons for his
assassination in October 1806.

It is therefore a grotesque misrepresentation of the situation to
accuse Dessalines of having 'set the Haitians upon the road to a caste
system', as Leyburn does.[15] Many writers have used the term 'caste'
to apply to the rigid system of stratification in colonial Saint Domingue;
some like Madiou in the nineteenth century and Leyburn himself in
the twentieth have used the term rather more loosely to describe the
two principal groups which composed independent Haiti.[16] It cannot
fairly be said, however, that Dessalines set Haiti on the road to a caste

system; in fact, as we have noted, he did all in his power to break down the barriers of colour and of wealth which Haitians had inherited from the colonial past. Leyburn himself states that Dessalines was 'tactless' enough to attack 'inherited privilege' and 'colour distinctions'. Insofar as we can talk intelligibly about a caste system in post-colonial Haiti, Dessalines was its adversary. The emperor certainly brought the question of social injustice out into the open, and was spokesman for the disinherited. It is always the lot of the oppressed to be accused of having initiated group antagonism, and of thereby disturbing the peace and the good community relations which had previously existed. Beaubrun Ardouin, one of the principal ideologists of the mulatto elite, also accused Dessalines of having pursued an impolitic and inhumane policy which prevented a fusion of the two groups. But the assessment of Thomas Madiou is more balanced: 'He conceived the generous and salutary idea, after the deportation of Toussaint L'Ouverture, of reuniting the two castes whose interests were the same, and of opposing them in a single body, to our oppressors; this was the constant and persistent idea of his whole life.'[17] Madiou went on to claim that just as Toussaint was the symbol of black supremacy, Dessalines symbolised an alliance between black and mulatto.

Militarism and politics

A further problem facing the newly independent state was what form of government to institute. The leaders of the national liberation struggle had not participated in the government of colonial Saint Domingue, except in its terminal stages. The wars of independence had resulted in the total elimination of the old elite group of colonial days. The administration of Saint Domingue under the French had been extremely centralised, with legal authority being concentrated in the hands of a military governor general who was responsible to the government in Paris. On the eve of the revolution the governor general 'had become the omnipotent agent of a centralisation *à outrance*', wrote Placide David.[18] Alexis de Tocqueville had already observed how the centralisation which was a lamentable feature of all French administration was magnified and exaggerated in the French colonies.[19] The leaders of the new nation were military officers and the type of authority which they understood best was that which is found in an army. The nation had gained independence as a result of thirteen years of fighting, and furthermore even after 1804 there was the continual threat of foreign military intervention. It is not therefore surprising to find that the form of government adopted in Haiti was military and authoritarian, clothed in the garments now of an empire, now of a republic, now of a monarchy. There was very little choice open to the leaders of the new black state, and it is surely a misunderstanding of the situation to suggest, as Leyburn does, that 'if ever a country had an opportunity to start absolutely fresh in choosing its own social institutions, Haiti had that opportunity in 1804 . . . the Haitians might (theoretically at least) have invented an entirely new little world of economic, political, religious and social life. All paths were open to them.'[20] No nation can begin absolutely fresh, and the viable courses of action open to Dessalines in 1804, with respect to the political institutions to adopt, were limited. In fact Dessalines became governor general on the pattern of Toussaint's 1801 constitution, but soon he was proclaimed emperor. The imperial constitution was, stated Dessalines, appropriate to the customs, usages and character of the Haitian people.[21] The government was, however, autocratic as well as being authoritarian, and Dessalines was not sufficiently sensitive to the opinions of his fellow generals. We have already seen how his economic policy in particular alienated important sectors of opinion. The *anciens libres* together with ambitious elements among the *nouveaux libres* determined to rid themselves of the emperor. An insurrection broke out in the South against the agent of the emperor, General Moreau, who was arrested on 8 October 1806; it was stated that he carried written instructions to exterminate the class of *anciens libres* of all colours. Most of the black and coloured generals supported the insurrection, and on 17 October 1806 the emperor was ambushed at Pont Rouge outside Port-au-Prince and shot dead.

II

With the death of Dessalines, Henry Christophe was proclaimed provisional chief of the government. Christophe was probably a *griffe* (born of mulatto and black parents) from the island of Grenada.[22] He fought in the early stages of the revolution with the British, and had spent some time in the United States. Christophe returned to become one of Toussaint's principal generals, and he fought under Dessalines during the last stages of the liberation struggle. Pétion and Gérin, together with a number of other officers, especially from the South and West, were, however, determined to limit the powers of the new head of state, and a constitutional convention was called in December 1806 at Port-au-Prince. A committee of nine under the chairmanship of Pétion put forward a draft constitution. 'It is', they declared,

an incontestable truth that the best system of government is that which, being best adapted to the character and to the customs of the people for whom it is made, must procure for them the greatest amount of well-being, but it is equally evident and certain that there are principles common to every good constitution. The most essential of these principles is the separation of powers, inasmuch as their concentration in the same hands is what constitutes and defines despotism.[23]

Christophe denounced the convention, and marched on Port-au-Prince. He found, however, that he was unable to subdue the South and West, while Pétion, a light-skinned mulatto born at Port-au-Prince in 1770, who was elected president in March 1807, could not defeat the northern armies. Fourteen years of civil war had begun.

Haiti and the black race

The spokesmen of the northern state and those of the republic agreed in seeing Haiti as a symbol of black dignity and black power in a world dominated by European nations. Noël Colombel, one of the principal apologists of Pétion's regime, reminded Haitians that they were the 'regenerators of Africa', and that their struggle represented a gleam of hope for two-thirds of the world.[24] Also from the republic F. D. Chanlatte claimed that the whole colonial edifice was perishing and that the nineteenth century would witness the liberation of men of all colours throughout the world.[25] The Comte de Rosiers, from Christophe's kingdom, urged 'the immense and unfortunate regions of Africa' to rejoice; the Haitian revolution marked the beginning of their redemption. He stated that the last gasps of the slave trade were the signal for the first steps towards the recognition of Haitian independence and he called upon philanthropists to strive for a full recognition of this independence.[26] Haitian writers rejected the theories of racialism which suggested that the races of the world are mentally or intellectually different in any significant respect, and claimed that theories of racial inferiority had been invented by white colonists to 'justify' the system of slavery. These theories were thus nothing more than ideologies, in the pejorative sense of the term. Juste Chanlatte argued that the physical differences between the races were largely the result of varying climatic conditions, so that the human species is better able to survive in the environment in which it finds itself. A system as oppressive as slavery in the new world could be defended only on the basis of extravagant ideas and diabolical cunning: 'To deny with respect to ourselves the unity of the species, to suggest in fact our inferiority, was to legitimate in some sort of way the traffic of the traders in human flesh, and to constitute in principle the right of slavery.'[27] Those people who attempted to justify the doctrines of racial inferiority by citing the indolence and the limited knowledge of the negroes ignored the fact that these characteristics are a direct result of slavery itself. The slaves were deliberately maintained in a state of ignorance, and their apparent laziness was a passive protest against the oppression under which they laboured.[28] King Henry had already insisted that mankind has a common origin, and that differences between the races are due not to inherent factors but are 'the result of civilization and knowledge'.[29] Haiti was, he claimed, by its very existence and by the progress it was making, conclusive proof against the racialist position. 'Instead of replying to them', he declared to the Haitian people,

we will make rapid strides towards civilization. Let them dispute, if they please, the existence of our intellectual faculties, our little or no aptness for the arts and sciences, whilst we reply to these by irresistible arguments, and prove to the impious, by facts and by examples, that the blacks, like the whites, are men, and like them are the works of a Divine Omnipotence![30]

The Chevalier de Prézeau in turn claimed that Haitians were proud of their colour and had no desire to become whites.[31] Haiti was thus seen as both a symbol and a proof of black dignity and of human equality.

Republican writers also denounced theories of racial inferiority. Félix Darfour, in his journal *L'Eclaireur Haytien*, argued that such theories were but the rationalisation of economic interest on the part of European nations.[32] In a series of articles on the book of Genesis, J. S. Milscent endeavoured to 'destroy the false opinion which the enemies of our race have tried to establish' on the basis of certain passages in this book. [33] He attacked the idea that the alleged degradation of Canaan was the origin of slavery, suggesting that the story was invented by Moses in order to explain or justify the system of slavery which already existed in his day.[34] Milscent insisted that differences in colour were due to the fact that God created men differently according to the climatic conditions in which they would live, so that men of all races were equal before him.[35] This belief led Milscent to attack colonial expansion as a usurpation which is contrary to the laws of God as they manifest themselves in the geographical separation of nations and continents. In the first number of his journal *L'Abeille Haytienne*, Milscent declared:

The establishment of European power in countries which the Supreme Being has separated from them by distance and by the barrier of the sea, is founded only upon usurpation. The divine hand, in distributing men in diverse zones, gave them an organisation appropriate to each temperature, and the whole must not submit to the laws of one of the parts of which it is composed. Only in situations when a country is found to be deserted is colonisation justifiable; to seize territory by slaughtering the native population is mere brigandage and gives rise to no valid claim upon that territory.[36]

Milscent therefore rejected any suggestion that Haitians needed to buy their liberty.[37]

There was, nevertheless, on the part of these Haitian writers a somewhat ambivalent attitude towards Africa. The mulattoes, of course, were partly of European origin and valued this link with Europe; most of the blacks were *créoles* and shared to some degree the colonial prejudice against Africa. While they denied vehemently any notion of the inherent inferiority of Africans, they often assumed that Africa was a barbarous continent and that the only civilisation worth considering in their own day was European. 'We realize what efforts we in turn must make', wrote King Henry to Clarkson, 'in order to fulfil your hope of being some day able to raise up Africa to the level of European civilization.'[38] Clarkson noted the fear entertained by Madame Christophe and her daughters of being confounded with Africans during their exile in Europe.[39] Even Félix Darfour, whose journal *L'Eclaireur Haytien* (which later became *L'Avertisseur Haytien*) adopted a somewhat *noiriste* position, assumed that the Africa of his day was deprived of civilisation and culture. The backwardness of the African people, however, was due to social and historical factors rather than to any inherent inferiority.[40] Darfour was himself born in Africa and he referred, in the early numbers of his journal, to Haitians as 'Africans'. He was rebuked for this by Milscent who stated that the term suggested a party spirit; Darfour subsequently agreed to cease describing Haitians as Africans.[41]

Baron de Vastey

It is, perhaps, in the writings of Baron de Vastey that this equivocal attitude towards Africa is best seen. Pompée Valentin Vastey was born at Ennery, near Marmalade in the northern part of Haiti, in 1781. He was the eldest son of a Frenchman, Jean Valentin Vastey, who came from Jumièges near Rouen. On leaving France in 1769 Jean Vastey stayed for some time in the southern city of Jérémie, where he met a coloured *créole*, Mademoiselle Dumas, whom he married. Although a mulatto, the young Vastey joined the army of Toussaint at the age of fifteen, and was from that time on associated with the cause of the *nouveaux libres*.[42] He was one of Christophe's principal advisors, and was tutor to the king's eldest son. Widely respected for his learning and his intelligence, de Vastey was hated and feared by the white residents of the kingdom. W. W. Harvey wrote of him:

His fierceness, his duplicity and his meanness, rendered him at once despicable and odious. He cheated whenever an opportunity offered, and afterwards boasted of his dishonesty. The hatred which he entertained towards whites of all nations rendered him sometimes an object of terror. Regarding them with utter abhorrence, he rejoiced to do them the most unprovoked injuries; and on one occasion he was heard calmly to declare that if he were allowed to follow his own wishes, he would massacre every white man in the Island.[43]

De Vastey became the official ideologist and apologist of the kingdom; his published works were distributed by the king and by the foreign minister, the Comte de Limonade. The views which de Vastey expressed can therefore reasonably be taken as representing in general the position adopted by the kingdom. With the fall of the kingdom in 1820 de Vastey was murdered by Boyer's troops and his body thrown into a disused well.

The colonial system, de Vastey maintained, was based upon the institution of slavery, which was in turn defended with reference to a theory of racial inferiority. The self-interest of the planters had led them to elaborate a racial theory which put the black man on a level with the beasts with the purpose of justifying their treatment of him as a beast.[44] De Vastey particularly criticised the clergy of colonial Saint Domingue for having been one of the principal instruments of colonial and racist propaganda. They continually preached the notion of white superiority and black submission. They told the slaves that it was necessary to suffer and to endure pain on earth in order to be happy in the next world. Clothed in the respectable garments of religion, they were sent out by the colonists to reinforce the degradation of the slaves. 'But', be continued, 'we have destroyed the toys of superstition with the chains of slavery.'[45] While colour prejudice was turned into an ideology of racialism in order to serve the interests of the colonists, there is, de Vastey suggested, a certain kind of prejudice which is natural and is common to all groups of men. It is natural for the members of any group to have a predilection for their own kind; black people are also prejudiced in this way, believing themselves to be more beautiful and more favoured by nature than are the whites. He went on to observe how artists and painters from Haiti portrayed God and the angels as black and the devils as white.[46]

As a result of the war of independence Haiti had become the symbol of black liberation; it was the land where the black man could walk erect.[47] Emerging from a background of oppression, it was the vocation of Haitians to lead the black race into a new era:

Black as we are and yellow in complexion, bowed as we have been for centuries under the yoke of slavery and ignorance, assimilated to the condition of the brute; how resolutely ought we to exert ourselves; how much of perseverance, wisdom and virtue is necessary for reanimating our race, to this moment enchained and in darkness.[48]

Furthermore, the independence of Haiti was seen by de Vastey as conclusive proof 'that Africa is capable of civilisation' and that there is no inherent difference between the various branches of the human race; all men are brothers and are members of a single family.[49] Like Chanlatte, he suggested that differences of colour stem from varying climates.[50]

De Vastey replied to those enemies of the black race who suggested that the African continent had always been sunk in barbarism and that a state of ignorance is inherent in the nature of its inhabitants. If these propagandists had forgotten that Africa was the cradle of the sciences

and of the arts, it was up to Haitians to remind them![51] Egypt was the
first civilised country in the world, and many African countries were
regarded as being far advanced in civilisation at a time when the Gauls
were still a barbarous and ignorant people.[52] The baron took particular
pleasure in pointing out to the former colonists how their ancestors,
the Gauls, were despised by their Roman conquerors, and how backward they were compared with many parts of Africa at that time.[53]
He used the findings of explorers like Mungo Park to refute the idea
that the Africa of his own day was totally uncivilised. 'From the record
of his journey', he declared, 'it can easily be seen that the Africans
are not at all as barbarous and as far from civilisation as our enemies
would have us believe.'[54] In fact many of these people were far advanced in civilisation. De Vastey attacked the false notion that African
government was despotic, which was an idea shared by many European
writers, including Hegel,[55] and he gave examples of mild systems of
government in the continent. Also the accusation of the Baron de
Malouet that African people are incapable of independence and are
naturally disposed to obey others was rejected. 'Do there not exist in
Africa', he demanded, 'an infinity of empires, of kingdoms and of
independent states?'[56]

I referred earlier to de Vastey's equivocal attitude towards Africa.
He clearly believed that to be civilised in the early nineteenth century
was to be like the Europeans. His argument was basically that Africans
were not inherently inferior to Europeans, that they were capable of
civilisation, and that, in fact, parts of Africa were not as different from
Europe as many people believed. Yet his general view of Africa was
that it was a backward continent, and that it was the vocation of
'noble and generous England' to carry civilisation to the people of
Africa through an enlightened colonial policy.[57] 'To civilise Africa',
he wrote, 'in bringing to it the sciences and the arts, in encouraging
agriculture and commerce; this glorious enterprise is appropriate to a
magnanimous and enlightened nation; it is appropriate in a word to the
great British nation.'[58] De Vastey went on to celebrate the founding of
Sierra Leone as an example of the colonial policy he had in mind.

As we shall see, de Vastey was in certain respects conservative in his
political ideas, criticising revolution, defending stability, favouring
royalty and aristocracy rather than democracy, and insisting upon a
policy of non-intervention in the internal affairs of other countries. His
views on Africa and the black race would clearly disqualify him for the
position of a father of *négritude*. Yet in a prophetic passage de Vastey
pointed to Haiti as the first fruit of a great colonial revolution in which
'five hundred million men, black, yellow and brown, spread over the
surface of the globe, are reclaiming the rights and privileges which they
have received from the author of nature'.[59] It was this conception of

Haiti's symbolic role which was to influence much political thinking within the country itself, and which was largely to determine the policy of the world powers towards Haiti during the years immediately following the declaration of independence.

Revolution in one country?

Although the policy pursued by the two Haitian states differed at certain points, as we shall see, there was a common core of agreed policy. In the first place both firmly rejected any possibility of reintroducing slavery, and also saw it as part of their mission to combat slavery and the slave trade wherever they still existed. Pétion gave encouragement and assistance to both Miranda and Bolívar in their efforts to free the South American mainland from Spanish control, and one of the conditions which he placed upon his assistance to Bolívar was an agreement to end slavery in the territories which the latter was seeking to liberate. In July 1816 Bolívar made his proclamation announcing the freedom of slaves in Venezuela. Pétion had, however, requested that his own contribution to the success of Bolívar's mission should not be mentioned, due to the possible international repercussions. Christophe supported and encouraged the work of Clarkson, Wilberforce and the abolitionists; he was nevertheless careful not to interfere with the Spanish slave trade. 'Though it is only with the greatest grief', he told Clarkson, 'that I can bear to see Spanish vessels engaged in the slave trade within sight of our coasts, it is not my intention to fit out ships of war against them because I should never wish to give our enemies any excuse for molesting us.'[60] It was a crucial principle of Christophe's foreign policy, in fact, to avoid giving any nation an excuse to interfere in the internal affairs of Haiti, and this demanded a conservative and cautious approach to international questions. Although Haiti had clearly placed the abolition of slavery at the foundation of national life, this did not mean that she would interfere in neighbouring colonies to secure abolition. One of the recurring themes in Christophe's letters to Thomas Clarkson is Haiti's refusal to become involved in the internal affairs of her neighbours. He stated a general principle of the kingdom's foreign policy:

Since the first Declaration of our Independence, the maxim of the government which preceded mine, as well as my own, has been not to interfere with the internal affairs of our neighbours. We have made this a fundamental article of our constitutions.[61]

The king went on to point out that the actions of Haitian governments had been in accord with this stated policy. The Spanish colony of Santo Domingo, sharing a common border with Haiti, had been left in peace, in spite of the fact that slavery was still being practised there. Henry reminded Clarkson that he had actually assisted the Spanish government with arms and ammunition. He attacked Pétion for giving support to Simón Bolívar and the South American liberation forces.[62] and explicitly dissociated the kingdom from disturbances which had occurred in some of the British colonies of the Caribbean:

How can anyone do us the injury of suggesting that we, who have so much reason to be grateful to the Government and people of England for the interest which they have always taken in our welfare, should ever seek to upset the Regime of the British colonies? Is it because these same colonies have experienced troubles and internal commotions? But these have nothing and can have nothing in common with the cause which we defended for more than 27 years.[63]

To show that he meant what he said, the king arrested a number of persons who were accused of planning to instigate a revolt in Jamaica.

The principles set forth by King Henry in his private correspondence were only an elaboration of article 36 of the 1807 constitution which stated that the government of Haiti would not disturb the regime according to which neighbouring colonies were governed. Baron de Vastey reiterated in his published works the policy of the kingdom on this matter. He insisted that the existence of Haiti posed no threat to powers with colonies in the region: 'we are no lovers of revolutions', he proclaimed, 'no one is more anxious to uphold, than we are, the stability of empires and of human things'.[64] He attacked the revised constitution of the republic which included an article (art. 44) allowing all Africans, Indians or their descendants to settle in Haiti and to become citizens after one year's residence. This article, de Vastey argued, was a violation of the principle contained in the act of independence which expressly forbids disturbing the peace or the domestic economy of other territories directly or indirectly. By article 44 Pétion's republic, he maintained, made a direct appeal to the black and coloured population of neighbouring countries to settle themselves in the country, 'a measure which tends directly to disturb the peace and internal government of those foreign colonies or countries'.[65] Despite these potentially revolutionary implications of article 44, article 2 of the republican constitution explicitly stated that the country must never attempt to conquer or to interfere with the internal affairs of neighbouring colonies.

The search for recognition

Although there was disagreement between the republic and the kingdom about the question of aid to foreign revolutionary movements, both states insisted that full and complete independence must be maintained, and that it was important to secure international recognition from the great powers as soon as possible. Informal negotiations had taken place between Pétion and the representatives of Napoleon, but they had come to nothing. With the restoration of the monarchy in 1814, agents were sent to meet with the Haitian leaders to attempt a reconciliation between France and her former colony. One of these agents, General Dauxion Lavaysse, was politely received by Pétion at Port-au-Prince; another agent, Medina, attempted to enter the northern kingdom through the Spanish part of the island. He was arrested and condemned on a charge of spying. He was carrying papers which indicated the French intention of splitting the mulattoes from the blacks and of restoring the colonial regime. The French plan further included distinctions among the mulattoes themselves. The first group, including Pétion and Borgella — 'toute fois que la couleur les rapproche de la caste blanche' — would be given full political rights. The rest of the light-skinned caste would be subject to certain restrictions; the third group, 'qui est moins rapproché de blanc que le jaune mulâtre', still less rights. Finally the blacks would be compelled to return to their former masters. This intention on the part of France was attacked by Christophe and by Pétion. 'We solemnly declare', ran the proclamation of King Henry,

that we will never become a party to any treaty, to any condition, that may compromise the honour, the liberty, or the independence of the Haytian people; that, true to our oath, we will sooner bury ourselves beneath the ruins of our native country, than suffer an infraction of our political rights.[66]

Christophe's council of state outlined the theory of a total war, distinguishing between 'les guerres politiques' in which the armies fight while the civilian population remains uninvolved, and 'une guerre d'extermination', when the very existence of a nation is at stake. In this latter case the whole people, including women and children, take up arms and all weapons of destruction become legitimate. It would be a war of ambush and guerrilla tactics, in which the enemy is attacked in the gorges and mountain passes of the difficult terrain.[67]

Pétion also issued a pronouncement against the French ambition of restoring Haiti to its previous colonial status, and announced that Haitians would resist by arms any attempt to conquer the country. 'Our independence has been the fruit of our exertions', he declared; 'without it, no security, no guarantee of our regeneration.'[68] The French government persisted in its efforts to persuade and cajole its former subjects into submission, and in 1816 two more agents, Fontanges and Esmangart, were sent to Haiti. King Henry resolutely refused to receive any communication which was not addressed from one sovereign to another. In a proclamation to the people he fiercely declared, 'Should the whole universe conspire for our destruction, the last Haytian will resign his last breath rather than cease to live free and independent.'[69] Pétion, who had agreed to meet with the agents, was no less firm in rejecting any compromise over the question of independence, and warned once more that anybody who attempted to invade the country would 'find on this land nothing but ashes mingled with blood, a destroying sword and an avenging climate'.[70] We may conclude that the public and official policy of both Pétion and Christophe was that national independence must be defended at all costs, and that recognition by France and by the other world powers should be secured as quickly as possible. The only major difference between the two governments was the willingness of the republic to pay compensation to the dispossessed planters. Christophe's letters to Clarkson indicate the concern of the Haitian king for a settlement with France. He even asked Clarkson to act as his agent in discussions with the French government. If complete and total independence were the only satisfactory solution for Haiti why, demanded the Comte de Limonade, had Toussaint himself not proclaimed independence and broken the final links with France? The foreign minister argued that although independence was the logical consequence of the 1801 constitution, neither Toussaint nor a sufficient proportion of the population at that time realised the necessity for taking this step. Some Haitians who had not really known what France was like still felt some loyalty to the metropolis, but 'this predilection exists no more'.[71]

Pétion's secret intentions

While the public and official policy of both the republic and the kingdom was that total independence must be maintained, it has been suggested that Pétion's private and secret view was that some kind of French protection or suzerainty would be desirable or at least acceptable. Baron de Vastey and other northern writers denounced Pétion as a collaborator with the French who was intending to reintroduce slavery, but this charge must be seen as a part of the royalists' campaign against the republic.[72] In a monograph of 1954, however, Leslie Manigat claims to produce evidence indicating that both Pétion and Boyer, his successor, were favourable to the 'return of the French' and to the recognition of the sovereignty of France.[73] For those who worship at the altar of national sovereignty this is a most serious accusation. The evidence marshalled against Pétion is inconclusive. It consists of an observation by a Frenchman in 1815 that the republic was ruled by *anciens libres*, many of whom were property-owners, and that in the republic 'the cause of liberty is defended with less zeal' than in the northern kingdom.[74] Much of the other evidence consists in similar kinds of speculation on the part of Frenchmen to the effect that Pétion might be favourable to some kind of French restoration, or to a 'rapprochement' with France. Unfortunately, however, Manigat does not seem to distinguish between a restoration and a rapprochement; Pétion was certainly in favour of a rapprochement, as indeed was Christophe. Manigat quotes the famous letter of Pétion to Marion of 25 July 1814 in which he wrote:

I can hardly believe that they [the whites] are so presumptuous as to imagine that they are able to take possession of this country and to make use of it, because we have already given them proof of what we are capable of when it comes to the preservation of our independence.[75]

But this letter was clearly destined for publication, and Manigat has already warned his readers that all published writings are liable to contain propaganda, and are thus less reliable than unpublished documents.[76] There is, however, in the Archives Nationales in Paris much stronger evidence that Pétion may have been willing to submit to French sovereignty in 1814. Dauxion Lavaysse wrote: 'On my arrival in Saint Domingue, they [the republican leaders] seemed disposed to recognise the sovereignty of France.'[77] Yet Pétion was inconsistent in this matter, and a few days after having 'consented to recognise the Sovereignty of France', he was talking of France selling Saint Domingue to the Haitians as she had sold Louisiana to the United States. This change of tune was ascribed by Dauxion Lavaysse to British intervention.[78] Manigat does not refer to these remarks, but quotes the report by Esmangart and Fontanges, where it was asserted that the republican leaders 'themselves have assured us' that at the time of the arrival of Dauxion Lavaysse 'everyone was disposed to submit', and that the situation was badly mishandled by the French delegation.[79]

Whether at this early stage in the discussion Pétion intended to accept French sovereignty is, of course, impossible to say. Perhaps he really believed that the best hope for the survival and prosperity of his class was to submit; on the other hand he may simply have been seeking to establish favourable relations with France, thus preventing an intervention by force, which was continually being advocated by part of the colonial pressure group in Paris and Nantes. After 1814, however, the public and private positions of Pétion would seem to have been identical — that a full recognition by France of Haiti's independence was a *sine qua non* of any agreement between the two countries. 'From the first moment', runs a confidential memorandum in the French archives, 'Pétion made it clear that he would reject any proposition which would not result in the recognition of Haitian independence . . . Pétion often repeated to Esmangart: "Concede independence; stipulate in this concession the conditions, and I shall sign." '[80] We may conclude then that while Manigat's assertions about the willingness of Pétion to submit to French sovereignty may be true of the period when he first met Dauxion Lavaysse, it was untrue of the subsequent period. Furthermore the evidence upon which Manigat bases his conclusion is by no means conclusive and he appears to have been assisted in coming to his conclusion by other factors; this is a matter to which I shall return.[81]

Compensation, recognition and foreign trade

Although Pétion demanded a recognition of full independence he was willing to pay compensation to the dispossessed French planters of Saint Domingue, and to sign a commercial treaty with the former metropolis. 'I proposed to your excellency', wrote Pétion, 'to establish the bases of an agreed indemnity which we shall solemnly engage to pay, accompanied by any just guarantee that may be required of us.'[82] Pétion and those influential in the republic were mostly *anciens libres* who had been property owners themselves in the colonial days. It is not, therefore, surprising that they were sympathetic to the plight of their fellow landowners. The official policy of the kingdom, on the other hand, where the *nouveaux libres* were more strongly represented, was uncompromisingly against such an indemnity. The foreign secretary, de Limonade, stated the royal position as follows:

Is it conceivable that Haitians who have escaped torture and massacre at the hands of these men, Haitians who have conquered their own country by the force of their arms and at the cost of their blood, that these same free Haitians should now purchase their property and persons once again with money paid to their former oppressors? It is not possible.[83]

He was, of course, wrong, for this is exactly what Boyer did, as we shall see. De Vastey agreed with de Limonade; the independence, liberty and prosperity of Haiti was achieved at the point of a sword. Everything that Haitians had was their own, and they owed nothing to the former colonists.[84]

Pétion and Christophe attempted, in their foreign relations, to secure international recognition of Haiti's independence. They also endeavoured to exploit the rivalries and antagonisms among the powers, as Dessalines had done, in order to prevent any alliance which might have as its purpose the subjugation of the country. The British, in particular, were keen to secure increased participation in the trade of Haiti, and both the northern state and the republic cultivated relations with the British. In 1807 the president of the senate, Théodat Trichet, went on a mission to England with the purpose of improving relations between the two countries and of securing recognition of Haitian independence. Christophe also made efforts to establish good relations with Britain. In December 1808 a British Order in Council opened the ports of Haiti to British ships. Owing partly to a United States and French embargo on trade with Haiti, the British achieved a near monopoly of Haitian commerce by 1814, and were in a strong enough position to persuade

Pétion to reduce import duties on British goods from 10 per cent to 5 per cent.

It was evident to the early rulers of Haiti that commerce was a necessary feature of the economic life of the country. Only a month after the death of Dessalines, Christophe, as provisional head of state, issued a proclamation abolishing all restrictions and exclusive concessions in foreign commerce, and offering full protection to foreign vessels. 'Each will be free to sell and buy on the conditions which he believes to be the most advantageous.'[85] The policy of the northern state in its early years was thus one of free trade and encouragement for foreign investment, but quite soon the policy was modified. Christophe introduced a tax on imported white sugar in 1808, in order to 'encourage national manufacturers', and to give the sugar industry 'all the protection possible'.[86] Nevertheless the northern state continued to place considerable emphasis upon the importance of foreign trade. De Limonade declared in 1811 that it was to the advantage of Haitians to exchange their products for the manufactured goods of Europe and that all persons concerned with commerce would be welcome in Haiti.[87] Later, however, efforts were made in the kingdom to decrease the degree of dependence upon foreign imports. De Vastey was particularly insistent upon the goal of self-sufficiency in essential foodstuffs. The colonial system had been based upon the export of crops like sugar, coffee, indigo and cotton; little attention had been paid to the production of goods for local consumption. This absurd system of growing only 'colonial products' and neglecting the cultivation of subsistence crops must be changed. Independence, de Vastey insisted, carried with it implications in the economic and agricultural field. 'A nation must be able to supply herself with everything she principally wants. If she depends for subsistence on foreign markets, she has no more her independence in her own hands.'[88] This changing emphasis in agricultural policy was closely connected to changes which were taking place in the system of land tenure, as we shall see.

Christophe was especially keen to establish friendly relations with Britain for purposes of trade, and also as a protection against French attempts at reconquest. The propaganda of the kingdom was consistently pro-British. It was the king's hope to secure a British guarantee for any future treaty with France. He applauded British philanthropists in their struggle against slavery and the slave trade. De Vastey praised the English as 'the principal power in Europe that took a lively interest in our fate',[89] and wrote approvingly of British colonial policy in Africa. Chanlatte also joined the chorus of praise.[90] We have already noted the king's strong denial of any desire to intervene in the affairs of British colonies, and the steps which he took to prevent a Jamaican revolt from being organised in Haiti. Christophe also encouraged

English school teachers to settle in Haiti and to help organise the educational system. He published a French translation of the Anglican Book of Common Prayer, and stated that he wished to make English the official language of Haiti.[91] Christophe's decision to transform the northern state into a kingdom in 1811 was probably influenced by the St James model, and de Vastey pointed to England as an example of a liberal monarchy. The attitude of Christophe and his associates towards England can hardly be explained simply in terms of *raison d'état* – as the policy of Dessalines could be. Undoubtedly Christophe was eager to secure British support against France, but his policy and pronouncements went much further than was required by this objective, and indicate a genuine admiration for that nation.

Land ownership and the plantation system

Although Pétion's republic and Christophe's kingdom both attempted to increase foreign exports, and allowed or even encouraged foreign merchants to operate in Haiti, they differed in their policy of land ownership. The republic remained faithful to Dessalines's prohibition of white ownership, by article 27 of the 1806 constitution. Christophe's northern state, on the other hand, omitted this prohibition in its 1807 and 1811 constitutions. Article 41 of the 1807 constitution actually guaranteed to foreign merchants the security of their property. It was, in fact, left to Clarkson to warn the king against the possibly subversive implications of foreign ownership, and to suggest that foreigners should be restricted to owning land in the trading cities of the coast.[92] The omission of Dessalines's prohibition of white ownership was by no means an oversight, and de Vastey attacked the position of the republic on this matter. The policy of excluding all white ownership was, he asserted, 'not only far from reasonable, but unjust, impolitic, and contrary to the laws of polished nations'.[93] It was reasonable and proper, he went on, to exclude French ownership, because France was still an enemy power, but this prohibition should not be extended to other foreign nationals. The republicans, in turn, defended the prohibition of white ownership as an article of faith. This prohibition, declared Hérard Dumesle, had become 'le boulevard de notre indépendance'.[94] Guy-Joseph Bonnet, one of the most influential politicians in the republic, also argued that Haiti must continue to restrict the ownership of land to nationals as long as the country remained economically weak and industrially backward.[95] This exclusion of foreign ownership of land was to remain a part of Haitian law (in a slightly modified form) until 1918, and was, as we shall see, a continual subject of debate throughout the nineteenth century, being frequently discussed in the context of the race question.

While the politicians of the republic and of the kingdom recognised the importance of foreign commerce, at least in the short run, changes were taking place which would have an effect upon the nature and extent of external trade in the future. The end of slavery and the resistance to forced labour by the population led to a gradual break-up of the plantation system. There was on the part of the former slaves an understandable dislike of labouring on large plantations, even if these were owned by the state or by black and coloured proprietors. The governments of Haiti were faced with a choice of either employing forced labour or breaking up the old estates among the peasants. On 31 March 1807 a law was passed in Christophe's northern state providing for the sale of state land to the people, though this law was not put into effect for ten years owing to 'important circumstances'.[96] Only a few days later the republic began to enact legislation which was to result in the granting and the sale of state land. The idea of breaking up the old plantations and distributing the land in smaller lots goes back at least to Polvérel's proclamation of 27 August 1793. Not only was emancipation decreed, but also there was provision for the division of vacant plantations and of conquered Spanish land among the former slaves.[97] During the presidency of Pétion over 150,000 hectares were distributed or sold to more than 10,000 persons.[98] Towards the end of his reign Henry Christophe began to put into effect the provisions which had been enacted earlier. He told Clarkson in 1818 that it was his intention further to 'augment the number of property owners', and that this policy had already had 'the most fortunate effects on our agriculture'.[99]

While Christophe's sale and granting of land benefited black and mulatto alike, the principal beneficiaries of Pétion's policy were the mulatto officers of the republican army. The British consul, Charles Mackenzie, observed in 1826 that very few of the large estates were in the hands of blacks, 'except perhaps in the Northern part of the Island formerly subject to Christophe, who bestowed properties indiscriminately on all without reference to complexion, who could bring forward the quantity of produce which he fixed as the return which ought to be made.'[100] Manigat suggests a number of reasons for Pétion's policy of land distribution and sale. In the first place it was likely to strengthen his own position vis-à-vis the senate and his other rivals within the republic; it might also strengthen the republic in its confrontation with Christophe's kingdom. Furthermore it would prevent the likelihood of revolution, would help to preserve the rule of the mulatto elite and would contribute towards a solution of the financial problems facing the government. Earlier critics and supporters of Pétion's policy had made the same points.[101] As Ardouin hinted, the move by Pétion would strengthen the landowning interest by adding to their numbers powerful military officers. It would also, according to Milscent, lead to the development of patriotism and a sense of national solidarity.[102] The policy, however, was opposed by Bonnet and by other members of the senate who were in favour of retaining the system of large plantations owned either privately or by the state. Bonnet further proposed to establish a state monopoly in the sale of salt, tobacco and timber, a policy similar to that which was later adopted by Salomon during the Soulouque regime. Bonnet's project failed due to pressure from important interests.[103] The land policy of Pétion was defended by his partisans as a natural consequence of the ideology of liberal democracy professed by the republic, while the state ownership proposed by Bonnet was said to represent an 'aristocratic' conception of society. In 1810 Bonnet joined Rigaud's secession in the South. It is not necessary here to enter into a detailed discussion of the land reforms undertaken in Haiti at this time.[104] The general effect of the reforms was to encourage the growth of subsistence agriculture together with the production of coffee for export, reducing drastically the production of sugar, which was most economically grown on the large plantations.

The colour question

It is sometimes suggested that the difference between Christophe and Pétion was essentially one of colour,[105] but this is a mistake. In the first place, blacks were in the vast majority in both parts of Haiti. Secondly the 1806 constitutional commission, of which Pétion had been chairman, was composed of four blacks and five mulattoes. The blacks included such important generals as Magloire Ambroise, David Troy and Guillaume Manigat; what is perhaps significant is that all four blacks belonged to the class of *anciens libres*. Certainly the majority of the high officers of the republican army were mulattoes while the majority of army chiefs in the northern state were black, yet most of Christophe's top ministers were mulattoes: Dupuy, de Vastey, de Limonade and Chanlatte. 'His Majesty's present Ministers', wrote Duncan Stewart to Clarkson, 'at least those on whom the great weight of the Government rests, are mulattoes and are very intelligent and well-educated men.'[106] The idea that there were almost no mulattoes in the North, owing to the fact that they had been 'destroyed' or had fled, is thus not accurate, and depends upon the authority of French supporters of Pétion like Liot, who had not visited the kingdom, and who relied for their information upon republican propaganda and upon the word of exiles. While the reports of Liot were exaggerated, there was, according to an English visitor to the kingdom in its last days, some discontent among mulattoes in the North owing to their 'being placed on an equality with blacks'.[107]

Colour distinctions were nevertheless a potential source of division among Haitians, and constituted thereby a threat to national independence. De Vastey warned his fellow mulattoes against being used by the French as instruments of their vengeance. Had not Rigaud been used by the French? Were not the mulattoes and black *anciens libres* the first to have collaborated with Leclerc's army? 'Oh Haytiens of my colour', he cried, '. . . will you always be blind to your true interests? Will you ever ignore the dictates of conscience?'[108]

Although the struggle between the two states was not basically caused by colour differences, this is not to say that accusations of prejudice were not made by one group against the other. There is hardly any dispute in Haiti into which this issue does not obtrude at some point. In one of his earliest pronouncements as head of state, Christophe denounced his opponents for having assassinated Dessalines together with more than thirty officers, 'only because they were black and enlightened'. The propaganda both of the republic and of the kingdom laid emphasis upon the absence of any colour prejudice in their respective territories. King Henry himself insisted that the cause of the blacks and of the mulattoes was one.[109] De Vastey argued that the conflicts between Toussaint and Rigaud, like those between Christophe and Pétion, were not essentially colour conflicts; blacks and mulattoes were on both sides. Being himself a mulatto he was particularly concerned to clear mulattoes of the charge of being responsible as a group for the policies of Rigaud and Pétion. He further stated that it is reasonable that a black rather than a mulatto should be head of state, as fourteen-fifteenths of the population of Haiti were black.[110] De Vastey accused Pétion of choosing his diplomatic representatives from among the most light-skinned group, of giving all positions of power at home to mulattoes, and of fanning the embers of colour prejudice for his own ends.[111] In his appeal to the citizens of the republic to reunite with the kingdom the Chevalier de Prézeau insisted that black and coloured Haitians were brothers belonging to one family,[112] while the foreign secretary, de Limonade, warned against the 'Machiavellism' of the French government which was attempting to exploit colour differences in Haiti for its own ends.[113] The apologists of the republic for their part stated that there was no colour prejudice to be found in the South and West, and that Haitians in the republic lived as a single family.[114] They denounced Christophe for nurturing a prejudice against mulattoes[115] and attacked de Vastey for 'misrepresenting the facts' and for 'plunging into the depths of ideology'.[116] Within the republic itself the colour question raised its head in the dispute between Darfour and Milscent. We have already noted the disagreement between these editors about whether Haitians could properly be called 'Africans'. Darfour suggested that among some of his fellow citizens it was possible to detect prejudice against the blacks.[117] Although Darfour was by no means an overt supporter of Christophe (this would not have been tolerated by the republic), there is a noticeable absence of anti-monarchical diatribe in *L'Eclaireur Haytien* and in its successor *L'Avertisseur Haytien*. Also Darfour's strong anti-French position has perhaps more similarity to the sentiments of Christophe than to the policy pursued by the republican government.[118]

Although the policies pursued by Pétion tended to benefit the *anciens libres* while those of Christophe served also the interests of a small elite among the *nouveaux libres*, the division between the northern state and the republic was not basically the result of a struggle between economic classes, as the war between Toussaint and Rigaud had largely been. Nor was it a dispute resulting from differing conceptions of government, though it was on this level that most of the propaganda was put forth. It was rather a struggle which stemmed from regional and personal loyalties. The army leaders of the North, in general, believed that their interests lay with Christophe, while those of the South and West were suspicious of Christophe, and it was this which led them to formulate a constitution which would limit the power of the president (who was likely to be Christophe), giving considerable power and patronage to the senate.[119] The constitutional issue, and the ideological conflicts which this engendered, were not, then, the principal cause of the war between the two states. Those involved in the civil war were not the kinds of fool who, according to the poet, contest over forms of government!

Constitutional differences

The form of government adopted in the northern state was, on the surface, quite different from that of the republic. The republican constitution of 1806 attempted, as we have seen, to limit the power of the president by creating a powerful senate, having control over declarations of war, national defence, treaties, appointment of civil servants and of military officers. It was composed of twenty-four members nominated, in the first instance, by the constituent assembly in three groups, the first having nine years' tenure, the second with six years, and the third with three years. From then on, one-third of the senate would retire each three years, and new senators would be elected for a nine-year period. These senators were to be chosen from among military officers and civil servants, by the existing senate. The constitutional commission was thus eager to prevent the concentration of power in the hands of one man. Christophe's northern constitution of 1807, on the other hand, was frankly authoritarian and autocratic, giving extensive powers to a government which was controlled by one man. The president had life tenure, with power to nominate his successor from among the top military officers of the state. The president was assisted by a council of state composed of nine members, two-thirds of whom were to be army officers, all nominated by the president himself. Thus while the republic, professing a liberal democratic belief in the sovereignty of the people, a free press, and other such institutions, was a military oligarchy, the northern state was a military autocracy, soon to be transformed, by the constitution of 1811, into a monarchy. Republican propaganda concentrated much of its attention on the tyrannical and dictatorial features of Christophe's rule, contrasting it with the supposedly liberal regime of Pétion. 'Colombus', a foreign spokesman for the republican regime, emphasised that there were no classes in the republic, that all men, whatever their colour or former status, were regarded as equal and that the government of the country was formed from the mass of the people. Pétion himself asserted that ideas of monarchy, of hereditary nobility, of grades and distinctions were 'bizarre and unseemly'.[120] Hérard Dumesle stated that political society has always been considered as the result of a contract between the people and their leader, that sovereignty resides in the body of the people and that 'the voice of the people is the voice of God'. He furthermore maintained that social equilibrium was possible only if power were divided.[121] Other republican writers wrote of a social compact limiting the power of the government, and the house of representatives itself paid homage to the sovereignty of the people, referring in religious terms to its own role. The southern republic set up by Rigaud and other dissidents was, if anything, even more strongly influenced by ideas of the Enlightenment. In an implicit criticism of Pétion they proclaimed that the accumulation of all power in one person is what constitutes despotism, and insisted that the sole principle which they accepted was that of liberty. Rigaud himself was accorded the title 'le fondateur de la Liberté à Haïti'.[122] Even at this early date writers were critical of militarism, no doubt sensing the threat of black power which might result from a continued predominance of the army in government. Milscent insisted, for example, that 'the essence of society is civil' and that civil rank is as important as military rank.[123]

The ideologists of the northern kingdom, instead of unmasking the republican oligarchy for what it was, accepted the claims of writers like Colombus at their face value. 'Can folly be carried to a greater height', demanded Baron de Vastey,

than the attempt to confound rank, and establish a system of equality in society? Can the rich and the poor, the feeble and the strong, the brave and the coward, the learned and the illiterate, can they be regarded as equal? Do not the simple dictates of common sense proscribe this imaginary equality?[124]

The only kind of equality that has validity, he insisted, is equal rights before the law; other claims to equality are imaginary and absurd. He called upon the people of the South and West to 'annihilate this democracy which tends only to disgrace and debase you in the eyes of nations'.[125] De Vastey admitted that Haiti derived its origin as an independent state from a revolution, but so did many kingdoms in other parts of the world; the legitimacy of the northern monarchy could not therefore validly be questioned on these grounds. He also argued that monarchy was perfectly compatible with liberty; never had a people existed which was more free or had firmer possession of political rights than the English, and they lived under a monarchy.[126] The baron replied to those editors of newspapers and 'colonising system-mongers' in France who poured scorn upon the idea of a black kingdom and a black nobility. 'Is royalty', he demanded, 'the exclusive prerogative of a white complexion?'[127] W. W. Harvey, who lived in the kingdom during its last days, claimed that the king's autocratic and authoritarian system was based upon his belief that the population was unstable by character, averse to labour and tending to disorderly conduct; that therefore liberty must be contained within due bounds.[128]

Yet despite the aristocratic pretensions of the northern kingdom, what struck foreign visitors most was the egalitarian spirit of the people. Harvey noted how a secretary of state might easily be found sitting on a workman's bench talking to the workman. He was horrified by the tendency of servants, while waiting at table, to intervene in the conversation and make comments on the guests 'with a freedom at times quite provoking'.[129] This sense of equality and respect for personal liberty characterised all sectors of the community. One French captain noted in 1819 that guilds existed in the republic whose members took an oath never to perform domestic work, which they regarded as degrading. Candler, writing of a slightly later period, was struck by the sense of equality subsisting between servants and their employers.[130]

In the kingdom, then, there was a considerable spirit of equality in spite of the elaborate façade of aristocratic hierarchy, while in the republic a careful reading of the constitution as well as an examination of the practice, would reveal that, despite talk about the sovereignty of the people, real power was in the hands of a small self-perpetuating elite. The new constitution of 1816 adopted the idea of a life presidency from Christophe's 1807 constitution, and Pétion was proclaimed president for life with power to nominate his successor. The institution of life presidency so impressed Bolívar that he introduced it into the 1825 constitution of Bolivia, making specific reference to the Haitian model.[131] Christophe and Pétion both laid claim to that paternal relationship with the people which Dessalines had decreed.[132] The British consul, Charles Mackenzie, described Pétion's rule, from reports which he had heard, as 'a perfect despotism',[133] which may be something of an exaggeration, though it is nearer to the truth than the picture painted by republican propagandists like Liot and Colombel. In any case the difference between the kingdom and the republic, with respect to polity, was by no means as great as the ideologists of either side suggested, and it would be quite wrong to view the civil war as a struggle between democracy and aristocracy (as Madiou did[134]) or between liberal democracy and despotic autocracy (as Ardouin did[135]).

Why was it then, that so much of the war of words was conducted on the level of constitutional forms? It was largely done in order to disguise the fact that the struggle was little more than a contest between two self-seeking elites — a northern group of mostly black *nouveaux libres*, who had constituted themselves into a new elite, over against a group of mostly mulatto *anciens libres* from the South and West. Neither group was particularly interested in the welfare of the mass of former slaves, though both groups relied upon their support. It was necessary for the republican government to hoodwink its black masses into believing that Christophe was a tyrannical ogre who would drive the people back to work on plantations at the lash of the whip and take from them their new-found freedom, while the royal government endeavoured to persuade its black masses that republican democracy was weak and ineffective, and that Pétion was preparing to submit once more to French control. The conflict between Pétion's republic and Christophe's kingdom cannot, therefore, properly be seen as a struggle between two social classes; it was a struggle rather between two cliques within a single class. The attempt to picture Christophe as the representative of the black masses against the mulatto elite is as misconceived as the suggestion that Christophe represented a feudal aristocracy — which the new bourgeoisie led by Pétion was attempting to overthrow.

III

General Jean-Pierre Boyer, a mulatto, born in 1776 at Port-au-Prince, became president in 1818 on the death of Pétion; in the early years of his presidency he followed the lines established by his predecessor. He was, however, generally less respected as a man, and his skilful handling of internal problems and of foreign relations gave him a reputation for duplicity. The picture of Boyer, wrote an English resident in 1821, 'presents so many disgusting features of weakness and cowardice, allied to presumption and tyranny, so many proofs both of stupidity and licentiousness, that I turn from it . . .'[136]

Haiti and the black race

Boyer continued, at least for purposes of propaganda, to speak of Haiti as the symbol of black freedom, and gave support to a scheme for the immigration of negroes from the United States. 'Those who come', he wrote, 'being children of Africa, shall be Haytians as soon as they put their feet upon the soil of Hayti.'[137] He deplored the prejudice and misery under which these Africans in the United States groaned, and invited them to live in Haiti under 'a liberal and paternal government'.[138] Boyer believed that Haiti had a special responsibility to assist these blacks of the United States and together with some American philanthropists he set up a fund to pay their passage to Haiti, but his view of Africa was unambiguous. He saw the immigration of these American negroes into Haiti as an alternative to their returning 'to the barbarous shores of Africa, where misery or certain death may [*sic*] await them'.[139]

In the eyes of European and American writers and politicians Haiti remained a symbol of black power. On the one hand the abolitionists painted a rosy picture of Haiti as part of their propaganda in favour of the emancipation of slaves in the British colonies; on the other hand their opponents delighted in pointing out faults and failings of Haitian government and administration. Many of these foreign writers were quite frank about their ideological interests in Haiti. Clarkson, Wilberforce and their associates saw Haiti as a living example of what black liberation could achieve. W. W. Harvey made it clear that he viewed his book *Sketches of Hayti* as an argument for emancipation in the British colonies; Zacharie Macaulay stated that the history of Haiti furnished the strongest arguments in favour of emancipation.[140] Victor Schoelcher's interest in Haiti was also closely connected to his campaign for the abolition of slavery in the French colonies.[141] James Franklin, on the other hand, complained that accounts of Haiti had been 'too highly coloured by the zealous advocates of negro independence'.[142] Franklin stated quite clearly and explicitly that the purpose of his book was to benefit merchants, manufacturers, traders and capitalists who had not had the opportunity of visiting Haiti. He saw Haiti, not as an argument for emancipation, but rather as 'the beacon to warn the government of England against an experiment which may prove absolutely fatal to her colonial system'.[143] Boyer's Rural Code of 1826 was translated into English and published in London. It would, so the editor claimed in his prefatory letter to Earl Bathurst, be of interest to persons who were concerned with 'ascertaining the possibility of obtaining regular and steady labour, in tropical climates, without compulsion'.[144] Limitations on the free movement of rural labourers, and the punishments prescribed for vagrants and vagabonds, were noted. The code of labour, the editor perceptively remarked, was one which could only have been framed by a legislature composed of landowners who were also military leaders. Vagrancy bills were introduced in the Jamaican legislature in 1834 and 1839, but were disallowed by the British government.

Haiti was seen by the British government itself as a crucial experiment in slave emancipation which should be carefully studied. Instructions issued by the Foreign Office in London to the newly appointed British consul Charles Mackenzie stated that he should find out in detail the regulations issued by Toussaint 'by which he was enabled to enforce Agricultural industry among the Negroes of St. Domingo, after slavery had been abolished', and to compare the effects of the agricultural policy of Pétion's republic with those which resulted from the policy of the northern kingdom.[145] The British were, of course, well aware of the danger which an independent black country in the Caribbean posed to their own colonies, and had expressly forbidden by law any civil or commercial intercourse between Jamaica and Haiti (6 Geo. IV cap. 114 sec. 48). We have already noted that the assurances of Christophe and de Vastey on this matter must be seen as part of their policy of securing international recognition, as must President Boyer's prohibition of intercourse between the black republic and the European colonies of the Caribbean (with the exception of Curaçao and St Thomas). The British foreign secretary made it quite clear that even after recognition of Haitian independence, no Haitian consuls would be permitted to reside in the West Indian colonies.[146] The republic had, however, already become something of a haven for maroons. 'It is a certain fact', reported Mackenzie, on his arrival in Port-au-Prince, 'that a very large proportion of the population of this city consists of refugee slaves from the British colonies.'[147]

Recognition by France

French refusal to recognise Haitian independence was at least partly due to the fact that Haiti had become a symbol of black independence and of successful anti-colonial revolt. The French prime minister told the British ambassador that the black republic was a potentially dangerous example to the rest of the West Indian colonies, and that France's hesitation in granting recognition had been due to a fear of establishing this example.[148] Nevertheless the French government decided that it was best to come to terms with her former colony. A memorandum in the archives of the foreign ministry advised the king to embark upon 'un nouveau genre de colonisation, sans en avoir les inconvéniences et les dépenses'. In Haiti France should create 'la colonie commerciale'.[149] Esmangart argued strongly that France would lose nothing by recognising Haitian independence, and that a treaty could be negotiated which would be of considerable economic benefit to France. The word 'independence', he insisted, should not frighten the French unduly, for many of the benefits of colonialism could be perpetuated into the era of formal independence.[150] De Vastey had, however, already warned his fellow countrymen against dangers of neo-colonialism:

Independence, say the ex-colonists, is the *hobby* of this people; by means of a *nominal* independence, they might be led to anything. Well, let us grant them what they ask, and we shall immediately succeed in leading them wherever we wish![151]

Russia, Britain and other world powers had emphasised that they were unwilling to recognise Haitian independence until France had done so. It was suggested that such premature recognition might be interpreted by the former metropolitan power as un unfriendly act — though this did not prevent 'perfidious Albion' from recognising the independence of Mexico and other South American republics in 1823. Her refusal to recognise Haiti was attributed by Haitians to colour prejudice. 'It is evident', declared Boyer on 1 January 1824, 'that the outrage done to the Haitian character is a deplorable effect of the absurd prejudice resulting from differences of colour.' The exclusion of Haiti from the Panama congress of 1825, despite the aid which Haiti had given Miranda and Bolívar in their hours of need, and also the continued refusal of the United States to recognise Haiti, were similarly attributed (and rightly so) to colour prejudice.[152] In listing the aims of the congress, Bolívar suggested that greater unity among the ruling classes in the newly independent states of the mainland would liberate the continent from the fear of 'this tremendous monster which has devoured the island of Santo Domingo' and from the fear of 'the numerical preponderance of the indigenous inhabitants'.[153] Boyer came to the conclusion that a settlement with France was imperative for Haiti, and the search for such a settlement was a principal feature of his foreign policy. Haitian leaders were also convinced that French recognition would reinforce the hegemony of their own class. J. B. Inginac later stated that such an agreement with France would open the country to 'the way of civilisation',[154] a notion which included a strengthening of the position of the mulattoes.

Negotiations between the representatives of France and Haiti continued during the early twenties. With the uniting of Haiti under one government in 1820, and with the further annexation of the Spanish part of the island in 1822, the position of Boyer had been immensely strengthened. The Spanish part of the island had for some time been regarded by Haitian military and political leaders as their weak front. Any foreign invading army would be likely to land in the east, and having established a land base, would attack the black republic from the east. For reasons of foreign policy neither Christophe nor Pétion had thought it expedient to invade Santo Domingo. This cautious policy, however, gained for Haiti nothing but contempt. The fact that the Spanish part of the island had been unmolested for over twenty years, in spite of Haiti's military superiority, was, for the odious British consul Mackenzie, conclusive proof of 'the degraded imbecility of the whole of the black and coloured Governments'.[155] With the success of Bolívar's liberation movement on the mainland, Boyer felt able to annex the eastern two-thirds of Hispaniola. There was in this part of the island a considerable body of opinion in favour of union with Haiti. Franklin Franco distinguishes two groups at this time: 'the radicals', who included slaves and free blacks, many mulattoes and farmers from the northern part of the country, and 'the liberals', drawn from white and other elite sectors. The latter were concerned with political rights and independence, avoiding talk about racial issues, while the former were concerned also with social and racial equality. It was the radical group which favoured union with Haiti.[156]

A realistic appraisal of the situation by the French government led to a reluctant acceptance of the need to recognise the full independence of Haiti. In 1821 the French had proposed internal self-government for Haiti under French protectorate. This had been rejected by the Haitians. Nevertheless the French government persisted in its claim to suzerainty. The Haitian agents whom Boyer had sent to Europe in 1824, Rouanez and Larose, stated that they had no authority to discuss the question of suzerainty, though the impression of British diplomats in Paris was that the Haitians were willing to entertain the idea of French suzerainty. The French government in fact claimed in 1825 that 'The offer to recognise the suzerainty of France was indeed made several years ago by the government of Saint Domingue', but gave no further details.[157] Leslie Manigat has argued that Boyer and a number of his close associates were secretly prepared to accept some kind of French protection or even sovereignty. In the notes of a discussion held in July 1821 the Frenchman Liot stated that Boyer told him that he was privately willing to accept French protectorate or suzerainty, but that public opinion would not permit this concession.[158] It is possible that this was simply a diplomatic tactic by Boyer in order to keep on good terms with the French, but it is more likely that, as Manigat suggests, these were the genuine views of Boyer. But why would the president of an independent country be prepared to admit or even positively desire French protection? There are two principal reasons why Boyer might have wished to increase French influence in Haiti. In the first place the internal situation in the country, as we shall see, was delicate. Class and colour lines were hardening. The government of Boyer was composed almost entirely of mulattoes of the elite class. Pétion had been willing and able to incorporate a number of black generals into the power structure, particularly in the early years of his regime, thus preventing an open confrontation between blacks and mulattoes. Boyer, however, failed to achieve this compromise, and felt increasingly menaced by the possibility of a black revolt. A growth in French presence and power might enable Boyer and the mulatto clique around him to play off black against white, and so remain in the saddle. A second reason why Boyer might have welcomed French protection was that he may well have foreseen the way in which a small independent country in the Caribbean would be at the mercy of the world powers, particularly Britain and the United States. Foreign protection from one power might at least prevent arbitary intervention by others. Esmangart himself stated in 1818 that Boyer believed it was difficult for Haitians 'to sustain their independence without the protection of France'.[159] Interestingly enought these were, in essence, the two principal reasons which led President Salomon to offer a naval base to the United States in 1883, and to seek French or American protection.[160] Nevertheless it was clear to Boyer that any recognition of French suzerainty would be resisted by the mass of the Haitian people possibly to the extent of a violent uprising, and would thus actually precipitate one of the eventualities it was designed to avoid. He therefore decided to reject any suggestion of French suzerainty. Like Pétion, Boyer was prepared to agree to financial compensation to the dispossessed French planters of Saint Domingue, and in a royal ordinance of 17 April 1825 the French government recognised the independence of Haiti on condition that Haiti agreed to an indemnity of 150 million francs, and reduced customs charges on French vessels to half that paid by those of other countries.[161] These terms were eventually agreed to by the Haitian government, after a little sabre-rattling by the French navy. Other European powers swiftly followed the French lead, sending diplomatic or consular representatives to the black republic. Boyer's agreement to pay such a large indemnity had two principal consequences. The government made itself extremely unpopular at home when it tried to raise the money by taxation. Its failure to raise any substantial sum led to the government contracting a loan of 24 million francs in order to pay the first instalment of the indemnity. The second consequence was thus the beginning of significant foreign financial involvement in Haiti. The low customs duties on French ships resulted in a growth of trade with the former metropolitan power at the expense of trade with Britain and the United States, though there was a general decline in the value of imports and exports in the twenties.

It is possible to understand and explain the internal and foreign policies pursued by early Haitian governments, and the policies pursued by other nations with respect to Haiti, only if we take into account the ideas of race and colour held by the persons and groups involved. We may very well wish to deny that racial differences have any significant objective consequences — that is, apart from men's beliefs about these differences — but the ideas, true or false, which men have about race are potent in determining their attitudes and actions in the concrete situations which face them. On occasions racial theories, like other ideologies, are nothing more than camouflage cynically erected in order to divert attention from the real issues. At other times racial theories have been sincerely believed and colour prejudice has seriously been entertained. When this occurs, race and colour become powerful factors influencing the behaviour of individuals and groups. This chapter has also illustrated the importance of symbol and myth in political action. In proclaiming independence, and in maintaining it against the threat of invasion, Dessalines and his fellow generals were doing more than protecting their material interests. They were fiercely proclaiming and defending a legend — the story of a long but victorious struggle for black liberation against the forces of colonialism and slavery. France, Britain and Spain viewed with disquiet the emergence of Haiti as an independent country, seeing Haiti as a symbol of revolt against colonialism and of the assertion of black liberation and black equality. The economic importance of Saint Domingue was considerable but its importance as a symbol was perhaps equally great.

3. Pride and prejudice

1820-1867

Jean-Pierre Boyer's swift conquest of the eastern part of the island of Hispaniola in 1822 began two decades of relative peace and stability for Haiti; this was reinforced in 1825 by French recognition of the country's independence. This period is characterised by the concentration of power in the hands of a small elite. A split developed among the members of the ruling class, however, and in 1843 Boyer was overthrown. The disturbed period which followed this event saw a reassertion of black power culminating in the empire of Soulouque, which was, in turn, replaced by the regime of Geffrard in 1859. In this chapter we shall be concerned principally with the development of political ideas and their relationship to the events of the period. In the first place we shall note how the black leaders in the North and in the South took advantage of the split in the ranks of the mulattoes to assert their interests. In order to do this they frequently made explicit appeals to the masses on the basis of colour. Large landowners like the Salomons in the South had interests which were clearly distinct from those of the rural masses, whose support they desired. They succeeded in convincing many of these poor rural Haitians that the real enemy was the mulatto group, and that the blacks had a common interest in combating the mulatto hegemony. This family and others like it were clearly prepared to use the colour issue to re-establish their own position in the political life of the country. With Jean-Jacques Acaau the situation may have been somewhat different, insofar as he could with more justification claim to be a man of the people. But even he was by no means from the poorest class of peasant; also, like most other Haitian leaders, he was willing to invite foreign intervention in the affairs of Haiti in order to strengthen his own position. With the growing challenge of black power, the mulattoes sought to reinforce their hegemony, and particularly significant in this context was the elaboration of a mulatto 'legend' of the Haitian past by a succession of historians. Also important were the political and social ideas of Edmond Paul, whose writings were to provide much of the inspiration for the politicians of the Liberal Party in the succeeding period. A detailed discussion of these developments will be the concern of this chapter.

I

The power structure

Jonathan Brown described the Haiti of his day as 'a sort of republican monarchy sustained by the bayonet',[1] and he emphasised the fact that the government of the country was a military one in the fullest sense. In almost every field the civil authorities were subordinate to army officers, a system which, he claimed, operated as a 'perpetual paralysis upon the prosperity of the country'.[2] Another foreign visitor referred to Haiti as 'a military despotism in the hands of a single man'.[3] The whole island, divided into departments, arrondissements and communes, was controlled by military officers responsible to the president.[4] With a population of under 800,000 in the mid-1820s, the regular army numbered 32,000 men.[5] It was composed almost entirely of black soldiers; only in the very highest ranks were mulattoes in the majority.[6] Nevertheless, as one observer pointed out, if the trend were to continue, it would not be long before blacks controlled even the highest ranks; almost all the subalterns were black, as mulattoes tended to secure more lucrative civil occupations.[7] The mulattoes, however, remained in control of the national guard in certain areas; in Les Cayes, for example, the elite, not wanting to see a large black army on the doorstep, were prepared to man the militia.[8]

During the early years of Boyer's regime a growing number of peasants acquired smallholdings of land, and began to squat on vacant property. This meant that the larger landowners found it difficult to get agricultural labourers to work for them. In 1821 Boyer attempted to halt the trend, and stopped the allocation and sale of state land. This was followed in 1826 by his celebrated Rural Code, which was referred to in the previous chapter. Boyer and the clique of landowners around him enacted the code in order to maintain the supply of cheap labour, by attaching rural workers to specific plantations and by punishing vagrancy. Prior to giving an extended summary of the code, James Leyburn makes the astonishing judgment that the code was 'an attempt on a grand scale to order the life of all people for common prosperity'.[9] We might more accurately call it an attempt to order the lives of the majority of rural workers for the prosperity of the few large landowners. The project was, however, unsuccessful, and merely served to increase the hostility of the masses towards the regime. The shortage of rural labour led Haitians to consider the possibility of adopting some scheme of indentured labour from India or China.[10]

Foreign visitors to Haiti observed the dilapidated state of the large plantations, and the prevalence of smallholdings on which peasants grew enough to support their families, selling the surplus at the local market. 'Hayti abounds with these small proprietors', wrote Franklin, 'their patches of land, with their huts upon them, are generally situate in the mountains, in the recesses, or on the most elevated parts, or spots, as the poet has described, "the most inaccessible by shepherds trod". They are therefore lost for the purposes of agriculture.'[11] Much of the coffee and of the other crops exported at this time was also grown by these small farmers, rather than on large estates, and the coffee was gathered from trees planted many years earlier which were growing almost wild.[12] Franklin lamented the lack of interest among the peasants in growing crops for export, and also noted that they did not appear to be particularly keen on consuming imported goods. It was, in fact, according to this writer, Boyer's plan 'to keep his people ignorant of artificial wants',[13] a policy which, if successful, spelt doom for foreign speculators like Franklin himself.

Although considerable numbers of peasants were working small-holdings, large estates still existed, and were mostly in the hands of mulattoes, except, as we have already noted, in the North. The state also retained ownership of large areas, and this state land was augmented in 1822 with the incorporation of the Spanish two-thirds of Hispaniola. 'It is important to destroy all traces of feudalism in this part of the island', ran the preamble to a law of 8 July 1824, 'in order that the inhabitants, happy under a regime of liberal principles, may lose even the memory of their former subjection.'[14] All land was nationalised which had previously belonged (*a*) to the Spanish crown, (*b*) to the church and other ecclesiastical corporations, and (*c*) to private individuals absent from the country in February 1822 who had not returned by 10 June 1823. Exports in general declined in the period of Boyer's regime. The most dramatic development was the decline in sugar exports from two and a half million pounds in 1820 to six thousand pounds in 1842. Other exports, however, were more stable, and included coffee, cacao, cotton and timber; also tobacco from the eastern part of the island was a significant export in this period.[15]

Life and leisure under Boyer

Haiti was, in this period, a generally peaceful country, with very little violence or serious crime. Foreign visitors were struck then, as they are today, by this fact. Jonathan Brown claimed that murder and robbery were almost unknown, and that this 'should put to shame many a more civilised people'.[16] Apart from the years 1842–7 the country enjoyed political stability under three heads of state; Boyer (1818–43). Soulouque (1847–59) and Geffrard (1859–67). The 1843 revolution which overthrew Boyer was itself a gentlemanly affair between rival factions of the mulatto elite. 'This extraordinary mode of revolution-izing a country', wrote one British naval officer to another,

with scarcely any of the attendant scenes of Bloodshed, rapine, and violence (so common in such cases in European Civilized Countries) the ultimate success of which cannot be doubted; will present a case almost unparalleled in History and place the Negro in a more exalted station in the Scale of Civilization than it had hitherto been deemed capable of attaining to.[17]

Nevertheless in the ensuing period, when the colour issue became more salient, political violence increased. Both Soulouque and Geffrard were dictatorial (as Boyer had been), and ruthlessly suppressed all serious opposition.

The great mass of the population, being former slaves and descend-ants of slaves, was black. Many of these men owned tracts of land on which they cultivated crops for local consumption, and also coffee for export. Others rented land, or squatted on vacant plantations and on state land; others again worked as labourers on estates belonging to large landowners, or engaged in sharecropping. Surplus crops were either exported through speculators or sold at the local market. Women *marchandes* played an important role in the economic life of the small towns, where they controlled the retail trade.[18] Goods were carried overland by animals or by humans, but the general state of the roads in the large cities as well as in the countryside was deplored by more than one foreign visitor. 'It is almost impossible to describe the state of the roads', wrote James Franklin; '. . . there seems a disposition on the part of the government to efface every vestige of the former roads.'[19]

African traditions continued to predominate in the culture and customs of the masses in Haiti. The popular religion of the country was, despite all the efforts to suppress it, the Voodoo cult. We have already noted the opposition to the cult from early black leaders, particularly Toussaint and Dessalines. Boyer and the mulatto leaders were also opposed to the cult. The Roman Catholic religion was established as the official religion of Haiti, and was firmly under govern-mental control, with its clergy being moved from parish to parish according to the wishes of the government.[20] In fact the church was in considerable disarray. Many of the priests were imposters, others were racketeers. While Boyer was himself in favour of a concordat with the Vatican, some of his principal supporters, Inginac and B. Ardouin for example, had been influenced by French thinkers of the Enlightenment, and were 'fierce partisans of the civil power' (Cabon).[21] The govern-ment's dislike of Voodoo was only one aspect of its generally franco-phile disposition, particularly in cultural matters. Inginac, who was Boyer's personal assistant for many years, described the way in which he had endeavoured to suppress disorders of all kinds, 'but above all the dangerous superstitions of voodoo'.[22] General Guy-Joseph Bonnet, one of the leading figures in the republic, was particularly keen to root out African 'superstitions', and to replace them with European customs. He proudly recorded in his memoirs how he had tried to introduce the *calinda* dance, performed to the accompaniment of the violin, alongside the traditional African dances of the peasants performed to the beat of the *tambour*.[23] Bonnet and a group of elite Haitians, together with some French residents, founded in 1820 a society for 'decent entertainment' in Port-au-Prince. The purpose of the society was to organise dances and concerts in European style. At the opening ball, however, a fight broke out between a Frenchman and a Haitian which ended in bloodshed. This was the first and last function organised by the society. It was generally concluded, Ardouin wryly remarked, that there is 'an incompatibility of temper between Haitians and Frenchmen'.[24]

Haiti of the thirties, then, presents the picture of a predominantly agricultural country ruled by a small group of military officers and politicians, almost all of whom were light-skinned. These men mostly lived in the capital city, and were engaged in commerce; many of them also owned estates of varying sizes in the countryside. A rift between social life in the capital and the larger coastal cities on one hand and life in the rural areas on the other became increasingly evident in Haiti, as in other post-colonial states of Latin America.[25] The sovereignty of the people was proclaimed as a principle, but it was replaced in practice by 'the sovereignty of a ruling clique'.[26] The political principles proclaimed by supporters of the regime were generally conservative in tenor, particularly towards the end of Boyer's period in office. *Le Temps*, for example, adopted for its motto: 'Ameliorations are the work of time.'[27] The elite families of the capital were literate and many of their members had been educated in France. A number of weekly newspapers and monthly reviews were published, but their circulation was small, and the lifetime of many of them was short. Nevertheless these journals were read by most of those who were in a position to affect the policy of the government, and they were therefore not without significant political influence. The bookshops in Haiti compared favourably with those in the neighbouring British colonies.[28]

The colour question

We have noted the existence of small black elite group, particularly in the North; also there were in Haiti at this time a few poor mulattoes, but colour lines tended to coincide in general with class lines, reinforcing economic and social distinctions in the country. The long period of Boyer's government witnessed the concentration of political power and patronage in the hands of an elite group composed almost entirely of mulattoes. The president himself claimed, in a letter to Jeremy Bentham, that colour divisions and distinctions had been abjured for some years,[29] but foreign observers noted the discriminatory policy pursued by his government. Not only were the sympathisers of Christophe, like Prince Sanders and W. W. Harvey,[30] insistent on Boyer's colour prejudice; James Franklin, a British businessman, noted the 'acrimonious feeling' of blacks against what they believed to be unjust discrimination by the government of Boyer. He went on to say that a discriminatory policy was consciously pursued by the president and his associates, who seemed to believe that the best way to retain power was to keep the blacks in a state of poverty and ignorance.[31] A later writer, Jonathan Brown, stated that the mulattoes were pleased that Boyer had succeeded Pétion; this event suggested to them that 'the sceptre of power was not to depart from their race'.[32] Brown referred to the mulattoes as a 'caste' and noted the hostility which existed between blacks and mulattoes, claiming that the prejudice of the latter against the former was almost as great as had been the prejudice of the whites against coloured people in colonial days.[33] He saw Boyer's administration as an attempt to 'balance the different complexions against each other in such a manner as to prevent the blacks from acquiring an undue ascendancy in the government'.[34] John Candler was equally impressed by the importance of the colour factor in the politics of the republic, describing it as a heritage from the days of slavery and colonialism.[35] The French consul in Les Cayes also observed the mutual hostility of blacks and mulattoes, and claimed that black resentment was such that if they were to gain control in the South, 'all who are not of pure African race would be slaughtered'.[36] The British consul, Charles Mackenzie, noted the claim made by many mulattoes to superiority over the blacks merely on account of their colour. He further insisted on the serious nature of these tensions: 'I am sure', he wrote,

that in Haiti a well defined national spirit not only does not, but never can, exist so long as the passions, that now agitate all classes, maintain their ground – And yet it will be difficult to devise any means of speedily correcting them . . . for they are not recent – they are deeply founded on the old Colonial System.

Every important public post, he went on, had been entrusted by Boyer's government to mulattoes, except 'when some odious act of the Government is to be carried into effect'.[37] The job of collecting taxes to pay the French indemnity was, for example, largely done by blacks.

Among the black voices raised against this mulatto hegemony was that of Félix Darfour, the founder and editor of *L'Eclaireur Haytien*. We have already noted the *noiriste* position which he frequently adopted. In August 1822 Darfour addressed to the legislature an 'offensive and seditious' petition which undoubtedly contained suggestions of colour prejudice on the part of the government. The president himself denounced this 'new Christophe' who was attempting to foment discord and to set one group of Haitians against another. Darfour was arrested, tried and executed, and Boyer took the opportunity to round up some of his other critics.[38] J. B. Inginac later stated explicitly that Darfour had been attempting to stir up 'colour divisions', though Beaubrun Ardouin vigorously denied that he had been condemned because of his colour.[39] By 1843 Salomon *jeune* and a group of southern blacks could denounce Boyer for having reduced the blacks to 'the most complete nullity'.[40]

Even within the group of coloured Haitians, further significant distinctions based upon race were occasionally to be seen. In 1822 Boyer's armies had invaded the Spanish part of the island, and the job of formulating a legal system which would apply to this newly acquired territory was assigned to Bruno Blanchet. Born in 1760, Bruno, together with his brother Blanchet *jeune*, had been the victim of colour prejudice by whites during the colonial period, and had led a revolt in La Grand' Anse in September 1791. In December 1806 Bruno Blanchet was a member of the nine-man constitutional commission headed by Pétion, but in 1810 he joined Rigaud's separatist movement in the South. Although he was himself a light-skinned mulatto, he attempted to extend the prohibition of land ownership to include not only whites, but also *métis*, *mameloucs*, *quarteronnés* and *sang-mêlés*, that is any person with more than 100 'parts' white (out of 128 'parts').[41] Why should Blanchet have wished to exclude from the right of property persons who were practically indistinguishable from himself in appearance? It was probably not really a question of race or colour. In colonial days a considerable number of supposedly 'white' *créoles* were really of mixed blood, but had secured acceptance as whites. These men, among whom was the writer Moreau de Saint Méry,[42] were often the most vigorous proponents of white domination. It was probably this group (some of whom, now that the tide had turned, were prepared to acknowledge the fact that they were of mixed race in order to retain their property rights) against which Blanchet's proposal was directed. Luckily for them, however, he died in April 1822, before being able to put his proposals into effect.

II

Ideology and discontent

The government of Boyer was not only chosen from one section of the nation, the mulatto elite, but it constituted a clique within this elite.

The regime had been challenged from time to time since its institution by opposition groups, but in the mid-thirties these groups began to pose a serious threat to the government. Popular resistance to the regime was manifest, particularly in the South.[43] The opposition from within the elite was centred in the lower house of the legislature, and regarded itself as liberal and nationalist, arguing for a greater liberty of speech within the country, for increased protection for local industry and for the development of a truly national culture. The leader of this opposition group in the legislature was generally recognised to be Hérard Dumesle, the poet and orator, who continued to adhere to those liberal values which he had defended earlier.[44] Others who emerged as opponents of the Boyer government were the brothers Nau and Lespinasse, as well as the historian Joseph Saint-Rémy of Les Cayes.

In the literary and cultural field the journal *Le Républicain* (which later changed its title to *L'Union*) was a principal channel through which the ideas of Boyer's critics were expressed. Among the contributors to this journal, which began to appear in 1836, were Emile Nau (1812–60) and Beauvais Lespinasse (1811–63). Haiti was, for these mulatto writers a symbol of black rehabilitation, having a distinctive culture which derived from a fusion of European and African traditions. They warned against a slavish imitation of European writers and urged their fellow countrymen to take pride in their own nation. Yet, being almost all from the elite, these writers adhered to that view of the Haitian past which I have called the mulatto legend.[45] In economic affairs they advocated the development of local manufacturing industry and a move away from reliance upon the export of primary products.[46]

In the first number of *Le Républicain* E. S. Dévimeux stated that each people has a distinct vocation and that in this respect, as in others, the principle of 'the inviolability of nationality' must be maintained.[47] Emile Nau, in a later issue, pointed out that a necessary prerequisite of a national literature is a cultural tradition specific to the nation, with customs, tastes and passions peculiarly its own. In this context he contrasted Haiti with the United States. 'American society', he wrote, 'is only English society with modifications due to climate and to locality; it cannot therefore boast a national literature.' Haiti on the other hand, with its unique fusion of African and European genius, was in a much stronger position.[48] Yet Haitian writers were blamed by Nau and his fellow intellectuals for having failed to break away from the European pattern. A lively literature must reflect the sentiments of the epoch and the experience of the Haitian people: 'We say then to our poets or to those who aspire to be such: the source of your inspiration is within you and among you; apart from that you have no salvation'[49] Even the French language must be modified to fit the needs and aspiration of the people. There was, however, disagreement among these writers as to how far Haiti had moved along the path towards a distinct national character, and conflicting opinions were expressed on this subject in the columns of *L'Union.*[50]

Most of the writers associated with *Le Républicain* and *L'Union* were mulattoes; they nevertheless saw Haiti as the 'cradle of African independence' whose mission it was to 'carry the torch of civilisation into the midst of unfortunate Africa'.[51] In a famous passage Beauvais Lespinasse declared:

> But can we speak on the political state of Haiti, on the future of the Antilles and of the black race in America, without pausing to think of Africa? It is to Africa, our mother, that we owe the colour which is still, in the eyes of some nations, the emblem of inferiority. Hence, Africa must be the object of all our wishes, of all our desires, of all our hopes.[52]

These writers believed that it was the special vocation of Haiti to be at the head of African civilisation in the world and to take the initiative in all matters which concerned the advancement of the black race.[53] The pupils of the national *lycée* were told that the country must develop, not only because this would lead to material benefits, but in order to destroy completely the prejudice which existed against their race.[54] The partisans of slavery as well as the supporters of abolition had their eyes fixed on Haiti as evidence for the positions which they were adopting.[55]

In the cultural field, then, we find a movement on the part of a number of younger mulattoes against the francophile assumptions of Boyer's government, which had manifested themselves most clearly in the enterprises of Bonnet referred to above. We find here among this group the stirrings of a *littérature indigène* which were to become a significant current in the period of the American occupation.[56] In the more explicitly political sphere, the opposition voiced its criticisms of the government in the journals *Le Manifeste* and *La Sentinelle de la Liberté*. The ideas expressed in the columns of these journals were generally liberal and nationalist in spirit. *Le Manifeste* vigorously insisted upon maintaining the prohibition of white ownership of property. This Dessalinian provision was necessary in order to 'root out the colonial regime and all the evils which accompanied it'.[57] Against the argument that a change in the law would lead to an influx of foreign capital and thus to a growing prosperity for the country, an anonymous writer in the journal stated that Haitians must raise their own capital for development. It was precisely because the country was underdeveloped that such an influx of capital would be impolitic. What would be the result of a repeal of the prohibition? Foreign capitalists would buy the large estates and proceed to absorb the smaller properties. Haiti would return to a colonial economy and become the theatre of European commercial rivalry.[58] Many Haitians at this time were concerned also with the adoption of an ideology appropriate to economic development and progress. It was in this context that *La Patriote* argued in favour of Protestantism.

The writers of this group were thus advocates of economic national-ism, as well as of cultural autonomy. In constitutional matters they also maintained that Haiti should not slavishly copy the laws of other countries.[59] Dumai Lespinasse, the director of *Le Manifeste*, fiercely attacked the French consul Levasseur for his intervention in the internal affairs of Haiti, particularly criticising his involvement in an incident concerning the circulation of false money in 1841. He referred to the consul's conduct as 'crafty and criminal',[60] and legal action was taken against Lespinasse for the article. He persisted nevertheless in criticising the consul for his 'continual encroaching on our rights by a foolhardy and unwarrantable interference in our affairs', and compared his conduct unfavourably with that of the British consul.[61] In the elections of 1842 all three of the candidates supported by *Le Manifeste* were returned in the capital; they were Dumai Lespinasse, Covin *aîné* and Emile Nau.[62] The government was clearly unable to stem the growing tide of opposition.

The 1843 revolution and its aftermath

On 1 September 1842 a society was formed in Les Cayes called the Society for the Rights of Man and of the Citizen, under the leadership of Hérard Dumesle. A manifesto was issued which listed the grievances of the opposition. It attacked the ambition, cupidity, hypocrisy, deceit and other vices of the president and his entourage. There was, it declared, financial corruption in the administration of taxes and duties; in the army promotion was secured through nepotism; freedom of the press had practically disappeared; magistrates and judges had become mere creatures of the president. What was the cause of these faults? Too much power, it stated, was concentrated in the hands of the president and the senate: 'Under the influence of our vicious constitution, it has become impossible to reform the most crying abuses, it has become impossible to apply any satisfactory remedy to the general depravity.'[63] The group consequently called for far-reaching constitutional reforms, and for the setting up of a provisional govern-ment composed of five men. They were careful to include the black general Guerrier, in order to secure at least the benevolent neutrality of the black army leaders, particularly in the north and centre. Charles Hérard *aîné*, an army officer in charge of the artillery batallion in Les Cayes, was proclaimed 'chef d'execution de la volonté du peuple souverain'. Hérard came from a mulatto family and was the cousin of Hérard Dumesle, who himself became president of the society. The revolution had begun. Soon the revolt spread and Boyer abdicated. Taking what was to become a familiar presidential route into exile, he boarded a British ship bound for Jamaica. The new government issued a decree accusing Boyer, together with his close associates, of treason.

The revolution of 1843 thus represented a split in the camp of the mulatto elite. The difference between the two groups was more a question of personalities than of principles, though it was frequently formulated in terms of the latter. The new government of Charles Hérard paid little more than lip service to the principles of liberty which its members had enunciated while in opposition. The rift among the mulattoes, however, led to a revival in the revolutionary movement among the blacks of the South. The black generals Guerrier, Lazare and Gardel wrote to the French foreign minister, Guizot, complaining about the way in which 'petits mulâtres' had taken all positions of honour and power. 'We would rather be under the domination of the French', they continued, 'and preserve our positions and our property . . . If you do not come', the letter concluded, 'we shall hand over the island to the English.'[64] Once again the colour issue was seen to divide Haitians in such a way as to endanger the independence of the country. As we shall see, the black *piquet* leader Acaau was later to approach the British on the possibility of a protectorate. The southern insurgents, led by members of the Salomon family, who were large landowners in the region, denounced Boyer for having been 'the oppressor of the black class' and called upon the new government to give justice to the blacks. They appealed to Lazare to lead the black party; 'after God and Dessalines', they told him, 'we recognise only you'.[65] The rumour was circulated that the government of Hérard was likely to destroy the small landowners, and, in an attempt to prevent the revolt from spreading, the government issued a proclamation denying any intention of interfering with smallholders. 'One of the principles of our regenerative revolution', ran the government statement, 'has had for its object the maintenance of and respect due to property and to acquired rights.'[66] The government also abolished the tax on the export of primary products, which had been particularly unpopular among the cultivators of coffee. In a further attempt to suppress the southern revolt, the government arrested a number of the leaders, including Salomon *jeune*, who was denounced by the mulattoes for wishing to 'annihilate the coloured population'. Hérard and his associates also attacked the rebels for attempting to rekindle caste hatred.[67] The arrest of these black leaders was the signal for renewed outbreaks of violence in the South. Many of the peasants were armed solely with wooden pikes, and became known from this time on as *piquets*. The leaders of the revolt were Jean-Jacques Acaau, D. Zamor and Jean Claude, three black peasant farmers who had formerly been soldiers. The demands of Acaau and the other leaders included respect for the constitution by the government, the release of the Salomons and the ending of martial law. There are, however, indications that the movement had goals that were more revolutionary that these explicit demands would indicate. According to Thomas Madiou the movement had for its unacknowledged purpose the destruction of mulatto power and the election of a black president. The movement further intended, according to both Madiou and Ardouin, to confiscate land from the rich of whatever colour, and to distribute it to the workers. They ascribed to Acaau the principle that 'all poor mulattoes should be considered as blacks, and that all rich blacks should be considered as mulattoes'.[68] In Port-au-Prince rumours were spread by the Ardouin brothers (who had returned to Haiti after the fall of Charles Hérard in 1844) that Acaau would massacre the mulattoes, who consequently called for his execution.[69] Acaau himself, 'chef des réclamations de ses concitoyens', as he was known to his supporters, denied engaging in a 'war of caste', and insisted that 'we call all men our brothers without distinction'.[70] Although he adopted a generally patriotic rhetoric, it appears that he was prepared to accept some form of British protection or suzerainty for Haiti, in exchange for material support from Britain.[71]

Owing partly to the revolt in the South, and partly to the declaration of independence by the Spanish-speaking eastern part of the island in February 1844, the new government had suffered a decline in prestige. The attempt to reconquer the east led to a resounding military defeat. The government introduced a new constitution which was ultra-democratic in form, but it was largely a façade behind which real power was controlled by a small group of mulattoes headed by Hérard Dumesle. The black army officers became apprehensive, believing that the new government intended to undermine their position, and the colour question became the arbiter of political developments. In the debate on the new constitution an interesting symbolic confrontation took place between a number of black deputies who argued that the flag should be changed back from blue and red, horizontally placed (which had been the flag of Pétion's republic), to the black and red, vertically placed (which had been the flag of the empire and of the northern kingdom). Majority opinion in the assembly was in favour of retaining the republican red and blue, which remained the flag of Haiti until the Duvalier era.[72]

Military defeat in the east, black discontent in the North led by General Thomas Héctor and Deputé Bazin, and the *piquet* revolt in the South, together with the subversive activities of former supporters of Boyer, led to the fall of the government of Hérard. The new president was Philippe Guerrier, an illiterate black general, eighty-seven years of age: real power, however, was in the hands of a group of mulatto politicians, which included many of the former supporters of Boyer. 'Beaubrun Ardouin governed behind the mask of Guerrier', wrote Madiou; 'he dreamed only of vengeance at this time; he had no other programme.'[73] The system whereby a black president was controlled by mulatto politicians became known as *la politique de doublure*, the politics of the understudy. In the South the government managed to get the support of General Lazare, who was denounced by Acaau for his change of face,[74] but another black general, Louis Pierrot, discontented with this *politique de doublure*, declared the separation of the North. Pierrot was a nationalist, a northerner and a *noiriste,* believing that real power ought to be in the hands of the blacks. He succeeded to the presidency at the death of Guerrier in 1845. The colour issue had by this time become so explosive that the new president decided to pass a 'race relations' act:

Any person whatever who indulges in idle talk about colour likely to spread dissension among Haitians and to provoke citizens one against another, will be arrested, put in prison and delivered to the courts . . . [75]

Pierrot attempted to establish northern black supremacy in the internal affairs of the republic, and, as we shall see, firmly asserted Haitian sovereignty in external affairs, particularly in his relations with the French. On 1 January 1846 the president announced his intention of reconquering the eastern part of the island, but an army revolt put an end to his regime, and the Ardouin brothers returned to political power and influence on the coat-tails of Jean Baptiste Riché, a vigorous septuagenarian black general, who 'speaks only of fêtes and balls' and himself 'dances like a young man'.[76] Riché introduced a new constitution, which went back in essentials to the 1816 constitution of Pétion, but the burdens of office combined with his energetic social life proved too much for him and his death in the following year led to a further crisis of succession. Neither of the two rival candidates for the presidency could secure the required majority, and a compromise candidate, General Faustin Soulouque, was elected president in 1847.

Dominican independence and the race question

Although Boyer's invasion of the eastern part of the island in 1822 had been encouraged by a number of Dominicans,[77] the Haitian occupation was not universally accepted among the Spanish-speaking population. Resentment mounted during the 1830s and a movement for independence was founded. As we have seen, the fall of Boyer in 1843 and the renewed outbreak of civil conflict which followed this event proved a propitious moment for a military coup in Santo Domingo and for a declaration of independence. Official proclamations denounced the Haitian tyranny and the failure to respect the cultural heritage and the religious beliefs of the inhabitants of the eastern part of the island.[78] In the official pronouncements there is no explicit reference to racial or colour factors; the new regime rather went out of its way to reassure the large black minority that its rights were to be secured.[79] This was important, as a fifth column of blacks within the new state would have weakened significantly its ability to resist subsequent Haitian invasions. Roughly one-sixth of the population was black, with a high proportion living in the city of Santo Domingo itself, where blacks and mulattoes constituted the majority of the population.[80] An American representative claimed that many of the very black negroes of the Dominican Republic were not favourably disposed towards Haiti, and might be heard saying 'soy negro, pero negro blanco', or 'aunque tengo el cutis negro mi corazón es blanco'.[81] A substantial number of eastern blacks actively supported the independence movement and were rewarded by the new government. The newly independent republic was not, however, without its racial and colour problems, and in 1847 Joachín Puello, the minister of the interior, together with three of his brothers, was accused of planning to massacre all the whites, local and foreign, and to unite the country once more with Haiti.[82]

Despite the avoidance of talk about colour and race in official utterances, private and diplomatic correspondence, together with foreign observations, reveals the importance of these issues. The French consul general in Port-au-Prince informed the foreign ministry in Paris that large numbers of mulattoes had come to him, asking him to recommend them to the junta in Santo Domingo and expressing their joy at the prospect of living under a French protectorate.[83] A French-speaking mulatto doctor writing from Santo Domingo in the following year saw the issue of separation very much in terms of colour. J. H. Fresnel denounced President Pierrot for having 'stirred up the blacks against the coloured people',[84] and claimed that the latter group now had little influence in Haiti. He called for an 'alliance between brown and white' as the only hope for the future.[85] Later, in 1858, now resident in Guadeloupe, Fresnel argued for a French protectorate over the whole island, claiming that without it the elite of both parts would be 'absorbed by the uncultured, ferocious and savage masses who form the majority of the two populations'.[86] He advocated a policy of foreign immigration, but insisted that this should exclude Africans, who could contribute nothing to the regeneration of Haiti, and who would bring with them 'the vices, the laziness, the idleness, the ignorance, the fetishism, the superstitions and the barbarous practices of the savage populations of Africa'.[87] Yet, interestingly, Fresnel favoured the immigration of coloured and black people from the United States, who had

in the past proved themselves a great asset to Haiti.[88] In these statements of Fresnel we see illustrated the subtle distinction between race
and colour which is the theme of this book. On the cultural level he
shared the belief of almost all educated Haitians, black and mulatto,
that things African were barbarous; with respect to the internal issues
in Haiti he sided with the mulattoes, seeing the *noiristes* as constituting
a threat to European civilisation in the country; yet on the purely
biological level he was convinced of the fundamental equality of the
races, being himself a member of the black race.

Fresnel's views were undoubtedly shared by many other mulattoes
on both sides of the border. In 1843 Admiral Alphonse de Moges had
observed how the Spanish-speaking population of the East was 'weary
of the African yoke', while a note of 1852 in the French archives
refers to the 'profound aversion to the pure African race of the West',
to the respect for Europe and to the consequent willingness of the
Dominicans to accept European domination.[89] The Dominicans themselves, in seeking United States recognition and support, made explicit
reference to the racial issue. J. M. Caminero, who later became foreign
minister of the Dominican Republic, told Secretary of State Calhoun
that in freeing itself from 'the Haitian Negroes', the new republic had
'thus diminished the force of the bad example offered by those negroes';
its firm establishment, he claimed, would therefore contribute to
stability in those territories where slavery still existed.[90]

If the Dominican authorities were coy about public reference to
racial and colour issues, the same could not be said of black Haitian
governments. In a thinly veiled attack upon France, Pierrot denounced
'the enemies of the African race', who continued to struggle against
'the complete emancipation of the blacks and of their descendants';
these people were attempting to find means of dividing Haitians, thereby undermining their national independence. 'See how they evidently
protect the insurgents of the East', he continued, '. . . it is then necessary
for us constantly to be on our guard against colonial Machiavellism.'[91]
The president took the opportunity of expelling from Haiti a French
citizen named Dubrac for having attempted to sow seeds of division
among blacks and mulattoes.[92] This was the occasion on which he
issued his decree against persons who raised the colour issue, to which
I have already referred.

Under President Riché there was something of a reconciliation with
the French consul, despite the latter's dislike of the Ardouin brothers,
whose 'hostility towards foreigners' he noted.[93] Faustin Soulouque's
determination to reconquer the eastern part of the island brought
Haiti once more into conflict with France (and also with other powers
who were hoping for some stability in the region). Soulouque expressed
his fears to the British consul that some foreign power would establish

itself in the East and thereby endanger the security of the empire.[94] In 1861 Haitian fears were realised when General Santana took the Dominican Republic back into the Spanish empire. Beaubrun Ardouin saw the matter in racial terms:

Placed already between two Spanish colonies – Cuba and Porto Rico – where the horrible system of African slavery reigns, this people which belongs to this race by its origin, by the blood which flows in its veins, cannot regard with indifference the return of the neighbouring territory to the dominion of Spain.[95]

We shall have occasion to note throughout this study how questions of race and colour have continually entered into relations between Haiti and her eastern neighbour. In this early period many Haitian mulattoes (taking a position different from that adopted by Fresnel) were as keen as were the blacks to secure the unity of the island. While the former saw the issue in terms of increasing the boundaries of the black republic, the latter believed that the relatively high proportion of light-skinned people in the former Spanish colony would help to rectify their own minority position in the western part of the island. Beaubrun Ardouin however, in reaction to the murder of his brother by Soulouque, had argued that Britain and France should act together to secure the independence of the Dominican Republic. Such a step would increase the likelihood of European influence on the island, would strengthen the position of the mulattoes and would contribute to 'the development of our civilisation'.[96] The most influential and articulate Haitian mulattoes adopted a position significantly different from that taken by Dominican mulattoes on the question of race. These Haitians, despite their prejudice against blacks, generally regarded themselves as members of the black race and were committed to a belief in racial equality. Dominicans, on the other hand, have frequently taken up explicitly racialist positions, claiming to belong themselves to the European race. The question of civilisation against barbarism was for the former one of culture, but for the latter one of genetic origin. It was not until the period of the United States occupation that race became a divisive factor in Haiti itself. The Spanish restoration in Santo Domingo lasted only a short time, and the Dominicans once more declared independence in September 1863.

Soulouque and Geffrard

With the election of Soulouque the *politique de doublure* was once again at work, but this time it was to rebound upon its promoters.[97] After some months in office, Soulouque began to assert his authority, and in April 1848 he took vigorous steps to eliminate actual or potential opponents, most of whom were mulattoes. Soulouque was proclaimed Emperor Faustin I in 1849 and he reigned for ten years. Although he identified himself in general with the black tradition, he relied to a considerable extent upon mulattoes in his administration, among whom were his foreign minister the Duc de Tiburon (L. Dufrène), Baron Emile Nau and Thomas Madiou. The leading ministers of Soulouque's government were Freemasons and his reign also saw an increasingly open practice of the Voodoo cult. Nevertheless the government claimed to be Catholic, and was concerned to encourage the development of an indigenous clergy. A leading cleric of the period was Abbé Moussa, an African from Senegal, who was for several years a favourite of the imperial court.[98] Partly with the aid of a paramilitary force known as 'zinglins' Soulouque managed to clip the wings of the regular army. He also suppressed the *piquets* in the South and executed Pierre Noir, their leader.[99] Soulouque's finance minister was Salomon *jeune*. Louis Etienne Lysius Félicité Salomon was born in June 1815 in the southern city of Les Cayes of a respectable black landowning family. He joined the army and became interested in politics at an early age. He attempted to introduce a limited form of state ownership by decreeing a state monopoly in the export of coffee and by organising state-owned commercial houses to handle all imported goods. The purpose of these moves was to undermine the power of local and foreign speculators and to increase state revenue, but opposition to the proposals (particularly from foreign businessmen and diplomats) forced the government to free coffee from state control. Salomon was rather popular with foreign residents, 'particularly the members of the old commercial houses, who were witnesses of his administrative capacity, and benefitted largely from it, when he was Minister of Finance and Commerce . . .'[100] British merchants were also favourably disposed towards the emperor himself.[101] It would thus be quite misleading to think of these black leaders as economic nationalists whose policy constituted a serious threat to foreign interests in Haiti. The racist press of Europe and North America, however, heaped scorn upon the black emperor, though he was in many respects a skilful politician, a sincere patriot and an astute diplomat.[102]

Soulouque's unsuccessful attempts to conquer the Dominican Republic, which constituted in his view a potential base for foreign invaders, and thus a threat to Haitian security, weakened his government, and in 1859 a conspiracy led by General Fabre Nicolas Geffrard brought an end to the empire. The new president, Geffrard, born in 1803 at L'Anse-à-Veau in the South, was an elite *griffe*, who returned to the constitution of 1846 with a few modifications. Although the form of government was republican, the country continued to be ruled by a small group, many of whom were army officers who had also been influential in the administration of Soulouque. Some foreign observers were unduly impressed by the constitutional façade, and overemphasised the transition. A Jamaican visitor to Haiti wrote:

> The reign of barbarism and tyranny which prevailed under the auspices of Faustin I has happily been brought to a close, and that of progress has been fairly inaugurated by the genius of a man as remarkable for his patriotism, as for sound judgement, benevolence and fixity of purpose . . . The policy of President Geffrard is to restore and foster civilisation.[103]

In the field of religion and education Geffrard pursued a vigorous policy which has had important effects on the social development of Haiti. In 1860 his government reached agreement with the Vatican, and a concordat was signed. 'Let us hasten', urged Geffrard, 'to remove from our land these last vestiges of barbarism and slavery, superstition and its scandalous practices.'[104] The president was thinking principally, of course, of the Voodoo religion which had flourished during the reign of Soulouque. E. Heurtelou, one of the leading journalists of his day, ascribed the continued power of Voodoo – 'that savage barbarous religion of Africa' – to bad Roman Catholic priests who had discredited the church.[105] From this time onwards the Roman Catholic church played an increasingly important role in the life of the country. Many of the principal schools were run by religious orders, and were staffed mostly by Frenchmen, thus tending to reinforce the francophile prejudices of the elite. As early as 1843 the French naval commandant in the Antilles, Alphonse de Moges, was attempting to convince the French government that it was possible to 'retake Haiti' in a peaceful manner, by sending missionary priests.[106] Geffrard reorganised the medical school, founded a law school and established some state *lycées*. He also encouraged the immigration of American negroes to assist in a projected revival of cotton production. Among these Americans was the Reverend James Theodore Holly, who founded the Anglican church in Haiti, and in 1874 became the first bishop of L'Eglise Orthodoxe Apostolique Haïtienne.[107] A committee was set up in Boston to organise the immigration of coloured United States citizens to Haiti. In his preface to the *Guide to Hayti*, which was addressed to these potential immigrants, President Geffrard wrote:

> Listen, then, all ye negroes and mulattoes who, in the vast Continent of America, suffer from the prejudices of caste. The Republic calls you . . . The regenerating work that she undertakes interests all colored people and their descendants . . . Hayti . . . will be a formal denial, most eloquent and peremptory, against those detractors of our race who contest our desire and ability to attain a high degree of civilization.[108]

The colour question continued to be central to the political and social life of the country. Many mulattoes from the elite group saw the accession of Geffrard as an opportunity to reassert that political supremacy which they had lost in the years following 1844. An abortive coup, led by members of the Salomon family in 1862, was designed to halt this growth in mulatto power.[109] A foreign visitor remarked upon the importance of the colour question at this time, claiming that all Haiti's recent revolutions had been 'simply a contest of races', while Sir Spencer St John, British minister in Haiti during this period, observed the way in which the social life of the country was affected by colour distinctions. At the parties and balls given by Geffrard there were often only two or three black ladies and perhaps a hundred mulatto ladies. Although the proportion of black men at such functions was larger, their presence was evidently due to their official positions.[110] Many Haitian writers themselves drew attention to the divisive effect of colour distinctions at this time; this was said to be one of the factors which caused the country to stagnate. Despite these colour distinctions within the country, Haiti continued to be seen as the symbol of black liberation, by mulattoes as well as by blacks. After the execution of John Brown in the United States, in December 1859, flags in Port-au-Prince were flown at half mast, and the presidential family attended a solemn requiem mass in the cathedral; Geffrard also laid emphasis upon the importance of unity between Haitians of all shades.[111]

The tranquillity of the country was once more disturbed in 1865 by a revolt in Cap Haïtien, led by a mulatto general, Silvain Salnave, which received some support from the United States. It was put down with the help of a British warship, and Salnave fled to the Dominican Republic. Salnave and one of his chief supporters at the time, Demesvar Delorme, were accused by the government of having planned 'to hand over a portion of national territory' to a foreign power (the United States) — something Geffrard himself had possibly been planning three years earlier.[112] The British government, which had been supporting Geffrard, was worried by this accusation which was subsequently confirmed by the American secretary of state.[113] In 1867, however, Geffrard was finally overthrown and was replaced as president by Salnave.

The noiriste *protest*

The frustrations of the black population, which had manifested themselves spontaneously and violently in the years following the fall of Boyer, increasingly affected the ideology of the period. *Noiriste* writers praised Dessalines and called for the complete rehabilitation of the liberator of Haiti. In an effort to placate this group, the government of Charles Hérard awarded a pension to the emperor's widow, and stated that 'despite the errors into which this illustrious citizen was plunged, these never could expunge from the hearts of Haitians the memory of the conspicuous services which he rendered to his

country'.[114] This somewhat grudging recognition by the mulatto regime
of Hérard was, however, soon superseded by the more generous law of
Pierrot, which fully acknowledged the services rendered to his country
by the emperor. Furthermore a memorial service for Dessalines was
held in the parish church of Les Cayes, at which the address was given
by Salomon *jeune*. The emperor was 'vengeur de la race noire':

Homage, homage, glory to Dessalines! No one, before or after him, has done more
for the children of Africa. In making Haiti a free, sovereign and independent
state, he assured to black and brown men of all countries a part of the earth
where they could realise the dignity of their being.[115]

The slaughter of the French, commanded by Dessalines in 1804, was
'mesure grande, terrible, sans doute, mais nécessaire'.

The person of Dessalines became a matter of acute controversy, and
the opinion which a person voiced on the emperor was largely governed
by his contemporary political allegiances, which were themselves
closely associated with the colour question. In 1861, for example,
a debate raged in the columns of *L'Opinion Nationale* about the proposal to erect a monument to Dessalines, the project being supported
by Septimus Rameau, one of the black founders of the National Party,
and opposed by a number of mulattoes. Not all the mulattoes opposed
the project, however: E. Heurtelou, for example, editor of *Le Progrès*,
was generally favourable to the idea, though he carefully distinguished
between Dessalines the liberator and Dessalines the 'despot', according
to the mulatto version which I consider below. An interesting aspect
of the controversy was the protest by the French consul against the
erection of a monument to one who had slaughtered so many Frenchmen. Geffrard told Levraud that of course it would be quite wrong for
the government to give its official patronage to such a project, but that
as a Haitian citizen he would himself contribute to the fund. In his
account of the whole affair, written from exile, Salomon misrepresents
the situation, by giving the impression that 'Heurtelou, mulâtre' was
opposed to the erection of the monument. This, of course, would
fit in better with Salomon's *noiriste* preconceptions.[116] A clear and
amusing indication of the mythological and ideological status given to
Dessalines was the extraordinary *volte-face* by Dorvelas Dorval between
1858 and 1861. In an 1858 article, written while the black emperor
Faustin was ruling Haiti, Dorvelas Dorval praised Dessalines as a martyr;
just three years later, when the mulattoes were in control of the government, he assailed Dessalines as one who 'perished a victim of his
tyranny'.[117]

In the period under consideration, from the fall of Boyer to the
advent of Salnave, Salomon *jeune* emerged as the leading ideologist
of the *noiriste* faction, insisting that the significant divisions in Haiti
were based on colour. 'By the fact of the difference of colour', he

wrote in 1861, 'Haitians are divided into two castes: the black party which forms the majority and the mulatto or coloured party'; this latter caste had within it a clique, led by President Geffrard, which was small in number but politically powerful, and which had as its aim 'to stultify and subjugate the blacks', in order to maintain permanent control of the country. Any resistance which the blacks put up was condemned by these politicians as a plan to exterminate the coloured population. Geffrard was the principal object of Salomon's wrath; he had, according to his critic, dismissed blacks from important offices in order to replace them with mulattoes, and he had deliberately encouraged the immigration of light-skinned negroes from the United States rather than blacks.[118] Salomon was, as we shall see, to come to power later largely on the basis of this *noiriste* position, and it is interesting to see how black politicians from the middle and upper classes have consistently used the colour issue to divert attention from the question of economic class, and to convince the black masses that their interests are the same as those of these leaders themselves.

III

Thomas Madiou

The regimes of Soulouque and Geffrard witnessed the appearance of a number of important works on aspects of the Haitian past. In 1847 Thomas Madiou published the first part of his *Histoire d'Haïti*, this being followed in 1848 by volumes II and III.[119] Madiou was born in 1814 at Port-au-Prince, but was sent away to France at the age of ten for his education. He became interested in history and, returning to Haiti in 1835, published a number of articles on Haitian history. From 1837 to 1841 he was personal secretary to Inginac, chief minister in Boyer's government, but managed to separate himself from the regime before its fall in 1843. He became a teacher and was appointed director of the *lycée nationale*; he resigned in protest against the massacres by Soulouque in 1848. Nevertheless Madiou was soon brought back into public affairs by the emperor, who appointed him editor of *Le Moniteur*, the official government journal. He was made ambassador to Spain by Geffrard and became secretary of state for education in 1866. His close association with Geffrard's government led to the confiscation of his property by Salnave. He returned to favour and became secretary of state for education under Saget. He retired from public life, but was brought back by Salomon, who was an old friend of his, and appointed secretary of state for justice, war and the navy. He died in 1884.[120]

Although a mulatto, Madiou was never totally committed to the

mulatto clique or cliques, as his association with the regimes of Soulouque and Salomon will indicate. His writings on the Haitian past,
though liberally sprinkled with value judgments, personal reflections
and practical lessons for his readers, were never simply an elaboration
of the mulatto version of Haitian history. He was not, however, a
historian interested in the past for the sake of the past, and made it
clear to his readers that a knowledge of the past is important in order
'to direct a society in the ways of progress'.[121] Madiou saw his historical
writings as a work of piety and patriotism. 'History', he wrote,

consolidates the independence of a nation. A people which does not know its
traditions is without a love of its fatherland. This people, being attacked by
foreigners, will defend only its material interests; vanquished, it submits to the
yoke of conquerors without regret for the past.[122]

He saw Haiti, founded as a free homeland for African people, as a repayment to the people of Europe for the oppression which they had
inflicted in the past, and for their destruction of the indigenous Indians.
The emergence of Haiti constituted, furthermore, a refutation of the
view that certain parts of the globe should be restricted to particular
races; the globe belongs to the whole human race. Madiou also believed
that important lessons can be drawn from a knowledge of world history,
in particular the fact that civilisation progresses because of the movement of populations and the blending (*fusion*) of races.[123] This belief
in the benefits of racial mixing became a familiar aspect of the mulatto
ideology, for obvious reasons. It would be quite wrong to think that
Madiou, who himself managed to avoid a narrow commitment to the
mulatto groups of his day, ignored the importance of colour distinctions in the history of Haiti. Quite the reverse: each of his three volumes
contains an appendix giving the colour of the characters mentioned in
the text. Furthermore, his explicit recognition of the colour question
and his reference to the presence of two 'castes' in post-colonial Haiti
was especially objectionable to the mulatto elite. Madiou saw the
rebellion headed by Acaau as a reaction against mulatto domination
under Pétion and Boyer, stating that 'colour remained the criterion
of social, administrative and political distinctions'.[124] He thus saw the
colour factor as important, but he refused to paint the history of Haiti
according to the 'official' mulatto version. In particular, as we have
already seen, his assessment of the emperor Dessalines was somewhat
out of line with the accepted mulatto view,[125] and his judgment of
Christophe was regarded as excessively lenient. The French writer
Bonneau accused Madiou of attempting to rehabilitate Christophe
in order to ingratiate himself with Soulouque.[126]

The mulatto legend

It is against the background of Madiou's three-volume history that we must see the historical writings of Alexis Beaubrun Ardouin and Joseph Saint-Rémy, who emerged as the principal vindicators of the traditional mulatto elite version of the Haitian past. Saint-Rémy stated, in his prolegomena to *Pétion et Haïti*, how his original intention had been to write a simple biography of Pétion; but the numerous errors in Madiou's *Histoire d'Haïti* had caused him to extend his work into a more general history.[127] Also throughout Ardouin's principal work there are critical and even hostile references to Madiou. Together with a number of other writers — including J. B. Inginac, G.- J. Bonnet, B. Lespinasse, S. Linstant de Pradine and Céligny (sometimes spelled 'Céligni') Ardouin — Saint-Rémy and Ardouin set out to establish, and particularly after the publication of Madiou's *Histoire*, to re-establish, a legend of the past which was to form part of a whole mulatto ideology. What these writers present is legendary, in the sense that it is a stylised version of the past, which is presented for its exemplary value — for its practical implications in the present.[128] Furthermore it forms part of a more comprehensive outlook on the world which is connected to certain suggested patterns of action in the present. It is therefore part of an ideology, and is presented in order to explain and justify the predominant position enjoyed by the mulatto elite, and thereby to consolidate its position. The past is being used as a weapon in the controversies of the present. When, in a later period, the black legend is elaborated by writers like Janvier, Charmant and finally by Duvalier, we find the controversies of present-day politics being fought out in terms of conflicting interpretations of the past. There is very little of that 'dead past' which, according to Michael Oakeshott, is the necessary material for a specifically *historical* interest in the past — an interest in the past for the sake of the past.[129] Most of the incidents, struggles and confrontations since colonial days still have, or are thought to have, practical implications for current politics. A person's understanding of the past will therefore be influenced by his present convictions; his revised assessment of the past might very well imply, or be thought to imply, a modification in his political commitments.

This practical approach to the past, which is characteristic of most Haitian writers, and particularly so of those mulatto historians whom we are considering in the present section, suggests certain similarities to what Herbert Butterfield has called 'the whig interpretation of history'. 'It is part and parcel of the whig interpretation of history', he writes, 'that it studies the past with reference to the present.'[130] Such an approach to the past is exemplified in a writer like J. R. Seeley, who stated that the purpose of studying history is to be 'wise before the event' and to help men in solving political problems in their own day.[131] In a recent book, N. W. Heer has illustrated the way in which Soviet historians have viewed the past and its relationship with the present. The historian has no right to be interested in the past for its own sake, but has a duty to investigate the past in such a way as to guide and direct the formulation of party policy in the present.[132] The historian is also bound to portray the glories of the past in an exemplary manner, so as to inspire those later generations who did not experience the events of the revolution first hand.[133] Historians, however, are potentially dangerous: 'They are capable of upsetting everything', declared Khrushchev in 1956; 'they must be directed.'[134]

Exponents of the legend

Beaubrun Ardouin and Joseph Saint-Rémy were the principal exponents of the mulatto legend. Ardouin was born at Petit Trou de Nippes in the department of the South, in 1796; Céligny and Coriolan Ardouin were his brothers. The latter died in 1836 at the age of twenty-four; Beaubrun and Céligny were closely associated with political developments in Haiti for many years. Beaubrun, after working as a printer, studied law and became an *avocat*. With his brother he was a supporter of Boyer. Both brothers were accused of treason by the liberal revolution of 1843 and fled the country. We have noted how they returned to power during the regime of Guerrier, and later under Riché; further, they were implicated in the election of Soulouque in 1847. In August, 1849, however, Céligny was shot by Soulouque, and his brother resigned in protest from his position of ambassador to France. Beaubrun was appointed again to this post by Geffrard, but returned to Haiti owing to ill-health, and died in 1865.[135] Ardouin's principal work was his massive eleven-volume *Etudes sur l'histoire d'Haïti suivies de la vie du général J.-M. Borgella*, published in Paris from 1853 to 1860. He had, however, published earlier a *Géographie de l'île d'Haïti* (1832) which was prefaced by a 'précis de l'histoire d'Haïti'; he also edited a work by his brother Céligny entitled *Essais sur l'histoire d'Haïti* (1865). The second of the great mulatto historians of this period was Joseph Saint-Rémy, who was born in Basse-Terre, Guadeloupe in 1816, of free mulatto parents. The family moved to Les Cayes in the South of Haiti, claiming the right of citizenship as persons of African descent, according to the provisions of the republican constitution of 1816. The young Joseph was sent to Paris where he studied law, returning during the latter part of Boyer's rule to practise as an *avocat* in Les Cayes. His sympathies were with the liberal revolution of 1843, and his attachment to the regime of Charles Hérard led to his arrest, imprisonment and banishing by Pierrot. He returned to Haiti at the accession of Soulouque, but soon left again for Paris. In 1853 he returned to practise law in the city of Gonaïves, but died five years later at the age of forty-two.[136] Saint-Rémy's five-volume work *Pétion et Haïti* was published from 1853 to 1857; also he wrote *La vie de Toussaint L'Ouverture*

(1850), edited two historical works and published a number of articles and pamphlets.

What, then, is the structure of the mulatto legend of the past, and how did it fit into the wider context of a mulatto elite ideology? These writers had a practical rather than a purely academic interest in the past, believing that a knowledge of the past helps a person to act wisely in the present; they thus saw their work as a practical and patriotic contribution to political life. They attacked the colonial regime and laid emphasis upon the importance of national unity. All Haitians belong to a single family, and all are descendants of the African race. The evils in the Haiti of their day were confidently ascribed to the colonial regime. The mulatto picture of the past usually played down the significance of colour distinctions among the black and coloured Haitians, ascribing the divisions of the past and of their own day to other factors. Haitians had a common enemy in the whites, who had done their best to encourage colour divisions among them by their actions, and to exaggerate the importance of these divisions in their writings. The whites had occasionally succeeded in using the ignorant blacks as instruments of their policy, but the true patriots, the mulattoes, had resisted the advances of the foe. Toussaint in particular was accused of having become a tool of the whites and of harbouring a passionate hatred of mulattoes. Dessalines is portrayed as despotic, barbarous and ignorant; Christophe was also despotic and prejudiced against the coloureds. Pétion, on the other hand, was everything that is virtuous: liberal, humane, democratic, mild, civilised, honest, as was Boyer, his lineal successor (though there was some disagreement on this latter point, as we shall see.) Two of the greatest tragedies in the past were seen to be the schism of the South under Rigaud in 1810, and the split between the mulattoes culminating in the revolution of 1843. The lesson which these two events are supposed to demonstrate is that mulatto disunity leads to the possibility of black power. In the cultural field the mulatto legend portrays Voodoo as a survival of barbarism and superstition; for most of these writers, civilisation meant European civilisation. They attacked militarism in politics, which breeds autocratic government.

The outline of the mulatto legend as presented here is expressed in very general terms; as we shall see, there have been mulatto writers who disagreed with particular aspects of the picture. Also I am not at all suggesting that the judgments made by these writers were uniformly false; much of what they said about the Haitian past could well be accepted by historians who were less committed to practical politics than these men were. The general effect of the mulatto version of the Haitian past is, however, to encourage Haitians to unite under the leadership of the most patriotic, civilised and technically qualified group in the country, to legitimate the mulatto ascendancy in the social and economic field, and to lend weight to their claim to guide and control developments in the political sphere.

The colonial past and the race question

In the first place, then, these writers had a practical interest in the past. Ardouin stated that he wrote from a Haitian point of view. He believed that 'the past is the regulator of the present as of the future', and saw his work as preparing materials which would serve his countrymen in the future. His *Etudes* was thus 'a patriotic work'.[137] Also, as the first generation of Haitians died, it was, he maintained, the sacred duty of their countrymen to record and hand on to future generations the story of past deeds.[138] This role of history, as the means by which younger generations who did not experience at first hand the revolutionary struggle might be instructed and inspired, is of course similar to the part which history plays in the Soviet system. The route from slavery and colonialism to emancipation from the European yoke was, for Ardouin, more than the achievement of men, it was a work of divine providence;[139] Lespinasse agreed that in the revolutionary war 'the work of God shows itself in all its majesty'.[140] Saint-Rémy declared that he approached his work with a 'heart full of religious patriotism', pointing out that it is the task of the historian to praise the good actions of men and to blame their bad actions, so that the teaching of the past will be fruitful in the present.[141] General Alibée Féry, a mulatto who had supported the 1843 revolution, stated that the study of history is necessary for the politician, and that active involvement in politics is helpful for the historian. Historical plays about the mulatto heroes of independence, such as *Ogé, ou le préjugé de couleur*, were produced in order to 'develop noble sentiments' among those who attended, 'and to show them, by the history of their own country, all that is absurd and odious in colour prejudice'.[142]

The ruthlessness of the colonial system was emphasised by these historians. In 1854 Emile Nau published his *Histoire des caciques d'Haïti*, drawing attention to the virtual extermination of a whole nation by the Spanish invaders. 'Can we ignore the origins and the past of our country', he demanded, 'the story, so pathetic and so lamentable, of this interesting people, whose last offspring were companions in servitude of our first ancestors on this soil? The African and the Indian have been enchained.'[143] The judgments by these historians of the colonial regime were understandably harsh. Ardouin asked his readers to excuse the 'energetic' tone of his language when dealing with 'the detestable colonial regime', which was the evident cause of all the evils which the black race had suffered.[144] The colonial oligarchy

stopped at nothing in their exploitation of the African race, declared
Saint-Rémy, and in order to 'legitimate the violation of all the principles
of natural law, the intellectual and moral incapacity of this race was
proclaimed aloud'.[145] Lespinasse also pointed out that his own generation was too close to the system of slavery to be able to judge it
coldly.[146]

The Saint Domingue revolution was therefore seen by these writers
as a rejection of colonialism and as a vindication of the black race.
Although mulattoes, and some of them in their physical appearance
hardly distinguishable from Europeans, they proudly proclaimed their
membership of the African race. Ardouin wrote as a 'descendant of
this African race which has been so long oppressed',[147] and he concluded his *Etudes* with praise to the children of Africa of whatever
class.[148] Haiti remained for these writers the symbol of black dignity
and racial equality, and the story of the Haitian past was therefore
seen as a defence (*plaidoyer*) of the black race.[149] Saint-Rémy spoke
of Pétion as belonging to the African race,[150] and reminded his readers
that Egypt, which had been populated by blacks, had been the centre
of a great civilisation. The study of history thus demonstrates that
'each race has its civilisation without ceasing to belong to the great
human family'. There are no inherent fundamental differences between
the races; such physical differences as there may be are superficial and
due largely to climatic variations.[151] These writers, then, regarded the
record of the Haitian past, and indeed the whole of human history, as
conclusive evidence for the unity of the human race, and therefore as
an implicit condemnation of all theories of racial inferiority and all
manifestations of colour prejudice. We have already noted Lespinasse's
insistence upon Haiti's African connection; he was equally firm in his
assertion that 'humanity is a great family of brothers'.[152] Ardouin
stated that the purpose of his writing was to bring before his fellow
citizens the glorious actions of their fathers in breaking the chains of
servitude, and thereby 'elevating to their true dignity men who had
for too long been ignored'.[153]

In his analysis of colour prejudice, published in 1841, S. Linstant
insisted upon 'the unity of the human race', and traced colour prejudice
in Haiti back to the class structure in France.[154] He saw theories of
racial inferiority as attempted rationalisations of the injustice practised
by the colonists who tried to maintain that nothing good or civilised
could come out of Africa. In fact, Linstant insisted, Egypt, which was
populated by negroes, received from them a part of its civilisation.[155]
But why, he demanded, had Africa failed to progress since that time?
The development of slavery, he argued, led to a suspicion of commerce
and of trade by the African people and, as commerce is the normal
manner by which civilisation is propagated, the continent did not

progress. Nevertheless Linstant maintained that the interior of Africa, which had known less of slavery, was more civilised than the coastal strip.[156] In a comparative critique of colonial systems Linstant suggested that, while British colonialism was characterised by pragmatism and enlightened self-interest, Spain took a maternal attitude towards her colonies which manifested itself in a more humane treatment of slaves. 'Religion', he declared, 'is the greatest cause of this mildness.' Yet this by no means abolished colour prejudice in the Spanish colonies.[157]

Caste, colour and national unity

Up to this point there is very little difference between the official mulatto legend and the story of the past as recounted by Madiou. Both versions of the Haitian past stressed the importance and desirability of national unity, but their assessment of the situation as it actually was during the period of independence differed significantly. Madiou, as we have seen, believed that there were serious divisions among the population in post-colonial Haiti which justified the use of the term 'caste' to describe them. He had referred to 'the rivalry which existed between the two castes, black and mulatto [*jeune*], forming the Haitian nation'.[158] Ardouin objected strongly to applying the concept of 'caste' to the situation in Haiti after independence. During the colonial regime it was possible to speak of castes, but after the abolition of slavery in 1793 'the *interests* have always been *the same* for all men of the black race'.[159] Having the same interests, blacks and mulattoes cannot be described as distinct castes. One might legitimately refer to a person as being black or mulatto, just as one could refer to an Englishman, a Scotsman and an Irishman, but they do not have different interests and therefore cannot be said to form castes. The term 'class' might properly be used to describe blacks and mulattoes, but it is clear from the context that Ardouin meant by class simply a descriptive category, and not a significant social division. He denied any serious rivalry between Haitians of different complexions; they all had the same civil rights and the same interests. Ardouin insisted that it was quite wrong to deduce a general rivalry between blacks and mulattoes from a few isolated incidents,[160] and Linstant denied the existence of a privileged class in independent Haiti.[161] Saint-Rémy also insisted, 'I belong to no caste, to no sect . . .'[162] It was essential for the apologists of the mulatto ascendancy to deny the existence of a mulatto ascendancy, portraying Haiti as a country of equal opportunity, where the most competent man gets to the top – or at least to the position of advisor to the man at the top! We shall have occasion to remark later on how it is often the most extreme defenders of the mulatto and the black ideologies who deny the existence of significant colour distinctions in the country.[163]

The mulatto ideology, then, emphasised the common interest binding together all Haitians, and denied the existence of rigid caste barriers. The colonial system had been responsible for such divisions in the past, and during the revolutionary period the French had attempted to perpetuate group antagonisms, and thus to divide and rule. Toussaint Louverture became, according to this view, the instrument of the whites. The thesis that there were serious colour antagonisms in Haiti in the period since independence, which resulted in the black masses being oppressed by a small caste of mulattoes, had also been canvassed by European writers like Victor Schoelcher. Saint-Rémy accused him of attempting once more to divide blacks from mulattoes in the interests of the whites. It was Schoelcher's own people, the whites, who were 'the source of all the evils' of Haiti. They had armed the mulattoes against the blacks and had stirred up the blacks against the mulattoes.[164]

The mulatto legend and the revolutionary wars

In the mulatto version of the Haitian past, then, national unity was not only an important aim to be pursued, but was, in substance, a present reality. The caste divisions of colonial days had ended in 1793, or at least in 1804. In order to establish the reality of national unity and to vindicate the mulatto ascendancy, it was important for these writers to show that, even prior to independence, it was the *affranchis* who had led the struggle against colonial oppression, and that they were the true pioneers of liberation and independence. In their consideration of the colonial and revolutionary period, these writers were particularly interested in the role played by this group of free coloureds, the most powerful of whom were mulattoes. Ardouin frankly recognised the fact that the *affranchis* were to some extent divided in their loyalties. He pointed out that many of this group were landowners and even slave owners, and that as such they had 'an interest in maintaining the colonial regime'.[165] Nevertheless, over against this common economic interest which the *affranchis* had with the *blancs*, there was the racial discrimination under which they laboured, which bound them to 'the unfortunate slaves'. This meant that the *affranchis* 'had a powerful interest in being reconciled with the latter [the slaves] and uniting with them to break the colonial yoke'.[166] Ardouin saw this dual interest as explaining the apparently ambivalent position taken by the *affranchis* in the conflicts and confrontations of the revolutionary period. The common interest with the slaves proved to be the more powerful, and although this group had to act in a manner which was politic, it was this predominant interest in overthrowing colonialism which was a constant factor influencing their actions and commitments.[167] Ardouin laid considerable emphasis upon the disabilities suffered by the *affranchis* under the colonial system, thus indicating their common lot with the slaves as an oppressed group. He also failed to give sufficient weight to the fact that most of the powerful members of this *affranchi* group were mulattoes, while the vast majority of the slaves were black. Saint-Rémy was, if anything, even less balanced in his discussion of the role of the *affranchis* in colonial Saint Domingue than was Ardouin. He wrote of this group as being 'composed of mulattoes and blacks' who were engaged in small-scale farming and in manual work,[168] thus seriously misrepresenting the true colour and economic situation. His picture of colonial Saint Domingue certainly overemphasised the disabilities suffered by 'this poor caste of coloured people',[169] in comparison with the lot of the slaves. Lespinasse, in turn, stressed the moral effects of racial prejudice in the colony, which the *affranchis* suffered together with the slaves. The humiliation of the black race was to be found not so much in the chains and in the physical suffering of the slaves as in the moral pains and woes inflicted upon the whole non-white population of Saint Domingue.[170] Bonnet suggested that the slaves and the *affranchis* were bound by a common interest, and that the whites pursued 'a single end: the maintenance of slavery by the destruction of the coloured people'.[171] For these men the early heroes of Haitian independence were Ogé and Chavannes, and it was part of the mulatto legend that the *affranchis* were struggling not only for their own civil rights but to secure 'the general liberty of all the children of Africa'.[172] At a banquet in support of Hérard Dumesle, presided over by Honoré Féry in 1839, toasts were drunk 'in memory of Ogé and Chavannes, these first martyrs of liberty', but no mention was made of the black leaders.[173]

For the historians we are considering, then, the *affranchis* were portrayed as a suffering and oppressed group, and they furthermore suggested that this group of free coloureds was the truly revolutionary group in the colony. Lespinasse claimed that the slave revolt of 1791 was essentially due to mulatto inspiration. In fathering the mulattoes, the white colonists had literally sown the seeds of their own destruction! The mulattoes received education from their white fathers, and being imbued with a love of liberty they had passed this on to the blacks, their brothers. The blacks, in turn, took the lead when it came to the question of independence, and passed on to their mulatto brothers a realisation that liberty could be secured only by political independence. Unity of purpose was thus achieved, but it was the mulattoes who initiated the movement which culminated in 1804.[174] Saint-Rémy suggested that Pétion began the war of independence by his revolt against the French in October 1802.[175]

The mulatto version of the past, portraying the predominantly mulatto *affranchis* as the leaders in the revolution of Saint Domingue, was necessarily critical of the role played by Toussaint Louverture. While these writers saw Toussaint as one of the greatest national leaders, and pointed to him with pride as a vindicator of the African race, they nevertheless attacked his supposed prejudice against mulattoes, and his too great reliance upon the whites. For Ardouin, Toussaint became 'the blind instrument of metropolitan policy'.[176] He re-established a despotic system of government and attempted to revive the plantations with the aid of the whites. He became, in fact, the principal agent of the counter-revolutionaries.[177] Saint-Rémy's description of Toussaint is full of both admiration and condemnation.[178] He particularly attacked the black general's prejudice against mulattoes, and his 'league with the colonists to re-establish slavery under the form of the glebe'.[179] Rigaud, rather than Toussaint, emerges as the true radical – the more determined enemy of the whites and the advocate of full independence. Madiou was criticised for suggesting otherwise.[180] Saint-Rémy insisted that the war of the South between Toussaint and Rigaud was not at all a war of colour, though he accused the former of attempting to turn it into such.[181] In his *Souvenirs historiques*, published posthumously, Guy-Joseph Bonnet also ascribed colour prejudice to Toussaint, referring to him as 'an ensign whose very presence was an incitement to hatred against the mulattoes'.[182] Lespinasse diverged somewhat from the accepted mulatto picture of Toussaint; although, together with Rigaud and Sonthanax, the black general could justly be accused of originating civil strife among Haitians, he must be recognised as among 'the most ardent defenders of liberty' as 'the soul of our independence'.[183]

The emperor Dessalines was pictured by most of these writers as fierce, tyrannical and opposed to the interests of the *anciens libres* of all colours. But he was nevertheless seen as a great general and as a father of Haitian independence, and was honoured as such.[184] Dessalines, however, had failed to move on from independence to create a viable political system. His despotic government was resented by all Haitians, not least by 'the black masses of our countryside', who 'in the impartiality of their understanding, in the recesses of their hearts', could not but celebrate his death with joy. He suffered the death reserved for tyrants.[185] According to Bonnet the emperor's reign was characterised by 'disorder, waste, immorality, violence'.[186]

Christophe, Pétion and the mulatto version

The mulatto historians whom we are considering were particularly concerned to present a 'correct' interpretation of the conflict between Christophe's northern state and the republic. Pétion was the heroic figure *par excellence*; not only had he initiated the war of independence, but he had also founded a liberal and democratic republic. Christophe, on the other hand, was the embodiment of all that was worst in the Haitian political tradition. He was arbitrary, unpredictable, colour-prejudiced and conspiratorial. There is little to relieve the grimness of the picture; Christophe does not even find a place among the principal fathers of national independence. Ardouin saw Christophe as the inheritor of that unfortunate 'aristocratic' tradition which emanated from the North.[187] In contrast, the South was democratic but unstable (which helped Ardouin to account for the schism of Rigaud in 1810). It was the West which was the centre of enlightened democracy, tempered by the practice of government. The principal cause of the civil war was Christophe's determination to assert the northern tradition and return to arbitrary and autocratic government, in the face of the demand by enlightened citizens for constitutional checks upon the power of the executive. 'The civil war was ignited by the disastrous ambition of H. Christophe', wrote Ardouin in 1832.[188] This struggle between liberty and democracy on the one hand and despotism and autocracy on the other was 'the *unique* cause of this war'.[189] It was, he insisted, only an ignorance of the facts which could lead anyone to suggest that the war was a war of colour or of caste. In this matter Ardouin and Madiou were, as we have seen,[190] at one. Nevertheless Ardouin went on to argue that Christophe was in fact prejudiced against mulattoes, and that he set out in 1812 to exterminate all persons in this group of whose loyalty he could not be assured.[191] Yet the king had also put to death many blacks in his kingdom, and Ardouin was eager to point out that opposition to him came from blacks as well as from mulattoes.

In contrast to the cruel and arbitrary Christophe, Alexandre Pétion appears as the paragon of virtue — honest, courageous, mild and moderate. The policy of the republic was entirely free from colour prejudice or discrimination. Ardouin was particularly concerned with the question of property. Pétion's 'generous' policy of land distribution and sale was proof of his democratic spirit.[192] Also it was an act of wisdom, preventing the growth of a powerful group of army officers who were jealous of the land owned by the *anciens libres*. The senate was criticised by Ardouin for its opposition to Pétion's move, and for wishing to maintain the large plantations intact rather than finishing with the colonial system. Pétion's policy was 'democratic', while the position of Bonnet and the other senators was 'aristocratic'.[193] Nevertheless Ardouin was quite clear about the proper limits of this 'democracy', and was violently critical of the demands made by Acaau in 1844, which were based upon 'the communist doctrine of the division of property'.[194] The republican insistence upon the exclusion of white ownership of land was judged by Ardouin as 'an urgent political necessity', in a situation where foreign property owners were likely to undermine national unity.[195] He also defended Pétion's offer of compensation to the dispossessed French planters. This offer was just and proper, embodying the principle of respect for property 'upon which the entire social order depends'.[196]

Writing soon after the assassination of his brother Céligny by Soulouque in 1849, Beaubrun Ardouin strongly reiterated his fear of 'socialist or communist doctrines', but now argued that the only way to prevent anarchy in the country was by lifting the ban on foreign ownership of property in Haiti. The most likely way for this to be achieved was by European recognition of Dominican independence; the firm establishment of an eastern neighbour which allowed foreign investment in land would in turn force Haiti to follow suit. Only with the help of Europeans, and of 'the class of coloured people' which formed a necessary and inevitable intermediary between whites and blacks, could the country be civilised.[197]

The picture of Haiti under Pétion and Christophe painted by Saint-Rémy is substantially the same as that presented by Ardouin. In his *Essai sur Henri-Christophe* of 1839, Saint-Rémy made great protestations of objectivity: he was, he declared, a stranger 'to the passions which divided our fathers'.[198] Yet he denounced Christophe as 'the tyrant of the north', 'a second Caligula' who had no other principle of government than terror.[199] The position which Christophe adopted in 1806 was 'despotic', and it was clearly he who was the aggressor.[200] Nevertheless the republican constitution, in reaction to the despotism of Dessalines and the claims being made by Christophe, erred by giving too little power to the executive.[201] Christophe's tyrannical regime, having no respect for liberty, returned in effect to the system prevailing in the days of colonialism.[202] Pétion, on the other hand, was 'almost a god to his fellow citizens'.[203] Saint-Rémy, however, disagreed with Ardouin about the wisdom of excluding white ownership of land. In the early days, this provision had the appearance of reason, but since international recognition had been accorded to Haiti, it had become unnecessary. The presence of white residents would introduce 'an element of civilisation' into the country.[204] We shall observe how this issue of foreign ownership was to divide opinion in Haiti throughout the nineteenth century, and to cut across party and colour loyalties.

Rigaud's return to Haiti and his schismatic movement in the South in 1810 was the subject of mulatto concern, for it represented a serious division in the ranks of the mulatto elite and strengthened the relative position of Christophe. Rigaud's heroic role during the revolutionary period, however, led Ardouin to adopt an 'indulgent' attitude towards his later actions, which were the result of misguided ambition. But providence was watching over the republic; Rigaud died and power in the South passed to General J.-M. Borgella, who, fully aware of the menace of Christophe's northern state, led the South back into the republic.[205] Borgella thus emerged as one of the great symbols of mulatto unity in Haiti, upon the basis of whose life Ardouin wrote his *magnum opus*. Saint-Rémy also criticised Rigaud's schismatic movement in the South, although there were extenuating circumstances. His early death, however, was providential and unity was once more established in the republic.[206]

Pétion was, then, the hero *par excellence*, but upon whom did the mantle fall? The division among the mulatto elite during the presidency of Boyer led to a difference of opinion on this point. Ardouin, faithful to the Boyer administration to the end, insisted that Boyer was the lineal and legitimate successor of Pétion, and that the policies carried out by the former were fully in accord with the principles established by the founder of the republic. Boyer was 'the emulator of Pétion' and 'his magnanimous successor'.[207] Boyer continued the work which Pétion had begun, and the peaceful unity of the country in 1820 on the death of Christophe was a conclusive vindication of 'the superiority of a legal regime over despotism, of justice over tyranny'.[208] Lespinasse, Dubois and Saint-Rémy, however, having supported the opposition in the period before 1843, were less concerned to picture Boyer as the legitimate successor to Pétion; they saw rather the spirit of the founder as inspiring the liberal and democratic movements of 1843.

Perhaps the absurd climax of the mulatto legend during this period is to be found in an article by Senator D. Trouillot entitled 'Résumé de la vie politique des cinq premiers chefs de la race africaine qui ont commandé en Haïti'. Toussaint was 'hypocrite et méchant', who aspired to power solely for personal ends, who betrayed his people and who had to expiate his crimes in the French fort of Joux. Trouillot paid tribute to Dessalines for declaring independence but saw his assassination as the just reward for his tyranny. Rigaud was praised for his early activity but criticised for his schismatic movement in the South; if it had not been for the noble disinterestedness and patriotism of Borgella, this action of Rigaud would have led to the victory of Christophe, 'the Nero of Haiti', whose bloody appetite had led him to slaughter 'almost all the coloured class' in the North. When Trouillot came to Pétion he was almost lost for words: 'le souvenir de ses vertus me ravit en extase'.[209]

Legend and ideology

The mulatto version of the past, then, has certain definite features which fit into a wider ideology. This ideology views Haiti as a symbol of black dignity, where black and mulatto – all sons of Africa – live in harmony under the leadership of the most enlightened class, which is that group descended from the *anciens libres*. Ardouin wrote: 'As these citizens formed the most enlightened class in the nation since the independence of the country, they were naturally called to occupy a large number of public offices, in concurrence with [he added, perhaps as an after-thought] those emancipated in 1793.'[210] These writers thus defended an oligarchical system of government parading under the banner of democracy and equality. They were afraid of the populism of Acaau and of militarism in government, which usually implied black power; the army was one of the few channels along which a black from a non-elite family could rise to power.[211] All notions of racial inequality were rejected by these men; there are no significant differences between the various branches of the human family. Yet Madiou and Saint-Rémy argued that the mixing of civilisations and races leads to strength and progress. Referring to the countries of Western Europe, Saint-Rémy demanded: 'Was not the primitive blood of the races of these different countries mixed with the blood of conquering races?'[212] The mulatto ideology, while denying the existence of superior races, has no doubt that there are superior civilisations. These writers saw the Europe of their day – and France in particular – as the model to be followed. Religion, family life and the property system lie at the basis of social life, according to Ardouin. In these matters the civilisation which Haiti must aspire to follow is that of Christian nations, and of France above all, rather than adopting or encouraging the customs of Africa.[213] They believed Africa to be barbarous, or at least relatively backward, and they were generally in favour of rooting out those customs and beliefs in Haiti which derived from Africa. The Voodoo cult was condemned by Ardouin as harmful for progress and civilisation; it 'perpetuates barbarism in the black population'. He insisted, of course, that superstition was by no means an invention of the black race, but was characteristic of Europeans of previous ages.[214] Some reservations need to be made about the position of Lespinasse with respect to the role which African beliefs and customs play and should play in Haiti, and at this point he diverged from the mainstream of mulatto ideology.

The radical dissociation between biology and culture which is characteristic of these mulatto historians was, as we shall see, shared by most black writers in nineteenth-century Haiti. Nevertheless the peculiar combination of racial pride and colour prejudice was a distinguishing feature of the mulatto position, though the colour factor was rarely stated explicitly and was translated into language about the most 'competent' and 'able' group, which was usually nothing more than a euphemistic expression for the mulatto elite. Perhaps the most interesting elaboration of this ideology is to be found in the writings of Edmond Paul, to whom our next section will be devoted.

IV

Edmond Paul

In this final section we shall consider the ideas of Edmond Paul, who was one of the most significant political thinkers in nineteenth-century Haiti. Born on 8 October 1837 in Port-au-Prince, he was the son of General Jean Paul, an active politician who was one of the two principal contenders for the presidency in 1847. In 1852 the young Edmond went to Paris as a student. In 1870 he was a deputy for the capital; banished by Domingue, he returned under Boisrond Canal to become one of the leaders of the Liberal Party in the legislature. Together with Anténor Firmin he was one of the principal black members of the predominantly mulatto Liberal Party. With the election of Salomon in 1879 Edmond Paul went into exile with other leading Liberals, and he supported the invasion of Miragoâne in 1883.[215] After the fall of Salomon in 1888 he returned to Haiti for a short while; he was elected senator in May 1890, but died in Kingston, Jamaica, on 17 June 1893.[216] Paul's most interesting books were published during the Geffrard regime, and the position which he later adopted was to a considerable extent based upon the ideas enunciated in the early sixties. It is therefore appropriate that we discuss his contribution to Haitian political thought in this chapter.

Land ownership

The question of the foreign ownership of land remained a live issue throughout the nineteenth century in Haiti. A Jamaican visitor to the country, who was 'chemist and geologist to the Republic of Haiti', stated in 1861 that any attempt to change the laws restricting whites from owning land in the republic would have 'very evil consequences', and would imperil the whole Geffrard regime. The 'enlightened portion' of the Haitian people believed that these restrictions should be removed; 'the masses of the people', he went on, 'are not prepared for so momentous a change'.[217] In 1860 an anonymous tract was published in Paris under the title *De la gérontocratie en Haïti*; it was probably written by two Frenchmen, Viellot and Labordère, who had spent many years in the country. The writers argued that the mulattoes are the racial group most suited to the Caribbean, and that neither black nor white would survive long in the climate. Also the pamphlet suggested that the presence of hard-working, disciplined, monogamous white peasants in Haiti would have a beneficial moral and genetic effect. From this basis the authors developed an attack upon the prohibition of foreign owner-ship of land in the republic. Article 7 of the constitution was thus attacked as the most absurd plank in the policy of the 'ultra-blacks'.[218]

In reaction to this anonymous pamphlet and to similar arguments Edmond Paul enunciated in the early sixties a coherent theory of economic autarky. Paul insisted that the law against white ownership of land raised two fundamental issues: what is a nation? and what is legislation? He argued that Haiti as an independent nation symbolised black dignity and the equality of the races; these principles lay at the very basis of the idea of Haitian nationality. 'To accord the right of property to whites', he maintained, 'while colour prejudice is still prevalent, would be to renounce the end which the nation pursues.'[219] When colour prejudice is a thing of the past, and when there is no longer a significant opposition between the interests of black and white, only then should Haiti think of modifying its law on this matter. Is it not the case, he demanded, that throughout the world, and 'up to this day, the prosperity of the whites is founded on the degradation of the blacks'?[220] The consequences of modifying the prohibition of foreign ownership would be the end of the small landholder; economic slavery would replace the legal slavery of former days, and money would be the tyrannical master. Paul told his readers that they should concern them-selves not only with the abolitionist writers of a previous era, but also 'with Hugo, de Lamartine, de Lamennais, Michelet and Madame George Sand, who have depicted the sufferings of the white proletariat'.[221] A similar condition would come about in Haiti if the legal restriction on foreign ownership were removed. The Haitian state was thus, for Paul, based upon a belief in racial equality and human dignity; an influx of foreign capitalists would undermine this conception. Further-more it is the purpose of legislation to preserve the integrity of the nation, and this is what the law against foreign ownership did.

Economic development and autarky

Perhaps the significance of Edmond Paul derives from the fact that he linked his ideas about the foreign ownership of land in Haiti to a theory of economic development, and he argued that industry must be devel-oped as a necessary support to agriculture.[222] Very often writers who defended the prohibition were concerned simply to protect the vested interests of the *gérontocratie*. Paul saw the question in a larger context of the accumulation of capital. Adopting the theories of Michel Chevalier, the French Saint-Simonian economist, he argued that the government should play an active role in the economic development of

the country by encouraging the growth of local industries, and furthermore that such a programme could be financed basically from within
the country itself; the role of foreign capital should be subordinate and
minimal. In the first place, he observed that much local capital was
exported and invested in Europe where it was thought to be safe. He
criticised the lack of patriotism in these Haitian investors, but stated
that the government could do much to remedy the situation. He did
not believe that the government should directly take on the role of sole
entrepreneur in normal circumstances; intervention of this kind 'can
be justified only by the complete abdication of private initiative'.[223]
Direct subsidies to private industry are by themselves also insufficient
to stimulate economic growth, and to 'wake the people from their long
slumber'.[224] What, then, is the role of the government in economic
development? Paul suggested that the state should go into partnership
with private enterprise in those areas where development is needed,
and be willing to take much of the burden of risk which is involved
in the growth of new industries. If the government did this, it would
'in one move increase job opportunities, inspire confidence in local
capital and attract foreign investment'.[225] He was thus prepared to
accept, at least as a temporary measure, a limited role for foreign
capital, so long as it was subordinate to local capital. While the country
should move in the direction of economic self-sufficiency, it would not
be wise to attempt to create the closed commercial state of Fichte in
a single generation.

Paul was fully aware that national independence requires economic
independence, that economic independence implies economic growth,
which depends upon industrialisation, a necessary condition for which
is the accumulation of capital. This is, as we have already noted, to be
achieved partly by government partnership with private investors, local
and foreign. This participation by the government would encourage
private investment. The necessary state capital could be raised by extra
taxation and by increased duties on imported goods. This latter step
would not only raise capital but would provide protection for newly
founded local industries.[226]

Another step which the state should take to stimulate economic
growth was the encouragement of technical and scientific education.
It is all very well for a country to boast of a rich literary tradition, but
'in our epoch a nation counts for more in the world by its industrialists
than by its writers'.[227] Edmond Paul emerges as the Lord Snow of
nineteenth-century Haiti, in his discussion of the 'two cultures'! With
such dependence upon foreign countries for relatively simple manufactured goods as soap, candles, ink, paper, cooking oil, bricks, shoes,
clothes, glasses, etc., can Haiti afford poets? 'Today what we need are
engineers, builders, industrialists, science teachers.'[228] Paul asserted

that it was clearly against the interests of the rapidly developing metropolitan countries to encourage this kind of development in Haiti. They were concerned to get coffee, cotton, sugar and other primary products; they were quite prepared for the black people of Haiti to have 'academies, museums, conservatories, observatories, gardens, theatres and a palace'. They did not want to see a programme of scientific and industrial education which would lead to economic development in countries like Haiti.[229]

Paul argued, in later publications, that the absence of industry was not only fatal to the material well-being of the country, but that it had a harmful effect upon the development of knowledge and understanding among the people.[230] He thus saw industrialisation as a means whereby Haiti could achieve economic self-sufficiency, together with a higher standard of living and a growth in the intelligence of the people. He also saw the need for agricultural reform, which should accompany industrial growth. For too long Haiti had 'wallowed in the colonial rut'. The primitive methods of cultivation must be replaced; agriculture must be mechanised.[231] Also the small farmers should be encouraged by government loans, rather than being continually harassed by excessive taxation.[232]

The reforms in the Haitian economy which Edmond Paul advocated were, he believed, urgently required if the country were to be saved from underdevelopment and dependence upon foreign countries. This economic dependence would in turn lead to political and military intervention by foreign powers in the affairs of the black republic. Vital decisions affecting Haitians would be taken not at home, but on the banks of the Thames and of the Seine. It is economic and financial considerations which determine the course of political events; stocks and shares have won or stopped battles, they controlled the Eighteenth Brumaire.[233] He claimed further that political intervention would end with annexation, and from exile he viewed with alarm President Salomon's creation of the national bank in 1880, depending as it did largely on foreign capital. It would become, he asserted, a Trojan horse which would vomit into the midst of the country foreigners who were bent on annexation.[234] His warning was prophetic; United States financial interest in the reformed Banque Nationale was one of the factors, though not, as we shall see, the principal factor, behind the American invasion of 1915 and the nineteen years of military occupation.

Power, colour and competence

It is thus clear that the kind of economic reforms contemplated by Edmond Paul would need to be spearheaded in Haiti by the state. But what were the chances of any Haitian government adopting the policies which he suggested, and what were the bulwarks in the way of reform? Paul's analysis of the political problems of the country therefore forms an integral part of his economic and social theory. Paul frankly recognised the existence in Haiti of a deep social rift between the mass of the people on the one hand and the elite on the other. This reflected itself in the politics of the country and constituted a danger to Haiti's independence. The political system had in the past led either to government by a small clique of self-interested politicians or to military dictatorship in the name of the masses; both types of government were powerless to effect significant changes in the economic sphere. Paul believed that the era of politics was over; government must be entrusted to experts and technocrats. Only then would social and colour barriers be removed and the country be set on the road to progress and true independence.

In the first place, then, Paul's analysis of current politics recognised the existence of two castes. On the one hand there were the mulattoes, who were the enlightened party, on the other the blacks who were the party of force. When in power, the former group found itself powerless, while the black regimes were frankly reactionary or incompetent. Like the movement of a see-saw, the ineffective Machiavellism of the mulatto minority had prepared the way for the vandalism of the black majority, which in turn led to a further reaction. From its very birth the government of the country had swung from powerlessness to incapacity and back.[235] For Paul, Dessalines was the symbol of the barbarous and ignorant black search for power. He was 'a man without political skills, without ideas, without insight, with no notion of how to conduct affairs of state, a stranger to law and morality, fierce in his conduct, barbarous and at the same time mysterious in his designs'.[236] The ghost of Dessalines had haunted the country since its foundation. This same spirit had manifested itself in Acaau and Soulouque, both 'abortive and monstrous products' of popular movements.[237] The current situation in Haiti, as seen by Paul, did not allow for successful government by the masses. 'The supremacy of numbers', he argued, 'assures the supremacy of ignorance.'[238] Yet Paul was by no means an uncritical adherent of the mulatto legend and vigorously criticised Geffrard's regime as 'the most pernicious' despotism in the history of Haiti, and he was particularly indignant at Geffrard's dependence on British military assistance.[239]

How was Haiti to escape from the dilemma which faced her in the political field, and to bring to an end the fratricidal strife which was fatal to the independence of the country?[240] In the first place Paul had great faith in the power of education to undermine these divisions, which were, he thought, based upon ignorance. It was education which would bring about concord, abolish castes and establish that equilibrium which was so necessary for the future of the country.[241] This somewhat naive faith in education led Paul to elaborate a theory of government by experts, similar in many respects to the ideas of Saint-Simon.[242] Government by the enlightened, by experts, should replace government by politicians. The opening sentence of one of Paul's books proclaims: 'The era of politics is past',[243] and he went on to insist that industrialisation will mean the dethroning of the political in favour of the technical; the government of men, replaced by the administration of things. 'Power to the most competent' was therefore the slogan adopted by Paul; it was the battle cry of the Liberal Party.[244] Government must be conducted by the most enlightened section of the community in the interests of the whole community. The masses were said to be incapable of participating constructively in politics owing to their ignorance. Paul defended a system of enlightened despotism in which the people would be ruled by a paternalistic head of state. Of Pétion he wrote: 'He was a despot, but good. At his death, it has been said that the Haitians lost their father.'[245] This paternalistic Saint-Simonism was an enduring feature of the mulatto ideology through the nineteenth century into the twentieth. Writers like Justin Dévot and L. J. Marcelin manifested the same tendency, as did Max Hudicourt and Jules Blanchet in the twenties and thirties of this century. The Parti Socialiste Populaire of 1946 was the residuary legatee of the mulatto ideology of the nineteenth century.

In the half-century following the death of Henry Christophe colour divisions in Haiti became increasingly bitter and explicit. The long regime of Boyer, when patronage and power were concentrated in the hands of the mulattoes, led to a violent black reaction in the years from 1843 to 1847, culminating in the regime of Soulouque. Nevertheless mulatto control of the national sector of the economy left them in a permanently strong position and enabled them to reassert their political power under Geffrard. The French recognition of Haitian independence in 1825 had been followed by a similar recognition by other European powers, and the threat of military intervention in Haiti receded. This was certainly one of the factors which led to the irruption of colour divisions among Haitians at this time and to the virtual absence of that sense of racial unity which was a feature of the early years of independence. Mulatto dominance in the economic field and their long tenure of political power were accompanied by the development of an ideology and an associated legend of the Haitian past. In the following chapter we shall witness the elaboration of a competing black ideology, and note how the colour divisions in the country manifested themselves in the activity of two political parties.

4. Liberals and Nationals

1867-1910

The return of the mulatto elite to political power under Geffrard proved to be short-lived, though their long-term control of the educational system had been secured by the Concordat of 1860. The years following the fall of Geffrard in 1867 saw a further polarisation of the black and mulatto elites and their manifestation in two political groups, the predominantly mulatto Liberal Party, and the preponderantly black National Party. During the 1870s and into the 1880s these two parties battled for supremacy in the electoral, military and intellectual fields. In answer to the mulatto ideology elaborated in previous decades, Louis Joseph Janvier, Alcius Charmant and others outlined a black ideology and an associated black legend of the Haitian past which conflicted at crucial points with the mulatto view. This chapter examines the ideological conflicts among Haitians in the context of growing governmental instability and increasing foreign intervention. The second part of the chapter deals with the writings by Haitians of all colours who defended the African race against its European and North American detractors, and who saw in Haitian independence a symbol and an effective proof of black equality. Finally we shall note that despite this insistence on independence by theorists of every hue, there was on the part of politicians from all sides a readiness to compromise the autonomy of the country by inviting foreign intervention rather than allowing their political opponents to gain power.

I

Presidents and parties

With the fall of Geffrard political power passed into the hands of General Silvain Salnave, who had led a prolonged struggle against Geffrard from the North. Although he was himself a light-skinned mulatto, Salnave received considerable support from the black masses of the North and of Port-au-Prince, many of whom believed that he was black. In fact, so light-skinned was Salnave that he was denounced by his opponents as not being genuinely Haitian at all. 'There is no African blood in his veins', declared Michel Domingue.[1] Nevertheless Salnave is generally associated with the *noiriste* tradition in Haiti. Among the president's principal supporters was Demesvar Delorme, a black politician and novelist born in 1831 at Cap Haïtien, who had accompanied the mulatto general in his struggles against Geffrard. Delorme, however, soon quarrelled with the new president and vigorously denounced him.[2] Delorme later returned to active political life as one of the leaders of the National Party. Salnave, who for almost the whole of his period in office had to contend with guerrilla opposition from the *cacos*[3] of the North, was eventually driven from the capital in 1869, captured and executed. That Salnave had enjoyed popular support from the urban poor was generally agreed. Victorin Chevalier declared that the government was 'the expression of the needs, the sentiments, the interests of the masses', and that to wish for its overthrow was to desire the annihilation of a whole people.[4] Even unsympathetic critics of the mulatto president acknowledged his popularity among the urban masses, which was due to the way in which he appealed to their 'dangerous spirit of social levelling'.[5] His *cacos* opponents came on the other hand mostly from the black and mulatto *classe intermédiaire*. It is noteworthy that the politically active among the rural population of the nineteenth century appear to have come not from the poorest class of landless workers, but from the rural middle class of *habitants*. This class played an important role in Haitian politics during the *cacos* rising under the American occupation, and as we shall see it was from this *classe intermédiaire* that François Duvalier recruited many of his most loyal supporters.[6] Fidel Castro in Cuba also secured a significant following from this peasant class in his armed struggle against Batista.[7] The Haitian post-colonial experience in this matter would seem to substantiate the assertion of Eric Wolf that the middle peasantry, with secure access to land of its own which it cultivates with family labour, is one of the few rural sections with sufficient resources to sustain a rebellion.[8]

After the fall of Salnave in 1869, Haiti was ruled by a constitutional president, Nissage Saget, an elite *griffe*, who distinguished himself by being one of the few heads of state to have served his prescribed term of office and then retired. It was during the presidency of Nissage that the Liberal Party under the leadership of Jean-Pierre Boyer Bazelais and Edmond Paul emerged as a powerful force in the country. Nissage was succeeded by his friend Michel Domingue, a black general. Effective power, however, was in the hands of the new president's nephew, Septimus Rameau, who gathered around himself a number of predominantly black politicians opposed to the Liberals, who were to form the basis of the National Party. Domingue's period in office is noteworthy owing to a huge loan which he was able to raise in Paris. The overthrow of Domingue and Rameau in 1876 spelt the return of the mulattoes to political power under General Boisrond Canal, but a growing hostility between the followers of Boyer Bazelais and those of the president led to a split in the ranks of the Liberals, and to the victory of the National Party in the elections of 1879. Delorme was elected president of the assembly and Salomon *jeune* returned to the country to become president.

After some abortive attempts by the Liberals to overthrow Salomon from within the country, a group of exiles led by Boyer Bazelais invaded Haiti from Jamaica, probably with British encouragement. They landed at Miragoâne in March 1883, and risings against the government occurred in other southern cities. These latter risings were successfully put down by the government, as was an attempted coup in the capital, but Miragoâne survived a siege until early into 1884. Eventually shortage of supplies and the spread of disease forced the Liberals to surrender, their leader, Boyer Bazelais, having died in the siege.[9] The principal events of Salomon's presidency were an agricultural law, distributing some state land to the peasants and allowing foreign companies to own property in Haiti, and the founding of the Banque Nationale with financial assistance from France.

Under Salomon the colour question once more became acute, though even at this time the coincidence between political party and colour was by no means complete. Two of Salomon's principal supporters, Frédéric Marcelin and Callisthène Fouchard (a former Liberal) were mulattoes, while two of his chief opponents, Edmond Paul and Anténor Firmin, were black. Marcelin was, however, denounced by his fellow mulatto Hannibal Price for his collaboration with Salomon. 'You are an undisguised scoundrel', wrote Price, 'because you, as a mulatto, serve a negro government . . . Being a mulatto, I am sure that you have a horror of negroes, *just as I have*.'[10] Firmin, on the other hand, complained that his National Party opponents in the elections of 1879 at Cap Haïtien spread the rumour that he was 'a mulatto, as clear-skinned as a white man' in order to persuade the black northerners to vote against him.[11] Regional loyalties as well as colour factors played a significant role during these years and further complicated the political situation. Salomon was never, for example, able to obtain firm support from the people of Cap Haïtien, where he was obliged to maintain a strong garrison 'owing to the well-known hostility of the population of that town to the existing government'.[12] It was, in fact, a northern alliance, including Firmin, Nord Alexis and Cincinnatus Leconte, which brought down the Salomon regime in 1888.[13] Though as we have seen[14] he had in the past been associated with the blacks and was regarded with fear and suspicion by most mulattoes,[15] Salomon claimed to be without prejudice. In his independence day speech of 1880 the president declared that although he had become in the eyes of many the symbol of discord and division, he intended to pursue a policy of national unity.[16] He had been called 'mangeur des mulâtres', but he rejected the accusation, pointing to the fact that his own children were mulattoes. Co-operation between blacks and mulattoes was essential for the future of Haiti, he insisted.[17] In a speech at Jérémie in 1884 Salomon drew attention to the fact that many of his ministers and officials were mulatto, as was the army chief in Jérémie.[18]

In the years following 1888 the relationship between colour and political allegiance was even more complicated than it had been in the preceding decade, and there was disagreement among Haitians as to whether the old Liberal and National parties had survived the death of their respective leaders, Boyer Bazelais and Salomon.[19] Nevertheless unscrupulous politicians were able from time to time to appeal to colour prejudice in order to undermine the influence of their opponents and to strengthen their own positions. The most likely successor to Salomon in 1888, the mulatto general Seïde Télémaque, was assassinated and a struggle broke out between two black generals, F. D. Légitime and Florvil Hyppolite. After only a few months in office Légitime, who was accused of being 'a manikin in the hands of the mulattoes',[20] was overthrown by Hyppolite, who remained in power until his death in 1896. Hyppolite was a friend of Edmond Paul and had generally been associated with the old Liberal Party. He nominated as his secretary of state for finance and foreign affairs Anténor Firmin, who managed by skilful diplomatic manœuvring to resist United States demands for the cession of territory. However, under Hyppolite's successor, Simon Sam (1896–1902) and during the struggle for power between Nord Alexis and Firmin in 1902, German involvement in Haitian affairs increased.[21] Alexis, an octogenarian black general, became president in 1902. Son of Baron Nord, a dignitary in Christophe's kingdom, Alexis became a soldier at the age of nineteen. He was aide-de-camp to Pierrot and in 1865 he assisted Salnave in the defence of Cap Haïtien against Geffrard and the British. He was exiled by Domingue, returned under Canal, but after two years left for Kingston where he remained until 1879. Twice imprisoned by Salomon, Alexis was one of the leaders of the successful rising in the North which overthrew Salomon in 1888. He was appointed by President Hyppolite to an administrative post in the North, where he remained for fourteen years. While his predecessor T. S. Sam had been denounced for alleged prejudice against mulattoes, and François Manigat had been attacked for wishing to turn Haiti into a country occupied solely by blacks,[22] President Nord was in turn accused by his opponents of being under the control of mulatto politicians, and of adopting policies prejudicial to the blacks. Pierre Frédérique maintained that 'the colour question formed the dominant spirit of the government of Nord Alexis'; also Alcius Charmant portrayed the president as a monkey and denounced him as the '*grand pontife du vaudouisme*'.[23] Nord Alexis further antagonised *noiriste* opinion by his massacre of the poet Massillon Coicou together with members of his family in 1908. A rising in the South during the same year led to the demise of Nord Alexis, who was replaced by another black general, Antoine Simon. The new president was at first welcomed, particularly by *noiristes*, but his signing of the McDonald contract in 1910, which gave extensive rights to an American company to build a railway and to cultivate land each side of the line, alienated a significant body of supporters including Dr Rosalvo Bobo and Pierre Frédérique. Simon's regime collapsed in the face of a *cacos* rebellion in 1911.

The colour question

Haitian writers, black and mulatto, who acknowledged the existence of a colour problem in the country usually traced it back to the colonial period. According to Emmanuel Edouard, the poet, it was the French colonial system which had established the basis of a caste system, with the three principal castes being denoted by the criterion of colour. Although he recognised that there had been mulatto slaves and free blacks in colonial Saint Domingue, their number was negligible.[24] After independence the caste system had, in the opinion of Edouard, been replaced by a black and a mulatto spirit which insisted on seeing all political problems as colour problems. The question asked in Haiti about a prospective head of state is, he maintained, never whether he is capable but what is the colour of his skin. Edouard asserted that colour prejudice had played a central role in Haiti from colonial times and that at the time of independence it was the mulattoes who had introduced 'the politics of colour' into the new nation.[25] Although economic divisions had to some extent complicated the situation in the country by cutting across colour distinctions, it would, he stated, be a great mistake to think that colour was no longer important.[26] The division between the Liberal and the National parties in his own day was fundamentally a question of colour:

Every Haitian knows that in Haiti the words 'Liberal Party' signify 'Mulatto party', party which desires the preponderance of mulattoes in the government of the country . . . Everyone knows that the words 'National Party' mean 'black party', party which desires . . . the preponderance of blacks, the immense majority of Haitians, in the conduct of public affairs.[27]

Some mulatto writers, like Joseph Justin, also argued that colour prejudice was the fault of 'certain ignorant mulattoes, conceited and sterile, who despised the African blood which flowed in their veins'.[28] Justin further pointed to the importance of colour in determining political allegiance in Haiti at this time, ascribing political divisions to 'the spirit of caste'.[29] Yet, as has already been observed, the political situation became more complicated towards the end of the century, and by 1909 the black historian J. B. Dorsainvil could fairly state that although colour differences reinforced by educational and other factors were socially significant, they were not clearly reflected in the political alignments of the day.[30]

The only Haitians to deny the importance of the colour factor in the political and social life of the country were the more extreme ideologists on both sides (especially the mulattoes[31]), and also those Haitians who were writing works of propaganda for foreign consumption. Among black writers there was a general recognition of the importance of colour prejudice in Haitian history. Particularly during the regimes of Nissage and Boisrond Canal, when the blacks were politically as well as socially discriminated against, black writers denounced colour prejudice in the country.[32] After 1879, however, when the political pendulum had swung in their favour, many black writers played down the significance of the colour question. Apologists of the National Party denied that it was a black party; it was, insisted a writer in *L'Avant-Garde*, 'composed of people of all shades'.[33] Frédéric Marcelin, while fully recognising the significance of colour prejudice in Haitian history, claimed that the National Party was 'an explosion of popular sentiment' directed against the exclusivism of the Liberals; Boyer Bazelais was 'le chef exclusif d'une caste'.[34] Armand Thoby, a mulatto Liberal who had been a minister in the government of Boisrond Canal and who had opposed the *bazelaisiste* faction of the party, drew attention to the fact that the National Party was strongest in the department of the North, but agreed that it was a coalition party comprising men of widely differing political opinions, whose unity consisted largely in their opposition to Boyer Bazelais.[35] This view was restated by the black historian Antoine Michel, who also ascribed the unity of the Liberals to a personal dislike of Salomon.[36]

The ultranationals

Although it cannot be said that the National Party held a single coherent ideology, nor indeed that it was totally agreed on policy matters, there was within the party a group of *noiriste* ideologists who were sometimes known as 'ultranationals' or 'piquets doctrinaires'.[37] The leading writer in this group was undoubtedly Louis Joseph Janvier, and its principal organs were *L'Œil* and *L'Avant-Garde*. Most mulatto supporters of Salomon like Marcelin and Fouchard were obviously opposed to this group, while Delorme and Salomon himself took a somewhat equivocal position on the assertions and demands of these men.

The *noiristes* wished to establish a 'black' view of the past which ascribed the evils of Haiti to the selfishness of mulatto politicians and to the weakness of those black heads of state who were prepared to play *la politique de doublure*. The principal villains were Rigaud, Boyer, Dumesle, Geffrard, and of course Boyer Bazelais in their own day. The *noiristes* were often critical of professional politicians, believing that the country is best governed by a strong but paternalistic head of state constitutionally responsible to the people. They were in general favourably disposed towards the army. Janvier and the ultranationals were bitterly critical of the Roman Catholic church, arguing that it was fundamentally opposed to the development of a national feeling in the country. It should, they believed, be replaced by an Erastian form of Protestantism. The fact that many of these writers were active Freemasons reinforced their anti-clericalism. The *noiristes* claimed to speak for the masses against the elite, for the country against the capital, and they fully subscribed to the populist slogan of the National Party, 'The greatest good for the greatest number'. These writers were generally nationalists, opposed to any change in the law prohibiting the foreign ownership of land in Haiti, and they argued that the economic development of the country should be based upon local capital. Although they believed in racial equality, they were generally hostile to African traditions and customs, insisting that Haiti should develop according to a European pattern. In these economic and cultural matters Janvier and the *noiristes* were in agreement with many Haitian mulattoes, and their arguments will be considered in the sequel. It might perhaps be worth emphasising here that neither the National Party nor the ultranational wing of the party believed in 'a return to Africa' in any sense of this phrase. Present-day black writers who see in the National Party the precursor of the ethnological movement in the occupation period and of the ideas of the *Griots* group are merely elaborating a legendary past in order to legitimate their contemporary commitments.[38]

Louis Joseph Janvier

The principal writers who were responsible for the elaboration of the black legend of the Haitian past, in the period we are concerned with in this chapter, were L. J. Janvier, Alcius Charmant, Antoine Michel and J. B. Dorsainvil. Janvier was born in 1855, the son of a Protestant tailor and the grandson of a peasant.[39] He studied medicine and political science in Paris, where he became a defender and apologist of Haiti in general and of the Salomon regime in particular. Most of his adult life was in fact spent in Europe as student, exile or diplomat. He died in March 1911. Janvier was a firm defender of the economic and political independence of Haiti and assailed theories of racial inequality which were current among European writers of his day. The latter aspect of Janvier's work will be considered in the second part of this chapter. Here we shall be concerned with Janvier as the ideologist of the ultranationals and the self-appointed spokesman of the black peasant. Janvier, recognising the importance of land ownership to the peasant, was particularly concerned to advocate the breaking up of large estates and the extension of the system of peasant smallholdings.[40] Dessalines had, according to Janvier, intended 'to divide all the state lands among the soldiers of his army, blacks and mulattoes', and it was for this reason that he was killed.[41] Janvier commended Pétion for his policy of distributing land and compared him favourably on this matter with the black Christophe.[42] Boyer, however, was fiercely attacked as 'a tyrant' who had 'abandoned the excellent democratic system instituted by Pétion' for a feudal, aristocratic conception of society unsuited to the needs of the Haitian people. By his Rural Code of 1826 Boyer had reintroduced serfdom, checking economic growth and 'sterilising the nation'. Furthermore this president had reinforced colour prejudice against the blacks.[43] It was in Janvier's view the black heads of state who had in general been favourable to a policy of land distribution and this is why, after the fall of Boyer in 1843, the peasant masses had supported them.[44] Salomon himself was praised for having reintroduced a policy of land distribution by the law of February 1883. 'Never was a political measure more opportune, more just, more fraternal and more wise.'[45] It was according to Janvier largely their opposition to this measure which led the mulatto Liberals under Boyer Bazelais to invade Haiti in the following month.[46] Janvier defended the *piquets* against their critics. Those who had written the history of this unfortunate group were 'their enemies or their assassins'.[47] These poor peasants were merely struggling for justice against their oppressors in the only way which was open to them.[48] Janvier urged the *piquets* to support the government of Salomon against the Liberals 'the sons of Boyer and of Bazelais, our heriditary enemies'.[49]

Janvier denied that colour prejudice was a significant factor in the Haiti of his day, insisting that the 'puerile, mean and absurd distinctions of caste or of colour have almost completely disappeared'.[50] He claimed that living in Haiti he had never heard mention of colour prejudice before the age of twenty, and that he had never experienced discrimination either in Haiti or in France on the basis of his colour.[51] He therefore denied that the split between Liberals and Nationals had anything to do with colour; there were, he insisted, men of all colours in both parties.[52] His main reason for adopting this unrealistic position was the desire to project a favourable picture of Haiti for foreign readers and to portray the Salomon regime as a government of national unity, entirely free from prejudice. How, he demanded, is it possible for a black to entertain colour prejudice when it is against him that such prejudices are directed? Was it not the case that Salomon had shot blacks as well as mulattoes?[53] Yet when writing controversial tracts addressed to his fellow countrymen Janvier was less coy about admitting the existence of colour prejudice in Haiti. He attacked the self-styled superior origin of his Liberal opponents – 'this stupid colour prejudice which blinds you'.[54] In spite of his many valuable insights, Janvier was in this matter as in some others patently dishonest and unreliable.

The black legend

The view of the Haitian past as outlined by Janvier received further elaboration and development in the period. As we have seen, Janvier's insistence on the centrality of the land question led him to place Pétion on the side of the angels, and this clearly constituted a weakness in the black legend. Later writers have remedied this deficiency.[55] Alcius Charmant, a black journalist from Jacmel, whose loyalty to the Salomon regime was somewhat ambivalent,[56] drew attention to the fact that there were in Haiti two political schools, divided according to the different judgments which they made of the heroes of national independence. 'Indeed', he wrote,

the mulattoes, due to a spirit of colour solidarity, exalt beyond measure the merits of Ogé, of Chavannes, of Rigaud, presenting these men with a halo of martyrdom in the cause of our independence . . . The other school, on the contrary (and impartial history sanctions its judgment), represents Dessalines as the organiser of the revolution . . . they are able to see in Alexandre Pétion only a traitor and a man of vulgar ambition.[57]

Charmant pointed to the four chief causes of the ills afflicting the country: colour prejudice, the ignorance and greed of heads of state, the authoritarian tradition and the ignorance of the masses. It was these factors which enabled mulatto politicians to rule behind the façade of an ignorant black general – *la politique de doublure*.[58] Black writers of this period were eager to support the rehabilitation of Dessalines as the true hero of national independence. He was, for Massillon Coicou, 'Le bras fort qui ceignit la race en agonie'.[59] The 'Liberals of 1806' were reproached by other *noiristes* for having assassinated the emperor, while Pétion and Boyer were blamed for having inaugurated a fratricidal struggle between blacks and mulattoes.[60] Henry Christophe was, on the other hand, praised as an inventive genius, a new Peter the Great. 'If our men of state had continued the work of Christophe', declared Emmanuel Kernizan, 'Haiti would be one of the richest countries on earth.'[61] The black legend of the past was carried out into the battle-field of contemporary political strife, and voters were urged to support

those candidates who were dedicated to continuing the black tradition.[62]

A series of articles in 1909 by the mulatto ideologist Auguste
Magloire, in his journal *Le Matin*, called forth replies from Antoine
Michel, J. B. Dorsainvil and other black historians. They pointed out
that Magloire was merely the latest in a long line of mulatto historians
whose interest in the past was a practical one. They attacked the
affranchis of colonial days for their narrow and selfish policies, they
criticised Pétion and assailed Boyer, whose long regime had brought
forth nothing of value.[63] These men rejected the charge that they
themselves were prejudiced. 'This tendency to accuse of having colour
prejudice all those who tell the truth about Pétion', remarked Michel,
'is an old game.'[64]

The anti-clerical campaign

Janvier and the ultranationals maintained through the 1880s a vigorous
and bitter attack upon the Roman Catholic church in Haiti. They saw
the Concordat of 1860 as the surrender of an important aspect of
national life to a foreign power. They opposed the Roman Catholic
church on a number of grounds, and underlying their attack is the clear
recognition that the clergy tended to reinforce the mulatto hegemony
in the life of the country. As we shall see, these writers were by no
means defenders of the Voodoo cult,[65] but were either Freemasons or
Protestants.

The presence of a foreign ecclesiastical system in Haiti, staffed largely
by Bretons and controlled from Rome, was seen as humiliating for
Haitians, who had fought hard for their political independence.[66]
Religion is an important aspect of national life which exercises an
enormous influence on the development of the individual citizen. It
was therefore said by these writers to be dangerous to allow this institution to pass into foreign hands.[67] The archbishop of Port-au-Prince,
Mgr Alexis Guilloux, was accused of having organised 'a vast plan of
politico-religious domination for Haiti'.[68] The state was to be subor-
dinated to the church and the young people of the country were being
encouraged to give more respect to the local parish priest than to the
civil magistrate.[69] The Concordat was said to be the root of the trouble,
and a campaign was mounted to abrogate this treaty with the Vatican.
Salnave was praised for his opposition to the Concordat, but with his
death Haitians had become slaves of the priests, who with their holy
water and their false blessings were robbing the poor people of the
country.[70] The Concordat had enabled the clergy to constitute 'a
veritable state within the state'.[71] A further accusation was brought
against the Roman Catholic church, that it was opposed to the de-

velopment of a black clergy, preferring to import *petits Bretons.*[72]

Janvier accepted and sharpened many of these criticisms of the Roman Catholic church. By its very nature that church undermines patriotism. 'From the political point of view', he wrote, 'Catholicism is the negation of patriotism; from the religious point of view it is fetishism accepted because it is respectable.'[73] Janvier maintained that the Concordat had introduced into Haiti bigotry, ultramontanism and clericalism, and he warned that Haitian governments were increasingly coming under the control of foreign clergy.[74] Nothing was more deplorable and degrading than the sight of a worthy Haitian civic figure paying homage to a foreigner.[75] Janvier reiterated the charge that the Roman Catholic church was prejudiced against the black man. Catholicism, he cried, after having enslaved the blacks had been responsible for their degradation and for the development of colour prejudice.[76]

Janvier also opposed Roman Catholicism because he claimed that it was the enemy of economic development, encouraging in people an irresponsible attitude to life. In this matter Protestantism was said to be infinitely superior to Catholicism, providing an ideology and an incentive for capitalist development. The Protestant is thrifty and self-reliant, he does not waste his money on carnivals and other frivolities. Protestantism permits free discussion, encourages private initiative and could become a powerful factor of social development in Haiti.[77] The Protestant is almost always a more practical worker and a better citizen that the Catholic.[78] Janvier also claimed that Protestantism was more suited to the African temperament than was Catholicism, and was in many parts of Africa a valuable means for introducing the population to Western culture.[79] The kind of Protestantism which Janvier wished to see established in Haiti was of a severely Erastian kind, where the clergy, even in matters of doctrine, would be controlled by the temporal government.[80]

Together with many of the National Party, Janvier was closely associated with the Masonic movement. Throughout the nineteenth century Freemasonry had a considerable influence in Haiti, having been founded in colonial days. By the 1840s every small town had its Masonic lodge; 'tout le monde est maçon', declared Schoelcher. The Roman Catholic church attacked the Masonic movement and refused to allow funerals to be conducted with Masonic symbols present in the church. Spencer St John recalls how during the regime of Domingue a funeral procession carrying such symbols was refused entry into the Roman Catholic cathedral and made for the Anglican cathedral, where the funeral was conducted 'with banners displayed and every other masonic sign in full view'. Bishop Holly was himself a Freemason.[81] A split among Haitian Freemasons in 1884, when posters bearing the slogan 'A bas le Grand Maître de l'Ordre' had appeared in the capital, gave an opportunity to Mgr Guilloux once more to attack the movement.[82] The editor of *L'Œil*, L. Prost, replied to the archbishop, pointing out that Salomon himself was the Grand Protector of the order, and that all the members of the cabinet were Freemasons. An attack upon the order was therefore tantamount to an attack upon the government.[83] Growing discontent with the Salomon regime had manifested itself in a schism in the Masonic movement. Fénélon Duplessis, a former Grand Master, led the opposition to Salomon, and referred to the 1888 revolution as 'une revendication politique et maçonique'.[84]

Although many of Salomon's supporters were anti-clerical, the president himself managed to remain on fairly cordial relations with the Roman Catholic archbishop. The National Assembly passed a resolution in September 1881 calling for the end of the Concordat, but Salomon did little to disturb the position of the church. In fact he re-established the government grant of 20,000 francs to the Grand Séminaire. Mgr Guilloux wrote during the second year of Salomon's presidency: 'Never have my relations with the state been more easy than since the arrival of General Salomon to the presidency.'[85] Nevertheless the government was keenly aware of the clerical issue, and Thomas Madiou, the secretary of state for cults, stated in his official report to the legislative assembly in 1882, 'In a free independent state like Haiti, the Government is unable to permit any power whatever to escape its jurisdiction.'[86] There was friction between the church and state particularly over the question of the relationship between civil and church marriages, and the church was denounced for the familiar crime of attempting to establish 'a state within the state'. The clerical issue continued to raise its head from time to time during the years which followed the overthrow of Salomon, particularly in the context of a demand for a *clergé indigène* and of resentment against ecclesiastical control of the greater part of the educational system.

Mulatto liberalism

The period from Salnave to Simon saw a marked development in the ideology of the mulatto elite. The general pattern of this ideology had been established in the previous era with the early writings of Edmond Paul and those of the mulatto historians. The *noiriste* regimes of Salnave and Salomon and the populist writings of the ultranationals led to a firm reassertion by the Liberals of their slogan 'Government by the most competent'.

The more strident voices among the mulatto ideologists denied the existence of a serious colour problem in the daily life of the Haitian people. Léon Laroche claimed that there was no evidence to suggest the existence of colour prejudice in the country.[87] 'Blacks and mulattoes, we form a single family', wrote Arthur Bowler;

Go to our country, visit our towns and our countryside – wherever political passions and bad faith have not perverted judgment and reason – you will find the spirit of unity and concord which is to be expected from men who are born of the same mother, and who share a joint inheritance.[88]

J. N. Léger also insisted that there was no such thing as racial or colour prejudice in Haiti and that in the home and in the school all colours mixed freely. 'The only distinctions admitted are those established by intelligence, probity and courage.' Justin Dévot and Léon Audin both denied the existence of significant colour divisions and criticised any use of the term 'caste' to describe social groups in Haiti. The latter, however, coyly admitted that especially with respect to marriage there are 'certain individual preferences for this or that shade of skin', but he boldly declared that colour prejudice does not exist in Haiti.[89]

The mulatto ideologists were keen to deny that colour was the criterion for membership in that elite which they believed should control political power in the country, and they claimed that in the past as in their own day blacks as well as mulattoes were to be found in this class. Armand Thoby believed that Haiti had been fortunate in possessing an enlightened and energetic elite, composed of blacks and mulattoes, who were the defenders of political liberty.[90] Writing from the *canaliste* wing of the Liberal Party he attacked despotism, stating that in Haiti it would never lead to enlightened government. Representative and parliamentary government, on the other hand, is 'la véritable école politique des peuples', which will lead to a government of the most capable.[91] He maintained that the assassination of Dessalines had been a natural consequence of his tyranny and was the work of blacks as well as mulattoes, refuting the accusation by the spokesmen of *le piquétisme doctrinaire*[92] that it had been the result of a mulatto conspiracy. In this early period it was in fact the mulatto leaders Pétion and Boyer who really cared for the masses and not the black leaders.[93] Yet conditions were such in the Haiti of his day that it was impossible to secure the election of a mulatto head of state, and Thoby asserted that *la politique de doublure*, whereby elite politicians acted behind the front of a black president, had therefore become necessary.[94] Hannibal Price also reinforced a mulatto view of the past by ignoring the contribution of Toussaint and Dessalines to the independence of Haiti, referring rather to the work of Ogé and Chavannes.[95]

Léon Laroche attacked Toussaint, Dessalines, Christophe, Soulouque, Salnave and Salomon, praising Pétion, Boyer, Riché, Geffrard and Nissage. These latter 'also belonged to the black race but were not barbarians'. Laroche in common with many of his contemporaries saw politics in Haiti as a struggle between a despotic tradition with its roots in Africa and the ideas of liberty, equality and fraternity which derived from the French revolution.[96] The latter tendency was represented by the Liberal Party and to a lesser extent by the National Party also, both of which stood for civilised principles and worked towards the common good. The despotic African tradition was embodied in a faction, the *piquets*, led by President Salomon, who was accused of conducting a war of caste by stirring up the blacks against the mulattoes.[97] This charge was also brought against Salomon by Hannibal Price, who in an open letter to the president declared: 'You have brought to birth in the hearts of the blacks of Haiti a fierce hatred of all those of their compatriots of a different colour who have shown in public life patriotism, talent, honour.'[98] Laroche put forward an explicitly racial theory of politics, arguing that the mixing of races leads to national development. Europe, he maintained, owes 'its perfection' to the various invasions from Asia, while Africa's backwardness was ascribed to its relative isolation. He therefore advocated increased intercourse between Haiti and the outside world, a policy adopted by the Liberal Party, in contrast to the National Party, which was said by Laroche to be in favour of the isolation of Haiti in a black civilisation.[99] Laroche's racial theories carried him even further. He argued that because Haiti is composed of blacks and mulattoes, the ideal president would be a *griffe* who, being 'black in skin but mulatto in origin', would symbolise the unity of the nation. He maintained that in the history of Haiti many of the best presidents had in fact been *griffes*, mentioning Riché, Geffrard and Nissage.[100] This idea of the *griffe* as the typical Haitian was reasserted by Léon Audin.[101] Laroche's derogatory description of Salomon's physical appearance contains further evidence of his own prejudice. He wrote of the president's 'thick woolly hair . . . his mouth circumscribed by his tight flat lips, and bearing the characteristic wrinkles of wickedness'.[102] A similar racialism is evident in the neighbouring Dominican Republic, where the mulatto politician Gregorio Luperón maintained that a *raza mixta* of European and African was particularly suited to the climate of the Caribbean. He further ascribed the barbarous behaviour of 'the savage General Heureaux' to 'his descent which is from Haiti'.[103]

Most of the spokesmen of the Liberal Party avoided explicit references to racial and colour factors, insisting that they were a truly national party whose policy was enlightened and progressive. J. P. Bazelais had claimed in 1870 that the party believed in a transformation of all classes in the community, and particularly of the masses, by a serious reorganisation of public education. Under the leadership of the most enlightened elements of the population the whole country would benefit.[104] Against the tendency of the National Party to argue in favour of a strong head of state, the Liberals maintained that important powers should reside in the legislative assembly, which should be controlled by the enlightened elite of the country. Under the Liberal Party the government had been in the hands of such an elite, declared Boyer Bazelais from Miragoâne in 1883, but 'Salomon has replaced them by the incapable, the vicious and by men from the lower orders. Salomon has rebelled against the law which requires that in every society there is a privileged group whose role it is to direct the lower classes'.[105]

While many of the Nationals looked favourably on the Haitian army as a symbol of equality and channel whereby the sons of the poor could rise to prominence,[106] the Liberals were for the same reason suspicious of militarism. In general they were in favour of reducing the power of the army and of introducing into Haiti a system of civilian government. 'We belong to the democratic school, one of whose most cherished hopes is the suppression of standing armies', wrote Thoby in 1870.[107] *Le Messager du Nord* (edited by Firmin) however, denied that it was part of the policy of the Liberals to abolish the army. 'It is', the newspaper insisted, 'possible to have a good army without tolerating arbitrary action by the military authorities.' Elsewhere Firmin suggested that the danger of national independence being achieved by force ('and unfortunately this is the only means of obtaining it with dignity') is that effective power then falls into the hands of the military leaders who led the independence struggle.[108]

Science, literature and politics

The Liberal Party slogan 'Government by the most competent' was frankly elitist and anti-populist in its implications. Many mulatto writers claimed that contemporary European social science lent support to their position. L. J. Marcelin, for example, insisted that 'a knowledge of sociological laws' was necessary for the successful practice of politics,[109] and in a later work he attempted to outline a synthetic philosophy along lines similar to those followed by Herbert Spencer in England.[110] Justin Dévot claimed that a scientific understanding of society, as advocated by Emile Durkheim, would lead Haitians to see that the political system was the result of social conditions in the country.[111] These writers pointed to the importance of the economic structure of the country, arguing that any renovation of the politics of Haiti must be based on reforms in agriculture, industry and commerce.[112] L. J. Marcelin, E. Mathon, L. C. Lhérisson, E. Ethéart and others put these ideas into practice when in 1892 they joined together to found an Ecole Libre Professionnelle. The object of the school was to teach young Haitians useful knowledge, and thereby to combat idleness, the great evil which was afflicting the country.[113] The syllabus would be divided into three parts, *classique*, *moral* and *civique*, and there was to be a strong emphasis upon practical skills like agronomy, technology and design. Moravia Morpeau had already pointed out in 1889 that trade schools would provide the government with men who were interested in public peace and who would defend 'the established order of things'.[114] Such schools would allow able children from the poorer classes to become trained in some useful profession, and thereby be diverted from revolutionary activity. The young Sténio Vincent was under no illusions about the purpose of the school, as is clear from his speech on the occasion of the opening ceremony. 'Perhaps all our great evils', he declared,

issue from the complete absence of any serious organisation of work to the profit of these inoffensive popular classes, who are too easily exploitable and are able to become fierce instruments of disorder . . . Young men from the elite understood that there is here an imminent public danger. From that time they have undertaken a remarkable work: the foundation in this city of an Ecole Libre Professionnelle.[115]

Vincent assailed the majority of the traditional elite, however, for their voluntary isolation from the rest of the nation, for their vanity and for the disastrous rivalries which undermined all co-operative efforts.[116] Other writers of the period called for the development of a strong middle class which would ensure a degree of social mobility. J. B. Dorsainvil believed that such a class would act as a stabilising force in the country by securing 'an equilibrium' between the rival elites.[117] The idea was taken up by J. C. Dorsainvil in his 1908 articles in *Le Matin*: it became a familiar feature of the *Griots* ideology of the post-occupation period and continually reappeared in the election speeches of François Duvalier in 1957.[118]

In 1892 the Société de Législation was founded by a group of intellectuals including Stéphen Preston, J. N. Léger, Georges Sylvain, Justin Dévot, Frédéric Marcelin, Louis Borno and Solon Ménos. The group was concerned to examine Haitian laws, proposing reforms where necessary, and to consider the wider aspects of political, economic and social life in the country. The Société had as its general object 'the introduction of civilisation in this land', and its members believed that this could be achieved only by formulating laws which were in harmony with the mores of the people.[119] They were therefore also interested in reforming the customs of the people. The Société held regular meetings and their journal, *La Revue de la Société de Législation*, was the principal means by which they hoped to exert influence upon the legislative process and upon public opinion.

The closing years of the nineteenth century saw in Haiti something of a literary revival with the founding of *Jeune Haïti* and *La Ronde*. 'La génération de La Ronde' included the poets Georges Sylvain, Edmond

Laforest, Charles Moravia and Louis Borno, critics Seymour Pradel and
Dantès Bellegarde, and novelists Frédéric Marcelin, Fernand Hibbert
and Justin Lhérisson. Perhaps the most influential member of the group
was the poet Etzer Vilaire, who was born in April 1872, the son of a
Protestant schoolmaster in the southern city of Jérémie. Vilaire in
many ways typified the attitudes and prejudices of the more enlightened
section of the elite of his day. Although, like the mulatto historians
Ardouin and Saint-Rémy, he was proud to be 'a descendant of the
black race', his cultural orientation was European and his political
sympathies were with the elitist Liberals. The evil afflicting Haiti was
ascribed to ignorant and brutal heads of state recruited from the army,
and 'derives principally from the unfortunate conditions of our ethnic
formation'.[120] The writers of *La Ronde* entertained a romantic despair
for themselves and for their country, claiming to be those 'who have
suffered as one rarely suffers at our age, who have shed tears of
blood'.[121] Their critics, however, called their writings a 'littérature
d'évasion' which failed seriously to come to terms with the social and
economic problems facing the country, being the product of a small,
self-centred and privileged minority.

Beyond colour

Although the colour question played a central role in the politics of
Haiti in the period from Salnave to Simon, and although much of the
literature of the time exemplifies the antagonism between blacks and
mulattoes, it would be wrong to suggest that all the writers of this
period were obsessed with the colour issue, or that they were disguised
protagonists in the battle. The mulatto writer Joseph Justin, for
example, while recognising the importance of colour prejudice in Haiti,
ascribed the blame to many of his own colour.[122] Justin also attacked
the selfishness of the elite which dominated the social life of the
country, and called for a more responsible attitude by the members of
this class, a theme which was to become familiar during the early years
of the American occupation.[123]

Perhaps of particular interest from our point of view are those who
allied themselves with political groups the majority of whose members
were of a colour different from their own. Joseph Anténor Firmin is
an outstanding example of such writers. Born in October 1850 at
Cap Haïtien, Firmin became a school teacher, lawyer and journalist.
Although he had supported Salnave in 1867, he associated himself with
the Liberal Party in the seventies. His sympathy for the Liberals was
largely engendered by his admiration for the ideas of Edmond Paul.
Firmin founded *Le Messager du Nord* in 1878, and was a Liberal candidate for the legislature in 1879; but with the victory of the National

Party he retired from public life. In 1888 he joined the successful movement against Salomon and became a cabinet minister under Hyppolite. Firmin was a formidable defender of Haitian independence, and gathered around himself many young disciples who supported his bid for the presidency in 1902. Firmin was however, out-manoeuvred by Nord Alexis and went into exile until the fall of Alexis in 1908, when he returned for a short while. He died in St Thomas in September 1911.[124] Firmin defended Christophe against the charge of having been prejudiced against the mulattoes and maintained that the colour question was the keystone of Boyer's government.[125] Salnave was portrayed as 'the idol of the masses', while Boisrond Canal was condemned for his practice of giving all lucrative posts to mulattoes.[126] Firmin's association with the Liberal Party suggests an admiration for Boyer Bazelais and Edmond Paul, who were 'the most remarkable men that Haiti has possessed'.[127] In general his interpretation of the Haitian past is remarkably free from colour prejudice, and from legendary domination.[128] The same might be said of the black writer Roche Grellier, whose *Histoire d'Haïti à l'usage des écoles* and its abridged version designed for primary schools, both published in 1893, were harsh on black leaders like Soulouque and Pierrot, and referred favourably to Pétion and Geffrard.

Frédéric Marcelin was, on the other hand, a mulatto who belonged to the National Party. Marcelin was born at Port-au-Prince in 1848, the son of a businessman, and was sent to school first in Port-au-Prince and then in Paris. Under Salnave he became secretary to the embassy in Washington and was a deputy during the regime of Domingue, being a friend of Septimus Rameau.[129] During the presidency of Boisrond Canal he was in exile in Jamaica, but returned to Haiti to become deputy for the capital under Salomon. He was the principal link between the government and the business community of Port-au-Prince.[130] Marcelin was minister of finance under Hyppolite, and after some years in France, where he published a number of novels and essays of social criticism, he returned to occupy the same post under Nord Alexis. He died in Paris in 1917. Curiously enough the political path followed by Marcelin was precisely opposite to that followed by Firmin. The former passed by easy stages from the National Party into the camp of Alexis, who was generally regarded as being anti-*noiriste*. Firmin passed from an early association with the predominantly mulatto Liberal Party into the government of Simon Sam, later holding a diplomatic post under the supposedly *noiriste* regime of Antoine Simon. The crossing-over point for both men was the regime of Hyppolite, in whose cabinet both men served. Marcelin was critical of the more extreme wing of the National Party, however, and assailed Janvier's *Les constitutions d'Haïti* (for which the author had received a subsidy from the

Haitian government) as a work which, owing to a blind desire to make
systematic generalisations, 'tramples on history and on truth'; it was,
pronounced Marcelin, 'a work of combat, not a product of scientific
reasoning'.[131] Marcelin's more sympathetic judgment of Beaubrun
Ardouin is significant. Although the mulatto historian was 'not sufficiently detached' and was too much influenced by his milieu, 'he is
nevertheless absolutely impartial and of good faith'.[132] Marcelin was
furthermore denounced by his antagonist Hannibal Price for despising
'les nègres d'Haïti', about whom he was accused of having said, 'the
most enlightened among them will only ever be a savage more or less
well-dressed'.[133] Though Marcelin denied having said this, it is the case
that in many of his writings he adopted positions which were more in
line with those of other mulatto theorists than with those of the black
members of the National Party, with whom he was politically allied.
Like other creative writers of this period, Marcelin took up the call
for a truly national literature, which had been issued in an earlier
generation by Emile Nau and his associates. 'Our literature', he declared, 'must generally find a greater source of inspiration in our
history.'[134]

II

Having indicated how colour was a major factor contributing to the
deep divisions existing in Haiti in the period from Salnave to Sam,
I shall move on to discuss ideas and attitudes about race which united
Haitians of all shades. In the first place there was a unanimous rejection
of European theories concerning the racial inferiority of the black man,
and an assertion of the fundamental equality of the human races. In
this context Haitian writers pointed to the origins of civilisation on the
African continent. Secondly there was a general acceptance in this
period of European cultural, religious and political ideas and institutions; this involved holding a low opinion of those elements in
Haitian culture which originated in Africa, particularly the Voodoo
religion. Nevertheless there was among Haitians considerable interest
in and support for the Pan-African movement of the late nineteenth
and early twentieth centuries. Thirdly there was general accord upon
the importance of maintaining Haitian independence, though disagreement about the necessary conditions of this independence. The
disagreement, however, which was particularly significant in the
economic field, cut across the colour line and also across the political
division between Liberals and Nationals.

Racial equality

While the phenomenon of racial and colour prejudice goes back many centuries, it received a fresh impetus in the nineteenth century. In France, Germany, England and the United States biological and anthropological data were used to turn racialism into a 'scientific' theory. In 1853 Arthur de Gobineau had begun to publish his *Essai sur l'inégalité des races humaines*, in which he maintained that, whatever the origin of the human race, 'it is certain that the different families are today absolutely separate'.The black race is at 'the foot of the ladder' and is 'incapable of civilization'. He believed that the inferiority of black people was based upon biological factors.[135] The less-known but hardly less influential Edinburgh anatomist Robert Knox also insisted upon the importance of biological factors in determining racial differences. 'Race is everything'. he wrote in 1850. 'Literature, science, art – in a word, civilisation, depends upon it.'[136] James Hunt, president of the Anthropological Society of London, asserted the impossibility 'of applying the civilisation and laws of one race to another race of men essentially distinct'.[137] He defended the notorious Governor Eyre of Jamaica, who was himself a member of the Anthropological Society, and he criticised the anti-slavery laws. 'Our mistaken legislature', he wrote, 'has done the Negro race much injury by their absurd and unwarrantable attempts to prevent Africa from exporting her worthless or surplus population.'[138] The Paris Anthropological Society, which was founded in 1859 by Paul Broca, subscribed to the belief that blacks and whites belong to different species, and that this involves a basic inequality of the races. The article 'nègre' in P. Larousse's *Grand Dictionnaire Universel* criticised philanthropists who 'have tried to prove that the negro type is as intelligent as the white type'. The racial factor was given considerable prominence in historical studies at this time,[139] and in 1871 Ernest Renan declared that the conquest of an inferior race by a superior race was perfectly understandable; he went on to claim that, as blacks were designed by nature to be labourers, so whites were a race of masters and soldiers.[140] These racialist sentiments were reflected in the imaginative literature of the period.[141] French nineteenth-century racialism was strengthened by the social psychology of Gustave Le Bon, and translated into a demand for the revision of colonial policy; the formerly accepted goal of assimilation was denounced for failing to take account of fundamental racial differences.[142]

Frequently writers who put forward theories of racial inferiority cited Haiti as evidence in support of their position. Gobineau stated that the manners of the Haitian people were 'as depraved, brutal and savage as in Dahomey or among the Fellatahs', and he pointed to Haiti as an awful example of what happened when European forms of government are imposed upon people of a different race. Later Léo Quesnel declared that the inability of the Haitians to constitute a stable society was confirmation of the theory of racial inequality.[143]

There were also current in Europe and North America accounts of Haiti which were clearly written from the standpoint of a belief in the racial inferiority of the blacks. Perhaps the best known of these accounts was *Hayti: or the Black Republic* by Sir Spencer St John, who had been British minister in Haiti for a number of years. 'As a rule', he declared, 'the abler a negro is, the more wicked and corrupt he appears.' He went on to state that, on the basis of his knowledge of Haiti, 'I now agree with those who deny that the negro could ever originate a civilisation, and that with the best of education he remains an inferior type of man.'[144] He further maintained that black people are 'incapable of the art of government'.[145]

It was against the background of this kind of writing that Haitians in the period we are considering felt it necessary to vindicate the black race and to assert the fundamental equality of the human races. They accepted the association between Haiti and the black race, and believed that the history of their country, as they understood it, constituted evidence for the equality of the races. Haiti, insisted Janvier, is for the black race 'the sun which rises on the horizon'.[146] J. N. Léger stated that Haiti had a sacred mission to rehabilitate the whole black race, and Emmanuel Edouard saw the little republic of Haiti as a representative of the whole black race,[147] as did the poets Massillon Coicou and Tertulien Guilbaud.[148] *Le Justicier* wrote of Haiti as 'l'avant-garde de l'Afrique posé sur le chemin de la porte d'or',[149] while the journal *La Fraternité*, published in Paris from 1890 onwards, claimed to be the 'organ of the interests of Haiti and of the black race', thus associating the two in the same way that Hannibal Price did in his book *De la réhabilitation de la race noire par la république d'Haïti*. President Salomon was therefore reflecting this belief when he attacked the Liberal invaders of Miragoâne as not merely enemies of their country, but of their race.[150] It is, however, noteworthy that in this period, as in earlier periods of Haitian history, mulattoes as well as blacks claimed that their country was a symbol of black regeneration; a writer as bitterly anti-*noiriste* as Georges Séjourné could refer to Haitians as constituting 'a branch of the immense African race'.[151]

The writers whom we are considering in this chapter – black and mulatto alike – thus linked their defence of the negro race with their discussion of the Haitian experience. From what has already been said, and from what will follow, it is evident that these writers must be seen principally as apologists – not simply because of their polemical orientation, but because of the fact that their purpose was basically to persuade European readers that Haiti was a 'civilised' country and that black people are capable of civilisation *according to European criteria*. These writers rarely challenged the superiority of European culture and they minimised the role of African elements in the heritage of the

Haitian people. It is not until the period of the United States occupation that we find an explicit and widespread challenge to European criteria and a positive appreciation of the African contribution to Haitian culture.

Africa and the origins of civilisation

The Haitian writers of this period were then agreed in rejecting theories of racial inferiority and ideas of significant differences between the races. Throughout human history, asserted Anténor Firmin in his celebrated treatise *De l'égalité des races humaines*, published in 1885, different races have assumed leading positions from time to time, but 'the actors are all equal in dignity'.[152] All men are, he stated,

endowed with the same qualities and the same faults, without distinction of colour or anatomic form. The races are equal; they are all capable of achieving the noblest intellectual development, as they are of falling into the most complete degradation.[153]

Those who spoke of the inferiority of the black race, he pointed out, insisted on comparing the most backward African tribe with the most cultivated European nations; but there are in fact Mongolian and white nations very much more backward than most of the people of Central Africa. Certainly, he stated, some nations are superior to others in terms of their culture and civilisation, but this has nothing to do with race, a word which implies a natural and biological fatalism.[154] Other Haitian writers agreed that any lack of development in their own country or in Africa was due to a lack of favourable conditions rather to any inherent inability on the part of black people; the notion of racial inferiority was, they insisted, wholly without scientific foundation.[155]

Hannibal Price argued that the savage condition of many African countries was no indication of the inferiority of the black race; all men are endowed with the same human nature.[156] Price pointed to Haiti as a country in which the black race has demonstrated its equality; the troubles from which the republic suffered were not different in kind from those which are evident in European history.[157] He further observed that racial theories were largely developed as an ideological support for the institution of slavery:

The colour question, the affirmation of an *inherent* inferiority of the man with black or red skin, *prejudice*, in short, was nothing other than a calculation of egoism, a kind of convention in the past among slave owners to quieten their consciences and to veil their crime from their own eyes.[158]

Slavery, while it represented for the black man in the New World three centuries of torture, might also be seen as the means whereby he entered modern civilisation. 'In working for the white man', wrote Price, 'the negro received from him the light. This was not the intention of the slave owner, it was the will of God.'[159] The system of slavery therefore contained within itself the seeds of its own destruction, and yet theories of racial inferiority survived the abolition of slavery, and Alcius Charmant found it necessary to combat the assertion that the institution of slavery had degraded the black man in such a way as to leave an indelible mark of inferiority.[160]

A number of writers, then, pointed to the African origins of European civilisation. Firmin insisted that Egyptian civilisation is the fountainhead from which sprang the Greek and Latin cultures, and that the development of the arts and sciences among white people of the West rested upon an African foundation.[161] Caucasian presumption, he observed, could not abide the idea that the whole development of human civilisation originated with a race which they considered to be radically inferior to themselves. The picture of Rameses II, however, manifests 'a beauty which is more similar to the black type than to the white'.[162] He argued that the historical researches of Champollion and others showed that the Egyptian and Ethiopian people formed a single race. 'Without doubt', he continued, 'one can stop here, and, supported by such authorities, can affirm that the ancient Egyptians, the true *Retous*, were black Africans . . . I consider this, for my part, as a major point against the doctrine of the inequality of the races.'[163] Dr Casseus also, after quoting the views of ancient authorities like Herodotus, maintained that Egyptians were negroes and also that remarkable scientific developments, including the discovery and use of iron, had taken place in the Africa of this early period.[164]

Yet these writers believed that the early black civilisation of North Africa had declined, and they saw little of value in the Africa of their own day. Moravia Morpeau stated that Egypt, which had been the centre of a great civilisation, was in his day a mere shadow of its former self; it was Europe which was enlightening the world with religion and science; tomorrow, he predicted, it will be the turn of the American continent.[165] The fact that civilisation had declined in Africa was, of course, no evidence for the inferiority of black people. These Haitians recognised the historical and biological links which existed between the population of their own country and that of Africa, but most of them denied that this physical link has any significant consequences in the social, cultural or political fields. The people of Haiti were described as 'a branch of the European tree grafted on to the enormous trunk of Africa'.[166]

The backwardness of modern Africa

Haitian writers of the late nineteenth century were thus interested in

Africa from two points of view. In the first place many of them insisted that civilisation had originated in Africa among the black race, and that this fact will refute any idea that the race is inherently inferior to other races. Secondly they accepted the general picture of the Africa of their own day as a savage and uncivilised continent which can hope to progress only by accepting contemporary European culture. Seldom do we find complimentary references to nineteenth-century Africa, and most of the Haitian writers of this period wished to dissociate their country as far as possible from its African past. In literature, music and religion, in politics and law, it was the European model which was conscientiously followed.

It is not surprising to find the mulatto writers Léon Laroche, Justin Dévot, Seymour Pradel and Hannibal Price arguing that the valuable elements, worthy of development, in Haiti are European rather than African in origin. Laroche eulogised the influence of France in Haiti. The blood of Frenchmen is mingled with that of Haitians; the intellectual life, language, law and customs in Haiti derive from France.[167] Dévot in his textbook on civic education stated that it is France which has nourished Haiti with its literary, social and political ideas. Elsewhere he declared that 'our political institutions, our legislation, our administrative organisations, our customs, our social patterns, our official language even, were made in France; she has been our educator'.[168] Haiti was for Etzer Vilaire 'Bastard daughter, alas, of proud Europe'.[169] Price believed that the African element was more numerous in the South and West of the colony of Saint Domingue than in the North, and that for this reason the people in these two provinces 'were less civilised, less intelligent, than the corresponding caste in the North'.[170] The poet Seymour Pradel ascribed the love of liberty in the country to its European heritage; the despotic tendencies were 'héritage transmis par atavismes africaines'.[171] Another perceptive observer of Haitian life, Dr Léon Audin, acknowledged the importance of African elements in the life of the people, picturing the Haitian temperament as 'a bizarre combination' of European and African features, and ascribing what he called 'le résignation' which was characteristic of the Haitian to his African past.[172]

It is important to note how black leaders and publicists of the period voiced similar views on Europe and Africa to those quoted above. Demesvar Delorme, in a letter to Salomon in 1867, made it clear that in his view Haiti should follow a European pattern of development, while in his novels and other literary work there is little reference to Africa or even to Haiti itself; as Price Mars has observed, his novels are set in Turkey, Italy or France rather than in the Caribbean.[173] Janvier manifested a similar orientation; all the institutions and customs of Haiti were, he argued, modelled on those of France. It is necessary for Haitians to 'struggle against the African element, the fieriness and appetites of which are well-known'.[174] He maintained that the Haitian youth of his day was familiar with all the latest scientific and literary trends in Europe, and that the Haitian literature which had been born was a daughter of the French. He went as far as to assert mendaciously that French was the only language used in Haiti and that 'all the peasants understand it'.[175] In legal as much as in literary matters Europe was the model. 'We Haitians', he told the electors of Port-au-Prince in 1907, 'have always copied England or France and not Africa, in the text of our law; we must then always imitate France and England, and not Africa, in the execution of our laws.'[176] Anténor Firmin, who is sometimes said to have moved from liberalism to nationalism, claimed in the latter period of his life that Haitians were more 'French' than Martiniquans or Guadeloupians.[177] The *noiriste* writer Charmant pointed to the need for a people to study its historical development if it is properly to understand its political institutions, but he did not suggest in any way that this might involve a knowledge of Haiti's African past. In fact he declared that

in spite of the laws of atavism . . . we bear very little resemblance to the primitive peoples of Africa, either in physical beauty, in spirit or in intelligence. Further-more, one can recognise that between the black race of Haiti and the Latin part of the white race, there is a certain affinity with respect to civilisation which is not to be found among other people of the black race.[178]

In his speech to the Universal Congress of Races at London in 1911, the former president F. D. Légitime admitted that it was possible to find in Haiti 'certain traces of African fanaticism, but', he went on, 'this is only a lingering relic of ancestral traits which a people does not easily suppress'.[179]

Voodoo

Among these traits not easily suppressed was of course the Voodoo cult. There was among Haitian writers in this period, black and mulatto alike, a certain reticence about discussing the question of Voodoo. Many extravagant and wildly inaccurate accounts of Voodoo ceremonies had been propagated in Europe and it is hardly surprising that Haitians, sharing the beliefs and prejudices about European civilisation which we have noted, wished to refute these sensationalist reports. Often, how-ever, they went further and actually denied the existence of the Voodoo cult when writing for European audiences. Although at times Janvier recognised the contribution which Voodoo had made to the struggle for independence, providing a source of solidarity and a means of communication for the slaves of Saint Domingue, he insisted that the old African dances associated with the cult 'have completely disappeared in the towns as well as in the country'.[180] Bénito Sylvain and J. N. Léger both denied the significance of the Voodoo religion in Haiti, stating that it was practised only by a few people and that it had lost its power.[181] Within Haiti itself, however, such denials were useless in the face of the evidence. An intermittent battle was waged against the Voodoo cult not only by the Roman Catholic church and the mulatto elite, but also by many black writers. The bishop of Cap Haïtien denounced the cult as diabolic and idolatrous; as long as this 'ignoble African paganism' continued to exist in Haiti 'it is in vain that we pretend to pass for a truly civilised nation'.[182] In February 1897 Mgr Kersuzan issued strict instructions to his clergy to impose severe penances on those confessing Voodoo practices, and reserving the absolution of 'magiciens et bocors' to the bishop. A 'Ligue contre le Vaudou' was founded, and the journal *La Croix* was largely devoted to attacks on the cult. Writers from the ultranational group fully accepted this position. *L'Œil* declared that it was important to put obstacles in the way of the cult's progress among the people who were trying to rid themselves of 'the heavy burden of their origin' in order to march in the way of progress.[183] *L'Impartial* also called for the extirpation of Voodoo by means of Christian evangelisation and instruction of the masses.[184] J. F. Thalès Manigat in his *Conférence sur le vaudoux* denounced 'this abominable sect which our ancestors introduced into the country', and which was, according to Manigat, 'in full recrudescence'.[185]

Léon Audin, addressing the Société de Législation in 1904, recognised the widespread practice of Voodoo, not only in the countryside 'but in the suburbs of Port-au-Prince itself'. Yet he portrayed Voodoo as primarily a form of amusement, with music and dancing combined with a communal feast. He quaintly admitted that the ceremony preceding the killing of the animal 'is not absolutely in proportion to the end proposed, the preparation of a meal', and he lamented the alcoholism and state of hysteria which frequently accompany the ceremonies. Yet he saw these features as peripheral to the real social function of Voodoo and believed that it was possible to purify the practices by removing those elements which carry over the barbarous spirit of past times, transforming Voodoo into 'a simple popular dance, joyful and decent'![186]

Haitian writers, then, generally accepted the picture of contemporary Africa as an uncivilised place, believing that it would benefit from contact with Europe. Frédéric Marcelin, for example, wrote of a future black civilisation in Africa, but insisted that European influence was a necessary condition for such a development.[187] Other writers went further and explicitly defended the colonial policy of the European powers. Bénito Sylvain attacked the brutal and cruel aspects of the European colonisation of Africa, which was being justified according to false theories of racial inferiority, but the partition of Africa, accomplished in a humanitarian manner, 'would be the most magnificent work — the most meritorious and the most fruitful — of modern civilisation'. It was, he declared, high time that the darkness of a barbarous Africa was dispersed by the invasion of European powers, led by France — the country which best understood the magnificent role of coloniser.[188]

The Pan-African movement

Believing that their country was the symbol of black regeneration, it was natural that Haitians should have played a leading role in the Pan-African movement which began in the closing years of the nineteenth century. President Nord Alexis wrote to Emperor Menelek II of Ethiopia in 1903 stating that, by its progressive development, an autonomous Haiti had conclusively established 'the moral perfectibility of the whole African Race'.[189] Relations between the two black nations were strengthened by the energetic activity of Bénito Sylvain, who visited Ethiopia and was the Haitian delegate to the Pan-African Congress of July 1900. Although Sylvain moved away from the extreme paternalism of his early days as editor of *La Fraternité*, his basic attitude towards Africa remained the same. While he continued to attack the brutal treatment of Africans in 'the colonies of exploitation', he believed that a good colonialism was possible, in which the natives would be civilised and eventually assimilated.[190] While this position appears somewhat naive, looking back from the standpoint of the 1970s, it was by no means rare among colonial subjects; there is more than a trace of it in René Maran's 1937 preface to *Batouala*, and it would appear to be a view which is still held by Aimé Césaire. Yet Sylvain's attitude towards Europe was ambivalent, and he observed how nine hundred years of Christianity had failed to develop a truly civilised community. 'In shamefully abusing the material power which assured her a baneful mastery in the art of killing', he observed, 'Europe constitutes a terrifying danger for the whole of humanity.'[191]

The Pan-African Congress, held in London in 1900, comprised a number of eminent black delegates from various parts of the world. Henry Sylvester Williams from Trinidad was one of the leading voices, and there were representatives from the United States and Liberia as well as from the Caribbean. Sylvain gives an account of the proceedings in *Du sort des indigènes dans les colonies d'exploitation*. The Congress appealed to 'civilised countries' to provide facilities for the education and development of backward people of the black race, and warned the world that 'the problem of the 20th century is the colour question'.[192] In 1906 Sylvain founded an organisation called L'Œuvre du

Relèvement Social des Noirs, under the protection of the emperor of Ethiopia and the president of Haiti, together with the heads of state of practically every power in Europe. The patron of L'Œuvre was Pope Pius X and its orientation was explicitly Christian. The three aims of the association were:

1. To combat colour prejudice *by every peaceful means.*
2. To work loyally to establish a satisfactory *modus vivendi* between the European colonists and the African natives, by a wise conciliation of industrial and commercial interests with the principles of Christian brotherhood.
3. To furnish the most advanced blacks with the opportunities to prove their aptitudes and to contribute in an effective manner to the progress of civilisation.[193]

Members of L'Œuvre would keep a watchful eye on the abuses of colonial power, as they saw it, as well as combating racial theories in articles and books. Furthermore they planned a series of literary and artistic exhibitions of African works as well as study voyages to the continent. *La Revue Haïtienne*, published in Paris at the beginning of the century, took at times a rather more radical position with respect to European colonialism. It urged the blacks of Africa to 'take up their rights and liberty' and to 'chase the savage and criminal oppressor from their territory'. Are there, the *Revue* asked, no descendants of Toussaint and Dessalines in Africa? It took as a motto '*L'Afrique aux africaines*'.[194]

While it is thus generally true to say that Haitian writers in this period regarded the Africa of their day as relatively uncivilised and believed that the European pattern should be followed, there are to be found occasional hints of a different approach. On one occasion when President Salomon was referred to by one of his opponents, in derogatory terms, as an African, Janvier exploded: certainly he was an African as all Haitians were, and 'we do not deny our origins'. He went on to refer to Haiti as 'notre *petite Afrique*'.[195] In a plea for the encouragement of African immigrants, 'Amicus' (probably Alcibiade Pommayrac) claimed that Haiti needed to be strengthened with 'the blood of the ancestors; with that of young Africa'. He pointed, in anticipation of the *négritude* writers of the following century, to the vigour, the simplicity, 'the primitive spirit full of integrity, of the principles of order and obedience' which characterise the people of Africa. These were the only immigrants which Haiti could successfully assimilate. Yet the author saw these Africans as being engaged in manual labour on public works, and the virtues which he saw in these men were those which an enlightened employer might hope for in his workers. Auguste Rameau alluded briefly in 1894 to the project for founding an 'Association Africaine' in Haiti, though it does not appear to have been visited with much success.[196] Later Massillon Coicou, in his 'Lettre à Pétion Gerome', reminded Haitians of their African past, arguing that any race which is ignorant of its origins is doomed.[197] Even with respect to the Voodoo religion it is possible to find the beginnings of a more sympathetic approach by Haitian intellectuals. In his 1906 introduction to *Mimola*, Antoine Innocent pointed to the fact that the origin of belief in the Voodoo spirits was the same as that of belief in all supernatural beings.[198] The early articles of J. C. Dorsainvil in 1907–8, as we shall see, also suggest a new approach to these questions.[199] Yet favourable references to Haiti's African heritage are difficult to find prior to the period of the American occupation, and, particularly in the case of Janvier, they by no means reflect the settled views of the writer himself.

National independence

Many Haitian writers of the nineteenth century believed that the independence of their country was of significance for the whole black race, and must therefore be maintained at any cost. Haiti was 'the common homeland of negroes and mulattoes' and the only corner on earth where they could demonstrate their aptitudes and prove 'the perfectibility of our race'.[200] The land which blacks had conquered with their blood and watered with their sweat must never be allowed to pass into foreign hands, for it was part of the national vocation to safeguard 'the *autonomy* and the *affirmation* of the black race'.[201] Joseph Justin insisted that there is no inherent difference between the human races and that the social *milieu* was all important; therefore Haiti had a mission to accomplish. 'We must free ourselves from all foreign will, from all interference in our affairs', he wrote. 'It is independence which characterises our political existence, our personality.'[202]

There was considerable disagreement about the conditions necessary for retaining an effective independence. Some writers continued to defend the prohibition of foreign ownership of land, arguing that any modification of this law would lead to excessive foreign involvement in the life of the country. I have discussed this whole question in some detail elsewhere.[203] Here I shall merely emphasise that the division of opinion on this matter cut across colour lines and party affiliations. While it is true that the ultranationals, led by L. J. Janvier and Edouard Pinckombe, were against any modification of this law, they were unable to persuade the leadership of the National Party to adopt such an uncompromising position. Neither Delorme nor Salomon himself was willing to exclude the possibility of allowing foreign ownership in future.[204] Though in his Liberal period Anténor Firmin warned against a change in the law prohibiting foreign ownership, urging President Boisrond Canal to wait, he later argued for such a change in the interests of economic development.[205]

The question of land ownership was of course only part of the wider problem of the economic strategy to be pursued by a small developing nation. The radical view was stated by Janvier, who insisted that the fields, forests and mines of Haiti must be developed by citizens of the country with local capital, and that Haiti should be prepared to accept a slower rate of growth rather than achieving more rapid development by handing over the resources of the country to foreign capital. As we have seen, Janvier insisted on the need for an ideology of economic development based on the Protestant ethic. At the other extreme we find Emmanuel Edouard positively inviting French capitalists to 'undertake the peaceful and economic conquest of Haiti'.[206] He argued that French investment in the black republic would be of benefit to both countries.

Most Haitian intellectuals during these years adopted positions in between the two extremes represented by Janvier and Edouard. It would perhaps be true to say that there was a gradual movement away from economic nationalism, with more and more writers advocating a change in the law which prohibited foreign ownership, thus encouraging foreign investment in Haiti. Antoine Laforest, director of *Haïti Littéraire et Sociale*, mounted a positive campaign to change the law, and even a writer as strongly nationalist as Rosalvo Bobo favoured United States investment in the country. There was, however, disagreement about which foreign nations were most likely to assist the country in a beneficial way. Linstant Pradine, Emmanuel Edouard and Léon Laroche, for example, were strongly pro-French and often adopted a hostile attitude towards Germany, Britain and the United States.[207] On the other hand Frédéric Marcelin, in *Une évolution nécessaire*, urged that Haiti should recognise the growing power of the United States in the Caribbean and come to terms with this fact.

Latin or Anglo-Saxon

During the presidency of Nord Alexis a vigorous campaign was conducted by a group of publicists, centred on the journal *Le Matin*, in favour of 'Anglo-Saxon' rather than 'Latin' values. It was argued that the Latin mentality discourages work, while for the Anglo-Saxons 'their life is, in effect, made of work and activity'.[208] The Americans and the British were praised for their *particularisme*, that is, for the spirit of individual initiative that prevailed among them. 'We know already that Anglo-Saxon societies owe their superiority precisely to the preponderance of private life over public life.'[209] It is not the job of the state to become involved in religion, commerce or industry, but 'to assure free play in these diverse spheres', insisted Senator Déjoie Laroche. In order to transform society, he went on, it is necessary to change its conception of itself, and consequently its thought and action. Anglo-Saxon countries which believe in individual self-help must be the model.[210] One writer observed how the trade union movements in these countries differed from French syndicalism in their concern for improving the conditions of individual workers rather than attempting a reconstruction of society in a communalist direction. It was further suggested by the writers of *Le Matin* that independent and objective social science would lend support to their belief in the superiority of Anglo-Saxon attitudes.[211] Defenders of the French connection, including Georges Sylvain, Léon Audin, Windsor and Dantès Bellegarde, who formed the Alliance Française, accepted, in general, the liberal individualism of their adversaries. They argued, however, that particularism was not the preserve of any single ethnic group, but was the product of historical circumstances. Audin observed how certain nations which had originally be communally organised were being transformed by 'the substitution of the power of the individual for that of the state'.[212] He was especially fascinated by the economic and military development of Japan, whose recent victory over the Russians had caused considerable interest in the non-European world.

A further aspect of the debate between those who argued for the superiority of the Anglo-Saxon world and their adversaries was centred on education. The former insisted, as Edmond Paul had done in an earlier generation, that there should be a shift of emphasis away from classical to scientific and technical studies.[213] As we shall see this shift was actually put into effect during the United States occupation, and led to bitter resentment from traditionalists.

These domestic disputes clearly had international implications. President Nord's supporters claimed that his entourage, which included Frédéric Marcelin and Louis Borno, was engaged in establishing a new order of things, 'in which American ideas, progress and civilisation, would take the place of old European influences'.[214] Furthermore, *Le Matin* received significant financial backing from members of the Syrio-Lebanese community. Many of those who took the pro-Latin side in the debate were secret or open supporters of Anténor Firmin, who was denounced by Nord for the familiar crime of having planned to hand over the country to foreigners and for having been backed by the French and the Germans.[215] The division among the Haitian elite on this question thus provided an opportunity for foreign powers to intervene further in the affairs of Haiti by backing rival candidates for the presidency. As Leslie Manigat has pointed out the dispute over the relative merits of Anglo-Saxon and Latin culture must also be seen in the context of the contest between France and the United States for control of the Banque Nationale.[216]

III

The erosion of independence

Very few Haitian intellectuals can be found who argued explicitly that the country should abandon its independence and seek the protection of a strong world power, though as we have seen there were those who advocated courses of action which might be said to have had the same effect. Yet despite this determination to defend the independence of Haiti in theory, the practice of politicians was quite otherwise. Geffrard, as we have seen, had invited British assistance in putting down the revolt led by Salnave in 1865, while Salnave in turn had sought assistance from the United States in return for the offer of a naval station at Môle St Nicolas. Nissage offered the Môle to the British, while Domingue suggested some kind of British protectorate over the southern province, and contracted a loan of fifty million francs from France, in 1875.[217] Domingue was also accused of having offered territory to the United States on an earlier occasion.[218]

Salomon perhaps went further than any other president in this period towards ceding Haitian territory and inviting foreign intervention in the affairs of the black republic. In May 1883 he had confidential talks with the United States minister in Haiti, J. M. Langston, in which he stated that he wished to put his country 'in such relations positive or practical with the Government of the United States of America that the protection of such government would be assured us'. He offered to cede the island of La Tortue suggesting that a United States mission visit Haiti immediately to discuss the details.[219] Late in the same year Salomon offered to cede the Bay and part of the peninsula of Môle St Nicolas to the Americans in exchange for diplomatic support and military assistance, but no final agreement was reached.[220] At the same time, Salomon was asking the French to establish a protectorate over Haiti,[221] and in 1884 sent General François Manigat to Paris in a renewed search for French protection and support, in exchange for commercial favours. He also introduced into the country a significant foreign influence in founding the so-called Banque Nationale with French capital, Boyer Bazelais denounced this action of the government: 'Salomon, the apostle of evil, in decreeing the Banque, has delivered our country to the whites.'[222] Although it may be said in Salomon's defence that no cession of territory actually took place, and even that the president had no real intention of parting with territory, yet merely to make offers of this kind was inviting intervention. A further mitigating factor was the need for international support in resisting the demands by the British in connection with the Maunder claim; and the threat of a British seizure of the isle of La Tortue. Nevertheless assistance in defeating his Liberal opponents was a major consideration, as he himself stated.[223]

After the fall of Salomon, Légitime was accused by his opponents of offering the Môle to the French, while Hyppolite made some kind of promise to the United States in exchange for military supplies during his struggle against Légitime. Nevertheless, after becoming president, Hyppolite, together with his foreign minister Firmin, managed to resist strong United States pressure for a cession of territory. In a speech made after his election to the presidency, Hyppolite denied that he had promised to cede the Môle, and explicitly linked his defence of territorial integrity with his racial identity. 'I am not white', he declared, 'I belong to the same race as you do; the day when there should be a question of such an act, I should prefer to see this country disappear like Gomorrah.'[224] Simon Sam was also widely accused of selling the country to foreign interests. A popular song of the period put the matter as follows:

> On the one hand Sam is butchering the nation,
> Stealing more than seventeen millions;
> On the other hand Leconte with Défly
> To foreigners was selling the country.
>
> For ever be cursed,
> O pigs of generals;
> There is no crime worse
> Than to ruin a people.[225]

Sam was succeeded by Nord Alexis, who was supplied with arms by German merchants. This was in fact the occasion for one of the most dramatic episodes in Haitian history. The supporters of Firmin, led by Admiral Hammerton Killick, captured a German ship carrying arms destined for Nord. The German government sent a warship, the *Panther*, to seize the Haitian flagship in reprisal, but Killick blew up the *Crête à Pierrot* and himself rather than surrender. After becoming president, Nord was faced with the problem of a growing number of Syrio-Lebanese merchants threatening to take over much of the retail and some of the wholesale commerce of the country. As was the case with British and German merchants in the country, the presence of these foreigners was frequently the occasion for foreign intervention. German and British merchants who believed that they had been unfairly treated in the Haitian courts appealed to their own governments, who were sometimes prepared to send a gunboat to extort compensation from the Haitian government.[226] In the case of the Syrians there was pressure from local merchants to limit their activities and to invoke earlier laws restricting foreigners, but foreign governments — particularly the United States and Britain — intervened to protect Syrians who carried their nationality. Nord himself, however, boasted that he was the protector of national independence;[227] nevertheless, Sténio Vincent was able in 1908 to lament the fact that much of the cultural and economic life of the country was under foreign control.[228] A similar pattern of foreign intervention is to be seen in the neighbouring Dominican Republic.

Under Simon, the Syrian question became somewhat less acute but, as we have already noted,[229] the government alienated nationalist opinion by granting extensive rights to a United States company under the McDonald contract. The government of Simon, however, managed to resist United States pressure for control of the Haitian customs, and French demands that the financial policy of the country be determined by the Banque Nationale, which was under French control. In reply to the latter demand, the Haitian foreign secretary Edmond Héraux reasserted the Dessalinian claim that Haitian independence was a symbol of black dignity and could not therefore be compromised.[230] Yet foreign pressure was maintained, and present-day writers have convincingly argued that it was at this period that Haiti moved decisively into the United States sphere of influence.[231]

Haiti in the period from Salnave to Simon was thus the scene of a battle for hegemony between the elite groups distinguished principally by colour. Although this conflict did not always manifest itself clearly in the narrowly political field, it is not difficult to see the battle proceeding just below the surface. The black elite was largely found in the rural areas and in Cap Haïtien, while the mulatto elite was centred on the capital and was strong in the southern cities of Jérémie, Les Cayes and Jacmel. The former were often landowners and the latter were, in addition, involved in commerce. The black elite looked to the peasants and to the army for support, and tended to parade a populist ideology. The mulatto elite relied on its ability to manipulate the constitutional machinery, with the aid of disaffected black generals, and propagated an explicitly elitist ideology. Writers from both groups, although they vigorously attacked all theories of racial inequality, were oriented towards European cultural patterns and tended to despise or ignore Haiti's African traditions. Black and mulatto authors competed in their protestations of patriotism and of the need to maintain an effective national independence, while both groups were on occasions prepared to invite foreign intervention rather than falling from power. This weakness was to prove fatal to the country's independence in the succeeding period.

5. Occupied Haiti

1911-1934

The fall of Antoine Simon in August 1911 inaugurated a period of acute governmental instability in Haiti. In the following four years, six presidents rapidly succeeded one another in office. No group within the country was capable of retaining political power owing to the deep divisions among the elite and to an increasing participation by the masses in the political life of the country. The ever-present colour question also served to divide Haitians into hostile groups, and gave politicians a stick with which to beat their opponents.[1] The situation was exacerbated by intervention in the internal politics of the country by the world powers. The existence of a large German colony in Haiti and the determination of the United States to gain strategic control of the Caribbean were among the principal destabilising factors. The American invasion and occupation of 1915 resulted in the re-establishment of the mulatto elite in office, and at first it looked as though the United States presence might aggravate the colour divisions which existed in the country. While large numbers of mulattoes collaborated with the invaders, the principal resistance in the early years came from black peasant irregulars. Yet among the first opponents of the occupation were such men as Elie Guérin, Moravia Morpeau and Georges Sylvain, who came from mulatto families. Also among the politicians there was a gradual disenchantment with the Americans; erstwhile collaborators Dantès Bellegarde, Sténio Vincent and Charles Moravia, among others, became critics of the occupation, and the nationalist front grew into a truly representative body. Race, the centripetal factor in Haitian politics, took precedence over colour with its centrifugal consequences. The clumsy actions of the Americans, who insisted on treating all Haitians of whatever colour as 'niggers', contributed to this growing solidarity. Paradoxically the Americans unintentionally succeeded, where Dessalines had failed, in uniting all Haitians under the name 'black'. The twenties saw a growing solidarity among Haitians; collaborators like Presidents Dartiguenave and Borno found themselves virtually isolated from national life, being maintained in office solely by United States military support. The literary and ethnological movements provided much of the intellectual stimulus for this revival of a national spirit based upon the conception of race; mulattoes were as much involved as blacks in these movements. At

142

last it appeared that the demon of colour had been exorcised from national life.

Yet the mulatto elite in its social and family life remained exclusive and continued to dominate the nationally owned sector of the economy. A new class was, however, emerging, whose members were unprepared to accept the old social system. These men came mostly from non-elite black families, and were frequently the products of the technical and professional schools set up by the Americans. Growing numbers of black teachers, doctors and lawyers were in evidence and it was they who provided the impetus for the *noiriste* movement of the thirties which culminated in the crisis of 1946.

I

Foreign interventions

In the previous chapter we noted the existence of a powerful German colony in Haiti. In order to circumvent the laws against foreign ownership of land, some Germans had married local women, and in 1912 a German school was opened in Port-au-Prince; this school would, in the words of the German minister, 'Germanize the descendants of Germans established in Haiti'. By 1914 the American State Department was informed that Germans controlled about 80 per cent of commerce in Haiti.[2] This growing economic interest had led in 1911 to German troops being landed in the capital to protect the property of their nationals. The United States minister in Haiti, H. W. Furniss, told the secretary of state, Philander Knox, 'Everyone knows of the complicity of the German merchants in the Leconte revolution and they also know that the Germans financed the Simon revolution of 1908 and the others before it, and doubtless will finance all those to follow.'[3]

Many Haitians also were disturbed by the growing power of the German colony, and one of them warned the British foreign secretary that the situation might lead Germany 'to seize and occupy a formidable stronghold in the Caribbean'.[4] The writer went on to ask Grey to use his influence to persuade the American government to intervene 'in view of prompting the restoration of order and peace by helping morally the National Progressive Party of which I am the leader'.[5] This party claimed to be the successor to the party which had been headed by Anténor Firmin, who had died in 1911 in exile on the island of St Thomas.

Germany was by no means the only country to show an interest in the internal politics of Haiti in this period. France continued to have important financial and commercial assets in the country, though she had lost effective control of the Banque Nationale to the Americans.[6] 'Every steamer brings experts of all nationalities who come to spy out the land', wrote the British diplomat Joseph Pyke in 1912.[7] The influence of the Syrian community continued to be a significant factor in Haitian politics, and was the cause of further foreign intervention. Persecution of the Syrians had abated somewhat during the presidency of Antoine Simon, but under Leconte the campaign against them had revived. The British in particular were keen to protect Syrian traders, many of whom were British citizens. As a British diplomat observed, these traders were some of the largest importers of English manufactured goods.[8]

In the second decade of the present century, however, the United States was the country most deeply involved in Haiti. We have already seen how during the previous century the Americans were eager to secure a naval base in the Caribbean, and how the Môle St Nicolas was one of the most favoured sites for such a base. With the completion of the Panama Canal in sight it became all the more important to obtain such a base and at the same time to prevent any further European penetration of the Caribbean. In 1903 the United States had secured Guantánamo Bay in Cuba as a naval base but, after some years, discontent with Guantánamo was expressed by military officers.[9] Interest in Haiti was therefore maintained for strategic reasons, and the United States invasion of 1915 can be seen as part of a whole strategy for control of the region. One American writer urged that the Monroe Doctrine implied that the country should achieve an absolute control of the Caribbean region and that this should be a fundamental principle of United States foreign policy.[10] In 1898 the Americans had secured Puerto Rico and Cuba; five years later they occupied Panama; in 1909 they invaded Nicaragua and in 1916 the Dominican Republic. In 1917 the United States purchased the Virgin Islands from Denmark.

Other factors influencing the American decision to invade were more narrowly economic. In 1910 an important concession had been granted to James P. McDonald to construct a railway and to develop land on each side of the line. It was suggested by the British consul that this contract was 'forced upon Hayti by the United States Minister on behalf of McDonald as an American citizen and that it will inevitably spell ruin to Hayti'. The nature of the financial guarantees which the Haitian government was pressurised into giving was such that the country would fall into the hands of her creditors.[11] Also in the years following 1910 United States bankers had gained control of the Banque Nationale. Although there were certain financial and commercial interests in the United States favourable to military intervention, it would, I believe, be a mistake to see this narrowly economic factor as the principal motive for military intervention by the United States

government. 'The major emphasis of the Wilson administration's
Haitian policy', writes Hans Schmidt, 'was on negative interdiction of
foreign interests, rather than on positive promotion of American economic imperialism.'[12] Nevertheless, the State Department relied heavily
on information supplied to it by Roger Farnham, who had significant
financial interests in the Banque Nationale and in other enterprises;
there can be no doubt that he was attempting to use the United States
government for his own purposes, but the government was also using
him. The policy of 'dollar diplomacy' involved encouraging Americans
to invest in Latin America in order to reduce the dependence of Latin
American countries on European capital, and thus to decrease the likelihood of European political and military intervention in the affairs of
the continent.[13] In fact the idea of an American bank in Haiti had been
suggested in 1905 by the United States minister in Port-au-Prince,
W. F. Powell, and the efforts of Farnham and the New York City Bank
to gain control of the Banque Nationale were supported and encouraged
by the State Department.[14] American policy was also influenced by
more general theories about the importance of sea power, and of
geographical contiguity, together with the doctrine of 'manifest
destiny'.[15]

There was thus an interaction between economic and financial
factors on the one hand and strategic factors on the other, but with
the latter being the more important reason for the government's
decision to invade. Also closely connected to the strategic factors was
the belief genuinely held by many Americans that they had a divinely
ordained duty of 'protection and regulation in regard to all these little
states in the neighborhood of the Caribbean', as President Theodore
Roosevelt had put it in 1904.[16] The United States wanted neighbours
who were stable, orderly and prosperous, and was prepared to take
steps to ensure that such was the case, both for American strategic and
economic interests and also for the good of these countries themselves.
There is a strong element of misguided altruism in much United States
foreign policy and it is particularly noticeable in the case of the Democratic Party. It is surprising that the Americans could, often with sin-
cerity, believe that they were in duty bound to maintain order and
justice in the Caribbean, while they were quite clearly incapable of
enforcing it in parts of their own country.

The occupation

The immediate occasion for United States military intervention was the
riot in Port-au-Prince which followed the murder by President Vilbrun
Guillaume of political opponents who had been lodged in the city
gaol. Guillaume was faced with a revolt in the North led by Rosalvo

Bobo and the prospect of an imminent rebellion in the capital. The likely consequence of these movements was the fall of his government and the accession to power of Bobo, who was generally disliked by the elite and who was believed to be anti-American, owing to criticisms which he had made of the McDonald contract. In fact, although Bobo opposed any suggestion of handing over customs control to the United States, he was by no means against foreign investment in Haiti. He went so far as to declare that the introduction of American capital into Haiti was 'one of my most ardent and constant dreams'; he believed that a large foreign loan was a necessary condition of economic development in Haiti.[17]

It was the the slaughter of 167 political prisoners on 27 July 1915 which precipitated the revolt against Vilbrun Guillaume in the capital. The president fled to the French embassy, which was eventually stormed by the crowd; he was hauled from the embassy and torn to pieces by the angry relations and friends of his victims. Crowds rushed through the streets clutching pieces of the former president. One man was seen with the thumb in his mouth crying, 'Voici ma pipe, m'ap fumin.'[18] It was at this juncture that the marines landed and began nineteen years of occupation.

It is not the purpose of this chapter to discuss in detail the policy pursued by United States officials in the period of the occupation, but simply to sketch the main lines of this policy, as a background against which developments in Haitian political thought and action may be understood. The Americans decided to adopt a system of indirect rule and looked for a likely candidate for the presidency of Haiti, who would be able to command a degree of support from local elites, but who would at the same time collaborate fully with the United States administration – that is, who would do as he was told. Many members of the elite, together with Syrian traders, had welcomed the American invasion, which had brought deliverance from political instability and from the rule of the potentially radical Rosalvo Bobo. They saw in the occupation a chance to re-establish the political hegemony of the mulatto elite which had been gradually eroded in the preceding decades. 'We are not at war with the United States', wrote Charles Moravia; 'the Americans are the enemies of a Sovereign Despotism and occupy the country to prevent its restoration.'[19] In a reasoned apology for the United States invasion Edouard Depestre argued that administrative confusion, financial irresponsibility and political instability in Haiti had led to and had justified foreign intervention.[20] Other elite Haitians, while secretly collaborating with and advising the Americans, refused to commit themselves publicly to the occupation. Jacques Nicolas Léger, who had been Haitian minister in Washington for many years and who had probably encouraged United States intervention, was approached by the occupying power as a possible candidate for the presidency. He was, however, acute and sensitive enough to realise that such collaboration would be deplored and denounced by future generations, and he politely refused the post. 'I am for Haiti', he told Captain Beach, 'not for the United States.'[21] Some elite politicians, including Moravia Morpeau, openly opposed the U.S.–Haitian convention in the senate; Morpeau declared that it would be a shameful day for the senate if it consented to such an abdication of sovereignty.[22] Other distinguished Haitians refused the ignominious office of puppet president, and the United States administration turned to Philippe Sudre Dartiguenave, president of the senate, whose 'election' was effected by the legislature, under the protection of American marines. The United States secretary of the navy, Josephus Daniels, and Robert Lancing of the State Department are both on record as having voiced doubts about the 'high-handed' way in which the election was conducted.[23] The rival candidate, Bobo, was regarded by the Americans as unreliable, despite his professed willingness to co-operate with the occupation forces. After the election he left Haiti for exile in Cuba; later he went to Jamaica and then to France, where he died in 1929.[24]

In 1918 a new constitution was promulgated which contained an article permitting foreigners to own land in the country, reversing a provision which went back to Dessalines.[25] This constitution, which according to the American presidential candidate, Warren Harding, was jammed down the throats of the Haitian people 'at the point of bayonets borne by U.S. Marines',[26] was largely the work of Franklin D. Roosevelt, then assistant secretary of the navy. The change in the constitution and the military presence of the United States encouraged new foreign investment in Haiti, and a number of American companies acquired land for agricultural development.[27] The policy of the occupation was in the first place, then, to encourage United States investment in Haiti. The technical and vocational schools set up by the Americans in Haiti were specially designed to train Haitians to fill middle level posts of a semi-skilled kind, particularly in agriculture. Dr George Freeman, who headed the Service Technique, told students:

when I first travelled over your country and studied your natural resources, I found valleys, rich in fertility, capable of loading thousands of steamers with cargoes of sugar, cotton, bananas, pineapples, and other fruits . . . How appropriately there sprung to my thought that expression of our Holy Master, 'The harvest is ripe but the reapers are few'.[28]

The Americans hoped that political stability and responsible government could be developed in Haiti on the basis of a new middle class, and it was the policy of the administration to encourage the growth of such a class. Arthur Millspaugh, for some years U.S. financial advisor in Haiti, referred to this explicit policy of the occupation, and in 1930 the Forbes Commission noted how this new middle class was being regarded by the old elite as constituting a challenge to its position.[29] As we shall see, many of those elite Haitians who at first welcomed the American invasion became increasingly disenchanted with their un-invited guests. The idea that a strong middle class in Latin America would provide the foundation for stable political democracy lay behind much of the policy of the Kennedy administration, and received academic support from such writers as J. J. Johnson and John Gillin.[30]

With respect to the Haitian armed forces it was American policy to develop a small efficient army, and to ensure that this army played no active role in the politics of the country. As we have already noted, there was a long tradition of militarism in politics, going back into the colonial period, when the French governor general was an army man. In this matter, as in many others, the American policy worked only so long as they were on the spot to enforce it.

The Americans, then, aimed to make Haiti a stable and subservient neighbour and a safe field for investment. It was, in the words of Millspaugh, 'a unique laboratory for social, economic, political and administrative paternalism'.[31] In the sphere of sanitary and medical services, road building and other public works and in technical education Haiti derived some benefit from the American presence; but even in these infrastructural fields the policy of the occupation was largely guided by the need to make Haiti an attractive country for private investment. In 1918 Dartiguenave's government declared war on Germany and was then able to seize German property and to intern a number of German nationals. After the war many German business-men were expelled from the country. The occupation also put an end to the privileged position which had been enjoyed by French commerce, thus leaving the field clear for United States economic penetration. Financial policy, which concentrated on the repayment of foreign debts, certainly benefited American capitalists; summing up the situation, Hans Schmidt has written, 'Occupation financial policy, like most facets of the occupation, looked first to American interests.'[32]

The nationalist reaction

The American invasion of July 1915 met with little military resist-ance,[33] but growing discontent on the part of the peasants, who were being compelled to work on road building, under the revival of an ancient system known as the *corvée*, resulted in the *cacos* rebellion of 1918, led by Charlemagne Péralte and Benoît Batraville. Péralte was born in 1886 in the town of Hinche, where his family owned land. He was a devout Roman Catholic as a youth, and attended the Collège St Louis de Gonzague in Port-au-Prince from 1900 to 1904. In 1908 he took part in a rising against the government of Nord Alexis, but when it collapsed he returned to Hinche. After joining the army he became commandant of the arrondissement of Port-de-Paix, but resigned from the army in 1915 and returned to cultivate the land in Hinche. Péralte was arrested by the Americans in 1917 for involvement in an attack upon the home of a United States officer, and was sentenced to five years' hard labour. He escaped from captivity, and was able to mobilise several thousand peasant irregulars.[34] The revolt took on such proportions that the local *gendarmerie* was quite incapable of dealing with it. Direct intervention by the United States marines was necessary, and reinforcements had to be rushed to the scene. In 1919 Péralte set up a provisional government in the north, and declared his intention of driving the invaders into the sea. 'Today our patience is at an end', he cried,

we demand our rights, unrecognised and flouted by the unscrupulous Americans who, by destroying our institutions, deprive the Haitian people of all their resources, and thrive on our name and our blood. With cruelty and injustice, the Yankees have for four years cast ruin and destruction on our territory . . . We are prepared to make any sacrifice to liberate Haitian territory.[35]

After considerable bloodshed and many months of fighting Péralte was betrayed by a member of his own family and was killed in November 1919. Resistance continued for some months under Batraville, who was killed in May 1920. The small pocket book which he was carrying suggests that he saw the *cacos* struggle in religious terms.[36]

Although military resistance was thus put down, political and journalistic opposition to the occupation increased. In fact the *cacos* rebellion and the ruthless way it was suppressed did much to stimulate opposition from the intellectuals. Such journals as *Haïti Intégrale*, *La Patrie*, *La Ligue* and *La Tribune* attacked the American occupation.[37] L'Union Patriotique, led by Georges Sylvain, Pauléus Sannon, Sténio Vincent and Jean Price Mars, was organised throughout the country, and in 1921 claimed a membership of 16,000.[38] The union demanded the immediate end to martial law, the abrogation of the 1915 convention which legalised the occupation, the calling of a constituent assembly and the 'withdrawal, within a short period, of the United States Military Occupation'.[39] Another group, L'Union Nationaliste, was particularly concerned about concessions of land which were being made to United States companies, and the consequent expropriation of the peasants. Percival Thoby called for the protection of small peasants and squatters against 'the tentacles of dollar imperialism'. He saw the introduction of North American capitalism in Haiti as the consequence of an extended campaign by Haitian publicists who had mistakenly insisted on 'the necessity of foreign capital for the development of our agricultural resources and the exploitation of our mines'.[40] Georges Séjourné claimed that a result of the expropriations would be the creation of a landless proletariat wandering from one factory to another. 'A people which alienates its land and relinquishes to foreigners the role of cultivator and exploiter', he declared, 'falls inevitably into economic slavery.' François Dalencour joined the chorus of protest, and attacked the law of December 1922 which made provision for the long-term leasing of land to foreign companies; it constituted nothing less than 'the legalised assassination of the Haitian rural proletariat'.[41]

Many of those elite Haitians who had at first welcomed the Americans went over to the opposition. Charles Moravia was imprisoned four times, and one visiting American remarked in 1925 that there were enough pressmen in Port-au-Prince gaol to start a school of journalism.[42] Educated and sophisticated Haitians objected to the vulgarity and to the racial prejudice of the Americans. Accustomed to thinking of themselves as the light-skinned aristocracy of the country these men now found that in the eyes of North Americans they were all 'niggers'.[43] Furthermore, they objected to the educational policy of the occupation, which laid emphasis, as we have seen, upon technical rather than upon traditional classical studies. One visitor noted the 'disrespect for the Haitian schools', and the consequent denial to them of 'any but the most meagre financial support'.[44] Dantès Bellegarde, for some time minister of education under Dartiguenave fought against this policy of the Americans, but without success.[45] The resentment of elite Haitians against the materialism of the North Americans is reflected in the novel *Le nègre masqué*, by Stéphen Alexis. Another writer, Jean F. Brierre, recalled the dismay of his fellow students, who had been brought up to translate the classical authors of Greece and Rome into French, only to be told 'all that is useless and absurd. You must earn a living.'[46] Similar objections to the growing cultural influence of the United States in Latin America were voiced by the Peruvian author F. García Calderón; North American influence was leading to 'the triumph of mediocrity, the multitude of primary schools, the vices of utilitarianism, the cult of the average citizen'.[47] Haitian intellectuals also complained about the increase in tax on imported pianos, while record players manufactured in the United States were easily purchased. Catts Pressoir criticised later United States assistance programmes for a similar 'prejudice against the elite', and for encouraging the growth of a clique of U.S.-oriented teachers, doctors and technical experts.[48]

Many Haitians who opposed the nationalist movements of the day nevertheless made professions of patriotism. In his journal *Le Courrier du Soir* Duval Duvalier applauded 'le véritable amour de la patrie'; the journal, however, attacked L'Union Patriotique, accusing its leaders of having selfish political ambitions.[49] The ideas of Duval Duvalier are perhaps of special interest as it is likely that he influenced the development of the young François. His writings are full of patriotic fervour, extolling the 'glories of the past', and reminding his readers of 'the love which we owe to our ancestors', for it is they who have helped to create 'le génie national'.[50] There is also in them a somewhat moralistic strain: the virtues of altruism, honesty and modesty are frequently commended.[51]

There were, however, in Haiti still those who were prepared to defend the American occupation. President Louis Borno, elected in 1922, was unapologetic about his role as puppet president. He persecuted his political opponents, and attacked 'the blind prejudice and the reactionary passions of nationalist extremists'. He pointed to the achievements of the occupation and referred to it as 'one of the most beneficent applications of that high Christian duty of assistance and mutual aid which is as mandatory among nations as it is among men'.[52] Borno was, of course, maintained in power solely by American arms, and both he and his patrons appear to have been unaware of the explosive state of affairs in 1929. The American high commissioner, in his report of January 1929, observed complacently that the peasants who had previously opposed the Americans were beginning to look on the occupation as a friend. 'The spirit of animosity', he went on, 'held, a few years ago, by a small group of Haitians against the Americans is gradually fading'.[53] Later in the same year, however, a demonstration by students of the agricultural college at Damiens led to nationwide strikes and demonstrations against the Americans and against the Borno government. At Marchaterre, in the South, United States marines fired on a demonstration of unarmed peasants, killing and wounding a number. President Hoover sent a commission of enquiry to Haiti to determine the causes of discontent and to advise on future policy. Meanwhile, after a brief interregnum, the nationalist politician Sténio Vincent was elected to replace Borno. Coming from an elite mulatto family, Vincent, after a brief period of collaboration with the Americans, had joined the nationalist movement. The leading contenders for the presidency were all committed to securing American withdrawal at the earliest possible moment.

The Forbes commission of enquiry criticised certain aspects of American policy in Haiti, and advocated a rapid Haitianisation of the higher ranks of the army. Vincent began negotiations with the United States government for the withdrawal of troops, and reached agreement with President F. D. Roosevelt in 1934.[54] Although Vincent claimed credit for securing the evacuation of the marines, proudly proclaiming himself as the second liberator of Haiti, the end of the occupation has also to be seen in the context of Roosevelt's so-called 'good neighbor policy'. The threat of European intervention had receded, a superficial stability had been achieved in Haiti, and a climate safe for American investment had been created. Continued military involvement by the United States was therefore unnecessary, costly and unwise.

II

The ethnological movement

The nationalists of the occupation period were concerned not simply with political liberation. Just as, in the previous century, the Napoleonic invasions of Germany had led Germans to delve into their folklore and into the established traditions of the peasants to discover the roots of their 'national identity', so in Haiti nationalism was closely connected to the ethnological movement. Appeal was made not only to a national literary heritage, but to oral traditions and to the language in which these traditions were passed on from one generation to another, the *créole* language. In his address to the inaugural meeting of the Société d'Histoire et de Géographie d'Haïti in 1925, H. Pauléus Sannon made this point:

all peoples instinctively go back to the past in order to search in their history for lessons of collective patriotism, for new rules of conduct, whether it be for the purpose of being able better to defend their threatened existence, or for re-covering more rapidly from their fall.[55]

But in Haiti this meant facing up to the deep division which had for over a century existed between the small 'cultured', educated and literate elite and the mass of poor illiterate peasants. 'Haitian society', declared J. C. Dorsainvil in 1909, 'has all the appearance of being composed of two juxtaposed societies.' On the one hand there was a selfish elite and on the other a stagnating mass living at the level of beasts.[56]

Justin Chrysostome Dorsainvil was born in Port-au-Prince in 1880, and was educated by the Frères d'Instruction Chrétienne and later at the Lycée Pétion. After studying medicine, he became a school teacher, then an official in the ministry of education; he died in 1942. In a series of seminal articles in *Le Matin* during the years 1907 and 1908, Dorsainvil had analysed the problems of Haiti. He pointed to the natural tendency of the elite to become a closed caste and he predicted that the middle class, based in agriculture, commerce and industry, would be the principal agent of social evolution in the country.[57] He argued that Haiti could be understood only in the light of its ethnic and historical roots. Although the human race is basically one, each ethnic sub-group has 'une physionomie spéciale' which it must conserve intact.[58] It is through a study of history that this ethnic identity is to be discovered, and in the case of Haiti the experience of slavery and the successful struggle against European imperialism has resulted in 'a new *créole* race'.[59] In these early writings Dorsainvil was clearly influenced by ideas of social psychology and evolution which were current in Europe at the time, and he referred in particular to the ideas of Le Play. He saw education as the means of developing the 'ethnic capital' of a people, and maintained that it must therefore be designed to suit that people's psychology.[60] There is in some of these writings an almost fatalistic strain which suggests that the life of the individual is determined by the ethos of the group to which he belongs; only in the case of the exceptional individual is escape from this collective fate possible.[61] Dorsainvil was one of the first Haitians to attempt a sympathetic understanding of the Voodoo religion, being particularly concerned to explain the phenomenon of possession in terms of current psychological theories. In his essay *Vôdou et névrose*, first published in 1913, he claimed that it is impossible to penetrate the mentality of the Haitian people without a profound study of their African origins.[62] These pre-occupation writings of Dorsainvil can clearly be seen to contain the seeds of the ethnological movement of the nineteen-twenties.

Dorsainvil's later writings develop the ideas outlined above. While not wishing positively to assert the physical or biological foundations of racial difference, he insisted, in a later work, that centuries of human history have diversified the races, so that 'each race has its own genius and it would be the most lamentable error to believe simply that it can assimilate itself by study or by imitation to the genius of another race'.[63] He spoke of a 'métaphysique raciale', and claimed that African people have a profound intuitive understanding of the world, 'which is not at all made up of abstract logic; which has, rather, its own affective logic, the logic of sentiment, allied to the primordial intuitions of the race'. The Haitian people basically form a branch of this African race. 'Personally', he went on, 'I am an African whom a historical accident has displaced from his original *milieu*.'[64] He attacked those intellectuals from the Haitian elite who wrote as though the black African slaves of Saint Domingue had simply perished on the plantations without posterity; their beliefs and traditions had in fact been perpetuated by the peasants of independent Haiti.[65] Dorsainvil wrote of the 'Guinean soul' of the Haitian people, which brought with it from Africa certain beliefs, attitudes and associated practices, and he saw the Voodoo religion as corresponding to certain psychological characteristics and needs of African people.[66] He assailed the education system in Haiti for having ignored racial factors and for having operated on the assumption that a group which had violently been uprooted from the soil of Africa could be turned into cultural Frenchmen. He thought that the individualism which was characteristic of European culture was inappropriate for the Haitian mentality.[67] While recognising the social and political role which the Voodoo cult had played in the Haitian past, and in particular its contribution to the revolt of 1791, Dorsainvil argued that its influence in his own day was harmful. It encouraged peasants to look for solutions to economic and technical problems in propitiatory sacrifices and in other cultic practices rather than in scientific analysis, and he referred to Voodoo as 'notre grand malheur'.[68]

Dorsainvil insisted that Haiti belongs neither to Anglo-Saxon North America, nor to the Hispanic South and Centre. Over a hundred years of independence had led to a specifically Haitian way of life, in which African traditions predominate. The colonial past had, however, left its mark, and although the principal economic influence in the black republic might be the United States, the Haitian soul is 'more at home on the banks of the Seine than beside the Potomac'.[69] Dorsainvil noted that Haiti was unique on the continent in having lost the whole of its dominant class during the struggle for independence, and it thus lacked that kind of continuity and contact with the former metropolis which the survival of elites had facilitated in the other independent republics of America.[70] The absence of such an elite stretching back to colonial times had also led to a certain social and political instability. Dorsainvil put forward some concrete proposals to remedy the defects which he had indicated. In the first place he advocated strengthening the independent peasants by appropriating more land for their use and by instituting regional development banks. Secondly he looked forward to the formation and growth of a strong middle class in the towns. These two classes might then provide the leadership which Haiti required, and also permit a degree of social mobility.[71]

From another standpoint Dr Arthur Holly had also considered the role of the Voodoo cult in Haitian history and had emphasised the African traditions of the people. He was the son of Jacques Théodore Holly, the first bishop of the Anglican church in Haiti.[72] Holly called himself an 'ésotériste', and expounded some of his peculiar ideas in a number of books and articles. He believed that individuals naturally belong to different classes, according to their psychological temperament, and that this temperament can be discovered by astrology.[73] Elites were therefore natural; but in Haiti the ruling class was a pseudo-elite, which was unqualified to rule and which had consequently brought ruin on the country.[74] Holly maintained that each race has its peculiar genius, which reflects itself in the psychological aptitudes of the people,[75] and he wrote of an African mentality which depends upon a mystical association between the individual soul and the collective soul. There are 'invisible forces which direct our destiny as a race', and which must be respected.[76] He therefore attacked those who allowed Haitian children to be educated by Europeans and criticised the work of church schools in the country. The Haitian was in fact in danger of losing his personality in an attempt to adapt himself to European civilisation; he must return to his African origins and particularly to the Voodoo religion. The Haitian should take pride in his African heritage, for all the speculative and physical sciences were born in Africa.[77] It is through the Voodoo religion in particular, however, that the African race has contributed to the progress of mankind, and Haitians must direct to Legba and to Damballah the prayers which well up in their hearts.[78] Holly adopted a *noiriste* position in Haitian politics and called for a restoration of the black and red flag of Christophe's kingdom, for esoteric and symbolic reasons.[79] There is some similarity between the ideas of Holly and the position of a defrocked priest of the Eglise Episcopale, Jonathas William, expressed in *Le bouc emissaire*.

The third and most important founder of the ethnological movement in Haiti was Jean Price Mars, who was born in 1876 at Grande Rivière du Nord. He was the son of a Protestant father Eléomont Mars and his Catholic wife Fortuna Dalcour Michel. After attending the Collège Grégoire and Lycée Pétion, he entered medical school in Port-au-Prince. He later studied in Paris where he gained his doctorate. A long and distinguished career as school master, university lecturer and rector, deputy, senator, presidential candidate, cabinet minister, diplomat and author, earned for Price Mars the title 'doyen of Haitian intellectuals'. He recently died at the age of ninety-two.[80] In his early writings Price Mars was especially concerned with defects in the educational system in Haiti, and called for the writing of school text books which would make sense to local children; all the books used in school were explicitly directed to French children. He further advocated the setting up of technical and agricultural schools throughout the country, and also a system of evening classes.[81] While he noted the attacks which had been made on church schools by some of his fellow countrymen, and the demand that their teaching should be more 'in harmony with our historic origins and with the democratic ends we pursue', he maintained that many church schools were doing a good job. In one of these early articles on education Price Mars cited the decline in ignorance and 'superstition' among Haitians as evidence for a belief in racial equality, and he criticised Christians for occasionally confounding Christianity with 'African idolatry', attacking the clergy for 'not always being sufficiently vigorous in their struggle against Voodoo'.[82] Clearly at this stage there was very little of that sympathy for the Voodoo religion and for the traditional culture of the Haitian peasant which was characteristic of his later writing. There was, however, a refusal to accept the idea that the French culture to which the elite aspired was sufficient to justify talk about the 'Latin mentality' of the Haitian people; the elite constituted only a tiny minority of the population. With respect to the majority, Price Mars quoted Sir Harry Johnson's observation that, apart from their language and their garb, the peasants differed in nothing from their African ancestors.[83]

During the first world war Price Mars elaborated his critique of the role of the elite. Although slavery had been abolished before independence, a rigid separation between the elite and the masses remained. Instead of providing leadership and guidance for the masses, the so-called elite formed a closed circle concerned with maintaining its vested interests. The peasants of Haiti on the other hand were living in conditions of great poverty, where women in particular were expected to do the work of animals. These peasants had, however, conserved many of the customs and traditions of Africa, and had been touched only superficially by western civilisation and by Christianity.[84] This latter point Price Mars developed in a series of lectures which were eventually published under the title *Ainsi parla l'oncle*. The book is a study of Haitian folklore and popular traditions, and the author laid great stress on the African contribution to the peasant culture of Haiti. Price Mars set his face firmly against the dogma of most elite writers that the country was a cultural colony of France. The daily life of the countryside – its religion, its customs, its proverbs and tales, its music and its whole ethos – is not French; it is the result of a mixture, but 'when we submit these traditions to a comparative examination, they reveal immediately that with respect to the greater part of them, Africa is their country of origin'. Price Mars rebuked his fellow intellectuals for their refusal to recognise this fact: 'Ah, I know with what repugnance I am greeted in daring to speak to you of Africa and of things African! The subject appears to you inelegant and entirely devoid of interest, is this not so?'[85] The majority of Haitians were descended from African slaves who were brought in great numbers from different parts of the continent, though mostly from the west coast. These Africans belonged to various tribal groups and spoke different dialects, but they shared similar beliefs and practices. The French anthropologist Maurice Delafosse had already drawn attention in a number of his works to the common traditions which existed among black Africans, who 'present a remarkable unity from the moral and social point of view'.[86]

In his book Price Mars assailed the 'bovarysme collectif' of the Haitian elite, who misconceived the true nature of their country. Negroes had been told that they had no history, no religion, no morals and that their only hope was to acquire these things from Europe. So Haitian intellectuals tended to deny or to ignore their African past, setting themselves the 'grandiose and absurd task' of becoming coloured Frenchmen. An indication of the sickness which afflicted Haitians of the upper classes was the fact that many mulattoes, in order to dissociate themselves from Africa, even pointed with pride to their bastard origin — to 'the turpitudes of colonial promiscuity, to the anonymous shame of chance meetings' — as a title to social superiority.[87]

Much of *Ainsi parla l'oncle* was devoted to a study of the religious beliefs and practices of the Haitian masses: the Voodoo cult. With Delafosse and Leroy, Price Mars insisted that traditional African religion was not 'fetishism' — the superstitious worship of material objects — but 'animism' or 'dynamism' — a belief that there is a spiritual power which manifests itself in the world through material forms, 'particularly in the great cosmic forces: the sea, the earth . . . '[88] Haitian Voodoo is a development of this African religion, and cannot simply be dismissed as superstition. Certainly, Price Mars agreed, there is very often a superstitious and magical element in the Voodoo cult, but so there is in Christianity and all religious practices. Superstition, he maintained, is the fatal corollary of religion.[89] Voodoo is in fact a religion with 'a theology, a system of representation thanks to which, in a primitive manner, our African ancestors explained the natural phenomena'.[90] Price Mars insisted that it is important to understand the nature and the strength of popular beliefs and customs in order to appreciate the consequent conservatism of the peasant, and the resistance which he will put up to 'hazardous enterprises of reformers-in-a-hurry'; these beliefs were for him both 'the charm and the horror of peasant life'.[91] This conservative populism is a characteristic political implication of 'folklorism'; it is to be found in much German thought, not only at the beginning of the nineteenth century with writers like Adam Müller, but also among Nazi intellectuals.[92] As we shall see, it is present in the writings of Carl Brouard and the *Griots* group in Haiti.

Price Mars also defended *créole* as the medium through which oral traditions had been preserved in Haiti, and pointed to its vivid and lively forms of expression. Perhaps one day the *créole* language would become a means of bridging the gulf which separated the elite from the peasant masses. He criticised Haitians of an earlier generation for having attempted in their imaginative literature to follow European patterns and he joined in the call for a *littérature indigène*, which by this time had become fairly general, particularly as we shall see from young writers of the elite.[93]

From what has been said about these three founders of the ethnological movement in Haiti, it will be clear that Holly was very much less critical in his appreciation of Voodoo that were Dorsainvil and Price Mars, whose writings could not be described as 'apologetic' in the way that Holly's can. Furthermore it is interesting to note that both Holly and Dorsainvil put forward those ideas which have come to be associated with the *négritude* movement in a much more forceful and explicit manner than did Price Mars, who was nevertheless accorded the dubious title 'Father of *Négritude*' by Léopold Senghor. The notion that African people have a personality which is peculiar to them and distinct from that of the white races is one which later became popular in the black francophone world. In 1930 two Haitians resident in Paris, a Doctor Sajous and Miss Andrée Nardal, founded *La Revue du Monde Noir*; this was followed by *Légitime Défense* and later by *L'Etudiant Noir*. It was among the black students of Paris that *négritude* as a movement was born. The three leading ideologists of the movement were Léon Damas of Cayenne, Aimé Césaire of Martinique and Léopold Sédar Senghor of Senegal. Although there were certain connections between the ethnological movement in Haiti itself and these developments in Paris, Césaire has recently denied that he was directly influenced by Haitian writers, and sees the growth of *négritude* among the black students of Paris as a distinct enterprise which stemmed from many common causes.[94]

A parallel movement occurred in the Spanish-speaking Caribbean with the Afro-Cuban literature, and with Luis Palés Matos and others in Puerto Rico. A common theme among these writers is the decline and decadence of the European world, echoing the theory of Oswald Spengler. Alejo Carpentier in an early novel describes the life of a negro boy who derived a sense of dignity from his participation in the Cuban Voodoo cult, *santería*. In the presence of North Americans, 'he felt real pride in his primitive life, full of complications and magic subtleties which the men of the North never understood'.[95] With these poets and authors there was the same emphasis upon the rhythms of music and dance, and the sensuousness of African life, which is to be found in the *négritude* writers of the francophone black world. The movement had similar political and social aspects in strengthening national resistance to the growing power of the United States in the region. In his poem of 1934, 'West Indies Ltd.', Nicolás Guillén tells the easy-going 'harmless negro':

> Take your bread, do not beg for it.
> Take your light, take your definite hope
> Like a horse by the bridle.[96]

The literary revival

The writings of Dorsainvil, Holly and Price Mars, particularly those of the latter, were enormously influential in moulding the ideas of the younger generation during the occupation period. Reinforcing the impact of these writers, there were important influences from overseas. In the first place there had been a revival of interest in Africa among European anthropologists, who emphasised the significance of the

African past, and the sophisticated nature of many supposedly 'primitive' beliefs and customs. Suzanne Césaire later pointed to the importance of Léo Frobenius for the black intellectuals of the time; also there were the writings of Maurice Delafosse.[97] Among authors and artists there was a renewed interest in Africa. René Maran's novel *Batouala*, which described the life of African people in French Equatorial Africa, received the Prix Goncourt in 1921,[98] and among artists there was a discovery of African sculpture and music.[99] A third factor was the new literary movement among the negroes of the United States and the associated development of jazz. Particularly important in Haiti were the poems of Langston Hughes, Countee Cullen and the Jamaican Claude McKay. Price Mars drew the attention of his contemporaries to these movements, and René Piquion translated their verses into French.[100] The parallel movement of Afro-Cubanism in the Hispanic Caribbean also contributed to the Haitian revival.

It may seem paradoxical, but the first young intellectuals in Haiti to have responded to these movements came from the mulatto elite. In 1925 *La Nouvelle Ronde* was founded as an organ of youth. The second number contained an article by Antonio Vieux and Philippe Thoby-Marcelin, in which these young writers accused their predecessors of slavishly having followed European patterns of literature, concealing their lack of originality by a superficial use of local colour. They pointed to the revival of negro art and music overseas, claiming that time was ripe for a reorientation of Haitian cultural forms. 'A specifically national literature must be created', they insisted, 'on the basis of an analysis of the Haitian soul.'[101] In 1927 two journals appeared for the first time, *La Trouée* and *La Revue Indigène*, sponsored by a number of young mulatto writers including Normil Sylvain, Emile Roumer, Carl Brouard, Jacques Roumain, Richard Salnave, Daniel Heurtelou and Max Hudicourt. These young men came from elite families, but were in revolt against the past, and indignant at the American occupation of their native land. All were nationalistic in spirit, and many of them turned in their poems, novels and critical works to the life of the Haitian peasant as representing that which is authentically and specifically Haitian. Though nationalistic, many of these men were, however, proud of Haiti's French connection. Normil Sylvain wrote of the black republic's 'glorious destiny to maintain, with Canada and the French Antilles, the traditions and language of France'.[102] The somewhat ambivalent attitudes of Haitian intellectuals towards France is similar to the Puerto Rican approach to the Spanish colonial heritage; in reaction to the heavy-handed North American presence, Caribbean nationalists sometimes found themselves taking refuge in the vestiges of an earlier colonial system.

Perhaps the most influential member of this group was Jacques

Jacmel?

Roumain, who had only recently returned to Haiti after many years in Europe. He had been born in Port-au-Prince in 1907 of a prosperous family. At an early age he went to Switzerland, and later to France, Germany and Spain; but he was anxious to return and join the nationalist struggle against the 'detested Yankee'.[103] On his return to Haiti in 1927 he immediately plunged into the political and literary life of the country. His writings were nearly always passionate and often wild. Consider, for example, his reaction to the occupation, in an article entitled 'In praise of fanaticism'! Patriotism, he maintained, is firm and reliable only when it is held instinctively, blindly, fanatically, so that no subtle reasoning can modify it. 'The fanatic', he went on, 'the instinctive patriot, the only true one, says: "I do not wish to know. Man, you are a stranger and you tread the soil that my father trod. Shut your mouth which overflows with sweet lies. It is no good. I hate you."' With Georges Petit, Roumain published a 'Manifeste à la Jeunesse', in which they stated that there are neither negroes nor mulattoes, neither rich nor poor, neither town-dwellers nor country-dwellers, there are only Haitians who are oppressed by the Americans and their lackeys.[104] It was writings like these which soon brought Roumain into conflict with the authorities. In December 1928 he was arrested, together with Petit and other nationalists. They were condemned to prison and fined. Roumain was released in August 1929, but arrested again in October for having planned a seditious meeting of L'Union Patriotique. In the following two years Roumain published three novels, two of which were concerned with the life of the elite in the capital, while the third was about the Haitian peasant.

The writers associated with the literary revival were, then, fiercely nationalistic, but they had also been influenced by the ethnological movement, and there is to be found in many of their writings a frank acceptance of Haiti's African heritage. Jacques Roumain based one of his best-known poems on the widespread belief among Haitian peasants that after death the soul returns to Guinea:

> It's the slow road to Guinea
> No bright welcome will be made for you
> In the dark land of dark men:
> Under a smoky sky pierced by the cry of birds
> Around the eye of the river
>   the eyelashes of the trees open on decaying light
> There, there awaits you beside the water a quiet village
> And the hut of your fathers, and the hard
>   ancestral stone where your head will rest at last.[105]

Léon Laleau too, from a slightly earlier generation, accepted the African past, referring to 'un peu de ce sang noir des races africaines', which circulated in his veins, while in 'Trahison' he lamented the unequalled despair and suffering which comes from attempting to

> tame with words from Europe
> This heart which came to me from Senegal.[106]

In his *Poèmes d'Haïti et de France*, published in 1925, Emile Roumer celebrated the beauty of the black women of Haiti, and poured scorn on the pomposity of that elite from which he had sprung.

Carl Brouard, perhaps the most interesting and gifted poet of this period, went further and embraced the Voodoo religion. In his review of *Ainsi parla l'oncle*, Brouard declared that 'voodoo is our only creation, it is the certain pledge of an architecture, of a literature, of a national mystique'.[107] Carl Brouard was born in 1902, the son of a successful mulatto businessman and a German mother. After spending a short time at the Collège Saint Martial, he attended a small private school, coming under the influence of Dr Catts Pressoir, whose family owned the school. In 1922 he went to Paris for a brief period, where he was drawn towards religious and mystical movements like theosophy and sufism,[108] which he attempted to integrate into the Catholicism of his home life and the Protestant influences of his school. It was this religious concern which led Brouard to embrace Voodoo. He became a devotee of the *loas*, and many of his early poems reflect this commitment. An example is his 'Hymne à Erzulie'.[109] He celebrated the glories of Africa, but unlike the writers of the pre-occupation period it was not the ancient African civilisation of the Nile which attracted him. Rejecting European criteria of 'civilisation', it was Africa the 'savage' and 'primitive' continent, standing apart from the sophisticated and decadent west, whose praises he sang:

> Drum
> when you sound
> my soul screams towards Africa.
> Sometimes
> I dream of an immense jungle
> bathed in moon-light
> with hirsute, sweating figures,
> sometimes
> of a filthy hut
> where I drink blood out of human skulls.[110]

In this period Brouard wrote of the 'nigritie' of the Haitian soul.[111]

Roumain too rejected Christianity and assailed the Roman Catholic hierarchy in Haiti for its collaboration with the American occupation, for its 'negrophobia' and for its perpetuation of a colonial mentality. 'If the American is the adversary of our material independence', cried Roumain and Petit, in their 'Manifeste au Peuple Haïtien', 'the white French clergy are the adversaries of our spiritual independence, and one of the means for keeping us under the colonial yoke.'[112] Brouard, Roumain and some other writers of this period combined a populist belief in the virtue of the masses with a call for leadership and order. Brouard's verses 'Nous' and 'Vous' reflect this romantic admiration for the simplicity of the peasant which is contrasted with the sophisticated corruption of the intellectual:

> Nous
> les extravagants, les bohèmes, les fous
> Nous
> qui aimons les filles,
> les liqueurs fortes,
> la nudité mouvante des tables
> où s'érige, phallus,
> le cornet à dés.
> Nous
> les écorchés de la vie, les poètes.

'Vous', on the other hand, is addressed to the poor masses of Haiti, to the beggar, the unwashed, the peasant with calloused feet who descends from the mountain with his garden produce:

> You are the pillars of the edifice:
> Disappear
> And everything will collapse like a house of cards.[113]

The masses form a great tidal wave, ignorant of their potential; rise up, he cries, and nothing will remain in your path which is not washed clean, bleached like a bone. As we shall see, Brouard's call for discipline, combined with this populism, exercised a powerful influence on the political ideas of the *Griots* group of the 1930s.

In this period also Jacques Roumain and Richard Salnave paid tribute to the fascism of Mussolini,[114] while Normil Sylvain called for a re-establishment of the notion of order and for a hierarchical society.[115] Max Hudicourt pronounced the people 'incapable of directing themselves' and attributed a revitalised Italy to the powerful and all-embracing government of the *Duce*.[116] Again Etienne Charlier attacked a politics of demagogy in which 'the people' becomes a god to which sacrifice must be done.[117] There was, therefore, even among those writers who had been influenced by the ethnological movement and whose political ideas contained a strong element of populism, a widespread call for strong leadership and for a regime of order and discipline. Those Haitians who were less influenced by the revival of folklore — Charlier, Hudicourt and later Jules Blanchet — developed a kind of Saint-Simonian socialism, advocating a system in which government would be conducted by experts.

III

The two principal intellectual movements of this period, the literary and the ethnological movements, can both be seen as part of a general reaction to the United States occupation. The two were obviously connected, yet they contained within themselves the potential for fresh conflicts. Most of those involved in the literary movement believed that Haitian life was a unique blend of African and French strands, and that a *créole* culture should be allowed to grow. They revived the ideal set forth by Emile Nau and Beauvais Lespinasse in the 1830s and 1840s. They accepted the fact that they were African by race, but believed that biological factors were of no objective significance in the development of culture; in this they were the true descendants of Firmin and Price. With many of the thinkers of the ethnological movement, on the other hand, a real discontinuity in the concept of race can be discerned. Race for them meant more than a biological category; it was also social and cultural. The fact that Haitians were fundamentally African had implications in the fields of culture and of social organisation. In the nineteenth century a principal conflict among Haitian intellectuals was between those who wished to follow European models (either French or Anglo-Saxon) and a small group who argued for the development of a specifically *créole* tradition. In the present century, however, the field of battle has shifted. Few Haitian intellectuals since the time of the American invasion can be found who *explicitly* accept the European model. The conflict in the twentieth century has been between those who insist that Haiti is essentially African and those who believe in a *créole* culture. This is at the level of theory; in practice many of the most vociferous Africanists have adopted European customs and prejudices.

The occupation resulted in the immediate re-establishment of the mulatto elite in office, but beneath the surface changes were taking place in the social structure which were to spell the end of mulatto dominance in the political field. Again, on the surface, the colour divisions which had been the plague of nineteenth-century Haiti receded and a new national unity emerged. Yet the very intellectual movements which helped to inspire this unity contained seeds of future conflict. The ethnological movement in particular contributed to a reinvigorated *noiriste* ideology, in which the black legendary view of the past was enforced by the new racialism of *négritude*.

A number of factors contributed to the emergence of *négritude*, but, when all is said, we must acknowledge the radical discontinuity in black thought which this ideology signifies. It involved an acceptance of the European racial myth that the races are significantly different, and represents a *volte-face* in the position which had throughout the previous centuries been argued by black and coloured writers. They had been almost unanimous in accepting the 'Credo' formulated by W.E.B. Dubois in 1920:

I believe that all men, black and brown and white, are brothers, varying through time and opportunity, in form and gift and feature, but differing in no essential particular, and alike in soul and the possibility of infinite development.[118]

A few exceptions may be found; Edward Wilmot Blyden, the West-Indian-born Liberian patriot, would be one of them. Born in St Thomas in 1832, Blyden is perhaps the true father of *négritude*, with his belief in the distinctness of the African race and in the importance of an 'African personality', together with his emphasis upon the peculiar social and political institutions of Africa which were related to this personality. Blyden's bitter criticism of the mulattoes would also qualify him as a *noiriste*, in Haitian terms.[119]

Why *négritude* emerged as a significant movement among black writers in the 1920s and 1930s is difficult to say. Certainly there were political events and tendencies which contributed to a fresh determination on the part of black people to resist European pretensions. The defeat of Russia by the non-European nation of Japan in 1905, the growing tide of Pan-Africanism, determined to oppose the more brutal aspects of European colonialism, and the picture of European nations tearing each other apart during the first world war — all these things played a part in the development of black awareness. But these occurrences do not account for the adoption by blacks of specifically racialist theories. Surrealism, existentialism and a new awareness of Africa among European anthropologists and creative writers certainly contributed to the development of *négritude*, but the birth of *négritude* must be seen as a rupture in black thinking. In the following chapters we shall describe the evolution of this idea and its impact on the course of events in Haiti.

6. Literature and dogma

1930-1945

The victory of Sténio Vincent in the election of 1930 marks a turning point in our story. As we have seen, he took a strongly nationalist position, as did all the principal candidates, and it was only a matter of time for the Americans to decide that the military occupation must come to an end. Under the occupation racial pride had taken precedence over colour prejudice and, despite many differences of opinion, the nationalist movement was able to unite Haitians of different colours and of divergent ideological commitments. The young Lorimer Denis drew attention to this 'profitable' aspect of the occupation, when he observed in 1932 that in the face of the invader Haitians had been forced to unify their interests and their efforts and had also been compelled to search within themselves to discover their collective personality.[1] With the removal of the common enemy in 1934, however, old antagonisms revived and new causes of internal conflict soon emerged. The nationalist movement, having succeeded in its primary task, divided into those who were basically in favour of preserving the status quo of bourgeois mulatto hegemony, and those who argued for a major shift in the distribution of economic and political power. Among the latter it is possible to distinguish those who conceived of the problem primarily in terms of colour, the *noiristes*, from those who saw the issue in terms of economic class, the socialists. They agreed that the old elite must be deprived of its privileged position, but disagreed about how this might be achieved and about the system which should follow. Also it should be observed that the socialists were themselves divided into Marxists and 'technocratic' socialists.

The socialist intellectuals of the 1930s came mostly from mulatto elite families and many of their assumptions are clearly influenced by their social origin. They were either wildly unrealistic in their assessment of the possibilities for social revolution at this particular period, or shrewdly aware that the rhetoric of revolution and class antagonism might provide a means by which they could gain political power and thus perpetuate, in the name of the proletariat, a mulatto hegemony. Most of them wrote from the comfortable homes of Pétionville and the Bois Verna, and their practical knowledge of the workers was

165

restricted to a nodding acquaintance with their servants and with the tenants on their country estates. Very few of them, for example, were prepared to involve themselves in the embryonic labour movement, preferring to write poems about the suffering of the masses. The *noiriste* writers, on the other hand, came mainly from the rising black middle class. This is not, however, true of all of them; one outstanding exception is Carl Brouard, who, like de Vastey and Pinkcombe in the previous century, might be called a mulatto anti-mulatto, and who came from an elite family.

In this chapter I shall outline the theories of these radical intellectuals and also look briefly at the ideologists of the mulatto establishment. There were in the period a number of issues and occasions when many politicians and writers found themselves compelled to take a stand on one side or the other, and it is particularly illuminating to examine the way in which theorists have responded to these concrete situations. In the second part of the chapter, then, after glancing at the varying responses in Haiti towards European fascism, I shall examine in some detail two situations of confrontation: the so-called 'anti-superstition' campaign of 1941–2, and the political crisis of 1946.

In the years following the departure of the United States marines the dominating figure on the political stage was undoubtedly President Sténio Vincent. He was an experienced and skilled politician who, despite his basically conservative and authoritarian stance, was able to retain support from a wide cross-section of Haitian opinion. Vincent's following included not only traditional mulatto politicians but also new voices from the black middle class and a number of socialist writers. In an earlier chapter we saw how, as a young man, Sténio Vincent had been one of the first in Haiti to note the significance of the rising middle class. His earlier experience stood him in good stead when it came to the business of forming a viable administration, and he was able, by an astute combination of patronage and threat, to secure support from many potential opponents. Carl Brouard linked his name with that of Salomon as 'the two great benefactors of the Haitian proletariat', and *L'Assaut* (directed by Jules Blanchet and René Piquion) cried 'Vive Sténio Vincent, protecteur intraitable des masses prolétariennes'.[2] Those who refused to bend, men like Jacques Roumain, were to be found either in prison or in exile. It is no coincidence that Vincent is one of the few mulatto presidents in Haitian history for whom François Duvalier had a good word to say.

Vincent was succeeded in 1941 by the Haitian ambassador to the United States, Elie Lescot. The new president, also a mulatto, was very different from Vincent, and soon began to antagonise important sections in the country. In particular his *mulâtrification* of the administration (as Etienne Charlier called it) and his support for the 'anti-superstition' campaign alienated most black intellectuals and his unsophisticated conservatism had the effect of forcing many of the more radical among Vincent's supporters into opposition. Looking back, however, it is possible to see the intensification of the mulatto hegemony beginning under Vincent, in particular with the dismissal of the black army chief Démosthènes Pétrus Calixte in 1938. A photograph of the higher echelons of the armed forces in 1943 reveals the virtual absence of blacks,[3] and a survey of the diplomatic corps, the higher civil service and the cabinet in these years confirms the impression of mulatto dominance. This policy of clumsy and open discrimination was a major cause of the uprising in January 1946 and of the consequent fall of Lescot.

In foreign affairs during this period Haiti followed United States policy in general. Relations with the neighbouring Dominican Republic, however, deteriorated during the early thirties. The census of 1935 recorded the presence of over 50,000 Haitians in the Dominican Republic, mostly engaged in the sugar cane plantations. There were undoubtedly many more illegal Haitian immigrants who managed to escape the census. Rafael Leonidas Trujillo, who had gained power in Santo Domingo in 1930, posed as the defender of Catholic values and of European culture against the 'barbarous' hordes of the black republic. His policy, designed to check infiltration from the west and summarised in his slogan 'desafricanizar las fronteras', culminated in the slaughter of thousands of Haitians in 1937. Trujillo introduced Japanese settlers into the border region as part of this same policy.[4]

I

Noirisme

Perhaps the most active and influential protest movement of the post-occupation years was that which centred on the *Griots* movement, and which I shall call *noirisme*. The movement owed much to J. C. Dorsainvil and to Jean Price Mars, but its members developed the ideas of these ethnologists and incorporated them into an older tradition in Haitian thought which went back to Janvier, to Salomon and even to the writers of Christophe's northern kingdom. These *noiristes* of the 1930s emphasised Haiti's African past, believing that as Haitians were basically African in their genetic composition their culture and social structure should be allowed to mirror this fact. In particular they insisted on the centrality of Voodoo in the life of the country, and they assailed the Roman Catholic church for its attempts to impose upon the country an alien European culture. Furthermore they saw the history of Haiti largely in terms of a struggle between a mulatto elite and the black masses, and they attacked the church as one of the principal means by which the elite was able to retain credibility. They thus revived the anti-clericalism of the ultranationals, with the additional accusation that the church's dominance in the educational field had led Haitians to despise their African past. Most of these *noiriste* writers came from middle-class black families and had received their education in Haiti rather than in France; they were doctors, lawyers, school teachers, and were determined to challenge the hegemony of the ruling elite, both in the ideological and in the institutional fields. They revived the populist rhetoric of Salomon's National Party, and believed that power should be in the hands of an authoritarian government composed of middle-class blacks acting on behalf of the masses whose basic interests they were said to share.

In the late 1920s a small group of young men known as *les Trois D* began to meet regularly to consider the implications of the ethnological movement for their generation and for their class. The three Ds were Louis Diaquoi, Lorimer Denis and François Duvalier. It was Diaquoi who was the driving force in the group. He had been born at Gonaïves in 1907 and after attending the Collège St Louis de Gonzague in Port-au-Prince, he became a journalist, frequently contributing to radical and nationalist newspapers. He died at the early age of twenty-five in 1932.[5] Lorimer Denis was three years his senior, the son of a black senator from Cap Haïtien; he was a student at the Law School in Port-au-Prince and became a practising *avocat* and journalist. He was director of the Bureau d'Ethnologie from 1946 until his death in 1957. François Duvalier was born in Port-au-Prince in April 1907 and was raised by Duval Duvalier, a teacher, journalist and justice of the peace. He attended the Lycée Pétion in the capital and later was a medical student. After qualifying in 1934 he worked in a number of hospitals and clinics and was assistant to the United States army medical mission from 1943 to 1946. During this period he spent a year studying public health at Michigan University, and returned to work with anti-malaria and anti-yaws campaigns. Under Estimé he was secretary of state for labour and public health; with the fall of the president in 1950 he worked with an inter-American public health project and became one of the leading opponents of President Paul Magloire. He was elected president of Haiti in September 1957, and became president for life in 1964. Duvalier was married in 1939 and was the father of four children, one of whom, Jean-Claude, has succeeded him as president for life.

A few months before his death in 1932 Diaquoi had announced the formation of the *Griots* group, which was later to welcome into its membership two important poets, Carl Brouard and Clément Magloire *fils* (later known as Magloire Saint Aude). The group took its name from a traditional African institution; the *griot* is the poet, the storyteller, the magician of the tribe, who perpetuates tribal customs, beliefs and myths.[6] These men contributed articles to *Le Petit Impartial*, *L'Action Nationale* and other journals of the day, and in 1938, with financial aid from Carl Brouard's father, who was mayor of Port-au-Prince, they founded *Les Griots*. The group explicitly acknowledged its debt to the pioneers of the ethnological movement, particularly to Price Mars. 'It is in his work', declared Diaquoi, 'that we find our Gospel.'[7] They continued to emphasise the African past of Haiti, and urged their fellow countrymen to cease attempting to be 'ridiculous little whites'.[8] Denis and Duvalier claimed that the Haiti of their day was still a prolongation of colonial society, and they called for a revolution in values which would involve 'a profound transformation in mentality' and a radical transfer of power.[9] The future president portrayed the sad fate of the black man in a world dominated by European values:

> I then recalled the route traversed by my ancestors
> of far-off Africa —
> The sons of the jungle
> Whose bones during 'the centuries of starry silence'
> Have helped to create the pyramids.
> And I continued on my way, this time with heavy heart,
> In the night.
> I walked on and on and on
> Straight ahead.
> And the black of my ebony skin was lost
> In the shadows of the night.[10]

Denis and Duvalier pointed to the 'splendours of the past civilisation' of Africa, and claimed that in their own day the black race was once more taking the lead in matters of art and music; there was 'a veritable renaissance of negro values in the world'.[11] These two writers insisted that the biology of a racial group determines its psychology, which in turn determines its 'collective personality'. The specifically African way of understanding the world is thus to be accounted for in genetic rather than in environmental terms.[12] Duvalier agreed with Gobineau that the races are significantly different from one another, and that this difference has its roots in biological factors. He conceded that the Haitian people are racially mixed, European and African, but nevertheless they are a people 'whose mentality is characterised by the predominance of the latter'.[13] It is, then, according to these two *Griots* writers, 'by the laws of ancestral heredity that the specific features of the forefathers of the most distant off-spring are preserved in the psychology of their descendants'. In particular the black man is characterised by an artistic temperament; 'sensibility forms the quintessence of the black soul'.[14] Duvalier and Denis reminded their fellow countrymen of the Pan-African movement, and of the growing anti-colonial campaign in Africa itself. They compared British colonial methods favourably with those of France, inasmuch as the former allowed for some emphasis upon traditional cultures. They pointed to the economic consequences of this anti-colonial movement which were disturbing the 'guardian powers', 'a movement which consists in systematically discarding the great metropolitan firms and replacing them by indigenous companies of commerce or industry, with a view gradually to recover industrial as well as agricultural exploitation'. They went on to denounce their fellow Haitians for a misplaced feeling of superiority from which they suffered with respect to Africans and for 'the stupid colonial prejudices which handicap us'.[15]

Kléber Georges Jacob, another associate of the *Griots* group, attacked those who refused to talk about 'race'. Although it is impossible to point to pure races 'in the zoological sense' it is undeniable that races, as social phenomena, each have a distinctive collective psychology.[16] In response to the racial obsession of the white world, he opposed a negro conception of race.[17]

The *noiriste* writers of the post-occupation years continued the re-evaluation of the Voodoo religion which had been initiated in the previous generation. Some echoed the sentiments of Carl Brouard and became devotees of the *loas*, others attempted a more objective study of Voodoo beliefs and practices. René Piquion expressed a desire to prostrate himself before the shrines of the African gods worshipped by his ancestors, and he attacked the role of Christianity in Haiti. The Christian ethic, with its teaching of patience, love and turning the other cheek, 'moulds despairing cowards rather than men'. The traditional teachings of the African religions are more robust and humane.[18] Such an explicit attack upon Christian moral teaching was rare, but, as we shall see, there were frequent criticisms of the role played by the Roman Catholic church in Haiti. Voodoo was, for Denis and Duvalier, 'the transcendent expression of racial consciousness before the enigmas of the world'.[19] It was a crystallisation of the origins and the psychology of the Haitian people, which 'perpetuates the African past'. This is certainly true, but it is more dubious to claim that Voodoo was 'the supreme factor of Haitian unity' and that it was the inspiration for Haitian independence.[20] It will be recalled that Toussaint, Dessalines and Christophe were fierce opponents of the cult and that since the earliest days it has been opposed by large sections of the elite, black and mulatto alike.

The colour question was, according to these *noiriste* writers, quite central in the history of Haiti, and they claimed that colour prejudice continued to be a powerful factor in their own day. In a series of articles entitled 'Satan conduit le bal', Louis Diaquoi asserted that colour prejudice lay at the very basis of the social and political life of the country. The politics of Haiti was a field of battle where the sides were drawn up largely on the basis of 'caste' (that is, colour). The mulattoes in general have united to obstruct the blacks, while the latter, sadly divided among themselves and jealous of each other, have delivered themselves over to an interminable war. Diaquoi denounced the religious and educational institutions of the country, particularly the large Christian schools like St Louis de Gonzague and Le Petit Séminaire St Martial, where there was 'a visible line of demarcation between the young black and the young mulattoes'.[21] He assailed the southern city of Jérémie as 'le boulevard du préjugé de couleur'.[22] Kléber Georges Jacob also claimed that colour prejudice had been 'responsible for our contemporary poverty as it has been the artisan of our waste'.[23] These *noiriste* writers thus confirm at least part of the thesis of this book, in their recognition of the importance of colour in Haitian politics and of the way in which the colour divisions have constituted a threat to effective independence.

These men were, however, victims of a legendary view of the Haitian past, and they further developed the black legend which they had received from the *noiristes* of a previous generation. Black leaders of the past were portrayed as the real defenders of the masses and as the true guardians of national independence, while mulatto leaders and politicians (frequently acting behind the mask of a black president, the so-called *politique de doublure*) had betrayed the people by feathering their own nests at the expense of the national interest. These writers were for Toussaint rather than for Rigaud; for Dessalines and Christophe but against Pétion and Boyer; for Acaau and Pierrot, but against Geffrard; for Salnave (one of the few mulattoes to appear on the side of the angels), Salomon and the National Party, rather than Boisrond Canal, Boyer Bazelais and the Liberals.

The *Griots* writers of this period evolved a whole political theory on the basis of their biological and social ideas. Duvalier stated that the social is prior to the political and that the political battles of the past must be seen as reflections of a struggle between social classes; *la politique de doublure* was evidently an attempt to appease the anger of the black masses.[24] Duvalier and Denis insisted that the solution to Haitian problems must be sought from within the country; government must be based upon the psychological and social realities of a particular people, which find their origin in racial characteristics. 'It is totally unscientific', they wrote, 'to confer according to our own good pleasure this or that form of government on a human group.'[25] Duvalier and those associated with him at this time claimed that political power should be wrested from the politicians of the old elite, and that an alliance must be forged between the rising black middle class and the masses. They surveyed the history of Haiti and saw political power monopolised by the largely mulatto bourgeoisie and employed in the interests of this small class. The younger *noiriste* writers took up the charges which had been made by Price Mars and Dorsainvil against the old elite, denouncing the selfishness and wickedness of this class. Karl Lévêque has recently drawn attention to the strongly moralistic tone of Duvalier's condemnation of the elite and to his call for a new, purer, austere elite in Haiti.[26]

The political theory of this group was, like that of many of their contemporaries, anti-liberal. Diaquoi assailed talk about liberty of the press, free elections and democracy as sordid tinsel designed to mislead the masses.[27] Liberalism, declared a writer in *L'Action Nationale*, 'is not an attribute of the Haitian temperament'.[28] Georges Jacob described republican institutions and democratic beliefs as constituting 'a cancerous virus' in Haiti, and providing a front behind which the interest of the masses had been sacrificed to those of the bureaucracy.[29] In a number of articles published in 1934 René Piquion argued that old ideas of liberal democracy must be replaced by respect for authority and discipline. He called for a system of dictatorship which he defined as 'reason and will allied to force in the service of the nation'.[30] While he rejected the idea that Italian fascism or German national socialism could be transplanted into the Caribbean, the system which he advocated for Haiti was in many respects similar.[31] 'Authority', he cried, 'is a sacred thing. Let us establish the mystique of authority. Force remains a beautiful thing, to be respected even when it crushes us.'[32]

Apart from constitutional changes, these thinkers demanded further concrete reforms, including a proper respect for the Voodoo religion, a new emphasis upon African culture in music, art and literature, a restructuring of the educational system and particularly a decreasing role for the Roman Catholic church in this field. The church was largely dominated by European clergy, and was regarded as the principal weapon employed by the francophile mulatto elite for maintaining the predominance of western culture in Haiti and for defending their own superior position. Georges Jacob insisted that all education must rest upon 'the history of the race', and he denounced the French clergy as a reactionary group which must be dissolved if progress were to take place.[33] Toussaint Louverture was portrayed in the schools as 'a French traitor' rather than as a Haitian hero.[34] Haitian children should also be encouraged in schools to have a proper respect for African traditions and for the beauty of the black person. The Caucasian somatic norm — *le canon grec*, as Duvalier called it — had been widely accepted in the established institutions of Haiti, and children were being educated with this image before them; all this must change.[35] For Magloire Saint Aude, the black race was 'the most beautiful race in the world'.[36]

The socialist protest

The socialists of the post-occupation period laid emphasis upon the economic basis of Haiti's problems, seeing the history of the country in terms of class conflict based upon the ownership of wealth rather than as a conflict between colour groups. In 1934 Jacques Roumain founded the Haitian Communist Party. The nationalism of the occupation period was, he claimed, a valid protest as far as it went; but its true foundation lay in the poverty and suffering of the masses, which were merely exacerbated by the military presence of the United States. The genuine popular protest had, however, been exploited by 'bourgeois' politicians for their own ends. Nevertheless the masses were, according to Roumain, beginning to see that the struggle against imperialism was only part of a larger struggle against capitalism, local and foreign. 'It is', he wrote, 'a fight to the last against the Haitian bourgeoisie and against the bourgeois politicians, valets of imperialism, cruel exploiters of the workers and peasants.'[37] The deep social divisions in Haiti and the phenomenon of colour prejudice were accounted for in economic terms. 'Colour prejudice', he declared, 'is the sentimental expression of the opposition of classes − of the class struggle − the psychological reaction to a historical and economic fact: the unbridled exploitation of the Haitian masses by the bourgeoisie.' He nevertheless claimed that the colour problem in Haiti was of exceptional importance because it was the means whereby politicians, both black and mulatto, were able to divert attention from the class struggle.[38] We have already noted that Roumain was considerably influenced by the ethnological movement, and we shall shortly consider the role which he played in the 'anti-superstition' campaign. Manuel, the hero of his posthumously published novel *Gouverneurs de la rosée*, states, 'I have respect for our traditional customs but the blood of a cock or a goat cannot change the seasons.' Although fiercely anti-clerical, Roumain claimed to respect religions, and told how he had written a life of Christ the revolutionary for his son 'because at that time, it was the best means of teaching him respect and love of man, hatred of exploiters, the dignity of poverty, the necessity of the "end of the world" − the world of oppression, of misery, of ignorance'.[39]

Roumain associated the interests of the Haitian masses with those of the proletariat in metropolitan countries, accepting the Soviet line on this matter. Stalin had written in 1918 that the Russian revolution had created a new proletarian front throughout the world, 'extending from the proletarians of the West, through the Russian revolution, to the oppressed peoples of the East'.[40] This was the period when many black intellectuals, including Richard Wright, Claude McKay and George Padmore, were attracted to communism.[41] In Peru, Mariátegui was also trying to make sense of the economic situation in his country and of its ethnic problems in the light of Marxist theory.[42] Roumain's Marxism, his concept of what today would be called the 'third world' and his hostility to official Christianity all emerge in one of his verses. In place of the sad spirituals, negro people would join 'the dirty Arabs', 'the dirty Indians' and 'the dirty Jews' in singing the 'Internationale':

> No, brothers, comrades,
> We shall pray no more.
> Our revolt rises like the cry of a stormbird
>   over the rotten splashing of the swamps.
> We shall sing no more our sad despairing spirituals,
> Another song shall surge from our throats.
> We unfurl our red flags
> Stained with the blood of our heroes,
> Under this banner we shall march,
> Under this banner we march.
> Rise, the damned of the earth;
> Rise, the prisoners of hunger.[43]

Roumain's most celebrated novel was about a young peasant who returned to his native village after spending some years in Cuba as a cane-cutter. He observed the fatalism and superstition of his fellow peasants, and attempted to show them how their situation could be improved. He set out to search for water, which was urgently needed in the community; having found a spring he organised the collective labour of the village to channel the water. Manuel, however, is killed as the result of a family feud. 'The mourning is sung that is the custom, with songs of the dead, but he, Manuel, chose a hymn for the living: the song of the *combite*, the song of the earth, of the water, of the plants, of love between the peasants, because he wanted — I now understand — that his death would be for you the rebirth of life.'[44] The message is clear: by social and political action men may become masters of their destiny — 'governors of the dew'. Although Roumain's later creative works are evidently inspired by his Marxism, it would be wrong to see them as mere political propaganda. He explicitly defended the *engagé* character of his work, and saw poetry as a powerful means of analysing and formulating 'the contradictions and antagonisms of the politico-economic structure of a society'. The poet, he went on, is 'at once witness and actor in the historical drama, . . . his art must be a weapon of the front line in the service of the people'.[45] The poet does not have the right, he maintained in criticism of the 'negative and anarchist' position of Magloire Saint Aude, 'to take refuge in the private property of a spiritual solitude'.[46]

Roumain spent most of the thirties in exile, returning to Haiti in 1941. After a period as director of the Bureau d'Ethnologie, he was appointed to a diplomatic post in Mexico; he died in 1944 at the age of thirty-seven. Jacques Roumain's influence, especially among the radical sons of elite families, was considerable, and the young writers associated with the journal *La Ruche* in 1945–6 looked to his life and work for inspiration. Marxism in Haiti was at this time, and in large part continues to be, a movement among intellectuals with no large following among the urban and rural workers. This judgment will, no doubt, be disputed by those involved in contemporary left-wing movements, but I believe it to be accurate. 'Every great class movement in history', observed Robert Michels, 'has arisen upon the instigation, with the cooperation, and under the leadership of men sprung from the very class against which the movement was directed.'[47] Of the departed Jacques Roumain, Jean F. Brierre wrote:

> And the light in which we march,
> We, who are called the living,
> Is perhaps only a golden trail
> Laid with the fruitful seed
> Of his apostolic word.
> Already the night falls . . . [48]

In the post-occupation period there were other tendencies in socialist thought. In particular there was a tendency towards a kind of Saint-Simonism – an attack upon unrestricted capitalism, combined with a belief in government by experts and technocrats, which should replace a bankrupt and outdated political system. This technocratic tradition in Haiti goes well back into the nineteenth century and is characteristic of certain writers who were associated with the Liberal Party, particularly Edmond Paul.[49] Writers of the thirties, especially Jules Blanchet, were socialists in the sense that they attacked capitalism and the system of liberal democracy which frequently accompanies it, and they saw the economic factor as the ultimately determining factor in human history. It is social reality which determines human consciousness.[50] Blanchet called for increased specialisation, because it is this which characterises advanced countries.[51] The state was seen, along lines similar to those sketched by Léon Duguit and Emile Durkheim, as a great public service corporation, which should play an active and creative role in planning the economy of the country.

Property, Blanchet insisted, is a social function, not an individual right, and is therefore properly subject to state control. He pointed to Italy and to the Soviet Union as providing examples of the way in which governments could intervene constructively by planning the economic development of a country.[52] 'The old notion of the liberal state has been amended', he wrote, '. . . The state has relinquished its passive role of policeman; its mission is to increase its duties, and its prime function is to organise.'[53] This economic and social planning was said to be more a matter of science than of art, and it therefore calls for the creation of cadres of technical experts who should control the state apparatus.[54] In order to achieve such a situation, correct ideology is necessary, for it is 'ideas that rule the world'.[55] Without doctrine, wrote Blanchet, 'action is precarious, fruitless, incoherent'.[56] Again we hear echoes of Saint-Simon, who declared that no new regime can be instituted 'without having previously established the new philosophic system to which it must correspond'.[57] Although it is proper to refer to the ideas of Blanchet as ideas of protest, he had, as we have seen, together with Piquion and others of this tendency, come to terms with the Vincent administration.

As with the political theory of Edmond Paul, this technocratic ideology of Blanchet had definite elitist implications. 'Power to the most competent' had been the slogan of the nineteenth-century Liberals. A suspicion of the masses is characteristic of this type of socialism in the occupation period and after, and contrasts strongly with the romantic populism of Brouard and the *Griots* school, which was to some extent shared by Roumain. In the war years, however, when Lescot's Haiti had allied itself with the United States in a battle against the dictators, 'democracy' became the order of the day. Blanchet insisted that the country must move towards a real, effective democracy which involves economic equality; 'formal democracy' merely secures legal rights without enabling people to exercise these rights and to benefit from them.[58]

From what has been said it will be clear that socialism in post-occupation Haiti by no means presented a united front nor a single ideology. The differences between socialists of this period will emerge when we consider some of the concrete confrontations in which they were involved, and particularly the crisis of 1946.

The mulatto reaction

The mulatto reaction to the challenges of *noirisme* and socialism can be seen in the writings of François Dalencour and Dantès Bellegarde, and also in the pronouncements of President Sténio Vincent himself. These men were strongly nationalistic in their rhetoric and condemned the *noiristes* for undermining the unity of the nation by their newly acquired racial theories. They themselves were generally pro-French and Catholic in cultural orientation, and they saw the 'return to Africa' as a flight from civilisation. The spokesmen of the mulatto elite were also suspicious of socialism, and they advocated a free market economy.[59] With respect to political ideas, however, they disagreed; while Dalencour and Bellegarde were prophets of political liberalism, Vincent practised and defended an authoritarian approach to politics. These mulatto intellectuals had been deeply affected by the United States occupation of their country. The fact of the white presence had hurt their national pride. While some of them had originally supported the Americans, seeing the invasion as a short-term intervention which would re-establish order and refurbish their own position as the governing elite, they gradually became disillusioned. As we have seen, the nationalist movement grew from strength to strength. Only those close to the collaborationist regime of Louis Borno were able to resist the tide and by 1930 they had become a discredited rump. Dalencour praised the military resistance of Charlemagne Péralte – 'he saved the national honour'[60] – and he attacked the alienation of Haitian land to foreign companies. He believed that agricultural self-sufficiency was the condition for an effective national independence and insisted that the small landholding was a vital aspect of this self-sufficiency. The great plantation was also seen as the enemy of liberty and democracy.[61] Another mulatto ideologist, Georges Séjourné, also wrote in favour of the small peasant.[62]

Despite his vigorous nationalism, Dalencour was, throughout his life, perhaps the most consistent and outspoken defender of the mulatto legend of the Haitian past and the larger ideology of which this legend was a part. As we shall see, his republication of the principal works of Ardouin and Saint-Rémy stemmed largely from this commitment. He denounced Christophe for having omitted the prohibition of foreign ownership from his constitutions; 'he could not have any real attachment to this land in which he was not born'. Dalencour referred to the 'shameful revolution of 1843', attacked 'the bloody despotism of Soulouque', and assailed Salnave and Salomon for engaging in 'disgraceful transactions' which had the effect of alienating national territory. On the other hand, 'the generous ideas' of Boyer Bazelais and Edmond Paul are praised.[63]

In response to the *noiriste* challenge these mulatto writers denounced the Voodoo religion as one of the principal causes of the backwardness of the country. Dalencour maintained that 'the disgusting African superstitions' which destroyed the critical sense of the masses were partially responsible for the weakness of the Haitian political system which in turn had led to the American occupation.[64] He advocated a ferocious war against the Voodoo religion with 'draconic penalties' imposed upon those found practising it.[65] Dantès Bellegarde also denied that the Voodoo spirits could ever be adequate objects of faith for the Haitian people.[66] The wider aspects of *noiriste* racism were attacked as unscientific and as undermining the unity of the nation. Bellegarde opposed the racism of the Nazis in Germany, linking it with the racism which was gaining ground in Haiti.[67] Haitians exist as an ethnic group which forms a nation, but there is no 'Haitian race', and although the biological origins of the people are largely African, their culture is

French.[68] He denounced 'the young aesthetes' who, 'clothed in the latest Paris fashions or dressed like the tap dancers in a Harlem night-club, believe it possible to impose upon their compatriots, writers, lawyers . . . the mentality or the religion of the fetishistic tribes of equatorial Africa'.[69] France was, for Dalencour also, the country to which Haitians should look as their spiritual home; it was the country of the 'declaration of the rights of man', of the abolition of slavery, a country without colour prejudice, where the black man could relax and be himself.[70]

From the standpoint of the practising politician, Sténio Vincent recognised the potential challenge which the more radical *noiristes* posed to his delicately balanced administration. He lamented the way that Haitians 'add racial pepper to every sauce', and claimed that their 'racial ideology' was out of touch with the harsh social and economic realities of their national situation.[71] Haitians should have better things to do than to substitute negro racism for white racism. 'It seems that nothing is able to check our racist mystique in its tragic and vengeful course.'[72] With Bellegarde, the president ridiculed the young *noiriste* intellectuals whose headquarters were in Paris. 'Which of them', he demanded, 'would have dreamed of actually going to some part of the Sudan or the Congo to enter into communion with the souls of our distant Mandingo or Bantu ancestors?'[73]

Dalencour and Bellegarde professed democratic and liberal principles in politics. The former claimed that Haiti illustrated the general law (later enunciated by S. M. Lipset and others) that political despotism leads to economic stagnation and that development is to be achieved by adopting democratic institutions.[74] These writers did not, however, see their liberalism as inconsistent with a belief in the vocation of the elite. In all countries, Dalencour maintained, it is normal to find a relatively small group which constitutes the true ruling class, but this class ought to form a single body with the mass of the people with whom it shares common interests. In Haiti however, this elite had become parasitic on the social organism.[75] Following the mulatto ideologists of previous generations Bellegarde emphasised the unity of the nation and the 'solidarity of economic interests'. While there are different 'social categories' in the country there are no deep divisions in the social structure of Haiti.[76]

Vincent was altogether less optimistic than was Bellegarde about the social situation in Haiti. He pointed to the deep divisions existing between the elite and the masses, and he continually reiterated his criticisms of the short-sighted and selfish attitudes of the former.[77] He denounced that 'passion de la politique' which he observed among many Haitians and he argued that it should be replaced by the taste for hard and honest work. Members of the elite still misdirected their energies into politics, literature and the liberal professions, leaving the productive fields of commerce, agriculture and industry to foreigners.[78] The president was also critical of the liberal democratic rhetoric and shared something of the authoritarian approach to politics which we have identified among the *noiristes* and technocratic socialists of the period. He urged his fellow countrymen to follow the authoritarianism of Toussaint Louverture;[79] he frequently pointed to the example of the Portuguese dictator Salazar and quoted with approval the sentiments of Charles Maurras on discipline.[80] The regime of Vincent owed much of its success to this critical approach to the traditional mulatto elite ideology and to his shrewd assessment of the role which the black middle class was beginning to play in the politics of the country.

II

Fascism and the Ethiopian crisis

As we have already noted there was considerable sympathy in Haiti for European fascism, among a number of different groups. They saw in fascism, and some of them also saw in Soviet communism, an alternative to the liberal democratic model which had widely been accepted as the one which should be followed in Haiti. Many *noiristes* of this period, with their anti-liberal and authoritarian rhetoric, were advocating a kind of fascism for Haiti. Some socialist writers of the twenties and early thirties thought of fascism and socialism as having much in common, while the Catholic right saw in fascism the only viable alternative to communism. Thus from differing standpoints fascism received wide support in Haiti in the years immediately following the election of Vincent.

The Catholic variety of fascism, represented by Mussolini, Salazar and later by Franco, received the best press. The racism of Hitler made him less palatable to the Haitian intellectual. The principal exception to this is to be found in the writings of Jean Magloire (who is not a Roman Catholic but an active member of the Anglican church). Hitler and Mussolini were for him 'the two great champions of European stability'.[81] Hitler was a 'grand réalisateur' who was wholly devoted to the honour of his country.[82] Italian, German and Portuguese fascism were seen as distinct, for 'fascism is not a dogma'; yet they shared the common feature of 'benevolent dictatorship'.[83] Magloire will emerge later in our story as a supporter of Estimé and as minister of the interior under Duvalier. Franck Mirambeau, who wrote for the same journal, *Maintenant*, praised Hitler and Mussolini for not having waited for the corruption of the masses before acting; their popularity among the people was due to their concern for social justice.[84] Max Bissainthe supported Franco because he represented the struggle against communism.[85] Gérard de Catalogne also defended fascism even after 1939. He was a champion of Action Française and was editor of the Catholic daily *La Phalange* for some years. On resigning from the editorship in 1941, he founded his own newspaper, *Le Soir*. He saw in Franco the creator of a spiritual reconstruction, and urged his readers to take inspiration from the Phalangist troops kneeling before the Holy Sacrament with rifle in hand.[86] De Catalogne linked Spain, Portugal and Italy with France as the defenders of eternal values. Liberalism, on the other hand, was denounced as the ideology of a new barbarism, by which an aristocracy of bankers and financiers was able to rise to power.[87] This familiar fascist rhetoric is also to be found in his books of this period.[88]

The francophile elite tended to support France against Germany in the European war, and were in something of a quandary when Mussolini joined Hitler. Their problem was soon solved, however, with the defeat of France and the setting up of the Vichy government, which paid homage to those ideals of discipline, authority and religion which they patronised. When the United States joined the war, President Lescot thought it wise for Haiti to join the allies. Jean Magloire celebrated the 'bien belle victoire' of the united nations in 1945. 'It is', he declared, 'the triumph of the democratic ideal and the end of all despotic tendencies.'[89]

A more serious embarrassment was, however, caused to the Haitian protagonists of fascism by the Italian attack on Ethiopia in 1935. A long-standing bond of racial unity tied the African empire to the black republic. The *noiristes* put race before political ideology and condemned the Italian aggression. The authoritarianism of Mussolini which had been celebrated by Piquion and Brouard was now seen in a less favourable light. Clément Magloire *fils* and René Piquion called upon Haitians to support 'notre congénère Hailé Selassie'.[90] 'Yes', cried Magloire, 'we are fanatics, the Ethiopian cause impassions us, and our faith in the victory of our Abyssinian brothers is blind.' The war, he urged, must be recognised as a racial war.[91] Duvalier and Denis also insisted that Haitian sympathy for Ethiopia was due to no geographical sentimentalism, but to the 'mysterious call of race'.[92] Carl Brouard condemned the neutrality of the other European powers as amounting to an assassination of Ethiopia. 'Shame, shame on white civilisation', he declared.[93] From the socialist ranks Jules Blanchet condemned the Italian aggression and Etienne Charlier founded the Ligue pour la Défense du Peuple Ethiopien in May 1935.

The Catholic elite remained fairly quiet on the issue, but there was clearly support for Mussolini in their ranks. *Le Temps*, directed by Luc Grimmard, who succeeded de Catalogne as editor of *La Phalange* in

1941, published an article in which Ethiopia was pictured as 'an anarchic country', while Mussolini was seen as the champion of western civilisation.[94] Nevertheless the government of Sténio Vincent condemned the action of Italy. Speaking in the name of 'the black republic of Haiti', General Nemours warned the League of Nations Assembly that what was occurring in Africa was a precedent for what would take place in Europe. 'I protest with all my might', he continued, 'at this attempt to crush an independent black people in a so-called colonial war.'[95] The Italo-Ethiopian war proved the occasion for a *prise de conscience* among black people throughout the world and for the manifestation of racial unity.[96] In Haiti itself race had by this time become a divisive factor, owing to the *négritude* ideology stemming from the ethnological movement, and many mulattoes sympathised with Italy in its struggle against that African 'barbarism' which they believed to be threatening their own country. Nevertheless the Ethiopian war was taking place many thousands of miles away and it was perfectly possible for respectable politicians to maintain a fairly detached stance on the matter. The chips were not really down.

The 'anti-superstition' campaign

Voodoo is a subject about which Haitians have been particularly sensitive since the early days of independence. Throughout the nineteenth century intellectuals of all shades either denied the existence of the cult altogether, or pronounced themselves totally opposed to it. The ethnological movement brought with it a re-evaluation of Voodoo, and on the part of a few an open participation in the ceremonies of the cult. The thirties saw an increasingly bitter conflict between a *noiriste* ideology which pictured Haiti as essentially African in its culture, and a nationalism which thought in terms of a *créole* culture, unique to Haiti, strongly influenced by French as well as by some African traditions; between a *noirisme* which, recognising the deep divisions existing in the country based largely on colour, insisted that political power ought to be in the hands of the majority, and a nationalism which denied the existence of a significant colour problem and which asserted that political power should be in the hands of the most competent, educated and enlightened section of the community and be exercised in the general interest; between, that is, those who believed in black power and those who were dedicated to the continued hegemony of the mulatto elite. This conflict manifested itself in a particularly acute form in the controversy concerning the so-called *campagne anti-superstitieuse*, conducted by the Roman Catholic church with support from the state, in 1941–2.

This campaign can be said to have been initiated by Monsignor Paul

Robert, bishop of Gonaïves, who in a pastoral letter of April 1941 pointed to the 'absolute incompatibility, the irreconcilable opposition, between Christianity and superstition'. He went on to state that the disastrous confusion between Christianity and superstition was the greatest obstacle to the reign of Christ in Haiti. By superstition he meant the 'collection of religious beliefs and practices which came from Africa'.[97] In the following week Elie Lescot was elected president of the country, and he made it clear that 'my government will be a Catholic government'.[98] In May a eucharistic congress was held in Gonaïves, whose central theme was the struggle against Voodoo. By September of the same year Archbishop Le Gouaze of Port-au-Prince could claim that over 100,000 people had taken the oath against Voodoo, and that the campaign was gaining momentum.[99] A special catechism was published, asserting that the *houngan* (Voodoo priest) was 'the principal slave of Satan', and that the *loas* (spirits) were representations of the evil one.[100] Hymn books were specially compiled for the campaign.[101] Mission services were held throughout the country in what the church newspaper, *La Phalange*, called this 'spiritual *blitzkrieg*'.[102] Although Voodoo practices had been illegal in Haiti for many years, and in 1935 the penalties had been increased,[103] the law was not strictly enforced. Lescot now gave explicit government support to the campaign,[104] which was, however, dramatically terminated after a church in Delmas, in the suburbs of Port-au-Prince, had been riddled with gunfire during a mission service conducted by Father Rémy Augustin on 22 February 1942. This event convinced even many Catholics that things had gone too far; it is possible that the government itself was becoming worried at the effects of the campaign. De Catalogne, who had kept a tactful silence during the height of the campaign, condemned the thoughtless and mistaken way in which many clergy had behaved towards the peasants.[105]

The 'anti-superstition' campaign caused considerable controversy in the press. In a series of articles, Jacques Roumain, at this time director of the Bureau d'Ethnologie, attacked the campaign. Although a Marxist, Roumain on this occasion found himself in a temporary alliance with the *noiristes*. The Haitian people, he maintained, are no more superstitious than the people of other nations, and the Voodoo cult is a vehicle for conserving the folk traditions of the masses. Are not the peasants of Brittany also superstitious? Breton priests do not need to come to Haiti to combat superstition. In any case, Roumain observed, the priest, by attempting to destroy religious objects, only strengthens popular belief in their power. When the peasants see the parish priest ordering a certain tree to be cut down, this is in their eyes clear evidence for the power of the *loas*. Roumain also accused some priests of stealing ethnological objects under the guise of the campaign.[106] He argued that

Voodoo beliefs like all religious beliefs are part of a false consciousness, and that they are destined to be replaced by a scientific world view. It is, however, education rather than persecution which will deliver the peasant from superstition; but this also requires 'transforming at the same time his material conditions'.[107] What was needed in Haiti was not an anti-superstition campaign but an anti-poverty campaign. Roumain applied orthodox Marxist analysis to the Voodoo religion, which was seen as the mere reflexion of the material process, of the mode of production, in the last resort. In its turn, he continued, 'this ideological superstructure reacts on historical development and often even determines *the form*'.[108]

Roumain also pointed to the political aspect of the campaign. We should not, he claimed, underestimate the importance of the fact that the French hierarchy was pro-Vichy and collaborationist, that it was 'part of the pro-fascist apparatus'.[109] The papal nuncio of the time, Monsignor Silvani, in an interview published in a Dominican newspaper, denounced the African superstitions of Haiti, and spoke of the Dominican Republic as 'a people on the road to progress led by an enlightened patriot Generalissimo Trujillo Molina'.[110] More important than the international political aspect of the campaign, however, was its significance in the internal struggle for power between the mulatto elite and new groups which were challenging their position. It was a desperate attempt by the francophile elite to maintain its superiority in the cultural field in the face of a growing working-class and peasant movement led by black intellectuals and of a socialist protest from within its own ranks. The collapse of the campaign clearly indicated the strength of the opposition, which was openly to assert itself in the election campaign of 1946.

The 1946 'revolution'

The victory of the allies in 1945 was hailed in many countries as the beginning of a new era; this mood was evident in Haiti, particularly among the young. President Lescot, as we have seen, had alienated many of the erstwhile supporters of Vincent. *Noiristes*, Marxists, mulatto liberals and young radicals were all discontented and strongly favoured a change of government. In 1944 L'Amicale, a black club, had been founded under the patronage of Emile Saint Lot, and in the following year Dr René Salomon, a rich black politician, formed Le Cénacle d'Etudes, which aimed to attract young intellectuals. Both groups wished to overthrow the Lescot government and to substitute a black administration. Cultural links were re-established with a liberated France, and André Breton, the founding father of surrealism, visited Haiti in December 1945; his presence provided the occasion for a reunion of radical intellectuals.[111] The new-year issue of the journal *La Ruche*, which contained reports of Breton's speeches, was seized by the police. The journal, which had been founded at the beginning of December, was run by a number of young men including Jacques Stéphen Alexis, René Depestre and Théodore Baker, and was vigorously critical of the government. On 7 January student and sixth-form demonstrations against the government took place, strikes broke out and many businesses closed. An army junta of three, General Franck Lavaud, Colonel Antoine Levelt and Colonel Paul E. Magloire, took power, and Lescot quietly left the country. The *créole* chorus was heard in the streets:

> Lescot, ou allé, ou allé, ou allé,
> Ou allé, Lescot, et ou pa di'm âyê.[112]

The actions of the students and strikers received wide support; many groups throughout the country believed that it was time for a change. A group calling itself the Parti Démocrate Unifié (composed mostly of mulatto intellectuals of the centre and left – Catts Pressoir, Louis Déjoie, Georges Rigaud, Etienne Charlier and others) called for a lifting of the state of emergency, for the release of political prisoners, and for freedom of speech, of the press and of assembly. There was a general demand for a new constitution; Charlier described the constitution of 1935 as 'typiquement fasciste, typiquement anti-démocratique'.[113] In the early weeks of 1946 there was a considerable degree of agreement among the various groups in favour of the revolution. Black and mulatto, Marxist and liberal, young and not-so-young formed a united front against the return of Lescot. A committee of public safety was formed, comprising seven blacks and four mulattoes. Discussing this early stage of the revolution, Charlier claimed that colour was not an issue, nor indeed was ideology. The question at issue was the setting up of a democratic regime which would respect civil liberties.[114]

Very soon, however, when it became clear that positive steps had to be taken to form a new civilian government, divisions which had their roots in the past began to manifest themselves. The Front Révolutionnaire Haïtien was formed as a federation of a number of distinct radical groups, and was dominated by blacks. The most important groups in the FRH were the Parti Populaire National (led by Daniel Fignolé, Emile Saint Lot and Clovis Désinor), the Ligue d'Action Social et Démocratique (led by, among others, Edner Brutus), the Parti Communiste d'Haïti (led by Félix d'Orléans Juste Constant, Max Ménard and Edris Saint-Amand), and the Parti Démocratique Populaire de la Jeunesse Haïtienne (led by René Depestre and the contributors to *La Ruche*). Saint Lot was the president of the FRH, with Juste Constant and Fignolé as vice-presidents. These groups were in general agreement that some radical changes were needed in the country and that these could be carried out only by an authentic representative of the people, that is by a black president. The PCH and the PDPJH were Marxist groups, while Saint Lot and Fignolé in particular were vigorously anti-Marxist. These ideological differences led to a split in the FRH at a later stage, which was deepened by disagreements about the best presidential candidate. The leading journals of the FRH were *Flambeau* (Saint Lot, Brutus, Désinor), *La Ruche* (Baker and Depestre), *La Nouvelle Ruche* (Depestre, Montasse, Alexis), *L'Intransigeant* (Paul Blanchet), *La République* (Marcel Vaval), *Demain* (Yvan Jeannot, Brutus, Love Léger), *Combat* (PCH), *Chantiers* (Fignolé), *La Fronde* (a weekly journal which seems to have been run by, and in the sole interests of, the Brutus family), and *L'Action Nationale* (Audain, Henock Trouillot, Duvalier, Denis, Morille P. Figaro).

The non-Marxist parts of the FRH clearly believed that the most important thing was to elect a black president; these groups rapidly developed a strongly *noiriste* position, and saw the election in terms of a battle between blacks and mulattoes. In a series of bulletins, the sponsors of *L'Action Nationale* argued the point. It was necessary for the presidential palace to be occupied by an authentic representative of the Haitian masses.[115] If this battle were lost by the blacks, they maintained, the only alternative would be to go back to Africa.[116] *L'Action Nationale* strongly supported the military junta and urged the population in the election of May 1946 to 'vote black'.[117] The colour question was not, they insisted, an invention of journalists and politicians to divide the people, as had been suggested; the truth was that the Haitian family has been divided for a very long time. 'What is a mulatto?' they continued; 'A man who thinks in every thing and in every way of his "clan". The mulatto is a mulatto before being a Haitian.'[118] Against the mulatto Marxists they argued that it was impossible to separate the question of class from the colour question in the history of Haiti; people may talk as much as they like about 'historical materialism' but the basic problem in Haiti was the colour problem.[119]

L'Action Nationale, together with the Mouvement Ouvrier Paysan (MOP), *La Voix des Jeunes* and *La Presse* supported as candidate for the presidency Démosthènes Pétrus Calixte. Born of black parents in 1896 at Fort Liberté in the northern part of Haiti, Calixte became an instructor at the Ecole Militaire in 1921. In 1934 he was appointed the first Haitian commandant of the Garde d'Haïti, but was removed from this position in 1938 by President Vincent, who believed that he was plotting to overthrow the government.[120] Calixte was described by *Flambeau* as 'one of the first victims of the bourgeois reaction and of the politics of *mulâtrification*'.[121] On the eve of the presidential election in August 1946 the MOP issued a statement to the effect that Calixte was the only candidate acceptable to the movement, 'no other candidate whoever he may be interests the MOP, nor can hope to obtain its support'.[122] The statement was signed by Fignolé, Désinor and Duvalier, and appears to have been designed specifically to harm Estimé. All of the signatories, however, were later to join Estimé's administration. It seems that this group of *noiriste* politicians who supported Calixte doubted whether Estimé was sufficiently militant on the colour issue, and in fact his government was later criticised by *Chantiers* (controlled by Fignolé) for having been too open to the old elite, who had lost none of the power which they had gained under Borno, Vincent and Lescot.[123]

While much of Calixte's backing came from Port-au-Prince, Estimé had a wide body of support from the blacks of the Artibonite and North, represented by such journals as *La Cité* (of Gonaïves), *La Masse* (of St Marc) and *La Lutte* (of Cap Haïtien). The regional factor played an important part in the election, with the predominantly mulatto PSP strongest in the South. Hostility towards the capital on the part of spokesmen from the provincial cities was a noticeable feature of the campaign, and the cause of Calixte certainly suffered from his being too closely associated with Fignolé and the MOP. 'A bas la Dictature de la Capital', cried the *Artibonite Journal*.[124]

Most of the FRH was in favour of Estimé, and many of those who preferred Calixte or Juste Constant were prepared to defend him when he was attacked by members of the mulatto elite. Dumarsais Estimé was born at Verrettes in the Artibonite Valley in 1900, the son of Florencia Massillon and Alcine Estimé. After attending primary school he went to the Lycée Pétion in Port-au-Prince, and later became a school teacher. He represented Verettes in the legislative assembly for many years, and had been secretary of state for education, labour and agriculture for some time under Vincent.[125] Estimé was thought to be generally progressive, and to be a defender of the interests of the masses and of the growing black middle class, though he was hardly a revolutionary by temperament. He had the support of a wide spectrum of opinion including writers of the radical 'right', like Jean Magloire and Max Bissainthe. Much of the rhetoric of his supporters was directed against the sins of the old elite. Edner Brutus wrote, for example, of the need to 'liquidate the bourgeois fifth column'.[126]

The Marxist groups in the FRH (the PCH and the PDPJH) were in favour of Juste Constant for president. He was secretary general of the PCH, and a priest of the Eglise Episcopale d'Haïti, in charge of the parish of Arcahaie, until he was put on the non-parochial list by Bishop Alfred Voegeli. Juste Constant was supported by Depestre, Montasse and most of the young radical writers associated with *La Ruche*. In April 1946, however, there was a split in this group. Théodore Baker and Gérard Martelly continued to publish *La Ruche*, while the majority of the group started *La Nouvelle Ruche*. This dispute was partly personal and partly a question of colour. Baker and Martelly were bitterly opposed to Estimé, 'authentic understudy of the Vincent–Lescot regime . . . a danger for the Republic . . . The life of Dumarsais Estimé is one of weakness, of disloyalty . . . and of a betrayal of the interests of the people.'[127] The Baker–Martelly faction was the only part of the FRH which actually attacked Estimé. As we shall see, the PCH and the PDPJH actually supported the new president after the election of 16 August.

One of the earliest parties to form in 1946, and one of the few groups to continue in existence through the Estimé period, despite two attempts to suppress it, was the Parti Socialiste Populaire. The leaders were left-wing intellectuals, and were almost all from the mulatto elite. Etienne Charlier was secretary general and others associated with the PSP were Max Hudicourt, Anthony Lespès, Jules Blanchet and Albert Mangonès. The group produced a daily newspaper, *La Nation*, as well as the journal *PSP*. In January 1946 the party issued a statement of its aims:

The PSP exists to assume the effective direction of the movement for the emancipation of the worker and peasant masses, and of the genuinely democratic portion of the Haitian intelligentsia, in the struggle which has begun for the inauguration of a New Society in which class privilege founded on the private ownership of the means of production and exchange will disappear.[128]

Most of the PSP leaders were Marxists of some variety, and they believed that class divisions, based upon economic factors, were fundamental, though some of them did not deny that colour divisions were also of importance in Haiti. These Marxist writers were insistent, however, that the colour factor was important only because people are misled into thinking that it is important. Only when people come to recognise economic divisions as the significant objective divisions in the country can they begin to tackle the real problem.[129]

The mulatto Marxists of the PSP were in general critical of those who raised the colour question in the election campaign, and interpreted any reference to colour as the attempt of a rising black middle class to divert attention from the real economic problem, thus furthering their own selfish interests. They saw Estimé particularly as representing this black *petite bourgeoisie*, and attacked him vigorously. It was the irrepressible Max Hudicourt who led the assault on Estimé. *L'Action Nationale*, *Flambeau*, *La République* and other journals of the FRH replied. They attacked what they called the racialism of Hudicourt; why should Estimé not live in the same comfortable, bourgeois sur-

roundings that the elite Marxists had lived in all their lives? Marcel
Vaval asserted that it was an affair of black and mulatto; 'Max Hudicourt', he went on, 'expends all the acrimony which a mulatto of his
type can have in his heart against a black like Estimé'.[130] The mulatto
novelist Philippe Thoby-Marcelin in turn attacked the black intellectuals
as racists; so the colour question became the great issue of the day.
Replying to the accusations of Marcelin, Roger Dorsainville declared:

We have, more than any others, suffered from the contempt and arrogance of
the Nazis of Haiti. And these Nazis resemble Monsieur Marcelin as brothers.
We have witnessed an unjust segregation depriving the most capable among us of
the possibility of their free development.[131]

As we shall see, mulatto groups continued to accuse Estimé of colour
discrimination during the period of his presidency, and the action of
the military in removing him from office in 1950 was generally welcomed by the PSP and by other mulatto factions. During the stormy
days of June 1946 Max Hudicourt further infuriated the radical blacks
by his proposal that the constituent assembly should be transferred to
the southern city of Jérémie, away from the heated atmosphere of the
capital. This suggestion was denounced by black leaders; Jérémie was
'the cradle of Rigaudism, the city of the most fierce sectarianism which
kindled the first fratricidal war in Haiti'.[132]

The PSP, generally Marxist and mulatto, sponsored as candidate for
the presidency a rather conservative black deputy from Les Cayes,
Edgard Nere Numa. He was a close associate of Louis Déjoie, the
dynamic and ambitious grandson of President Geffrard, who was a
candidate for the senate in the election of May. The PSP leaders clearly
realised that any presidential candidate with a hope of success at this
time must be black, and they also believed that the time was not ripe
for a socialist government. Numa was a widely respected politician, and
they thought that he would be a useful figurehead. To their opponents
this looked very much like *la politique de doublure*.

There were many other parties and factions in 1946 with their own
journals and with their favourite candidates for office. Liberal and
conservative groups included the Parti Libéral Socialiste of François
Dalencour, the Union Démocratique Haïtien of Serge Corvington and
F. Burr Reynaud, the Parti Populaire Social Chrétien of Edouard
Tardieu, and the Parti National Travailliste of Antoine Pierre Paul.
Journals connected with these groups included *La Forge* (Corvington),
L'Action Sociale (Tardieu), *La Bataille* (Georges Figaro, Milo Rigaud).
The latter journal backed Dalencour for president in April 1946, but
by August had decided that this was impossible, and had switched their
support to Numa. These groups tried hard to dissociate themselves
from the Lescot regime, but it was quite clear that the popular mood
was in favour of changes more radical than these parties were likely to

provide. Spokesmen of the Roman Catholic church urged their flock to 'vote Catholic', and supported conservative candidates such as Luc Dorsinville. During the exhilarating days following the fall of Lescot many trade unions sprang into action. It is possible to distinguish four groups of unions at this time. There was La Fédération des Travailleurs Haïtiens, which included railway workers and those employed in electricity, printing, copper mining. This group of unions was Marxist in orientation and was led by Edris Saint-Amand. The MOP under Fignolé had support among workers in the docks, water works, Bata shoe company, HASCO (Haytien–American Sugar Corporation) and in small manufacturing. L'Union Nationale des Ouvriers Haïtiens, which was affiliated to the United States AFL–CIO, had members in tobacco, tanning, customs and in the bakeries. There were also some independent unions, the most important of which were the chauffeurs and construction workers. Although total membership of trade unions was probably less than 10,000 the unions were strong in the capital, and were able to exert influence out of all proportion to their size. In the months following January 1946 a number of strikes took place and workers secured some improvement in their wages and working conditions.[133]

By the beginning of August 1946 about eight presidential candidates remained in the race, all but one of whom were black. Radical black politicians were supporting Juste Constant and Calixte and the less radical blacks were backing Estimé. Numa was promoted by the PSP and by a number of more conservative groups, represented by journals such as *La Bataille* and *La Garde*, the latter being an anti-socialist journal from Les Cayes, whose support for Numa was largely due to regional loyalties. Bignon Pierre Louis also had a fair body of support, which included the journals *Démocratie* and *Le Mouvement*, both published in the capital. The army leadership appears to have favoured the candidature of Estimé, believing that Calixte would be a puppet controlled by Fignolé and the MOP. Estimé received the requisite number of votes in the electoral college on 16 August 1946, and took the oath as president of the republic. In an effort to secure a wide body of support in the early days of his regime he included in his first cabinet Daniel Fignolé as secretary of state for education (who took with him Kléber Georges Jacob and Clovis Désinor as assistants); also he included Georges Rigaud, a mulatto leader of the PSP, as secretary of state for commerce (who chose Jules Blanchet and Anthony Lespès as technical counsellors). Calixte immediately issued a statement supporting the new president and announcing that he no longer regarded himself as a political leader.[134] Also Estimé received support from the small PCH. Odnell David argued that the Estimé government was pursuing a policy favourable to the masses and to the working class, and that if this regime were to fall there would probably be a restoration of the old order; the Communist Party ought therefore to give the government its support.[135] In March 1947 the PCH made an official statement backing the government, and dissolved itself the following month. René Depestre also saw the middle-class government of Estimé as the avant-garde of the proletariat, and of the peasants, which would prepare the way for 'a total transformation of the conditions of life and a general recasting of values'.[136] He was awarded a government scholarship to study abroad.

Georges Rigaud did not remain long in the cabinet and throughout the four years of Estimé's regime the PSP constituted the most vocal opposition. Political divisions followed colour lines in a way which they had not done since the time of Salomon.

The triumph of the *noiristes* in 1946 must be seen in the context of a changing class structure in Haiti and of a growing colour and class consciousness on the part of the black middle class. As we have seen, one of the principal effects of the United States occupation had been the development of a significant middle group, distinct from the old elite. It had in fact been the deliberate policy of the United States administration to create a strong middle class which would bridge the gulf separating the elite from the masses and thereby provide the basis for political stability. By 1946 this class had become a significant factor in the social and political life of Haiti. American sociologists Leyburn, Lobb and Simpson,[137] writing in the 1940s, had seriously underestimated the importance of this class. Their mistake is condoned by Wingfield and Parenton on the ground that 1946 was 'the date of the emergence of this class from an embryonic stage into a recognizable stratum'.[138] The middle class might have been unrecognised by these sociologists before 1946 but it was not unrecognisable. One of the principal criticisms levelled against Leyburn's book by Price Mars, in a review first published in 1942, was the fact that he ignored the existence of a significant middle class. 'It is incontestable that this class exists in respectable numbers', wrote Price Mars.[139] It was this mistake which led Leyburn to state that 'for the present and the near future it is safe to say there will be no more black non-élite presidents'.[140]

7. Authentics and their adversaries

1946-1957

In this chapter we shall be concerned with the development of political ideas in Haiti in the period from 1946 to 1957. After briefly discussing the course of events from the election of Estimé to the fall of Magloire, I shall examine in some detail three traditions of political thought, the *noirisme* of the *Griots* group, the Marxism of Charlier, Alexis and Depestre, and the mulatto 'liberal' ideology of François Dalencour, Alfred Viau and others. The final section will deal with the extended election campaign which lasted from the fall of Magloire in December 1956 to the election of Duvalier in September 1957; here we shall be concerned largely with the political programme put forward by Duvalier and the group with which he was associated.

I hope to show that as a result of the twin attacks of socialism and of *noirisme* during this period, the hegemony of mulatto liberalism was further eroded. The traditional mulatto position had already been weakened in the preceding period by the ethnological movement and by the writings and actions of Jacques Roumain and his followers. Under the Estimé regime, the *noiristes* were able to use the instruments of government — particularly the educational system — as a means of propagating their ideas for the first time since 1915. Yet the regime, believing itself to be dependent upon the good will of the United States, and upon some degree of co-operation from the business community, which was dominated by mulattoes, was fearful of a showdown and adopted a somewhat timid and ineffectual approach to the problem of mulatto hegemony. The regime of Magloire represents the last successful attempt by the old elite to reassert its political pre-eminence behind the mask of the black colonel. The fierceness of the election campaign of 1956–7 was due largely to a realisation on the part of both sides that a victory for Duvalier (or even for Daniel Fignolé) would entail a final collapse of the mulatto hegemony in the political field.

I

The election of Dumarsais Estimé as president of Haiti on 16 August 1946 signified a victory for the moderate *noiristes*, and in the months following the election Estimé managed to gain support, as we have seen, from most of the important black groups. Estimé's attempt to secure some support from the mulatto elite by the inclusion of Georges

Rigaud in his cabinet failed. Rigaud resigned in October and the Parti Socialiste Populaire formed the basis of opposition to the new regime. Estimé was widely accused by mulattoes of pursuing a policy based on colour prejudice,[1] and constant criticism and opposition from this quarter prevented him from carrying through all the measures which his supporters demanded. Fignolé and the Mouvement Ouvrier Paysan (MOP) became restless, and, together with Emile Saint Lot and other important black leaders, went into opposition. The president's attempt to modify the constitution and his conflict with the senate led to a constitutional crisis, which was abruptly ended by a military coup in May 1950. The same triumvirate – Levelt, Lavaud and Magloire – who had presided over the installation of Estimé thus effected his dismissal.

The military coup of 1950 was made possible by a number of factors. Estimé had not only failed to gain support from the powerful bourgeois class, but he had alienated much black support. In addition to this the world economic situation was not particularly favourable to the country, and the international fair organised in celebration of the bicentenary of Port-au-Prince had cost much more than it was worth. The action of the army in overthrowing the Estimé government was thus welcomed by many black politicians, like Fignolé and Saint Lot, as well as by big business, by the Roman Catholic church and by the mulatto Marxists of the PSP. The latter group attacked the suppression of public liberties, the banning of political parties and student associations, the closing of newspapers (including their own, *La Nation*) and the attempt to revise the democratic constitution of 1946, and they approved the army's coup.[2]

As a result of the coup, Paul Magloire became presidential candidate, posing as the 'apostle of national unity', who would once more bring together classes and colours which had been bitterly divided by the actions of the Estimé government. Magloire was the *caudillo* whose mission it was to restore unity to the nation; he attacked 'politicians' who had exploited the divisions in the country, securing and retaining power by 'the odious strategy of setting one group of Haitians against another'.[3] This call for national unity was in fact a mask behind which the elite together with a number of opportunist black politicians were able to return to power.[4] The Roman Catholic hierarchy had been particularly concerned about the way things had been going under Estimé. They were opposed to the patronage and encouragement given by members of his government to the ethnological movement. They were also afraid that his mild nationalism might eventually lead to the replacement of foreign ecclesiastics by nationals. Magloire was the answer to their prayers, and was received into the cathedral at Gonaïves by Bishop Paul Robert, with the words 'Art thou he that should come or do we look for another?' – words originally addressed by the disciples of John the Baptist to Jesus. Robert saw the *caudillo* as bringing 'a new liberation' and continuing the work begun by Geffrard when he signed the Concordat of 1860: Magloire was 'a saviour' who would redeem a country descending towards the abyss. The junta had already issued a decree on 29 June 1950 banning all manifestations of the Voodoo religion, which was hailed in *La Phalange* as a significant step towards freeing the Haitian people from their 'shameful servitude to African deities'.[5] With support from big business, the army, the church, the mulatto Marxists and the black opportunists it is not surprising that Magloire was elected with an overwhelming majority; he was in fact the only serious candidate.

Gradually, however, Magloire alienated significant groups among his original supporters. Duvalier and the hard core of Estimists were implacably opposed to the *caudillo* from the start. They were soon joined by Fignolé, who found that he had less influence in the new government than he had expected. In August 1952 Fignolé formed the Grand Parti National Démocrate, based upon the MOP. In its ideology it was 'anti-communist and anti-totalitarian', attempting to unite progressive elements among the elite with the urban proletariat.[6] Magloire became increasingly sensitive to criticism, and closed a number of journals, including *L'Action*, edited by Georges Petit. In December 1953 Fignolé and others founded the Ligue de Défense des Libertés Publiques, but a few weeks later its principal leaders were arrested and accused of inciting the army to revolt. Magloire attempted to reinforce his support from the business community. Leading businessmen, including Brandt, Madsen, Vital, Nadal, Deschamps and others, pledged their allegiance to the regime,[7] though the more liberal among the elite, led by Louis Déjoie, were increasingly critical of the government. By 1956, when Magloire attempted to achieve *continuismo* on the Latin American pattern, there was a formidable array of groups opposed to his regime. The *caudillo* began to pose as the defender of the black masses but he was too late. After failing to secure an extension of his term of office, he resigned as president, but attempted to retain power as provisional head of state with the support of the army. In the face of widespread opposition, however, Magloire decided to follow the well-worn presidential path into exile, while his police chief Marcaisse Prosper took refuge in a foreign embassy.

An interpretation of the 1950 coup d'état such as I have suggested has been called 'superficial' by Doubout and Joly in their interesting monograph on trade unionism in Haiti.[8] The more profound significance of the coup is, according to these authors, that it was a definitive break with the democratic and popular current in the revolutionary movement of 1946. Yet from what they themselves say about the repressive policy of the Estimé regime, this break had already been made. There was little danger of a powerful and independent labour movement significantly affecting the social and economic structure of the country under Estimé. The events of 1950 ought therefore to be seen as a struggle for political power between two rival elites; the 'superficial' interpretation is, in this case, the right one.

II

Duvalier and the black legend

Le problème des classes à travers l'histoire d'Haïti was written by François Duvalier and Lorimer Denis in 1946, being first published as a series of articles in the journal *Chantiers*. The journal was the official organ of the MOP, and the articles were dedicated to 'Daniel Fignolé, symbole des aspirations et des traditions de toute une classe d'hommes'.[9] In this essay, and also in the columns of the weekly journal *Les Griots*, founded in 1948 by Duvalier, Denis, André Séjour and Kléber Georges Jacob, the *noiriste* position received its most radical formulation. In *Le problème des classes* we find an elaboration of the black legend of the Haitian past, and an insistence upon the central role which colour has played in the history of the country.

Duvalier and Denis maintained that even in colonial Saint Domingue the prejudice of mulattoes against the blacks was a significant factor, cutting across the 'caste' division between slave and freeman. The free black was regarded as inferior by a light-skinned slave, and free blacks dared not have mulatto slaves working for them, owing to the pressure of public opinion. In the colony one-third of the property and one-quarter of the slaves were owned by the *affranchis*, who were mostly mulattoes. For Denis and Duvalier, Vincent Ogé was the symbol of *affranchi* class consciousness and of mulatto colour prejudice. No leader, they insisted, who was sincerely devoted to the cause of the masses could possibly emerge from that group. In this context the authors made an oblique reference to the party politics of their own day, and to the need for a leader who is the authentic spokesman of the black masses. Duvalier and Denis regarded the rivalry between Toussaint and Rigaud as essentially a war of colour, and they continually assimilated the distinction between *anciens libres* and *nouveaux libres* to the colour distinction between mulatto and black. They wrote about 'the class of mulattoes', and claimed that Rigaud's army and the South which he controlled were characterised by colour prejudice on the part of this class.[10] Dessalines was seen as the great champion of the masses. He was 'the first Haitian socialist', assassinated by the mulatto elite because of his policy of economic equality. In their brief sketch of the Haitian past Christophe and Pétion hardly received mention. The black

Christophe's possible complicity in the emperor's assassination, and the frankly elitist policy which he pursued, scarcely justify his inclusion on the side of the angels. Pétion's land distribution, on the other hand, had led Janvier to admit a certain admiration for the mulatto president. This admission, however, was something of an embarrassment to the *noiristes*. If Pétion could not be shown to be wicked, it was obviously thought best to ignore him.[11] The Dessalinian mantle in fact fell on Goman, who led a prolonged rebellion against Pétion in La Grand' Anse, and it was later taken up by Acaau and by President Pierrot. The advantage of these three men for the purposes of the black legend is that they did not control political power for any length of time, and the policy which they would have pursued is thus largely a matter of conjecture. Soulouque barely received mention, presumably for the same general reason that Christophe was omitted. Geffrard was elitist in his sympathies, though at certain moments he pursued 'a sort of policy of equilibrium'.[12] Elsewhere Duvalier was somewhat less charitable in his judgment of Geffrard, calling him 'a dangerous type of politician'.[13] A correct judgment about Geffrard became a matter of practical importance during the course of the election campaign of 1957, in which, as we shall see, one of the principal contenders was a grandson of Geffrard. In his message to the nation of November 1956, Duvalier linked the name of Geffrard with that of Salomon as the two governments which had inaugurated progressive policies, but later on in the campaign, in a message addressed to the people of the South in March 1957, Geffrard is referred to as having merely put into effect educational policies devised by Salomon.[14] The 'exception that proves the rule' in the black legend is President Salnave, 'the mulatto democrat', who was the idol of the black masses. Salnave's achievement in overthrowing Geffrard and in founding the National Party, together with his populism and his alleged practice of the Voodoo religion, probably account for his position of honour in the black legend. Marcel Vaval concluded his bitter attack on the mulatto elite with the words 'Vive Salnave!'[15] The short-lived regime of Salnave (1867–69) might well have evolved into a 'democratic dictatorship', if it had not been cut short by a revolution, according to Duvalier and Denis. The hero of *Le problème des classes* is, however, undoubtedly President Salomon, who ruled from 1879 to 1888. Under him the majority was able to take power. Salomon undertook a prolonged struggle against 'the eternal enemies of the masses', regrouping the blacks into a rational organisation based upon class loyalty.[16] After the fall of Salomon the blacks were out of power until 1908, when there was 'a real ascendancy' of this group once more with the election of Antoine Simon. After the fall of Simon, the blacks did not return to power again until 1946 with the advent of Estimé – this 'authentic son of the peasant masses'.[17]

Duvalier and Denis asked themselves why it was that the blacks, who form the vast majority of the Haitian people, have since 1804 been generally dominated by the mulatto minority. They listed a number of factors, including a lack of solidarity among the blacks and a selfish spirit which leads the more fortunate to despise their less fortunate brethren; they also referred to a lack of patience, to 'a spirit of equality which destroys the principle of hierarchy and the respect for traditions' and to a self-depreciation among the blacks which prevents their rise.[18]

There would appear to be some contradiction in the thought of Duvalier and Denis on the question of whether the black masses had ever enjoyed real power in the history of Haiti. When discussing Salnave, Salomon and Simon in *Le problème des classes* they suggested that the masses did enjoy such power under these presidents, though in a previous article they had insisted that the bourgeoisie had always been the real masters in the country.[19] Another significant feature of the black legend is the equivocal position adopted on the relationship between class and colour distinctions in the country. On the one hand there is explicit recognition of the fact that not all blacks have been poor and not all mulattoes have been rich. On the other hand this fact is frequently ignored, and class distinctions are assimilated to colour distinctions. This assimilation is not the result of an argued position, but is covertly performed. As we shall see, this was one of the basic criticisms of the black legend made by Price Mars in one of his last writings.[20]

Conflicts in religion and education

The elaboration of a black legend was only a part of the ideological concern of the *noiristes* in the period under discussion. They enthusiastically cultivated that 'véritable mystique' of race, the origins of which Duvalier and Denis had ascribed to the writings of Carl Brouard.[21] *Griots* writers called for the development of a 'conscience nationale', which would involve the acceptance of new values and a rejection of the old individualism and of the colonial mentality which was still a powerful factor in Haiti.[22] This national consciousness could be achieved only by a reform in the educational system. The *Griots* writers of the Estimé era therefore continued to press for those changes in school curricula and organisation which *noiristes* of the pre-1946 period had demanded. René Chalmers urged that history be taught in such a way as to develop a racial and national mystique, and to provide faith and inspiration for the future.[23] Marcel Vaval pointed out that many of the school text books indicated European and colonial values referring to 'our ancestor Charlemagne' and 'our homeland France'. Pictures and statues used in schools and churches portrayed the saints as white, and reinforced feelings of inferiority on the part of black people. Art teachers in the schools should encourage children to see beauty in the African face.[24] Price Mars, Hervé Boyer, Emmanuel C. Paul and others insisted that the *créole* language be officially recognised as a national language, and that it should play an increasing part in the education of young people.[25]

Duvalier and Denis listed five requirements of educational reform: (*a*) a rationalisation of the teaching programme so that it would be based upon 'our national and racial ideal'; (*b*) the teaching of courses in civics and in social ethics; (*c*) the use of the *créole* language in primary schools, and an increasing emphasis upon practical subjects like public hygiene; (*d*) 'the suppression of courses in religious instruction which do not correspond to any reality, and their systematic replacement by courses in national and racial morals'; and (*e*) the laicisation of teaching in Haitian history. 'The education of a people', they concluded, 'cannot be entrusted to foreigners without this people renouncing its historic mission.'[26] In an explicit attack upon the role of the Roman Catholic church in education, these two writers insisted that foreign clerics had sabotaged the teaching of Haitian history ever since the Concordat of 1860; this act of Geffrard had in fact established a 'colonial system of education' in Haiti.[27] Another writer denounced church schools as centres of prejudice.[28]

The conflict between clerics and *noiristes* was by no means restricted to the field of education. The *Griots* writers, for example, strongly supported Hubert Papailler, a Haitian priest who had been removed from his parish by Bishop Paul Robert of Gonaïves for having conducted the funeral of a Freemason. Max Cadet referred to Papailler as 'a victim of racial prejudice', and saw the manifestation of support from his parishioners as 'the signal of the struggle for religious independence'.[29]

We have already noted that the *Griots* writers and others connected with the ethnological movement defended the Voodoo cult, and criticised the Roman Catholic church for its attacks upon Voodoo. The controversy was revived in the late forties. The indefatigable Père Foisset launched a number of attacks upon school teachers of the *lycées* and upon the Bureau d'Ethnologie for attempting to erect Voodoo into a national religion.[30] Foisset criticised the official patronage which was being given to the ethnological movement by members of the government, singling out for particular condemnation a former minister of education. The church, he argued, was not against the study of folklore as such, and it has always tried to 'transform and Christianise pagan customs', but he asserted that the ethnological movement in Haiti was inspired less by genuine patriotism than by the vanity of 'performers', and by the greed and fanaticism of the devotees of the cult.[31] Duvalier and Denis replied to these charges, reproaching Foisset and other foreign clergy for sowing seeds of division and discord in the country, for undermining the culture of the people, and for keeping the peasant masses in a state of ignorance.[32] In his reply the French priest accused Duvalier and Denis of being themselves devotees of the Voodoo cult and 'theoreticians of neo-racism', regarding their article as 'a declaration of war'.[33]

In a report to the Vatican in 1947 Mgr Robert maintained that the struggle against superstition was 'the fundamental problem of the missionary apostolate in Haiti'; not only was the Voodoo religion an obstacle to the spread of Christian truth, it was also a major bulwark against social progress.[34] There is to be detected, however, a change of emphasis in the writings of Robert on the question of Voodoo in the period following *la campagne anti-superstitieuse*. By 1951 he had come to insist that Christians must seek to understand the mentality of the Haitian people, in order to find 'points of contact' between Voodoo and Christianity. He quoted *La philosophie bantoue* by Père Placide Tempels to illustrate the possibility of such an understanding.[35] In the following year he went as far as to assert the existence of 'authentic values' in Voodoo which need to be respected and preserved. He pointed to the similarity between the *wanga* of Voodoo and the Christian sacraments. 'There exist in Voodoo', he went on, 'practices which are able to assist us wonderfully in understanding the sense of the Christian calling and even of the priestly and religious vocation.'[36] Nevertheless, Robert insisted, Voodoo is a religion of African origin in which the Christian elements are purely superficial; the church must demand a total abandonment of paganism among its people.[37]

Apart from these controversies between representatives of the Roman Catholic church and of the ethnological movement, there was a general concern in Haiti in the period following 1946 about the domination of the church by foreign clergy. In September 1946 an article in *Le Mercure*, a pro-Estimé journal, called on the government to take action in the matter and to secure the appointment of Haitian bishops. A similar demand was made by the journal *Lumière* of Gonaïves. *Construction*, a journal controlled by Fignolé, also called for the promotion of local clergy to the highest positions in the church.[38] This demand for a national clergy was by no means restricted to *noiriste* writers. Even a journal like *L'Action*, edited by Georges Petit, which had published articles harshly critical of the Voodoo religion,[39] condemned the appointment of a foreign cleric, Mgr Cousineau, to the post of co-adjutor bishop of Cap Haïtien, as 'wounding to our national pride, because it amounts to a warrant of incapacity or ineptitude issued against our race'.[40] Gérard Gayot, in his demand for a *clergé indigène*, referred to three wars which Haitians had had to fight 'the war against the French colonists, the war against the American 'colons en kaki', and finally the war against the Breton colonists in cassocks.[41]

With respect to the Eglise Episcopale a similar demand was made for a Haitian bishop. 'It is high time', declared Marc Pierre, 'that we had a clergy: local, independent, autonomous.'[42] Yet, as we have seen, Episcopal clergy tended to be more sympathetic to the Voodoo religion, and to the ethnological movement, than did their Roman Catholic brethren. In fact, Foisset criticised the Eglise Episcopale for its position on this matter. A priest from that church replied in *Les Griots*, maintaining that the study of folklore is vital in order to understand the significance of popular beliefs and customs.[43] In honour of the bicentenary of Port-au-Prince in 1949, the Anglican bishop, Alfred Voegeli, an American, commissioned a number of Haitian artists to decorate the cathedral of the Holy Trinity with murals in the 'primitive' style. Prominent in the central mural, however, is the Masonic 'all-seeing eye'. It will be recalled that the National Party newspaper in the time of Salomon was called *L'Œil*, and that Bishop Jacques Holly was himself a Freemason and had been willing to conduct Masonic funerals in the cathedral.[44]

The economic base

The *Griots* writers of the late forties were increasingly concerned with the importance of economic factors in the life of the country. Denis and Duvalier argued that one of the chief causes of 'disequilibrium' in Haiti was the poverty of the masses, a poverty which is characteristic of all semi-colonial countries. In the history of civilisations, they continued, developments in literature and art are less significant than changes in the economic structure. In this context they claimed that the law passed by the Estimé government which established a minimum wage was of great significance.[45] As under-secretary of state for labour in 1949, Duvalier organised a National Congress of Labour, assisted by Clément Jumelle and others. Duvalier began one of his speeches at the Congress with a quotation from Salvador Allende, to the effect that national defence and well-being rest upon sound health services, and he gave details of the government's plan for a system of national insurance for workers.[46] Duvalier claimed, in his closing speech, that although the economic sphere ought not to be regarded as an end in itself, economic forces are powerful in influencing the life of a people. He called for a study of the real needs and aspirations of the various groups in Haiti, which could be achieved only by a 'bio-sociologie'. New forms of social organisation must be allowed to evolve which are peculiar to the Haitian situation, and legislation must be enacted which 'conforms to the Haitian mentality'.[47] Duvalier and Denis listed the achievements of the Estimé regime in the economic and social field: the establishment of a minimum wage, irrigation schemes, encouragement of industrialisation, development of hydro-electric power, urban reconstruction, improvement in water supply, maternity and child welfare schemes in rural areas, 'the utilisation of folklore material' and the construction of new schools.[48]

While the Estimé government cautiously encouraged the development of trade unionism, a somewhat paternalistic attitude was adopted. The mentality of the Haitian workers, insisted a writer in *Les Griots*, is different from that of workers in advanced industrial countries; they need to be guided and educated. The writer went on to criticise the unions for being more interested in political than in social questions.[49] The shadow of Fignolé and the MOP continually haunted the Estimé regime, and the Mouvement was eventually banned, together with the other independent unions grouped under the Fédération des Travailleurs Haïtiens.

The economic and social policy advocated by the *noiristes* of the post-1946 period was termed 'equilibrium'.[50] It was opposed to a policy of 'exclusivism' which was ascribed to the mulatto elite politicians. In fact the term 'equilibrium' was little more than a euphemism for black power. Joseph D. Baguidy made it clear that this 'equilibrium' or 'social balance' can be achieved only by destroying the economic basis of elite power. The Haitian bourgeoisie constitutes a caste whose power is founded on economic bases such as the ownership of land and control of the commercial sector; educational and cultural influences are secondary to this economic factor.[51] Hervé Boyer argued that this new equilibrium can be achieved only by encouraging small peasants to improve their productivity, and by setting up agricultural banks throughout the country to provide credit facilities for these small farmers.[52]

We thus find a continued development in political ideas in the period following 1946 among *noiriste* writers and among those who were to join together in support of Duvalier in the election campaign of 1956–7.

The Marxism of Etienne Charlier

Among Marxists of the post-1946 era Etienne Charlier stands out as one of the few writers who attempted seriously to relate Marxist theory to the realities of the Haitian situation, past and present. In his *Aperçu sur la formation historique de la nation haïtienne*, and in a series of articles published in *La Nation*, Charlier attempted a Marxist interpretation of Haitian conflicts. Although he was eager to point to the underlying economic factors which determined developments in Haiti since colonial times, he fully recognised the importance of colour and 'caste' divisions. He implicitly rejected the naive dogmatism of a writer like Joseph Déjean, who could blandly assert that in colonial Saint Domingue colour distinctions were 'absolutely secondary', and that social distinctions could be accounted for simply in terms of economic interests.[53] This position would preclude any satisfactory understanding of the role which was played by the *affranchis*, a group which, owning perhaps one-third of the land and one-quarter of the slaves, had economic interests in common with the whites, but which at crucial stages of the revolutionary conflict aligned itself with the *nouveaux libres*. Charlier insisted that 'in the last analysis' the ideological superstructure rests upon an economic foundation,[54] but he was equally clear that Haitian politics could not be understood simply in terms of class conflict; colour factors assumed in certain periods a central role.

Charlier argued that the Haiti of the early nineteen-fifties was a semi-colonial society, in which 'caste' divisions, associated largely with colour factors, were basic. He agreed with Christian Beaulieu that Haiti was in the process of becoming a society based upon class divisions, where social stratification would be regulated no longer according to criteria of colour, but by the economic role which the individual plays in the productive process.[55] Charlier, therefore, criticised the Estimé regime for having placed too much emphasis upon the colour factor. The resurgence of the colour question was, however, largely due to the policy of the Lescot regime, which had reversed the policy of 'equilibrium' pursued by Vincent. By equilibrium Charlier here meant that blacks from the elite and semi-elite were included in the Vincent government together with mulattoes.[56] The *mulâtrification* under Lescot led to the rise of the *authentiques* in 1946, who posed the social problem in terms of colour rather than class. Yet Charlier was compelled to admit that the *authentiques* of 1946 were not entirely mistaken in recognising the importance of colour at this period. Also Charlier conceded that the Estimé government had achieved something positive; in particular it had secured a 'revaloration du noir', which was important in Haiti, where for too long a 'western' conception of beauty had been accepted. Again the Estimé regime had reinforced the position of the small black bourgeois class, raising it to the level of the mulatto bourgeoisie.[57] In these respects Estimé had contributed positively to the development of Haiti. The retrogressive policy of Lescot had to some extent been reversed, and the relevant social question could now be seen once more in terms of economic rather than colour factors. The election campaign of 1956–7 and the victory of Duvalier, however, suggest that Charlier's analysis of the situation was deficient, in that it failed to recognise the continued centrality of the colour question in Haitian politics. We may even say that Charlier's own commitment to the Déjoie party exemplified this continued centrality.

Charlier extended his Marxist analysis of Haitian politics back to colonial times, and put forward an interpretation of the past which conflicted at certain points with the black legend. Charlier's position

was stated in his *Aperçu*, published in 1954. This essay led to a controversy between Charlier and Emmanuel C. Paul in the columns of
Le Jour and *Le Nouvelliste*. The bitterness of the controversy was out
of all proportion to the differences between the protagonists. While
on the one hand Charlier recognised the importance of colour in Haitian
history and was critical of the role played by the mulatto elite, Paul
for his part maintained that economic status rather than colour
determines class structure.[58] There was thus considerable agreement
between Charlier and Paul, who were both critical adherents of the
traditional legends. Paul attacked Charlier in particular for having
underemphasised the role played by the *marrons* in the revolutionary
struggle, and of having laid too much stress upon the revolutionary
contribution of the *affranchis*. He accused the mulatto Marxist of having
too much sympathy for Rigaud and for having dealt unfairly with
Toussaint. 'Is it not human to have such sympathies?' remarked Paul.[59]
Charlier denied that his work was inspired by colour prejudice, and
accused the group on whose behalf Paul spoke of believing that all
mulattoes are reactionary, and that all blacks are revolutionaries at the
head of the struggle for the emancipation of the masses. Charlier agreed
that he had not pictured Rigaud as a stupid and reactionary mulatto
but had attempted an objective account of the man.[60] He went on to
accuse Paul of failing to recognise the importance of the new black
elite of *nouveaux libres* which had established itself in the years following emancipation.[61] Charlier defended his assessment of the role of
the *marrons*, by arguing that, although these groups of *marrons* could
properly be regarded as representing the 'armed protest of the . . .
avant-garde of the masses of Saint Domingue against colonial oppression
and exploitation', it was by no means the only form which such protest
took.[62] In fact, he pointed out, in the years immediately before the
revolution of 1791 the most active groups of *marrons* had made peace
with colonial governments of the island. Yet he insisted that the whole
of his essay emphasised the important and central role played by the
masses in the struggle against the colonial regime.[63] Charlier maintained that not only had most Haitian historians, blacks and mulattoes
alike, been influenced by colour prejudice and therefore painted an
unbalanced picture of the past, but also that they had failed to take
into account the underlying structural factors determining the history
of the country. As a result of this, history tended too often to be the
story of great men, of heroes: Toussaint, Rigaud, Dessalines and
others.[64] The controversy between Charlier and Paul was, as I have
suggested, somewhat unreal; each was more concerned to attack the
legend which he imagined the other to be defending than carefully to
criticise what his opponent actually wrote. Neither adhered to the more
extreme version of the legend with which he was associated, and each

was therefore unjustly blamed by his critic for holding positions which he did not in fact hold. The encounter is nevertheless significant in that it illustrates well the propensity of Haitians to discuss the past in terms of competing legends which have practical consequences for the present, rather than in terms of a disinterested and dispassionate attempt to understand the past for its own sake.

Poetry and protest

Among the younger generation of the post-1946 period two Marxist writers deserve attention, they are Jacques Stéphen Alexis and René Depestre. The former, born at Gonaïves in 1922, was the son of the black novelist Stéphen Alexis; four years his junior, René Depestre, on the other hand, was the child of poor mulatto parents from Jacmel. Both men had been active in the editing of *La Ruche* and *La Nouvelle Ruche*, and had given a qualified support to Estimé after his election. Depestre saw the black middle-class government of 1946 as 'the avant-garde of the proletariat and of the peasantry of Haiti', which would prepare for a total transformation of the conditions of life and of social values.[65] Yet the bitter strife of January to August, in which the colour question reasserted itself, submerging all other loyalties, had led to a certain disillusionment in the spirits of these young men. The optimism of *Etincelles* was replaced by the more sceptical mood of *Gerb de sang*, a collection of poems written during 1946. In the latter volume it was an 'enfant des désespoirs féconds' who sang of a rotten world:

> Pourri le monde pourrie la chair pourrie la vie
> pourrie toute chose vue pourrie toute chose entendue
> pourris le bec des oiseaux la bouche des hommes
> pourris le museau des femmes les ongles des bêtes.[66]

Depestre and Alexis as creative writers were particularly concerned with the relationship between culture and the life of the community. They agreed that art must be concerned with real problems in the real world, and they had little time for the notion of 'art for art's sake'. Yet, for the creative artist, realism must be embodied in lively and imaginative forms which will be peculiar to the group of people among whom the artist lives. Alexis coined the phrase 'réalisme merveilleux' to describe the cultural contribution of Haitian artists to the modern world. This Haitian realism is a peculiar blending of traditions stemming from Africa, from the Caribbean and from Europe. 'Before all and above all a son of Africa', he wrote, 'I am nevertheless the inheritor of the Caribbean and the Amerindian as a result of a secret connexion of blood and of the long survival of cultures after their death. In the same way,

I am to a considerable extent the inheritor of old Europe, of Spain and of France above all . . .'[67]

Alexis's principal novels are concerned with peasant life in Haiti and he must be seen as continuing and developing the artistic tradition of Jacques Roumain. While there is in both writers a strong ideological motivation it would be a mistake to see their novels simply as channels for Marxist propaganda. Both writers have an ability to create living characters and to portray the charm and the tragedy of peasant life. In *Compère général Soleil* (1955), Alexis builds his story around the massacre of Haitian peasants in the Dominican Republic during the mid-thirties. The powerful influence of African traditions and customs on the life of the peasant is contrasted with the United States domination of urban culture which had begun during the occupation. Alexis pictures American cars as great frogs which crawl over the body of Haiti. 'The city dweller is the slave of the Americans, slave of the bureaucracy – some would go so far as to sell their wives – slave of his stomach, slave of all the big fish who oppress the people.'[68] Alexis's second important novel, *Les arbres musiciens* (1957) is about the so-called 'anti-superstition campaign' launched by the Roman Catholic hierarchy with support from the newly elected president Lescot in 1941. The campaign is associated in the story with the expropriation of peasants' land on behalf of an American-controlled company. In both novels Alexis pictures the peasant returning instinctively to his ancestral roots in times of crisis, and particularly to the Voodoo religion. Yet for Alexis, as for Roumain, this religion must be understood as the opium of an oppressed people. The *loas* rise up from the earth in Haiti because the earth is poor; when electricity and agricultural machinery appear they will die. 'The supernatural was the enemy of a free life. It paralysed men, alienated their courage and their spirit of resolution. All the *houngans*, high priests, parish priests and ministers trapped man in despair and resignation.'[69]

While he defended the general tradition of *indigénisme* in Haitian culture, and saw the ethnological movement as a valid reassertion of the African contribution to the life and traditions of the people, Alexis was critical of the *négritude* movement, as tending to 'conceal the reality of the cultural autonomy of the Haitian people'; he also declared war on the 'nationalistic and bleating folklorism' of the *Griots* school. The popular culture of the Haitian people – their dancing, music, poetry and folk stories have value only insofar as a more universal and dynamic content could be poured into their mould.[70] Elsewhere, however, he was prepared to generalise about the essentially practical orientation of negro art.[71] The 'marvellous realism' of the Haitians is universal in scope and humanist in content, but 'resolutely national in its form'. Each national culture, for Alexis, and for Depestre also, must be seen in the specific historical context out of which it emerges. Depestre criticised talk about 'black poetry' as mythical, owing to this lack of a historical and concrete dimension. Alexis insisted that although he and his fellow countrymen were indeed part of an international army fighting for a new humanism, they formed a Haitian battalion with its own peculiar history and characteristics, with its special contribution to make.[72]

For the Marxist writer there can be no going back on the past, and there is no place for that hatred of man, that hatred of self, that determination to demolish, which he believed to be characteristic of certain writers in the *négritude* tradition.[73] With this positive approach to the past − a past which though sometimes painful may nevertheless be seen to contribute in a constructive way to the present − there can be 'no rejection of the past, no need for "decolonization"'.[74] The 'marvellous realism' of Alexis contrasts strikingly therefore with the rhetoric of 'decolonisation' which is prevalent in the newly independent states of the Caribbean. The colonial experience has left indelible marks on the region which cannot be erased, though on the basis of these marks a new pattern can be drawn, and the post-colonial state which emerges will be significantly different from its colonial predecessor. Attempts to undo the past − to turn the nation into a *carte blanche* − are utopian in the worst sense of the word, and are (as both Burke and Marx realised) bound to fail.

Mulatto liberalism

Doctor Francois Dalencour was for many years the *porte-parole* of mulatto liberalism, and he continued his work into the 1950s. He saw himself as the heir of a great tradition going back to Ardouin and Saint-Rémy, whose major works he re-edited. The introduction to his edition of Ardouin's *Etudes sur l'histoire d'Haïti* begins with a eulogy to Edmond Paul and Boyer Bazelais, the liberal politicians of the second half of the nineteenth century. Why should Dalencour begin his introduction with a discussion of the work of two men whose significance lies in a period after the death of Ardouin? The reason is that for Dalencour, as for those mulatto historians whom we have considered in an earlier chapter,[75] the study of the past and the practice of politics in the present are hopelessly interwoven. A proper account of the past will reinforce the claims of the mulatto elite in the present. Ardouin's historical writings and Boyer Bazelais's invasion of Miragoâne were but parts of a single struggle. For Dalencour the great period of Haitian history was under Pétion and Boyer, when the mulattoes established themselves in power; apart from these two heads of state, only Geffrard, Nissage Saget and Boisrond Canal − all mulattoes − were beneficent.[76]

The short schism of the South in 1810–11 and the revolution of 1843, in both of which the mulattoes were divided among themselves, were tragic events, and it is significant that the hero of Ardouin's *Etudes* is General Borgella, who had led the South back into Pétion's republic, thus providing a united front against Christophe's kingdom. Of the very few pictures in Dalencour's edition of this book, two are concerned with the reconciliation of mulatto differences: the submission of the southern leaders to Pétion in 1811, and the reunion (in exile) of Boyer and the man who had been instrumental in deposing him, Hérard Dumesle.

Dalencour, then, regarded his historical writing and editing as providing a strong argument for his present commitment to political and economic liberalism. The Liberal Party of the nineteenth century had, however, in his opinion lacked a coherent ideology. 'It is this work of education – national, spiritual, liberal – that I have been engaged in over the past thirty years, and which I have progressively realised by my works of history, of school education and by a series of new editions . . .'[77] He argued against militarism in politics, and believed that a system of universal suffrage should be introduced in Haiti despite its relatively backward economic position and its high rate of illiteracy.[78] 'I dream of seeing you one day, dear Haiti', he wrote, 'resembling the great western democracies, the sublime models of democratic liberalism in the world.'[79] His lengthy *Philosophie de la liberté* sets forth the theoretical basis of his political creed.

Less committed to liberalism and democracy, and more explicitly and passionately concerned with the colour problem, was Alfred Viau. His view of the past was in line with the mulatto legend. Toussaint, cruel and vindictive, had been a puppet in the hands of the whites, and had 'laid the foundation of a colonial organisation'. In the war of the South he had introduced into the souls of black Haitians the germ of colour prejudice; black leaders like Dessalines, Christophe, Soulouque, Salomon and Estimé merely followed in his footsteps; Edmond Paul and F. D. Légitime were the 'exceptions that prove the rule'.[80] Viau saw two tendencies at work in Haitian history: *louverturisme*, which stood for the union of black and white against mulatto, 'to the detriment even of the sovereignty and independence of the country'; and *pétio-dessalinisme*, representing the union of black and mulatto Haitians against the whites, with the aim of achieving a complete independence of the country.[81] Viau ascribed the ills of Haiti to certain weaknesses in the character of the mulatto. Although he suffers from no inferiority complex because of his colour, he is too individualistic, lacking the gregariousness of the black, 'he does not have the clannish spirit, he fails to practise solidarity of colour', he chooses his friends according to common interests or to common social class rather than according to the colour of their skin.[82] Instead of praising the mulatto for his freedom from colour prejudice, Viau denounces him for his lack of solidarity and for his timidity in the face of the black.[83] Viau, whose son had been assassinated under Estimé, lived for many years in the Dominican Republic, where he became an apologist for Trujillo. He returned to Haiti and proclaimed himself a presidential candidate in 1956.

Although less fanatical in his adherence to the mulatto viewpoint, Dantès Bellegarde should also be mentioned in this context. As one of the leading intellectuals of his day, Bellegarde exercised considerable influence among the elite. In 1950 he welcomed the military coup, and he presided over the constitutional assembly at Gonaïves. He praised the military junta for defending order and liberty, and he expressed complete confidence in Paul Magloire. While reminding his audience of Haiti's declaration of independence made at Gonaïves in 1804, which marked 'the triumphant entry of a people of negro origin into the society of civilised nations', he insisted that the government must, by means of education and religion, liberate the country from 'degrading superstitions'. Another speaker at the assembly, Luc Fouché, in a thinly veiled attack on Estimé's *noiriste* supporters, denounced those who sought to undermine the unity of the nation by attempting to compartmentalise the population, which in fact belongs to a single community of origin.[84]

The Parti Populaire Social Chrétien constituted a distinct group in this period. It was founded in October 1946 by Edouard Tardieu, J. M. Lescouflair and Emmanuel Lajoie and can best be seen as developing out of mulatto liberalism. The views of the party, expressed in its journal *L'Action Sociale*, were inspired by the ideas of Christian Democratic parties in Europe and particularly by those of the MRP in France. These men defended the family and private property, but criticised unregulated capitalism and individualistic liberalism. Writers from this group rebutted the criticisms that Catholicism is inherently conservatism and that it encourages an attitude of resignation on the part of the masses.[85] While Monsieur Tardieu was engaged in political and journalistic adventures, Madame Tardieu maintained the family business, advertising her 'Produits Alimentaires' on the back page of *L'Action Sociale*.

III

With the fall of Magloire early in December 1956 there followed almost ten months of political instability and confusion; on departing for exile the *caudillo* had declared that the country was like a cigar alight at both ends. Nemours Pierre Louis, as president of the Cour de

Cassation, became the provisional head of state, but after a short period in office he was attacked by critics as 'the *alter ego* of Magloire'. In the face of mounting denunciations he resigned and was replaced by Franck Sylvain early in February 1957. The new provisional president began to make preparations for a general election, but was criticised for plotting to secure the election of Duvalier. After two months in office he was overthrown by the army under General Léon Cantave, who instituted a collegial government which was effectively controlled by the followers of Louis Déjoie and Daniel Fignolé, two of the leading contenders for the presidency, who had joined together to prevent the drift towards Duvalier. 'The monster Duvalier' was denounced in the *déjoiste* journal *Indépendance* for advocating the setting up of a military junta.[86] In May an attempt was made by the *déjoiste* elements in the government to replace Cantave by Colonel Pierre Armand, and on 25 May a pitched battle took place in the capital between rival groups in the armed forces. Fignolé joined with Duvalier and Clément Jumelle in an effort to block the growing power of Déjoie; Fignolé was made provisional president and Antonio Kébreau was appointed head of the armed forces. With less than three weeks in office, however, Fignolé was dismissed by Kébreau and sent into exile. The military junta under Kébreau proceeded to organise elections for 22 September.

During these ten months a large number of politicians came forward as presidential candidates; they included Alfred Viau, Auguste Fouché, Métrius Bonaventure, Julio J.-P. Audain, René Salomon, Clément Jumelle, Daniel Fignolé, Louis Déjoie and François Duvalier. Only the last three had any substantial following in the country; the others could have succeeded only as a result of some compromise among politicians and the military. Fignolé was a school teacher and union leader whose strength lay particularly among the urban poor and sections of the black middle class in the capital; his general position was, as we have seen, populist, anti-communist and *noiriste*. Déjoie had support from the majority of the business community in the capital and from the cities of the South. He also enjoyed strong backing from those elements in the Roman Catholic church which had supported Magloire. He was a light-skinned mulatto, the grandson of President Geffrard, and although generally conservative, he was favoured by many former members of the Parti Socialiste Populaire. Finally Duvalier had a strong following in the North and Artibonite and also had support from most of the black middle class in the capital. The election was bitterly fought, and the changing alliances among the candidates are to be seen as tactical moves designed to prevent their rivals from getting too powerful rather than as representing any genuine agreement on policy or programme.

The military junta under Kébreau was generally favourable to

Duvalier and was praised by his supporters as 'the ultimate hope of the Haitian people'.[87] By the time of the election in September only two effective candidates remained, Duvalier and Déjoie; Jumelle was still a candidate but lacked support from any powerful group. While irregularities no doubt occurred in the polling on 22 September, it is likely that Duvalier's victory reflected opinion in the country. The result was:

Duvalier	679,884
Déjoie	266,992
Jumelle	9,980

Déjoie had an overwhelming majority in Les Cayes, and also won Port-au-Prince, Jacmel, Port-de-Paix and Pétionville; he was, however, unable to secure a majority in any *département*, and all the seats in the senate went to supporters of Duvalier.[88]

'The activity of a generation', wrote Duvalier in 1948, 'is divided into two stages and two aspects. During the first half of the period approximately, the new generation propagates its ideas, its preferences and its tastes; finally these are realised and prevail in the second part of its career.'[89] Apart from a short period of ministerial responsibility under Estimé, Duvalier's contribution to politics in Haiti had largely been in the field of ideology rather than in practical politics. His election campaign was managed by the Parti Unité National, whose leaders included Marcel Vaval, Michel Aubourg, Jules and Paul Blanchet; and many of his speeches were written by Roger Dorsainville and by the former Communist Lucien Daumec, to whom Duvalier was related by marriage. Perhaps the most frequently recurring feature of these pronouncements is the claim to be the lineal successor of Estimé and to be fighting 'under the banner of *estimisme*'.[90] Again and again the name of Estimé appears; he had begun the revolution which Duvalier himself was to complete. The strident anti-clericalism of the late forties and the vigorous *noirisme* of the *Griots* doctrinaire were suitably toned down for the campaign, and Duvalier was careful not to alienate any potential support. Paul E. Magloire is almost alone as an explicit object of attack. The clergy, Roman Catholic and Protestant, were praised on a number of occasions for their zeal and hard work in the face of difficult conditions, for 'the evangelisation of our masses', and for their contribution to the 'spiritual evolution of the Haitian people'. He paid tribute, surely with tongue in cheek, to the work of the clergy of the south-west in rooting out 'superstitious practices'.[91] Duvalier insisted on more than one occasion that his studies in the field of ethnology were purely academic, and he defended himself against an 'insidious confusion between the phenomena which have been the objects of my study and my own religious convictions'. He pledged that his government would maintain good relations with the Vatican and expressed a 'profound respect for the social doctrine of the Catholic Church'.[92] Only rarely was there mention in these election addresses of the need for an indigenous clergy.[93] Although Duvalier himself refrained from criticising the Roman Catholic church during the campaign, his supporters occasionally attacked the hierarchy.[94]

While addressing the people of Gonaïves, the city of his former companion and fellow *Griot* Diaquoi, Duvalier referred to the need for a deepening of the 'prise de conscience racial'.[95] He spoke in Ouanaminthe of 'our tragic transplantation from Africa',[96] but he rarely raised the thorny question of colour in an explicit manner. Significantly it was in a speech at Les Cayes, the bastion of mulatto power, that Duvalier discussed this question. He insisted that, as a successor of Estimé, he stood for a policy of the greatest good of the greatest number 'without distinction of colour'. The revolution of 1946 symbolised the elevation of the masses, black, *griffe* and mulatto, and it witnessed a significant co-operation between Haitians of all colours. 'We are against colour prejudice', he declared, 'we shall combat it by any means in our power.'[97]

Duvalier's campaign speeches laid considerable stress upon the need for economic equality, and for an improvement in the condition of the 'exploited masses'.[98] With the fall of Magloire 'reactionary conservatism' had been defeated and political and legal inequalities had been suppressed; 'It is necessary to march now towards the suppression of economic inequalities.'[99] The candidate attacked a 'false negative liberalism'[100] and spoke of an 'economic democracy' which involved not simply political participation by the masses but a real share in economic power. 'A new equilibrium' must be established in society, he maintained.[101] Duvalier guaranteed freedom and protection to trade unions, assailing 'the forces of money' and the power of 'financial interests' in the country.[102] In these speeches one can see the influence of the *Panorama* group. In a statement of party principles, the Parti Unité National committed itself to a vigorous struggle against 'the dissoluteness of the satrapy, the machinations of the foreigner and the permanent menace of imperialism'.[103]

Together with the emphasis upon economic democracy, there were definite traces of the *Griots* ideology in the campaign addresses of Duvalier. He regarded his campaign as a 'crusade' inspired by 'a dynamic ideology'.[104] The doctrinaire of yesterday had become the presidential candidate of today.[105] He emphasised the importance of 'leadership' and referred to the influence which Kemal Ataturk had had upon his thinking.[106] There are, however, few suggestions of the kind of personalisation of power which was to occur during his term of office. Duvalier's understanding of the fact that Haiti was predominantly a rural country is reflected in many of his speeches. He praised the dignity of peasant life, attacking a philosophy of government which proclaimed 'the exclusive preponderance of the city dweller'.[107] Yet the PUN pointed to the central role which the rising middle class had played and would continue to play as the 'classe dirigeant'.[108] The old bourgeoisie had separated itself from the rest of the population and had divided the country by its selfishness.[109] Duvalier praised the army for having liberated the country from 'a system of slavery' instituted by Magloire and pledged his government's support for the great historical role which the army had played in Haitian life, promising to raise the pay of the lower ranks.[110]

The speeches of Duvalier and his supporters during the election campaign of 1956–7 gave scant indication of the policy which he was to pursue during his fourteen years in office, though they clearly reflect a shrewd assessment of the political situation at the time.

8. Culture and tyranny

1957-1971

François Duvalier was installed as president of Haiti on 22 October 1957 and remained in power until his death in April 1971. The present chapter will be concerned with the role which ideology has played in the politics of Haiti during these fourteen years. It is convenient to distinguish two periods, the first in which Duvalier was engaged in establishing his own position largely by reducing the power of a number of important groups in the country, and the second in which he attempted to effect an accommodation with these groups and to enlist their support. His avowed aim throughout his period of office was to achieve what he called a 'new equilibrium' in the country, by which he meant a major shift in power from the established, predominantly mulatto, elite to a new black middle class, which was said to act in the interests of the mass of peasants and workers from which its members had emerged. I have already drawn attention to the populist and *noiriste* ideas propagated by Duvalier and the group with which he was associated from the early 1930s onwards. In the present chapter we shall consider the further development of these ideas, and I shall attempt to estimate the extent to which they influenced the policy pursued by the government in these years.

Two interpretations of the Duvalier phenomenon are, I believe, equally mistaken. On the one hand he is portrayed as a cynical operator whose sole ambition was to gather maximal wealth and power to himself and his family; according to this view ideology was merely a camouflage which was employed to hoodwink the masses and to present an acceptable image to the world scene. The other view is that Duvalier was a blind and fanatical maniac whose actions were wholly determined by his esoteric interpretation of the Voodoo religion or by his socio-logical and biological theories of race. In this chapter I shall suggest that Duvalier came to power with certain ideals; he was genuinely concerned to forward and complete the work which Estimé had begun. The latter, however, had come to grief as a result of failing to appreciate the power situation in the country, or, if he had correctly understood the situation, of failing to deal with centres of opposition in a sufficiently vigorous and ruthless way. Duvalier was determined not to make the same mistake. His general aim, then, was to translate into practical policy that ideology which he had helped to develop since the time of the American occupation.

Duvalierism in practice

On gaining office Duvalier found that all his energies were absorbed by the urgent task of staying alive and of retaining office. Ideology had temporarily to be set on one side, except on those occasions when it could be used as a weapon against those groups which threatened the existence of his regime. The most striking example of this use of ideology can be seen in Duvalier's *kulturkampf* against the Roman Catholic church. After 1964, however, the president had successfully eliminated opposition groups; surely now he could turn to the positive programme of social, economic and cultural revolution to which he had committed himself. Unfortunately by this time Duvalier and the group around him had developed a vested interest in keeping things more or less as they were. Lord Acton's dictum about the corrupting tendency of power was once more vindicated. The *noiriste* and nationalist ideology of earlier days was relegated to the role of empty symbolism: the changing of the flag, the erection of a statue to the *marron inconnu*, the visit of Haile Selassie, the homage to Martin Luther King. Instead of representing, as outward signs, a genuine rehabilitation of the poor black Haitian and an effective independence in foreign and economic affairs, these gestures were substitutes for significant change. 'Mon gouvernement', confessed Duvalier to a close friend and former cabinet minister just before he died, 'n'a pas été ce que j'avais projeté.'

I have maintained elsewhere that it would be a mistake to think of Duvalier's regime as either totalitarian or fascist.[1] In the first place there has been no consistent attempt to impose upon the country a total ideology, or to dominate the whole life of the average citizen. Considerable areas of personal liberty remained for the vast majority of the population; only those interested, or thought to be interested, in political power and those who attempted to thwart the ambitions of local Duvalierists found themselves persecuted or killed. Thus Leslie Manigat's statement, 'such is the encroachment of politics on all aspects of life that if a man does not go into politics, politics itself comes to him', needs qualification.[2] It certainly applies to the elite groups in the cities and to the wealthy and powerful in the countryside, but not to the mass of the people. Manigat speaks about those groups to which he and his friends belong. This is not, of course, to say that the regime was not ruthless nor that it was not dictatorial; it was certainly both these things. Yet it was qualitatively different from modern totalitarian governments as manifested in Hitler's Germany, Mussolini's Italy or indeed in Castro's Cuba.

Again it is, on the whole, misleading to refer to Duvalier's regime as 'fascist', but the temptation to do so is, in the case of its opponents, difficult to resist on account of the emotive connotations of the term. Fascism emerged in Europe at a particular stage in the development of capitalism, when a revolutionary working class had become an effective challenge to the hegemony of the bourgeoisie. In the face of this threat, governments came to power which through a combination of terror and paternalistic legislation suppressed the revolutionary movement and used the instruments of state for preserving the basic economic structure which they inherited. The situation in Haiti in the 1950s was quite different from this. The small urban working class was led by the anti-communist Daniel Fignolé and constituted no real threat to the established economic system. Duvalier's government certainly used terror, but this was nothing new in Haiti; all previous governments had used it. Perhaps the distinguishing feature of the 1957 regime was that it was prepared to use terror against substantial sections of the elite, as well as against the unfortunate peasants. Other superficial similarities with fascism were the personalisation of power, the nationalist posture, and the revolutionary jargon combined with a basically conservative economic and social policy. The principal differences were that Duvalier represented, not a middle class threatened by a revolutionary working class, but one which was itself attempting to challenge the power of the old elite, or at least to muscle in on its privileged position. Also, as I have suggested, Duvalierism was not totalitarian in the way that fascism was. If a European pattern is needed, perhaps Bonapartism would be the most satisfactory one. But it is better to see the political tendencies which manifest themselves in post-colonial and economically dependent countries as *sui generis*. Duvalierism is to be seen as a further development of that post-colonial pattern which emerged in nineteenth-century Haiti and from which the country has not entirely freed itself. The Duvalierist phenomenon is allied to certain movements in Latin American politics, and perhaps constitutes a sort of model towards which many of the former British colonies in the Caribbean are tending. In this context the names of Forbes Burnham of Guyana, Eric Gairy of Grenada, Patrick John of Dominica and Robert Bradshaw of St Kitts come to mind; even the politics of post-colonial Jamaica and Trinidad show certain similarities to the Haitian pattern.[3] In all these countries, as in Haiti itself, ethnic or colour factors are readily available for exploitation by political leaders, so that the attention of the masses can be diverted from economic issues.

It is, furthermore, an error to believe that Haiti is a country 'where to speak of a "public opinion" is a misnomer' and 'where for all practical purposes any government can rule provided it has military support'.[4] This view, apparantly culled from journalistic and literary sources, is widespread and partly accounts for the belief that with the death of Papa Doc the Duvalierist regime would collapse. In fact, as we have noted throughout this study, there is a long tradition of popular participation in politics; it has manifested itself sporadically, however, and its importance has primarily been in removing unpopular governments. This occurred in 1946 and again in 1956. The extended election campaign of 1956–7 was conducted throughout the country and involved a very large number of individuals. Organised groups such as political parties, business organisations, trade unions and churches played an important role. As I hope to show in this chapter, Duvalier clipped the political power of these groups, but he was nevertheless acutely aware of the importance of that for which 'public opinion' is said to be a misnomer. The *tontons macoutes* were (and are) indeed an organ of repression, but they were also a means of recruiting support throughout the country. Duvalier's government enjoyed the support or the benevolent neutrality of a large part of the population who were shrewdly aware that their lot under a succeeding regime would probably be no better and might possibly be worse. It may justly be said that they were in many ways misled by propaganda, but this is true in some of those countries which enjoy a 'mature political culture'. Accounts of Haiti under Duvalier as a country in which five million ignorant discontented and rebellious peasants were forcibly held down by a handful of 'cutthroats' are the product of wishful thinking and bed-time reading rather than the conclusion of careful academic research.

The attack on the groups

I have suggested that the first seven or so years of Duvalier's period of office were characterised by a sustained effort on his part to secure his position by the elimination of potential centres of opposition. His most urgent task was to deal with explicit political opponents, many of whom rejected the result of the 1957 election and appeared determined to overthrow the new government in any way they could. Déjoie went into exile and the Jumelle brothers went into hiding where they attempted a violent overthrow of the government. Followers of these politicians were rounded up or harassed by the army, the police and by Duvalier's own private force known as *cagoulards* (hooded men), who were under the control of Clément Barbot. Real or fictitious bomb plots were exposed, and a small group of former army officers and American adventurers invaded the country and seized the Dessalines barracks in July 1958. The president himself led the successful resistance from the Palace.[5]

While conducting a violent – but necessarily violent – campaign against his political opponents, the president also began to deal with a potentially more dangerous threat, the army leadership. Duvalier must be seen as a man after Professor Kenneth Galbraith's heart, for in the early years of his regime there was a marked decline in the political power of the army, which was brought firmly under civilian control.[6] The president himself declared in his inaugural address as president for life in 1964: 'I have removed from the army its role of arbiter and balancing weight of national life, a role which made it swing from side to side according to its own interests.'[7] Undoubtedly the election of Duvalier in September 1957 had been facilitated by the army; it was facilitated but not effected by the army, and this was a distinction too subtle for the military mind of General Antonio Kébreau, who was heard to boast on a number of occasions that he had made a president and could unmake him. Even after the formal installation of Duvalier as president, Kébreau continued to act as if he were the real ruler of Haiti, and when he paid an official visit to the Dominican Republic he was received by Trujillo with all the trappings of a head of state. Soon after his installation Duvalier persuaded Kébreau that some of his immediate inferiors constituted a threat to his own position, and a number of officers including Colonel Frank Beauvoir were retired or sent as military attachés overseas. The general himself, now partially isolated, was politely informed in March 1958 that he too was in retirement and he fled to the Dominican embassy; he was soon made an ambassador. Maurice Flambert succeeded Kébreau. Later in the year Duvalier dismissed more army officers and then in December 1958 Flambert was replaced by Pierre Merceron. Although both these men were mulattoes, many of the newly promoted young officers were black. Throughout his fourteen years in power Duvalier maintained a continual watch upon the army leadership and thereby prevented it from becoming an independent variable in the political arena. Captain Francis Charles stated the Duvalierist position in 1968, insisting that the army should 'passively obey the civil power'. He went on to praise the government for having opened up the higher ranks of the armed forces to the sons of the ordinary people.[8]

During these early struggles Duvalier astutely secured the neutrality, if not the active support, of the Roman Catholic church and of the United States embassy. By appointing Père Jean-Baptiste Georges as secretary of state for education he appeared to be adopting a conciliatory approach to the church, and by inviting a United States marine corps mission to train the Haitian forces and by frequent denunciations of communism, he showed himself to be on the side of the 'free world'.

Having dealt with threats from political opponents and from the army, Duvalier turned to his erstwhile supporters, and decided to eliminate those who were not prepared to give unqualified support to his policies and practices. Government critics in the senate, led by Emmanuel Moreau, a priest of the Eglise Episcopale, and Jean P. David, either fled the country or were arrested. More important, the president began to be suspicious of the growing power of Clément Barbot. In the period of Duvalier's serious illness in May–June 1959, it was Barbot who effectively ran the country. The civilian militia, known as *tontons macoutes* (from the figure in folklore who carries off wicked children in the night), were under the personal control of Barbot and had been the instrument which the regime had used to suppress political opponents and to effect changes in the leadership of the armed forces. No successful attempt to depoliticise the army could have hoped to succeed without support from such a paramilitary organisation. Barbot had evidently enjoyed his short taste of presidential power and began plotting to assassinate Duvalier. Dr Roger Rousseau, a close friend of the president, warned Duvalier of a plot to shoot him during the Carnival celebrations of 1960, but he did not know that Barbot was behind the move. Rousseau was shot by Barbot before he could discover more. Barbot's close relations with the United States embassy and his general demeanour, however, led Duvalier to suspect his intentions, and he was arrested in July 1960 and sent to Fort Dimanche; he was eventually released and maintained a low profile for some time, attending church regularly. Late in 1962 he went into hiding and organised underground terrorist activity, which included an apparent attempt to kidnap the Duvalier children. He was killed in July 1963 in a gun battle with the militia. In the meanwhile Duvalier had taken steps to bring the *macoutes* under his full personal control. In November 1962 the *milice* was formalised by a presidential decree into the Volontaires de la Securité Nationale.

Duvalier's extended feud with the Roman Catholic hierarchy began in 1959 and continued until 1966; this was a conflict in which ideology played an important role, and I shall look in detail at the relations between church and state during this period in a later section of this chapter. What needs to be noted here is that Duvalier, believing the church to constitute a centre of opposition to his regime, dealt a number of blows to the political power of the hierarchy, which effectively removed the threat from this quarter.

Many of Duvalier's opponents were powerful members of the business community in Port-au-Prince. This group, composed principally of mulattoes, had since the early days of independence played a significant role in the politics of Haiti. Not only were they able to bring pressure upon governments from within – owing to the fact that the higher grades of the civil service were largely staffed by their families and friends – but they also used the instrument of the business strike to make their interests felt. Under Duvalier, however, the strike weapon proved ineffective due to ruthless action by the *macoutes* in forcing open the doors of businesses which closed, and thus leaving them to be looted. While the mulatto elite in the business community were almost all opposed to Duvalier, the new president attempted to secure support from the rich and extensive Syrio-Lebanese community. For the first time in Haitian history a cabinet minister was appointed from this community, in the person of Dr Rindel Asad who was made minister of tourism in 1958; Carlo Boulos became minister of health in 1959, and Jean Deeb was later appointed mayor of Port-au-Prince.

Looking back on the years following his election in 1957 Duvalier identified 'the reactionary forces' opposed to him as a certain faction in the army, the leading ecclesiastics, the propertied and commercial classes, and also politicians relying on support from the '*lumpenproletariat*'.[9] Under the latter head he was of course thinking particularly of Fignolé and his supporters. In the weeks prior to his election the army junta under Kébreau had done much to immobilise the 'Fignolist steamroller', and Duvalier kept up the pressure in the poorer parts of the capital city. In his early struggles against elite politicians and army leaders, however, Duvalier needed support from organised labour unions which remained relatively free to operate until 1963. During the nineteenth century there were no trade unions in Haiti of any importance,[10] but in 1903 a Syndicat des Cordonniers Haïtiens was formed, and in 1924 a Département de Travail was established. Under Estimé the labour movement grew significantly, and by 1947 Fignolé headed a federation of fourteen unions; two years later the number had increased to twenty-nine.[11] Independent unionism was, however, harassed by Estimé and suppressed by Magloire, but emerged again in 1956 with three distinct groups of unions: L'Union Intersyndicale d'Haïti (claiming thirty-three unions with a total membership of 22,000), La Force Ouvrière Paysanne with ten unions, and La Fédération Haïtienne des Syndicats Chrétiens with about the same number of unions.[12] Yet in 1960 union membership was probably one of the lowest among the nations of Latin America.[13] In general the unions refrained from frontal attacks upon the government, concentrating on particular issues where the interests of the workers were directly concerned. In November 1960, however, the UIH joined in support of the student strike and protested against the arrest of student leaders, but with little effect. Many leading unionists were arrested, others went into exile, but the UIH and the FHSC continued to exist as independent bodies and a number of successful strikes were organised by their constituent unions. In the middle of a general strike in December 1963 the UIH was dissolved by the government and its principal leaders were arrested; in the following weeks the FHSC was also dissolved. From this time onwards only those unions, like the chauffeur–guides, who were explicit supporters of the government, were permitted to operate; these remnants of the labour movement, centring on the journal *Panorama*, still constitute an interest group within the regime.

Duvalier, who came to power as an 'intellectual', had always been sensitive to criticism from this quarter, and was eager to demonstrate that his regime had backing from important and forward-looking elements among Haiti's writers and academics. In the early years of his government Duvalier valued support from the aged Jean Price Mars and from his son Louis Mars, who became foreign minister in June 1958. Yet the president saw the university and the teaching profession as possible centres of opposition, and in April 1959 he imprisoned the president of the National Union of Secondary School Teachers (UNMES). Later in the year it was the expulsion of Père Etienne Grienenberger, head of the Petit Séminaire St Martial and an influential figure in UNMES, which was the opening shot in the extended battle between Duvalier and the church. In the following year the student strike, which began in November 1960 and received qualified support from the church hierarchy, resulted in the permanent closure of the Université d'Haïti and to the founding of the Université d'Etat, which was to be firmly under government control. Duvalier also had to contend with a number of freelance intellectuals, many of whom had returned from periods of study in Eastern Europe or China. Some gave limited support to his government, while others were hostile. One of the most extraordinary events of the late 1950s was the bitter exchange between two former friends, the Marxist writers René Depestre and Jacques Stéphen Alexis, which I shall discuss in more detail later in this chapter. The incident led to a general discrediting of both men in the eyes of literate Haitians and to a consequent weakening of their influence. Yet Duvalier was still keen to show that there was intellectual backing for his regime, and he put pressure on a number of writers to make explicit professions of support for the government.

One of the most powerful factors influencing politics in Haiti during the present century has, of course, been the United States embassy. Although the United States government favoured the election of Louis Déjoie in 1957, they were not opposed to Duvalier, who appeared to be willing to co-operate with American interests in the country and to support United States policy in the international field. One of the key figures in persuading the embassy of Duvalier's acceptability was Alfred Voegeli, the bishop of the Eglise Episcopale (Anglican church), who was an American, and was a personal friend of the president. Voegeli warned the State Department in Washington that their belief that Déjoie would win the election was based on an imperfect understanding of the situation in the country on the part of the American embassy. At the suggestion of an Embassy official the bishop organised a dinner party at which the American ambassador was able to meet Duvalier, who astonished the assembled company by announcing his intention, if elected, of requesting a United States marine mission.

Many members of the Eglise Episcopale in the capital came from that black middle-class group which supported Duvalier, and a number of individual Anglicans were prominent Duvalierists, among them Emmanuel Moreau and Jean Magloire. After his election the new president stated that his government would 'preserve that Haitian–American unity which is for the mutual benefit of the two peoples'.[14] An incident under the preceding military junta, in which an American citizen had been killed while in prison, had led to some tension, but Duvalier agreed to pay compensation; Duvalier's offer of missile bases in May 1958 and his request for a marine corps mission to help train the Haitian army quieted American doubts. The fact that the invasion of July 1958 had been planned in Miami and had included two minor officials of the state of Florida led to further tension, but a more serious breach had already occurred when the American ambassador, Gerald Drew, had objected to the appointment of Antonio Rimpel as Haitian director of a development programme financed by the United States. The Americans also became critical of the activities of the *macoutes*. Then in his famous 'Cri de Jacmel' in June 1960, ghost-written by Clovis Désinor, Duvalier deplored the low level of American aid, blaming 'le grand et capable voisin' for Haiti's continued state of under-development. 'We are at the limit of our endurance', he declared, hinting that unless something were done Haiti might have to reassess her pro-western position in international affairs.[15] Barbot, who had been busy over the previous months cultivating American business and diplomatic contacts, remarked to a cabinet minister after the speech, 'Duvalier has gone mad.' A few weeks later Barbot was arrested, and relations between the United States and Haiti continued to decline.

United States disapproval was voiced over the 're-election' of Duvalier in 1961 for a further term of office and a number of incidents involving American citizens led to further differences. Successive United States ambassadors were declared *persona non grata* by the Haitian government. Duvalierists published articles criticising American policies and attacking the Puerto Rican model as 'a false example' for the rest of the Caribbean.[16] Trade delegations from Eastern Europe appeared in the country, and although Duvalier eventually instructed the Haitian delegation to vote with the United States on the expulsion of Cuba from the Organisation of American States at Punta del Este in 1962, relations between the black republic and her giant neighbour almost reached breaking point. Duvalier's dictatorship was clearly an embarrassment to President John F. Kennedy, whose Latin American policy in the face of the Cuban threat was designed to encourage liberal democratic regimes that would adopt a 'reasonable' attitude towards American investments and would follow a pro-western line in foreign affairs. The story of the co-operation between Kennedy and Juan Bosch of the Dominican Republic in order to secure the overthrow of Duvalier in 1963 is complicated and cannot be dealt with here.[17] The move failed and relations between the two countries reached their nadir. In July 1963 articles with a Marxist orientation were published in *Panorama*, a journal run by the Blanchet group. In the following months articles appeared on Lenin, on Eastern Europe and on China; a translation of one of Mao's poems was also published. In August 1963 Gérard Daumec wrote a violent attack on the United States entitled 'Les prisons de la Démocratie'. These journalistic exercises were clearly designed to warn the American government that Haiti might be pushed into the communist camp. Nevertheless Bosch fell in September 1963 and in November Kennedy was assassinated. 'The incorruptible Doctor François Duvalier'[18] had once more survived. From this time on, relations between the two countries began to mend, and with the visit of John D. Rockefeller in 1969 a new era of co-operation was inaugurated. President Nixon succinctly observed that 'we must deal realistically with governments in the inter-American system as they are'.[19]

II

The church–state conflict

Of all the conflicts and confrontations of the Duvalier era, it was in the field of religion and education that ideological factors appear to have been most prominent. We have noted how Duvalier and a number of the men whom he brought into his government in 1957 had been critical of the role played by the Roman Catholic church in Haiti, and in particular of the control which it exercised over many of the leading educational institutions in the country.[20] In certain cases their criticisms were based upon a belief in the importance of the Voodoo cult in maintaining African traditions and customs in the country. The *Griots* group saw the church as one of the principal ideological instruments by which a small francophile elite was enabled to maintain its hegemony. To this *noiriste* critique of the role of the Roman Catholic church was frequently linked the charge, formulated in the nineteenth century by Louis Joseph Janvier, that the existence of a body within the state owing allegiance to a foreign power undermined national unity and the sovereignty of the state.[21] This nationalist argument was also widely employed by writers who had little sympathy for the *noiriste* position.

In October 1957, for the first time in the history of Haiti, a Roman Catholic priest, Père Jean-Baptiste Georges, was included in the cabinet as secretary of state for education. The choice of the radical young priest served at once to demonstrate Duvalier's support for the growing number of Haitian priests in the church, and to allay some of the doubts in the minds of the hierarchy about the policy which the government would adopt towards the church. During the first months Duvalier did not want to alienate this powerful group.

It was not until August 1959 that the first blow in the battle between church and state was struck. On 12 August a presidential decree was issued banning the Union Nationale des Membres de l'Enseignement Secondaire (UNMES), on the ground that this teachers' union had become infiltrated by communist ideology, and that a direct connection had been established by the police between this organisation and recent acts of terrorism.[22] Four days later the secretary of this union, Père Etienne Grienenberger, superior of the Holy Ghost Fathers, and another priest, Joseph Marrec, were expelled from Haiti. Various reasons were given for the expulsions. Clément Barbot claimed that the two priests had omitted the president's name in prayers for the state, while Paul Blanchet maintained that Marrec had 'refused all collaboration with local authorities', and that Grienenberger had 'even infiltrated Haitian families, giving moral and material support to the enemies of the government'.[23] 'We were obliged', declared Blanchet, 'to take this measure of expulsion which is directed at two priests, in order to preserve the spiritual unity of the nation, because the two expelled priests had devoted themselves to a work of social disintegration.'[24]

Grienenberger was clearly a lively and influential priest, and a close friend of the former president Paul Magloire, who was actively opposed to the government of Duvalier. The reason for Marrec's expulsion is more difficult to discover. It is necessary to go back to the end of 1948, when a young Haitian priest, Hubert Papailler, was evicted from the parish of Petite Rivière de l'Artibonite, in the diocese of Gonaïves, for refusing to obey the directions of Mgr Robert. Supporting and advising the bishop in this case was Marrec. The action of the bishop was condemned by Max Cadet at the time in the columns of *Les Griots*, and Papailler was referred to as 'the victim of racial prejudice'.[25] Eleven years later Papailler had become influential in politics, and was a few months later to succeed Jean-Baptiste Georges at the ministry of education.

Archbishop F. Poirier, described as a stern unbending Breton, vigorously attacked the action of the government in a pastoral letter to all parish priests. 'We ask you to make known to all Catholics in your parish', he wrote, 'the exceptional measure which has been taken against two particularly worthy priests, who were truly incorporated into the life of the country.'[26] The archbishop claimed that he had not been consulted, as the terms of the 1860 Concordat stipulated that he should be. Paul Blanchet criticised the archbishop's remarks, referring to them as an open attack upon the sovereignty of the state. A warrant for Poirier's arrest was issued, but later suspended. Meanwhile, in the cathedral, a silent prayer meeting of protest was broken by by steel-helmeted police, several arrests being made. Five priests attacked the policy of the government in the columns of *La Phalange*, and the first round in the church–state battle was over. The generally defiant attitude of many Catholics was characteristically expressed by Père P. Halaby, who had received notice from the director general of education that he was no longer to teach religion in the *lycée*. 'I very much regret to inform you', he wrote, 'that as a teacher of religion I am responsible to his grace the archbishop and not to the Department of National Education. If certain Catholics and even certain priests have sold their consciences, Père Halaby has not yet arrived at this position.'[27]

Fifteen months later, in November 1960, the second round in the church–state contest was opened. The immediate occasion was a student strike which had been called in protest against the arrest of certain politically active student leaders two months earlier. On 22 November 1960 martial law was declared and the students were given a twelve-hour ultimatum to end the strike. Most of the student leaders, who were either in prison or in hiding, refused to return, and the university was closed one month early for the Christmas vacation. Moderate support for the students was given by the church and by *La Phalange*. On 24 November Archbishop Poirier was expelled from the country on the ground that he had given $7,000 to student communist groups. The papal nuncio complained to the government about the action, and Bishop Rémy Augustin was named apostolic administrator of the diocese of Port-au-Prince. The government refused to accept Augustin, who was arrested and later expelled from the country on 10 January 1961. Rome reacted to these events, and the pope declared that he was 'pained by the violation of the church's sacrosanct rights and by the unjust and inconsiderate treatment' of the archbishop.[28] All involved in the expulsions were excommunicated.

In the meanwhile three of the arrested students had died in prison, and the others refused to leave. On 1 December Joseph Roney, the leader of the students, left prison with the other students. The ministry of education, now in the charge of Père Hubert Papailler, issued a decree making parents responsible for the attendance of their children at school and at university, thus making it possible to punish the parents for the actions of their children. Also, in another decree, the old university was replaced by the Université d'Etat, firmly under govern-mental control. The rector of the university and the deans of the faculties were to be appointed by the president on the advice of the secretary of state for education. Further arrests were made in December 1960, including the veteran politician Georges Rigaud, and former senator Emmanuel Moreau, an Episcopal priest, who had attacked the government some months earlier, and who had been deprived of his senate seat. *La Phalange* of 7 January carried on its front page an open letter to the secretary of state for education from a number of priests, brothers and sisters, protesting against the decree of 15 December making parents responsible for the attendance of school children and students. One more edition of *La Phalange* appeared; the newspaper was closed by the government on 9 January and an extensive purge of school teachers was instituted. By the middle of January, twenty-five priests and twenty nuns were said to be under arrest. On 30 January Claudius Angénor was appointed apostolic administrator of the diocese of Port-au-Prince, and relations between church and state began to relax, though not before Mgr Robert, bishop of Gonaïves, had been forced to leave his diocese and go into retirement. The second round in the contest had come to an end, with the archbishop deported and the president excommunicated.

An uneasy truce lasted for over eighteen months, during which time the government turned to more pressing problems. In November 1962 Mgr Robert, who had been living outside his diocese in compulsory retirement at Pétionville since February of the previous year, was expelled from the country, together with three priests. The reason given for the expulsion was Robert's constant campaign against the practice of Voodoo in his diocese, and in particular the part which he had played in the campaign of 1941. 'Under the cover of the anti-superstition drive, Bishop Robert organised or tolerated the pillaging of archaeological and folklore riches of the diocese.'[29] All involved in the expulsion were excommunicated, and the papal nuncio, Mgr Ferrofino, was recalled to Rome. Undoubtedly the *macoute* leader in Gonaïves, Zacharie Delva, who was an active *houngan*, played a role in the expulsion of Robert. In the following month seven more priests were expelled for refusing to pray for the president. Two Haitian priests were by this time among the most active and influential exiles planning the overthrow of the Duvalier regime. Gerald Bissainthe headed an organization known as 'Jeune Haïti', while the former secretary of state for education, Jean-Baptiste Georges, was leader of a group of exiles planning to invade Haiti from the Dominican Republic. This fact did not help relations between church and state.

During 1963 the government was fully preoccupied with terrorists at home and with potential invaders from abroad, and there was no significant development in the relations between government and church until early in 1964, when Haiti ended its 1958 agreement with the Canadian Jesuits. A presidential decree denounced the way in which the Jesuits had caused trouble and confusion in Haiti and had discredited the country overseas. A communiqué from the Department of Foreign

Affairs and Cults stated that documents had been discovered which showed that the Jesuits and their allies were plotting to overthrow the government. The congregation, which had been staffing the Grand Séminaire and had also run Radio Manrèse, was expelled from the country, though the government hastened to reassure other Canadian religious orders that they would continue to be welcome, and that protection would be given to all clergy 'without distinction of nationality'.[30] The seminary was closed and the students were sent back to their homes and ordered to report daily to army posts. Later in 1964 the apostolic administrator of the diocese of Port-au-Prince, Mgr Claudius Angénor, was put under house arrest because of an appeal for leniency towards political prisoners which he had made to the president during the *Te Deum* marking Duvalier's election as president for life. Also in 1964 two church reviews, *Eglise en Marche* and *Rond Point*, were suspended and Catholic trade unions were disbanded.

In April 1964 the president called together first the Roman Catholic clergy, and then the ministers of other denominations, to receive from them a message of loyalty and support. Père Luc Hilaire, on behalf of the Roman Catholic priests, and Père René Gilles of the Episcopal Church made speeches at the respective gatherings. Dr Duvalier congratulated Gilles on having understood 'that all power comes from God and must be respected'.[31] At the end of April the head of the Episcopal church, Bishop Alfred Voegeli, whose attitude towards these gatherings had been noticeably cool, was expelled from the country. Formerly a friend and supporter of Duvalier, Voegeli had fallen victim in the drive to indigenise Haitian religion. Since the arrest of the Episcopal priest Emmanuel Moreau, relations between Voegeli and the president had been strained. The immediate occasion of the expulsion was a letter written by an Episcopal priest to Duvalier stating that his services were completely at the disposal of the government, believing that his duty to the state took precedence over his duties to the church. This letter happened to fall into the hands of the bishop, who insisted that this priest should not involve himself in politics, transferring him to the isle of La Tortue. This action of the bishop was seen by the government as conclusive evidence that he was conspiring to overthrow the Duvalier regime. He was expelled on the following day, and the lay chancellor of the diocese was also arrested. This person had previously been active in politics as a supporter of Clément Jumelle, one of Duvalier's principal opponents in the 1957 election, and his association with the bishop was interpreted as an anti-government plot. In spite of being unofficially warned by a leading member of the Volontaires de la Sécurité Nationale that action was soon to be taken against him, he failed to leave the country in time.

By 1965 Duvalier clearly felt enough had been done to reduce the political power of the Roman Catholic church, and of any other religious body which appeared to have political pretensions. Also the hold which the foreign clergy exercised over the church had been broken. The time had come for some constructive step to be taken in replacing the foreign bishops by Haitians, and in healing the breach with Rome. In October 1965 the Grand Séminaire was re-opened with a staff of Canadians from the Congrégation des Clercs du Saint-Viateur. Duvalier saw the reconstituted seminary as contributing to the policy of 'replacing a system of ideas foreign to the ideas and traditions of the nation' by one more in accord with these traditions.[32] Duvalier's insistence on a basically indigenous hierarchy coincided with a new emphasis in the Roman Catholic church on the importance of choosing local men to lead the church in places where this was possible, rather than perpetuating ecclesiastical colonialism. For example, the Vatican Council decree on missions (*Ad gentes*) envisaged the establishment of native churches in those areas which were the scene of recent missionary activity, stating that these churches should be 'sufficiently provided with a hierarchy of their own'.[33] More important than this theoretical statement was a real change in practical policy – more and more, throughout the world, native bishops were appointed in the place of missionary bishops. Duvalier's policy had become the church's own!

In June 1966 Pope Paul VI announced that steps were being taken to settle the differences between the government of Haiti and the Holy See; 'we are satisfied', he declared, 'that pending questions will soon find a satisfactory solution'. Mgr Antonio Samore was sent to Haiti as a special papal legate, and by October of the same year agreement had been reached. Mgr François Wolff Ligondé was enthroned as the first native archbishop of Port-au-Prince, and Haitian bishops were to fill all the other sees, except Cap Haïtien, where the aged Bishop Cousineau remained. Mgr M. J. Lemieux, formerly archbishop of Ottawa, was named papal nuncio and was formally received by President Duvalier in November 1966. 'In all humility', declared the president, 'we consider today's ceremony as a further proof of the legitimacy of our cause.' It was, he went on, a comfort to know that he could count on 'the support of the highest moral authority in the world'.[34]

The new hierarchy was obviously the result of a compromise between the wishes of the Haitian government and the desires of the Vatican. Although it would be wrong to think of the new appointments as merely political, the hierarchy is expected to give general support to the policies of the government. 'I can assure you', wrote Mgr Ligondé to the president, 'of our entire collaboration in the political, economic and social domain.'[35]

Duvalier stated that the new native hierarchy established in 1966 was the realisation of his 'dream' of *un clergé indigène*. 'The struggles which I have undertaken for the constitution of the church hierarchy', he wrote, 'were for me the reflection of the struggles of the nation for its independence and sovereignty.'[36] In a series of articles in *Panorama* Jules Blanchet outlined what he considered to be the role of the church in Haiti. In the past the church had been unresponsive to the needs of the poor, had reinforced social divisions and had adopted an attitude of non-cooperation with the government of Duvalier, which had been elected by a majority of the people. The new role of the church, a national and enlightened church, must be that of 'vassal to the Haitian state'.[37] Since 1966 relations between church and state have been cordial, although the Petit Séminaire St Martial was taken over by the government in 1971 and the Holy Ghost Fathers, who had run the college for many years, left the country. In recent years, following the death of François Duvalier, the hierarchy has occasionally made tactful and oblique criticisms of the more outrageous activities of some government ministers, but apart from this the church has generally given its support to the government.

Duvalier's attack on the Roman Catholic church was connected with his desire to modify the education system in Haiti. We have already seen how the *Griots* writers in earlier years had demanded changes which would give a greater prominence to national history and literature and which would lead Haitian children to take pride in their African heritage. In July 1958 Duvalier called for a great crusade against illiteracy and presented a bill to the legislature which would allow for primary-school teaching to be conducted in the *créole* language.[38] Article 35 of the 1957 constitution had already given a semi-official status to *créole*, which could be used in court cases and other official proceedings when citizens had insufficient knowledge of French. The preamble to a law of September 1963 drew attention to the need for 'national pride' and to the importance of 'our ethnic origins', and the law prescribed a greater emphasis upon the study of Haitian history in the school curricula.[39] In the field of education and literacy, however, little effective progress seems to have been made since 1957.

While Duvalier's policy in religion and education was bitterly opposed by most of the hierarchy and by the majority of foreign priests, it received a certain support from some local clergy. In recent years an increasing number of priests have become critical of church policy in Haiti. In particular the cultural imperialism of the Breton clergy has been under attack, and a more positive appreciation of the Voodoo cult has been evident. Gérard Bissainthe criticised the church for having tied Christianity too closely to western civilisation and culture, and for having equated African culture with paganism. It was in the context of this 'iconoclasm' that the persistence of Voodoo must be seen.[40] Claude Souffrant has argued that 'the fatalism of the Haitian peasant' is as much a result of the kind of Catholicism taught in Haiti as of the Voodoo religion. After analysing a number of *créole* hymns used by the church in Haiti, Souffrant concludes that 'a Catholicism of resignation' has been preached, according to which the peasant is told that his poverty and suffering are to be borne patiently.[41] Christian missionary policy is denounced as 'a veritable cultural aggression against the soul of a people'.[42] Even more radical criticisms of Catholic attitudes towards Voodoo have come from Laënnec Hurbon in *Dieu dans le vaudou haïtien*. In this book the author attempts to understand not merely the function which Voodoo had played in Haiti as the principal means whereby the Haitian peasant has been able to preserve his African identity, but also he has taken seriously the beliefs professed by the initiated. He argues that Christians should respect the beliefs and practices of Voodoo, just as they do in the case of the so-called higher religions. In the past the church's policy in Haiti has reinforced a feeling of cultural inferiority on the part of the masses.[43]

Anthropologists and ethnologists have generally been more sympathetic towards Voodoo than have theologians and ecclesiastics, though this is perhaps truer of foreign anthropologists than of Haitians, whose professional interest in perpetuating exotic practices is sometimes balanced by a patriotic interest in the future of their country. Rémy Bastien states that to his knowledge no *houngan* has ever sponsored a development programme, built a school or introduced improved agricultural methods. 'Vodoun will will remain the bane of Haiti and the arch-enemy of the progressive state', he wrote, 'until its clergy is curbed by a superior power and learns to cooperate with the rural teacher, the physician, and the agronomist.' Price Mars's own judgments on the role of Voodoo in Haiti were hardly less stringent.[44] In a recent essay Hurbon, together with a Guadeloupian co-author, has rejected the kind of 'development' which Bastien was assuming. Hurbon and Bébel-Gisler criticise the role of 'progressive' Roman Catholic priests like Père Ryo, and see the activity of Protestant sects in recent years as an aspect of United States penetration of Haiti. They see Voodoo performing somewhat the same role as was played, according to Frantz Fanon, by Islamic customs in Algeria prior to the revolution. It is a form of silent resistance by the masses to cultural domination. These authors therefore see many of the attacks on Voodoo (and on the *créole* language) by progressives as part of a campaign to lead Haiti into a situation of developed dependence on the capitalist west. They are, however, critical of the way in which Duvalier and others associated with the ethnological movement have used Voodoo as a means of political advancement for their own class.[45]

III

The noiriste *theme*

The development of what I have earlier called 'the black legend' of the Haitian past received some official support during these years. Duvalierism was portrayed as the 'synthesis of Dessalinism and Salomonism', and the president himself was said to be the first man in the history of the black race to have made a reality of *négritude*.[46] During his address to the Haitian people on the *jour des aïeux* in 1965,[47] Duvalier criticised the role played by the *affranchis* in colonial Saint Domingue, and he celebrated the work of the *marrons* who had fled into the hills to oppose the colonial regime. A governmental decree stated that the resistance of the *marrons* was the beginning of the movement which resulted in independence, and that all schools should be closed on the occasion of the inauguration of the monument to the *marron inconnu* in December 1968.[48]

Black writers during this period were critical of Pétion and Boyer for having planned to surrender Haitian independence, and for having effected land reforms in the interests of the mulatto minority. I concluded in an earlier chapter that there is some truth in the latter charge, and that with respect to the former charge the evidence is inconclusive.[49] Even if the mulatto presidents would have been willing to accept some kind of French protectorate, such a disposition was not substantially different from that of President Salomon. In his writings on the Haitian past Manigat is clearly assisted in coming to conclusions by his own *noiriste* position. In his monograph on Salomon, Manigat, who was in the early years a supporter of the Duvalier government, developed the legendary picture of the nineteenth-century president and his party. The National Party, according to Manigat, valued the African origin of Haitian culture and wished to cultivate in the Caribbean a black civilisation. Salomon was the symbol of black regeneration for the masses.[50] This view has been echoed by R. A. Saint-Louis.[51] As I have argued in a previous chapter this view of the National Party has no basis in fact and is the product of legendary writing.[52] Perhaps the most extraordinary piece of legendary writing on Salomon is by Max A. Antoine, minister of social security and labour for many years under both Duvaliers. 'Oh Salomon!', he writes, 'The active and doctrinaire youth of the working classes salute you, you are for them an idol.'[53] In the introduction to this book, Duvalier reminds his readers how the great spiritual forces of the national and ethnic past are able to edify the present. Antoine's heroes are Goman and Acaau, Dessalines, Pierrot, Soulouque and Antoine Simon, but above all Salomon, who is called a martyr who was sacrificed for the defence of his class.[54] In fact, as Antoine himself acknowledges, Salomon came from a rich landowning family in the South.

One of the most interesting ideological controversies during the Duvalier era was between René Piquion, dean of the faculty of letters in the State University, and Jean Price Mars, the *doyen* of Haitian intellectuals. In his open letter to Piquion of 1967 Price Mars attacked the interpretation of the Haitian past adopted by Piquion in his *Manuel de négritude*, where Price Mars was criticised for not having sufficiently exploited the colour question during his presidential campaign of 1930.[55] Price Mars disputed the assumption that the social question in Haiti could be reduced to the colour question. There had always been in the country since colonial days a number of poor mulattoes and rich blacks, so that the class and colour lines never coincided completely. In making this point Price Mars was challenging the *noiriste* legend which had in substance been espoused by Duvalier himself in his *Problème des classes*. The reaction from government circles was swift. Morille P. Figaro attacked the ideas of this 'old man in decline'.[56] As if to give official support to Figaro's attack, he was in the same week appointed minister of the interior. In a speech of 1957 Duvalier had named Price Mars as one of the decisive influences in his life, but in a 1967 reprint of the speech the name of Price Mars was omitted.[57] Piquion's reply to Price Mars reiterated the *noiriste* view of the past.[58]

As I have already observed, Duvalier enjoyed support from a number of Marxists in the early years of his regime. Although tolerating Marxist propaganda, he kept a wary eye upon the activities of these men. Whether the president himself engineered the split between Alexis and Depestre is not certain; in any case he was the sole beneficiary. In an extraordinary newspaper article Depestre denounced his fellow Marxist and former friend as 'a shameful *déjoiste*', and an opportunist of the right;[59] this was in response to the accusation that he himself had succumbed to flattery from the Duvalier regime. 'René Depestre', wrote Alexis, 'has in effect in my opinion a strong propensity to an emotional character; self-control and the objective analysis of a question are sometimes falsified by the unstable side of his dissolute personality.'[60] Alexis, while he denied having ghost-written speeches for Déjoie, insisted that the political programme of the industrialist was the only one which was likely to lead to 'the gradual economic independence of our country'.[61] In the course of their debate Alexis reiterated the Marxist interpretation of the Haitian past which had been set forth by Charlier and other writers of the PSP in a previous generation. According to this view Boyer Bazelais, Anténor Firmin, Edmond Paul and the nineteenth-century Liberal Party were the representatives of 'bourgeois democracy' who were opposed to the 'feudalism' of Salomon and the National Party; they were therefore seen as a progressive force, as indeed was Déjoie in their own day.[62] The controversy between Alexis and Depestre had begun when the former had been omitted from the Haitian committee of the Société Africaine de Culture, which included among its members Louis Mars, J. B. Romain, E. C. Paul – all supporters of Duvalier – and René Depestre. The exchange, which began on a mundane level, ended with Depestre referring to his former friend as 'un nègre démasqué' (a parody of the title of a book by Alexis's father called *Le nègre masqué*), and being himself denounced as 'le petit-bourgeois mulâtre'.[63] Charles Péguy once wrote 'tout commence en mystique et finit en politique', but in Haiti the movement is frequently in reverse.

By the early 1960s most radical politicians had decided to oppose the Duvalier regime despite occasional hints that the country might move in a socialist direction. In April 1961 Alexis, after a visit to Moscow, where he had signed the declaration of the eighty-one communist parties, landed near Jean Rabel in the department of the North-East with a small group of pro-Russian communists. The peasants, however, showed little interest in supporting this adventure, and the group was soon rounded up by the *tontons macoutes*. Alexis was put to death. Depestre, for his part, has lived in Cuba since 1960, where he has conducted a campaign of opposition to the Duvalier regime. In his address to the cultural congress of Havana in 1968 he denounced the *négritude* ideology of the regime as 'a delirious mystification' which has been used by the most reactionary sectors of Haitian society to serve their own interests.[64] Depestre also criticised 'the father of *négritude*' – Jean Price Mars – for having divorced the cultural and ethnic factors in Haitian history from their material basis; while it is possible to talk about French culture or even African culture, it is mystification to speak about black or white culture.[65] The *négritude* movement represented for him a legitimate literary and artistic revolt against the systematic denigration of African traditions in the Caribbean; it was a sort of 'cultural *marronage*' – a protest and a (sometimes irrational) flight from western culture.[66] The Voodoo cult also is seen as a gesture of defiance and a warning to the Christian west.[67] Depestre points to a cultural stagnation in the Caribbean (with the exception of Cuba) which he ascribes to the state of neo-colonialism. Although the Latin American revolution must be a cultural revolution, Depestre insists that the roots of the problem of 'identity' are to be found in the history of social relations in the region.[68] Yet Depestre rejects a central thesis of many *négritude* writers that the black man has a human nature peculiar to himself and significantly different from that of the white man; this idea he condemns as absurd. Furthermore the colour question in Haiti, while it is important, is not according to him a determining factor in the history of the country, but is rather to be seen as an ideological camouflage behind which two rival aristocracies struggle for power.[69] It is in the Cuban revolution that Depestre sees the legitimate aspect of *négritude* being realised.[70] Another mulatto Marxist, Antoine G. Petit, joins Depestre in attacking Price Mars, Dorsainvil, Senghor, Duvalier and other 'reactionary' apostles of *négritude*.[71] The communist opposition to Duvalier has been divided into a number of groups, but the principal ones have united to form the Parti Unifié Communiste d'Haïti (PUCH).

Duvalier himself constantly reiterated his criticisms of Marxism and his basic adherence to the western side in the cold war. In a message to the legislative assembly in 1966 he declared that his government stood for the 'defence of Christian civilisation against atheist materialism and the ideological intolerance of a levelling and inhuman communism'.[72] In the following year he stated that 'the doctrine of our forefathers existed before Marxism' and that Haitians 'have nothing to learn from anyone'.[73] Duvalier's words have been faithfully echoed by Gérard de Catalogne[74] and by René Piquion. The latter has emerged as the principal spokesman of Duvalierism on the ideological front. Piquion has been as consistent in his opposition to Marxism as he has been in his adherence to whatever government happened to be in power in Haiti.[75] He has restated the *noiriste* legend of the Haitian past, and in reply to Depestre has reasserted the relevance of *négritude* ideas in the modern world. Piquion recruits Manigat, Saint-Louis and Claude Souffrant in his polemic against Depestre.[76]

IV

Duvalier's 'mission'

A constantly recurring feature of Duvalier's presidential speeches and messages was the introduction of religious symbols to reinforce his claims to legitimacy. Even in his early writings it is possible to detect such a religious theme. Karl Lévêque has analysed the speeches and writings of Duvalier, pointing out the moralistic and mystical strains which frequently appear.[77] Duvalier portrayed himself as divinely chosen; his work was 'une mission sacro-sainte', and a crusade.[78] He often spoke of himself in the third person as 'un grand mystique', who embodied in his person the spirit of the nation. The mere fact that he believes something to be necessary for the country is enough, 'because I am Haiti'.[79] For several years cars carried the slogan 'To wish to destroy Duvalier is to wish to destroy Haiti.'

The claims to supernatural power and authority made by Duvalier himself fade into insignificance when compared to those made for him by his supporters. His office was an 'apostolate', and he was the instrument of the divine will, able to control the spiritual forces of the universe. Walter Préval, editor of *Le Nouveau Monde*, referred to Duvalier's 'eternal reign' in Haiti, comparing it to the universal reign of Christ.[80] According to another of his supporters, Duvalier entered into politics 'as others enter into religion'; he represented an insertion of the eternal into the temporal.[81] Pictures of Duvalier, carrying the words *Ecce homo* (traditionally applied to Christ), were familiar to those who visited Haiti in the late 1960s. Even slogans about the new dam at Péligre had mystical significance: 'Duvalier alone is able to harness the energy of Péligre and give it to his people.'[82] In 1967 Gérard Daumec edited the *Bréviaire d'une révolution*, containing the sayings of Duvalier and appearing in the format of a little red book similar to Mao's famous volume. Even more extraordinary was the *Catéchisme de la révolution*, compiled in 1964 by Jean M. Fourcand. Duvalier was here proclaimed to be the living embodiment of 'the five founders of the nation', Dessalines, Toussaint, Pétion, Christophe and Estimé. The seven Duvalierist sacraments are listed, and 'extreme-onction duvaliériste' is defined as 'a sacrament instituted by the people's army, the civil militia, and the Haitian people . . . to crush with grenades, mortars, mausers, bazoukas, flame-throwers and other weapons' the enemies of the state.[83] The Lord's Prayer, the Salutation to Mary, the Apostles' Creed, the Acts of faith, hope, charity and contrition are all used as the basis for Duvalierist mythology. The 'Lord's Prayer' begins:

> Our Doc, who art in the National Palace for life, hallowed
> be thy name by generations present and future,
> thy will be done in Port-au-Prince and in the provinces . . . [84]

Of course, the ascription of divine authority and supernatural powers to political leaders is a widespread phenomenon. The advent of Trujillo in the neighbouring Dominican Republic was said by his supporters to be the result of divine providence. 'God has sent him to us', proclaimed posters in Mussolini's Italy, and a version of the Lord's Prayer was used by the Hitler youth.[85] Up to the reign of Queen Victoria the most extravagant language was used in the liturgy of the Church of England, reflecting the doctrine of divine right, and even today the coronation service contains similar implications. It is, however, particularly in those situations where the habit of obedience has never been firmly established among the population, or has for some reason been weakened, that such exaggerated claims to divine patronage are thought necessary.

The claim by political leaders to possess occult powers and in some mystical way to embody the spirit of the nation is frequently made not only in so-called third world countries, but also in Western Europe.[86] In Haiti, Duvalier's claim to possess occult powers must be seen in the context of the Voodoo religion. From his earlier ethnological studies and from his experience as a country doctor, the new president understood the widespread and deeply rooted beliefs of the masses, and knew the power possessed by the *houngans* in the towns and villages of Haiti. Soon after coming to power in 1957 he eliminated a number of *houngans* who were unprepared to recognise his superior powers. Voodoo signs and ceremonies were frequently introduced into official proceedings, and the speeches and writings of the president contained unmistakable allusions to the cult. He was, for his followers, guided by the spirits of Boukmann, Padre Jean and Mackandal, early leaders of the cult.[87] The more bizarre stories, recorded by Diederich and Burt, of Duvalier meditating in his bath wearing a top hat, or sitting for hours trying to communicate with the severed head of one of his opponents, are surely fabricated.[88] Nevertheless the president himself cultivated the reputation for occult powers, and the accusation by foreign critics that he practised Voodoo only served to strengthen his authority among the masses. He frequently consulted Ludovic (Dodo) Nassard, a celebrated augur, though he appears to have accepted the auguries only when they agreed with his own assessment of the situation. Nassard himself also made sure to acquaint himself with the complexities of a situation by discussing the matter with some of the interested parties before disclosing his divination to the president.

One of the most extraordinary episodes in the fourteen years of Duvalier's rule was the changing of the Haitian flag. Since the death of Henry Christophe in 1820 the flag had been equal bands of blue and red placed horizontally; this had been the flag of Pétion's republic. Christophe's northern state retained the flag of black and red, vertically placed with black to the mast, which had been the imperial flag of Dessalines. The widely held belief was that on 18 May 1803 at Arcahaie Dessalines had torn the white band from the French tricolour, leaving a blue and red flag, with colours vertically placed, and that subsequently the blue had been changed to black. The black and red flag of Dessalines was associated with the *noiriste* position, and there was an attempt in 1844 by a black group to reinstate this flag in place of Pétion's blue and red. The attempt failed, and little attention seems to have been paid to the matter until the controversy was revived by Dr Arthur Holly during the occupation period.[89] He insisted that if the flag were to represent the two parts of the Haitian nation, blacks and mulattoes, the colours should be *black* and red. Also the colours should be placed vertically (standing up), symbolising in an esoteric way a beneficient influence, rather than horizontally (lying down), which showed a nocturnal or malevolent influence. Pétion had 'satanised the Republic', and this was reflected in his flag.[90] It was also widely held that the horizontally placed colours, sharing the mast, symbolised the fact that blacks and mulattoes shared power in Haiti, while the black and red, with black to the mast, represented the fact that the blacks should control power.

Duvalierists like Michel Aubourg asserted that the first flag of independent Haiti was the black and red, and campaigned for its restoration. The blue and red, they claimed, was invented by Pétion in 1807 and was the symbol of discord and civil war.[91] In the debate on the 1957 constitution there was a heated exchange over the proposal to change the flag to black and red, and eventually the proposal was dropped. One deputy declared, 'while we tolerate the red, it is necessary that the black be attached to the mast, because it is the black who is attached to the true countryside of Haiti'.[92] Duvalier himself insisted, even after the 1957 constitution had been promulgated, that the black and red was the flag created by Dessalines at Arcahaie, and that it was 'the legitimate flag of the State of Haiti'.[93] It was, however, only in 1964 that Duvalier felt strong enough to impose this flag on the country, and thus symbolically to consummate the victory of the *authentiques*, which had been begun by Estimé in 1946.

The transfer of the remains of Dumarsais Estimé to a shrine on the site of the *Bicentenaire* in 1968 was also the occasion for a reassertion of *noiriste* ideology. In the course of his address Duvalier attacked 'le groupuscule de mulâtres et assimilés noirs' who wished to take political power and to impose upon Haiti 'the inhumanity of their borrowed occidentalism'. Estimé on the other hand stood for the culture of the ordinary Haitian and for the interests of the greatest number.[94] The ceremony included a number of Voodoo symbols.

Other occasions on which ideology has played a role have been the erection of the statue to the unknown *marron*, the homage paid to Martin Luther King and the visit of Emperor Haile Selassie of Ethiopia. The unveiling of the impressive monument to the *marron inconnu* was for Duvalier the realisation of a dream; it represented the pioneering role played by Haiti in the assertion of black dignity. 'We constitute for the negro-African masses of the universe', he declared, 'the highest exponent or a kind of common denominator of all national and racial consciousness.'[95] At the opening ceremony Paul Blanchet portrayed Duvalier as himself continuing the work of the *marron*.[96] In the homage paid to Martin Luther King after his assassination in 1968 Duvalier pointed to the fact that Haiti was the first black republic in the world, and he decreed four days of official mourning; one of the capital's streets was renamed Avenue Martin Luther King. Haile Selassie's visit to Haiti in April 1966 had also provided the opportunity for a reaffirmation of Haiti's claim to joint leadership of the African race, and indeed of the third world.[97]

In company with other populist dictators of Latin America, Duvalier frequently attacked 'politicians', distinguishing himself from them.

'We came to the management of the affairs of state', he declared on the occasion of the publication of a Hebrew translation of his *Problème des classes*, 'not as a wire-puller to play peanut politics, but rather as an intellectual. That is the difference between Me and the others.'[98] There was on the part of the president an acute realisation of the importance of propaganda. The slightest favourable reference to his regime from abroad was given great publicity, and even formal telegrams of greeting on the occasion of Haiti's independence day were printed in full in the national newspapers, taking up most of the space for the day.

We have already seen how during his election campaign Duvalier was projected as the spokesman of the masses, and this image was reasserted from time to time during his years in office. For Ulysse Pierre-Louis the Salomonist doctrine of the greatest good for the greatest number, revived by Duvalier, had led to an awakening of the social conscience of the peasants and of the rising middle class.[99] A similar claim was made by Hermann Louis Charles, who portrayed the Duvalierist revolution as a movement committed to 'a better distribution of the national wealth' and an increased participation of the masses and of the middle class in the affairs of the nation.[100] Duvalier himself claimed to be a product of the masses, whose policy was designed to eliminate economic and social inequalities.[101] His was a revolutionary government, and 'revolutions must be total, radical, inflexible'.[102]

The effects

Fourteen years of François Duvalier's iron rule saw few fundamental changes in the economic and social structure of Haiti. The black middle class was strengthened, and black domination of the military and of the civil service was reinforced. The political power of the mulatto elite was consequently eroded, although the control of the national sector of the economy, which they have shared for half a century with the Syrio-Lebanese, remained undisturbed. The general coincidence between colour and economic class, characteristic of the whole Caribbean region, continues. Recent developments suggest that little change has occurred in the social practices of this elite, and in the arrogance with which they treat their black fellow countrymen.

With respect to foreign influence in Haiti, Duvalier achieved only a temporary limitation of United States influence, and the accommodation which was reached with the Americans in the years following 1966 has opened the way to increasing United States penetration of the Haitian economy since 1971. Duvalier's vigorous policy towards the Roman Catholic church has, however, ended foreign domination of the hierarchy, and has secured the appointment of a national and generally subservient group of bishops. In recent years, though, the hierarchy has begun to make cautious criticisms of some of the more outrageous activities of government ministers, and clergy have been making comments on disputed issues of the day, such as the use of the *créole* language.

Perhaps the most significant result of Duvalier's 'revolution' will turn out to be the sense which was given to the mass of the peasants that they were really citizens and that what they did was important. The actual power which they possessed to influence the course of events was negligible, but the rhetoric of populism, the mass rallies and the countrywide organisation of the VSN may have led to a new consciousness on the part of the masses. If people are told often enough that they are important, they may begin to believe it.

How did Duvalier remain in power for so long, despite the confident predictions of the 'experts', and how was he able to institute a dynasty in Haiti? Duvalier's ruthless suppression of groups which might have challenged his position is certainly part of the answer, yet suppression and terror only partially explain his survival. His shrewd knowledge of the mentality and customs of the Haitian peasants and his recognition of the key role played by the middle class were important. A network of information and control which ran to the furthest corners of the country kept the president in touch with local developments. He frequently called peasants from remote villages to see him in the Palace, and would talk to them for perhaps an hour or two. The people he relied on in the country were often *houngans* or peasants from that intermediate class which has played an important part in the political history of Haiti.[103] Propaganda and the manipulation of the colour issue also contributed to Duvalier's continued rule as did the ineptitude of most opposition groups. He had been elected in 1957 with a considerable body of support, and even by 1971 there was little popular opposition to his regime among the masses. The state had never done anything significant to help the masses in the past, and Duvalier's inaction in this matter was no reason to replace his regime with one which might be worse and actually interfere in some important way with their pattern of life.

Colour, class and region played their part in determining political attitudes at this time. The vast majority of the light-skinned elite were opposed to the government, though most of them were prepared to reach some kind of compromise when they became convinced that they could not overthrow it. Duvalier's strength was among the black middle class and among the peasants in the country. The small black working class had no love for his regime, and the old black elite of the North saw Duvalier, during the election of 1957, as a means by which they themselves would continue to exercise influence. Duvalier, like Salomon before him, was never popular in Cap Haïtien, whose black elite families regarded him as an upstart.[104] When this group realised that they were unable to wield power through Duvalier they either went into exile or decided to lie low and hope for better days.

9. Conclusion

Father and son

François Duvalier died in April 1971, after having named his nineteen-year-old son, Jean-Claude, his successor as president for life. Despite confident predictions by foreign experts that chaos would ensue, the transition from father to son was accomplished smoothly. Exile groups were kept at bay by the United States naval forces, while the uneasy balance of power between the various military and paramilitary groups within the country enabled the dynasty to survive the crisis. A large number of important groups had an interest in keeping things more or less as they were. Those who wished for change were unprepared to risk a possible collapse of the whole system and were willing to bide their time. The policies which were pursued by the new government were in general a continuation of those initiated by François Duvalier towards the end of his period of office. Good relations with the United States, a continued strengthening of the bond between the government and the business community, local as well as foreign, and a relaxation of terror have been some of the principal features of government policy. Recent United States emphasis upon human rights has led to pressure being brought upon the Haitian government and to the release of some political prisoners. It is likely that there are still many such prisoners held in the country, though a large number have died in captivity. North American investment has increased considerably, particularly in the area of light manufacturing industries and assembly plants making use of cheap labour. In recent years contracts have been signed by the government with two large foreign companies for the investigation and possible exploitation of copper deposits. Overseas aid for the improvement of roads, harbours and other infrastructural facilities has been received. All these changes have led to a superficial prosperity for a minute (but important) sector of the population without having had any beneficial effects upon the living standards of the mass of rural dwellers.[1] The plight of the latter has in recent years grown even more desperate with extended droughts in the north-east and north-west of the country. The rise in world coffee prices has done something to ease the situation in certain areas, though much of the benefit has gone to speculators rather than to the peasant farmers. Emigration has continued, and today there are probably as many as half a million Haitians in the United States; also many thousands of Haitians are to be found in Canada, France, the French Antilles, the Bahamas, the Dominican Republic and Cuba.[2] As I have observed in previous chapters, migration is by no means a new phenomenon; during the present century Haitians have frequently gone to Cuba and to the neighbouring Dominican Republic in search of work, and political exile has been a feature of national life since the earliest days. Yet with the Duvalierist era the problem has reached new proportions. Large numbers of skilled and semi-skilled workers have left: for example, of the 761 doctors graduating from the medical faculty in Port-au-Prince between 1945 and 1968, only 242 were practising in the country by 1970.[3] As we shall see, most of the political literature of the period has been published abroad. This again is not an unusual feature of Haitian life; during the nineteenth century Edmond Paul, Louis Joseph Janvier, Anténor Firmin and other authors frequently wrote from exile.

Since the death of François Duvalier the *noiriste* and nationalist rhetoric of the government has been less in evidence, and the emphasis has been upon economic and technical development. Little has in fact been achieved in this direction, though the 'economic revolution' is a much-heralded aspect of the government's policy. Technocrats have been appointed to ministerial posts, and teams of international experts have been invited as part of the elaborate and expensive game which must be played in order to secure foreign aid.

With respect to the theme of this study some minor developments have taken place. It is my contention that the colour question remains important in the social life of the elite in particular, though many middle-class blacks are also eager for their sons and daughters to marry persons lighter than themselves. The public manifestations of colour prejudice were firmly put down under François Duvalier, but in recent years the mulatto elite seems to have become less guarded in the practice of its exclusive social life. In politics, however, colour, which has never been the sole factor determining allegiance, is less significant today than it was in the period from 1946 to 1966.[4] With respect to the African elements in the culture of the country, Haitian writers differ as widely today as they have in the past. On the one hand there are still the representatives of the *Griots* group who see the social problems of Haiti almost solely in terms of colour and race; on the other there are the liberal writers of the elite and one section of Marxists who deny that these factors play any significant role. In between these two positions are a large number of writers who acknowledge the vital role played by African culture in Haiti and the importance of the colour question, but who believe that it can be the source from which radical reforms can spring.

Neither of the extreme positions merits much serious attention. A recent representative of the *noiriste–négritude* position is Mesmin

Gabriel, whose curious esoteric works are reminiscent of the writings of Arthur Holly.[5] The position he maintains is somewhat eccentric and is of little practical importance today. At the other extreme is the mindless Marxism of Jacqueline Lamartinière and the Mouvement Haïtien de Libération. According to this view any recognition of racial or colour loyalties as having been significant in the politics of Haiti is 'metaphysical', and it is baldly asserted that 'racism must disappear' with the abolition of a capitalist economic system.[6] A fellow Marxist, René Depestre, is assailed for his belief that *négritude* ideas have had, in the past, a valuable contribution to make towards an understanding of Haitian history and social structure.

In between these two tendencies may be found a large number of authors. In Haiti itself the group of young writers associated with the weekly journal *Le Petit Samedi Soir* attempts to develop a radical interpretation of the *négritude* and *noiriste* traditions, offering some cautious criticisms of the administration. In the debate about the *créole* language, which broke out in the early 1970s and continued for some time, these writers, headed by Dieudonné Fardin, Jean-Claude Fignolé and Franck Etienne, have defended the use of *créole* in Haiti and have attacked those who (with support from the French embassy) have claimed that the only hope for Haiti is for the French language to replace *créole* as the language of the masses. These young writers have also developed a peculiar literary form which they call *spiralisme*.[7] With respect to the importance of *créole* and the role played by African traditions — particularly the Voodoo religion — this group finds support in the writings of two exiled Haitians, Claude Souffrant and, more important, Laënnec Hurbon.[8] The latter attacks the use which Duvalierism has made of Voodoo, but nevertheless believes that the religion must be taken seriously, and that it might very well provide the sources from which radical action will stem. He is critical of the way in which the Roman Catholic church and the French government assert that Haitians are poor and backward because of their failure to adopt the French language and ways of thinking and because of their adherence to the Voodoo religion. The refusal of successive Haitian governments to recognise *créole* as the official language of the country is ascribed to the determination on the part of the mulatto elite and the black middle classes to exclude the masses from effective participation in political life.[9] Paul Laraque, an influential poet and former army officer, now living in New York, accepts this general position. Voodoo and the *créole* language are seen as important insofar as they conserve the indigenous culture of the people in the face of cultural imperialism. He quotes Amilcar Cabral: 'Only those societies which preserve their culture are able to mobilise the masses, to organise themselves and to struggle against foreign domination.'[10]

While it is obviously the case that exiles are in general able to be more outspoken in their criticisms of life in Haiti and of the Duvalierist establishment than are residents of the country, perhaps the most damning condemnation of seventeen years of Duvalierism came from within the country itself. I refer, of course, to Jean-Jacques Honorat's book *Enquête sur le développement*, published in 1974. We are not here directly concerned with the specifically economic sections of this book, but the second half is principally devoted to a consideration of 'l'homme haïtien'. All those criticisms of Haitian social life which had been the stock-in-trade of Duvalier and his *Griots* associates since the occupation period are reiterated: the selfishness of the elite, the domination of the country by European values, the conservatism of the church, the 'cultural terrorism' of the educational system, the exploitation of the peasant by the speculator, and the role of the Chefs de Section as 'guard-dogs of a regime of exploitation'.[11] Religion, colour and language are seen as the principal instruments used by the elite in maintaining its hegemony. These criticisms, if true, represent a massive indictment of Duvalierism. The appointment of an indigenous hierarchy in the Roman Catholic church, for example, of which François Duvalier was so proud, is dismissed as superficial; the labour code and the rural code are implicitly condemned as ineffective. I am reminded of Selwyn Ryan's acid comment on the 'Perspectives for the New Society' issued by Eric Williams's People's National Movement of Trinidad in 1970: 'Unsuspecting readers would be surprised to learn that it was the manifesto of a government which has been in power for fifteen years.'[12]

One of the least satisfactory aspects of Honorat's book concerns the notion of 'la personnalité haïtienne'.[13] The term suggests some kind of essence which Haitians share and which ought to be manifested in their conduct. It is similar in some ways to talk about 'the new Caribbean man', which is found among black intellectuals of the new elite in the English-speaking islands.[14] The idea of the Haitian personality assumed by Honorat deserves the critique it has received at the hands of Charles Manigat, Claude Moïse and Emile Olivier.[15]

Adopting a somewhat similar position to that of Honorat is Leslie Manigat, who comes from a long line of black elite politicians, originally from the North.[16] Manigat collaborated with Duvalier in the early years of the regime, but fell from favour and left Haiti in 1963. Since then he has made a number of important contributions to our understanding of Haiti past and present. His recent pamphlet *Ethnicité, nationalisme et politique* is a sophisticated, illuminating and generally accurate analysis of the role which ethnicity has played in Haitian history, and in *Statu quo en Haïti*? we find a perceptive discussion of the various political forces at work in the country at the time of François Duvalier's death. Yet much of Manigat's writing is coloured by his *noiriste* preconceptions and by his manifest political ambitions; in a recent interview he thought it necessary for some reason to insist, 'my pen has never been a valet nor a mercenary'. Manigat's pamphlet *Maîtriser la conjoncture* is a rather shallow piece of writing and is characterised by a considerable amount of wishful thinking. Though he rightly points to the absence of a visible 'collective anger' in Haiti, he misrepresents the situation by suggesting that there is a 'non-acceptation profonde' of President Jean-Claude Duvalier even by those in government circles. Manigat is by no means unique in this respect, and it is possible to think of a number of other acute and intelligent academics who seem to lose all their balance and critical faculties when they enter the Caribbean political arena.

Most Marxist writers[17] are hampered in their understanding of the present situation in Haiti by their long absence from the country and because they feel a need to force Haitian reality into a Procrustean bed built at the British Museum in the nineteenth century and recently reconstructed in the Bois de Vincennes. Though they do not normally go as far as Lamartinière and deny the significance of colour divisions in Haiti, they tend to underestimate the continued strength of such divisions among important sectors of the population. In their criticisms of *noirisme*, as the attempt of a group of middle-class blacks to obscure the fundamental economic divisions in the country for their benefit, these writers are substantially right. Yet excessive attention is paid to a number of doctrinal and conceptual issues; whether Haiti is *really* feudal or semi-feudal, pre-capitalist or neo-colonial, and whether there can be said to exist a national bourgeoisie (in the Maoist sense) are some of the questions which divide Marxists. There is among most of them the general belief that if only these conceptual problems could be solved the diagnosis and prognosis of Haiti's ills would be clear and beyond doubt. Insufficient attention is paid to studying the concrete social, economic and political structure of the country. Gérard Pierre-Charles and Jean Luc, for example, have written about the economic and political problems of Haiti and much of what they say is true, but their work suffers from a determination to see Haiti in terms of categories which were developed in order to understand a quite different situation. As a result we find the former referring to Haiti under Duvalier as an example of '*créole* fascism' corresponding to a 'feudal or semi-feudal society' and exhibiting a 'medieval' form of government![18]

Caribbean colonialism

It would be a mistake to treat Caribbean colonialism as a single un-differentiated whole. Undoubtedly significant variations existed in the pattern of colonial administration. The presence of an important group of white residents clearly had an impact upon the colonial system which evolved; the explicit or implicit racialism which frequently justified alien rule needed to be modified in these cases. Again the natural resources of the territory influenced political and social developments; the need for external sources of cheap labour was, for example, greater in some colonies than in others, and the population structure today is partly a consequence of this need. The differing conceptions of colonialism entertained in the several colonising states of Europe and the modifications in the policies pursued by successive governments in the same colonising state all had their effects and made the situation in each territory unique. Yet these differences should not blind us to the significant common features which the European colonies of the Caribbean shared.

Colonial regimes are characterised by an authoritarianism in which important decisions are made not by the inhabitants of the colony but ultimately by individuals and groups often many thousands of miles away. Even when decisions are made locally they are made by administrators sent from the metropolitan country or by officials directly responsible to such foreigners. The lack of power and the absence of participation on the part of colonial people breeds an attitude of irresponsibility. The distant metropolitan government is often seen by the people as some kind of guarantee against excesses and injustices perpetrated by local white residents. The authoritarianism is, then, frequently paternalistic. Even today we occasionally hear of Amerindian tribes seeking an interview with the British queen in order to redress some grievance which they have against the United States government.

Colonial government is thus authoritarian and commonly paternalistic. The paternalism is an implicit rejection of the idea that the colonised have rights; rather they are granted favours. Demands for the recognition of rights when these would challenge the relationship of subservience are suppressed, often violently. Political paternalism is essentially repressive.

Colonial territories are also composed of a number of different ethnic groups. As Fanon has insisted,[19] there are at least two such groups, the colonisers and the colonised. But often colonial policy has encouraged or facilitated or compelled the immigration of ethnic groups other than those native to the territory. Slavery and indentureship are the most obvious ways in which this movement of peoples has occurred. The islands of the Caribbean are today populated by numerous groups who arrived in this way – Africans, Indians, Chinese, and Portuguese. The colonies and former colonies of the region are characterised by a high degree of social pluralism, in which divisions frequently reinforce one another; religious, economic and linguistic distinctions largely coincide with racial or colour distinctions.[20]

The only convincing arguments for the possession of colonial territories are economic and strategic. They must be thought by the colonising power to bring benefits to itself which compensate for the expense and inconveniences of empire, and which could not be easily secured otherwise. In those areas where European or North American states are able to establish military bases when needed, and to dominate the economy of a territory in their own interests, colonialism becomes an unnecessary luxury.[21] A dependent economy, then, is not a sufficient condition of colonial status, though it is a general feature of colonial territories. It is not possible here to enter into a detailed consideration of economic dependency, but in the Caribbean it has generally taken the form of a plantation economy producing a small number of crops for export to a single metropolis, and depending upon imports for some of its basic items of consumption.[22]

The contrast between the French policy of 'assimilation' and the British idea of 'indirect rule' is well-known and basically sound. Yet anyone who has experience of the British colonies of the Caribbean will know well the impact which certain British institutions and customs have had upon whole classes of colonial subjects. I remember an old Chinese resident of Tobago telling me, in response to a polite inquiry about the health of his Chinese wife, that she was on holiday in 'the old country'. 'In China?' I asked (not entirely in innocence). 'No, no', he replied with evident ill-humour, 'in England.'

Post-colonial politics

Authoritarianism, paternalism, irresponsibility, ethnic diversity, economic dependence and what we might call cultural imperialism are some of the features common to European colonial territories in the Caribbean. Post-colonial politics in the independent countries of the region must be understood as a development of, and in some cases a reaction to, these features. Haiti was the first non-European post-colonial state of the modern world; a consideration of the path which it has followed since 1804 and the problems which it has encountered in its 174 years of independence might be of interest to the more recently independent countries of the Caribbean region.

Authoritarianism has been a constant feature of Haitian politics since independence. Governments have been dictatorial and the pattern has been that of military command. Even when the head of state ceased being a military officer he continued to exercise authority in an arbitrary manner. At no time in the history of the country has there been a significant degree of long-term popular participation in the political process. The state is seen as something alien, and the average Haitian regards it as beyond his power to influence the activities of the government. He hopes only that it will remain distant from him, and interfere as little as possible with his life. 'Apré bôdié sé léta' ('after God comes the state'), an old Haitian proverb, refers not to the benevolence but to the remoteness and the unpredictability of God. *Bôdié* in the Voodoo religion is the remote creator who can normally be approached only through the mediation of the *loas* (spirits).

Authoritarianism on the part of the government and political irresponsibility or apathy on the part of the mass of the population have gone together in independent Haiti. Only when conditions have become intolerable, or when rival claimants to governmental power have appeared, did the mass of the people intervene and then merely to secure the transfer of power to a new dictator. The *cacos* and *piquets* bands which as we have noted in earlier chapters, were active in certain periods do suggest an occasional positive involvement in public affairs by small and medium-sized peasants. Yet their impact has been transitory. The *piquets* of the 1840s did help to secure the elections of black heads of state, but they were soon put down by Soulouque and their leader was executed. Salomon *jeune*, who had previously been one of the *piquets* leaders, had by this time found a comfortable niche as minister of finance in Soulouque's government. The *cacos* of 1867 secured the eventual defeat and execution of Salnave but there is little indication that subsequent governments gave them a better deal than they would otherwise have had. Sporadic military activity by peasants in the early years of the present century did not give them an effective voice in the government of the country and at most enabled them to get rid of a particularly unpopular president. Undoubtedly the centralised system of administration in Haiti, inherited from the French, has made it more difficult for popular participation to occur at the local level than is the case in some of the former British colonies. I have, however, suggested elsewhere[23] that one of the consequences of Duvalierism has been the beginnings of a new consciousness among the peasants and a growing belief that something can be done to affect the course of events. This is partly due to the countrywide organisation of the VSN and to the populist rhetoric of the regime. Also many groups, often associated with the churches, have been active in the countryside for some years, helping to organise development projects, co-operatives and the 'conscientisation' of the rural inhabitants.[24] Although the explicit political intention of the sponsoring agency has normally been conservative the unintended effects of these projects may turn out to be more radical than their patrons have calculated.

The paternalism of the colonial system was extended into the postcolonial period in Haiti. Dessalines, Christophe and Pétion were all referred to as 'father' of their people, as have been many subsequent heads of state. 'Papa Doc' was a title valued and cultivated by François

Duvalier and the myth was maintained that he had a paternal interest and concern for his people. Although the rhetoric is that of paternalism the reality is quite different; the state is very much less paternalistic than is the welfare state in Western European countries. The government has never seen its duties as including a responsibility for the welfare of its individual subjects in general, and a failure to recognise this fact has been one of the reasons why foreign observers frequently misunderstood the nature of Duvalier's administration and its prospects for survival. The fact that his government did almost nothing to improve the lot of the average Haitian was irrelevant to his claims to legitimacy. No government in the history of Haiti had done anything significant to improve the lot of the masses and this was not the criterion by which a regime was judged. At least Duvalier usually refrained from interfering with the life of the peasant, and this was all they could hope for from a government.

It has been one of the central themes of this book that post-colonial politics in Haiti have been strongly influenced by colour distinctions which have their origin in the colonial era. The ethnic factor has been a powerful one in most of the post-colonial countries of the Caribbean, and will be considered in the following section.

Two further features of post-colonial politics in Haiti seem to have set the pattern for other Caribbean territories. In the first place we have noted the continuance of a relationship of economic dependence on the former metropolitan power and later on other large powers. Despite efforts by Dessalines, Christophe and Pétion to move towards a situation of economic independence and self-sufficiency in essentials, Haiti soon succumbed to foreign domination of its economy. Serious steps had been taken in the early years, such as the prohibition of foreign ownership of land and the breaking up of many old plantations, which limited the scope of foreign intervention in the economic field. Nevertheless foreign merchants soon established themselves in the principal coastal cities and secured control of foreign trade. Furthermore the massive compensation to French planters of 150 million francs, agreed by Boyer in 1825 as a condition for French recognition of Haitian independence, led to further dependence. Although Haitian governments frequently raised import duties, the purpose was either to increase revenue or to protect some politically powerful producer; it was never part of a serious and consistent policy of economic development. The prophetic words of economic nationalists – Edmond Paul, Louis Joseph Janvier and others – fell on deaf ears. As French and British involvement in Haiti declined German and United States interest increased. In the course of our study we have noted how successive governments gave commercial privileges to foreign powers in exchange for material and diplomatic support against their rivals, and that these governments were often associated with one of the two colour groups in the country. Ethnic divisions made it difficult to achieve a degree of national unity sufficient to resist foreign economic domination and political intervention.

Haiti's experience in foreign relations has been in certain respects different from that which is faced by the post-colonial states of the 1960s. For a century and a half Haiti, together with Liberia and Ethiopia, were black sheep in a white diplomatic flock. In the early years Haiti constituted a distinct challenge to the slave-owning and colonising states, and needed to be continually on her guard against military attack. As the nineteenth century proceeded the threat came more from diplomatic and commercial sources, though frequently backed by the gunboat. There was no possibility of a 'third world' alliance of non-aligned nations at that time. Haiti's only hope was to play off one power against another and thereby to avoid coming under the control of any. This policy might have succeeded if internal divisions had not led politicians to invite foreign intervention in the affairs of the country in order to strengthen their own positions. Such potentially divisive factors are present in many of the more recently independent countries of the region and constitute a threat to their national integrity; the significance of these factors is not always fully recognised by the political leaders of the countries concerned. When the problem is recognised there is sometimes a reaction which consists in the misconceived attempt to impose a single culture and a centralised administrative structure on the territory. The attempt to impose such uniformity commonly leads to anxiety on the part of minority groups, and to the exacerbation of divisive tendencies.[25]

Secondly, with respect to what I have called 'cultural imperialism', Haiti has to some extent constituted a pattern which other nations have followed. Throughout the nineteenth century practically all educated Haitians unquestioningly assumed the superiority of European culture and institutions; as we have seen, even the concept of *négritude* was strongly influenced by western racial theories, by romantic anthropology and by European literary and philosophical fashions. In the Latin American nations Spanish culture has continued to dominate and the indigenous Indian customs have until recent years been despised. In the English-speaking parts of the Caribbean European cultural forms predominate and even the black power movements in Trinidad, Jamaica and the smaller islands which became popular in the late 1960s were strongly influenced by North American models. West Indian novelists and poets, including Vidia Naipaul, Edward Brathwaite and Derek Walcott, have vividly portrayed this feature of West Indian life.

Yet in Haiti, particularly in the countryside, there has been a stubborn though frequently unarticulated resistance to this cultural imperialism. It is reflected in the customs of the peasants and particularly in the Voodoo religion, which is a genuinely *créole* phenomenon. While Voodoo is basically a development of African religions, it has incorporated elements of Christianity as well as other practices and institutions which reflect life in the Caribbean. The militarism which is characteristic of Haitian history, for example, has affected the development of Voodoo, with such figures as 'Laplace' (from Commandant de la Place), and in the way in which the *loas* are commonly painted (in military costume). It would be a mistake not to recognise elements in the culture of other Caribbean territories which are genuinely *créole*, such as the Rastafarian groups in Jamaica, whose attacks upon 'Babylon' represent a genuine revulsion among ordinary poor Jamaicans against the western civilisation they have come to know.

In the introduction to a recent collection of papers, Professor Archibald Singham laments the way in which colonial intellectuals in the Caribbean have failed to advocate a genuine liberation of the people; they have been the purveyors of 'counter-revolutionary' ideas and spokesmen for 'petty-bourgeois' interests. Singham is himself a startling exemplification of these tendencies, not only with respect to his intimate collaboration with the conservative Jamaica Labour Party in the late 1960s, but also to his recently acquired 'Marxist' jargon. It is difficult to believe that anyone who knows the Commonwealth Caribbean islands as well as Singham does can talk of 'the revolutionary classes of workers and peasants', unless he is deliberately trying to mystify. As is clear from the excellent studies of Carl Stone and others, the workers and peasants in Jamaica (and this is generally true of the rest of the anglophone West Indies) are frequently discontented but are far from being revolutionary. All this is not, of course, to deny that Singham's assertions about the role played by intellectuals in the contemporary Caribbean are accurate.[26]

Violence and decolonisation

The history of Haiti over the past 174 years which I have sketched in the preceding chapters might properly be seen as a study in post-revolutionary politics. Much has been written in the last fifty years on the comparative study of revolutions, and more recently on wars of national liberation, but the emphasis has usually been on the causes and course of these movements rather than on their consequences. The present study has relevance to this latter aspect of revolution. One writer who has put forward certain hypotheses or generalisations about the relationship between revolutionary or liberation movements and the post-revolutionary consequences is Frantz Fanon. With much of his work on the phenomena of false decolonisation and on the new native elite which frequently takes over from the metropolitan officials it is difficult to disagree. The picture that he paints is one which reflects the situation not only in African countries such as Kenya and the Ivory Coast, but also in the recently independent states of the Caribbean. No one who has lived in the region for any length of time can forget the rhetoric of national unity, the flag and the anthem, that 'chauvinistic tenderness in keeping with the new awareness of national dignity' and the 'cult of local products',[27] by which the new elite justifies its retention of political power; these symbols of independence and liberation are the empty signs of a reality which is absent rather than effective sacraments of a reality which is present.

Fanon's analysis of post-colonial politics has been applied to the Caribbean by a number of political writers,[28] but with some of his main contentions they are not in full agreement. I am referring to Fanon's generalisations about the effects of violence in the struggle for decolonisation. I say 'generalisations' rather than 'hypotheses', but it is unclear whether he wished to assert universal laws which a single instance would serve to falsify, or general tendencies and probabilities. In any case what Fanon said about violence is relevant to the Haitian case.

Fanon's peculiar belief in the purifying effects of violent behaviour on the individual — as the means by which the colonised man 'finds his freedom', as an activity which 'restores his self-respect'[29] — is one which may properly be left to the social psychologist, and which need not detain us here. Fanon also insisted that violence 'mobilises' the people, that it binds the colonised together and increases their understanding of social realities.[30] Furthermore violence is said to help in 'the building up of the nation', so that the new nation is strengthened by the 'cement which has been mixed with blood and anger'.[31] Violent wars of liberation ensure that no one will be able to set himself up as a 'liberator', and it is the indispensable condition of a genuine liberation, without which there is 'nothing but a fancy-dress parade and the blare of trumpets'.[32]

In discussing the Haitian revolution we should be clear that it became a war of national liberation (in the sense of its leaders having for their explicit aim the full independence of the country) only in its final stages. Yet if we consider the struggle for independence which began in 1802, it is certainly true that the mass of the population became directly or indirectly involved in the war. It is also true that this mobilisation led to a unity among the colonised. Whether it led to an increase in understanding and consciousness on the part of the masses is doubtful. A successful revolutionary war is not usually conducted on the basis of democratic participation. As Engels observed, 'a revolution is certainly the most authoritarian thing there is'.[33] It is not calculated to increase critical understanding of and involvement in the making of political decisions.

The story of Haiti's early years suggests that the violent decolonisation struggle failed to bind Haitians together into an independent and united nation. Divisive loyalties based on caste and colour existing prior to the revolution (which were temporarily discarded during the war) emerged to play a central and destructive role in the post-colonial period. Furthermore, so far from the violent struggle preventing the emergence of 'liberators', it can be seen to have contributed towards the rise of the *caudillo* in a most direct way. Even when the mass of the population is positively involved in the revolutionary struggle, there is, in the case of a successful war of liberation, that authoritarian element referred to by Engels which is frequently perpetuated in the post-revolutionary situation. Surely Anténor Firmin's judgment, referred to in an earlier chapter, is sounder than that of Fanon:

The danger of national independence obtained by war — and unfortunately this is the only means of obtaining it with dignity — is that the heroes of this war necessarily become, after the victory, the effective representatives of power, having in their hands the military force which is the instrument of coercion at the same time as being the means of defence.[34]

A violent war of liberation thus provides no insurance against the development of a personality cult, and in the case of Haiti it was the basis upon which such hero worship was built. As we have seen, early military-political leaders posed as 'fathers' of their people; Pétion was called a 'god' and Dessalines became incorporated into the Voodoo pantheon as a *loa*. The Haitian interpretations of their past and popular mythology centres on the heroes of independence whose statues decorate the principal park in Port-au-Prince; one of the important national holidays is called the *jour des aïeux* (2 January) when these heroes are commemorated.

Militarism, which became an enduring feature of Haitian politics throughout the nineteenth century — and which, although originating in the colonial period, was strengthened during the violent struggles for liberty and independence — also contributed to the lack of economic development in the country. This in turn led to dependence on overseas markets and on foreign capital. As one acute and sympathetic observer of the Haitian scene remarked, the absence of manufacturing industries in the country after forty years of political independence and the consequent reliance on imports of basic consumer items may be ascribed to the fact that 'the energies of the country are entirely expended under an unhappy military system'.[35]

We may therefore conclude that the case of Haiti by no means supports the generalities about violence and decolonisation which

Fanon enunciated. Violence is certainly not a sufficient condition of genuine decolonisation; the case of Haiti is conclusive on this matter, and the post-colonial history of Algeria itself hardly substantiates Fanon's assertions. Whether violence is a necessary condition for such decolonisation would demand a study of *prima facie* counter-examples like Tanzania and Guinea. There may be cases where violence has led to genuine liberation, as in the former Portuguese colonies, and there are countless examples of peaceful 'constitutional decolonisation' resulting in a neo-colonial dependent state. Considered as universal hypotheses, however, Fanon's assertions on violence are certainly false, and as generalisations they are of dubious validity. The colonial situation and the policies pursued by the new government are very much more important than is the factor of violence in determining the features of the post-colonial state.

Ethnicity and conflict

I have not found it necessary, in the body of the book, to employ the concept of ethnicity. As recent work on the subject suggests, there is considerable disagreement about the use of the term.[36] If we mean by ethnicity the sentiment which binds individuals into self-conscious groups on the basis of some somatic, cultural or genetic characteristics which they believe they share and which they think to be significant, then the independence struggles between Leclerc and Dessalines were unambiguously ethnic; the divisions between blacks and mulattoes in the revolutionary and independence periods might also be called ethnic, being characterised by perceived somatic difference during the nineteenth century and in addition by supposed cultural differences in the period since 1915. The evidence in the preceding chapters illustrates the contention of M. Hechter that cultural (and we might add, racial and colour) differences between men assume major importance in the articulation of political demands only when they are reinforced by economic factors, or what he calls the 'cultural division of labor'.[37] This is not, however, the same as saying that ethnic solidarity only emerges when it is reinforced by antagonistic economic class divisions. Although in the colonial and revolutionary periods there was a cultural division of labour, certain occupations being effectively closed to blacks and mulattoes, there were many mulattoes (and some blacks) who belonged to that landowning and commercial class which lived by rent and profit and which was predominantly white. These men at certain crucial stages united with blacks and mulattoes of other economic classes on the basis of race to fight against whites of their own class. Again, in independent Haiti, as we have seen, the leaders of the rival political classes did not normally belong to different economic classes, but were different sectors of the same class; they did, however, frequently owe their specific employment or source of income at least in part to their colour. Blacks tended to patronise blacks and mulattoes tended to patronise mulattoes. Colour discrimination was practically institutionalised. The fact that 'the manifestation of ethnic solidarity appears to be a response to the perception of patterns of structural discrimination', in a particular instance, does not mean that 'traditional or primordial sentiment' plays no part in the process.[38] Black solidarity in Haiti after the fall of Boyer, for example, must be seen as a reaction to structural discrimination by the mulatto elite and by the mulatto-controlled government; but this raises the prior question, why did mulattoes discriminate in favour of mulattoes; why did they not treat blacks of their own class on equal terms? What led them to consider colour as a relevant factor in the allocation of resources or in the provision of employment opportunities? Any analysis would be inadequate which fails to recognise at this point the importance of primordial sentiment, based particularly on perceived somatic similarities as well as on family, personal or regional loyalties (factors which were themselves not unconnected to colour divisions). When systematic discrimination on the part of one group leads to these ethnic divisions being reinforced by economic class divisions, one can expect even more bitter struggles taking place between ethnic groups.

Ethnic allegiance, then, becomes a significant factor in politics when there is a 'cultural division of labor'. Two further factors which influence the strength of ethnic solidarity have emerged in the course of the present study. In the first place if one group of persons distinguished by a common culture or by perceived somatic characteristics begins to move into an occupation previously monopolised by another such group, the ethnic consciousness of this latter group will normally intensify and ethnic conflict is likely to ensue. Two examples from our study will illustrate this assertion. The liberation of some 450,000 slaves, most of whom were black, and their movement into the free labour market or into peasant farming, occupations which had previously been dominated by mulattoes and whites, led to a marked increase in mulatto ethnic solidarity, and ultimately to the assassination of Dessalines. The land policy of Pétion, which generally favoured the mulattoes, the collapse of the northern kingdom, and the Rural Code of Boyer together checked the movement of blacks into these areas and reassured the mulattoes. Only then do we witness a decline in ethnic solidarity among the mulattoes and the revolution of 1843, which resulted from a division in their ranks. Then again, during the United States occupation, the growth of a significant black middle class, which moved into the professions of teaching, law and medicine, previously dominated by mulattoes (and by a few members of the small black elite), contributed to mulatto ethnic solidarity and to the exclusivism of President Elie Lescot.

The second factor which appears to have affected the level of ethnic solidarity based upon colour differences in Haiti is the relative proximity and power of Europeans. While it is true that colonial governments and more often local white residents have occasionally pursued a policy of 'divide and rule' with success, colonial domination has often led to a front of inter-ethnic solidarity among the colonised. As colonies have moved peacefully towards formal independence inter-ethnic conflict has tended to increase. In the Caribbean the 1961 election campaign in Trinidad and the 1963–64 conflicts in British Guiana (later Guyana) might be cited as evidence. In those cases where independence is achieved through a violent struggle, as in Haiti, a fairly united front among the colonised may be maintained until the defeat of the colonial power. As ethnic solidarity on the basis of *race* declined in Haiti, ethnic divisions based on *colour* assumed a new importance. The two great occasions in Haitian history when racial unity has taken precedence over colour divisions were the struggle against the French in 1802–3 and the nationalist movement during the United States occupation. It would appear that among Afro-Americans the salience of ethnic divisions based upon colour is inversely related to the number and power of the white population as perceived by the Afro-Americans. When the overt white presence is small, as in Haiti, colour divisions are significant and conflict is likely. In countries where there is an economically powerful white minority, as in Jamaica, Barbados and some of the smaller islands, there is less antagonism between blacks and mulattoes; while in the southern states of the U.S.A., where whites constitute a powerful majority of the population, there is even less hostility between the various shades of colour in the negro community.[39] This is not, of course, surprising. When certain sections of the population are regarded by a privileged elite as belonging to a single category which is systematically discriminated against, it is likely that these sections will forget the potentially divisive factors which are present among them and will unite to combat a discrimination of which they are all the victims.

It would thus appear to be the case in Haiti that, while ethnic conflicts based on colour have led to the possibility of foreign intervention, foreign intervention has in turn resulted in the abatement of such colour conflicts and in the development of ethnic solidarity based upon race. Whether this pattern will recur in the newly independent English-speaking countries of the region is difficult to say. With respect to Trinidad and Guyana the presence of two large racial groups among the local population complicates the issue. In British Guiana (as it was then) the intervention of British troops in 1953 appears to have had the long-term effect of increasing the political significance of racial divisions, rather than of increasing the solidarity of the colonial population. In these two countries the absence of an ethnic factor which might serve as a basis for uniting the population makes local solidarity more difficult to achieve than in those countries like Haiti where ethnic diversity (based upon colour) is balanced by ethnic unity (based upon race).

Notes

Abbreviations

AAE	Archives du Ministère des Affaires Etrangères, Paris
AN	Archives Nationales, Paris
PRO	Public Record Office, London
USNA-DS	United States National Archives, Department of State, Washington D.C.

Note on system of reference

Since all books cited in the Notes are included with full details in the Bibliography, each book will be referred to by its full title only on its first appearance in the Notes. Subsequent references to a book will be made by short title and author's surname only; where there is reference to only one book by a particular author, second and subsequent references to the book will be by author's surname only. Thus O. C. Cox, *Caste, Class and Race* will appear after its first occurrence as 'Cox, p. 00'. Note that this system applies only to books; articles, which are not listed in the Bibliography, are cited in full at each occurrence, with the occasional exception of two nearly contiguous references to the same article.

1. Introduction

1 The failure to make this distinction impairs the otherwise excellent work of Sidney Mintz on Haiti; see S. W. Mintz, *Caribbean Transformations*, pp. 282ff. It is surprising that the contributors to J. H. Franklin (ed.), *Color and Race* do not take more trouble to distinguish the two concepts.

2 By this I mean simply that if an attempt were made to divide up the world strictly according to the criterion of biological descent, no clear-cut 'racial' divisions would result.

3 A person of this particular appearance, if his hair were curly, might be called a *griffe*.

4 For evidence of the widespread use of these categories of colour, see the following chapters. The first great Haitian historian Thomas Madiou lists the principal characters appearing in his book with their respective colours.

5 J. E. E. D. Acton, *The History of Freedom*, p. 284.

6 W. Connor, 'The politics of ethnonationalism', *Journal of International Affairs*, 27:1 (1973), p. 9.

7 Toussaint Louverture to Colonel Vincent, 29 Thermidor, l'an VII (15 August 1799), AAE, Mém. et Doc., Haïti 2, f. 330.

8 Granville to Canning, 13 January 1825, PRO, FO 27/329.

9 'Haïti', *Revue des Colonies*, juin 1836, p. 531.

10 A. Césaire, *Toussaint Louverture*, pp. 21–2.

11 Eyre to Cardwell, January 1866, *Parliamentary Papers*, 1866, xxx (3682), p. 3.

12 J. T. Holly, *Anglo-African Magazine*, I (1859), p. 364; D. A. Payne, *History of the African Methodist Episcopal Church*, p. 477; cf. M. Fordham, *Major Themes in Northern Black Religious Thought, 1800–1860*, pp. 104ff, and Duncan Macleod, *Slavery, Race and the American Revolution*, pp. 153ff.

13 Cf. Y. Gindine, 'The magic of black history', *Caribbean Review*, 6:4 (1974), pp. 25ff; B. Mouralis, 'L'image de l'indépendance haïtienne dans la littérature négro-africaine', *Revue de Littérature Comparée*, 48 (1974), pp. 504ff; N. Raventós de Marin, *Haití a horcajadas de su independencia en la visión de Alejo Carpentier*.

14 A celebrated black Haitian lady now living in Paris called to see a friend of mine recently in Port-au-Prince; the boy who works in the shop came round into the office and told my friend that there was a *blanc* to see him. Her 'afro' hair style, mode of dress and the fact that she spoke in French led the boy to think that she was foreign. The incident is amusing because the lady in question is a *mambo* (priestess) in the Voodoo cult and a great propagator of Haitian culture in France.

15 J. C. Dorsainvil, 'Des idées collectives, II', *Le Matin*, 8 janvier 1908. F. Douglass to J. Blaine, 8 January 1891, USNA-DS, Diplomatic Dispatches, Haiti 25.

16 M. A. Lubin, *L'Afrique dans la poésie haïtienne*, p. 9. Jonathan Brown, writing in 1837, observed a similar tendency: 'The citizens of the republic . . . assume that this country is a brilliant point in the system of nations, diffusing to them illumination and happiness, and that all the kingdoms of the earth are clustered around it, eager to enjoy its smiles and participate in the favors which it bestows' (*The History and Present Condition of St. Domingo*, II, p. 277).

17 Both these poems are quoted by Lubin, but he fails to note the striking contrast in themes. 'Claude Fabry' was a *nom de plume* used by Arthur Bonhomme, who was associated with the *Griots* group, and became a cabinet minister under Duvalier.

18 Ussher to Lord Aberdeen, 17 August 1843, PRO, FO 35/26.

19 For Coleridge's account of the relationship between economic, cultural and constitutional forms in early nineteenth-century Britian, see his essay *On the Constitution of the Church and State according to the Idea of Each*.

20 This is roughly the position maintained by Etienne Charlier; see pp. 200ff below.

21 O. C. Cox, *Caste, Class and Race*, pp. 153ff.

22 K. Marx, *The Poverty of Philosophy*, pp. 140 and 195. Elsewhere, however, Marx suggests that insofar as there is no national bond uniting families with common interests and no political organisation by which they express this unity, there is no class (*Eighteenth Brumaire of Louis Bonaparte*, in K. Marx and F. Engels, *Selected Works*, I, p. 303). It is misleading of

Gramsci to assume that 'every party is the expression of a social group, and of one social group only' (*Selections from the Prison Notebooks*, p. 148). It may be the case that a party defends the interests of a particular social class, but a social class is not a social group, and there are few parties in the modern state which are the expression of only one social group.

23 K. Marx, 1869 Preface to *Eighteenth Brumaire*, in Marx and Engels, *Selected Works*, II, p. 222. Marx does, however, in this case, see the competing groups among the elite as representing classes, 'the free rich and the free poor', though these were not the principal antagonists in the class conflict in ancient Rome.

24 S. W. Mintz, 'The rural proletariat and the problem of rural proletarian consciousness', *Journal of Peasant Studies*, I (1974), p. 316. Cf. also R. Stavenhagen, *Les classes sociales dans les sociétés agraires*, p. 35.

25 By *noirisme* I mean a belief that it is the blacks, in the history of Haiti, who have been the real defenders of national independence, and that it is they who, being the vast majority of the population, should control political power. *Négritude* is the doctrine which asserts that people of the black or African race have certain peculiar psychological characteristics, and that these are reflected in the culture of black people. There is a more extended discussion of *négritude* at pp. 152ff below. *Noiriste* writers of the period of the United States occupation incorporated *négritude* ideas into their ideological position, but *noirisme* existed throughout the nineteenth century apart from *négritude*.

26 See David Nicholls, *Economic Dependence and Political Autonomy: The Haitian Experience*, pp. 9ff.

27 L. F. Manigat, *Ethnicité, nationalisme et politique: le cas d'Haïti*, p. 30

28 There is a brief discussion of this point in David Nicholls, *Three Varieties of Pluralism*, pp. 45ff.

29 In G. Pierre-Charles (ed.), *Política y sociología en Haití y la República Dominicana*, p. 38.

30 E. Rodríguez Demorizi (ed.), *Papeles de Pedro F. Bonó*, pp. 393ff.

31 R. Rotberg, *Haiti: The Politics of Squalor*, pp. 20ff and 347ff; cf. David Nicholls, 'A scientific study of Papa Doc', *Government and Opposition*, 8:3 (summer 1973), pp. 385ff.

32 The term 'third world' is, however, somewhat misleading even in our own day, suggesting as it does the existence of three distinct worlds. The countries of the so-called third world have, in general, been a dependent extension of the economy of the 'first world'. I use the term in the text to mean the countries of the three continents, Africa, Asia and South America (including Mexico, Central America and the Caribbean), which share a colonial background.

33 F. H. Bradley, 'The presuppositions of critical history', in *Collected Essays*, I, pp. 1ff. Ernst Troeltsch, *Protestantism and Progress*, pp. 1ff; also *Gesammelte Schriften*, III, p. 169.

34 K. Kautsky, *Foundations of Christianity*, p. 12. For an elaboration of the distinction between a historical and a practical interest in the past, see M. Oakeshott, *Rationalism in Politics*, pp. 137ff, and earlier, *Experience and its Modes*, pp. 102ff.

35 E. D. Genovese, *In Red and Black*, p. 10. Cf. also Louis Althusser, who writes: 'true ideas always serve the people; false ideas always serve the enemies of the people' (*Lenin and Philosophy and Other Essays*, p. 24). What Althusser means by 'true ideas', within the context of his own system of ideas, however, is anyone's guess.

36 G. W. F. Hegel, *Political Writings*, p. 145.

37 D. Riesman in D. Lerner, *The Passing of Traditional Societies*, p. 3. When asked what he would do if he were manager of the radio station, the exasperated victim of this enquiry replied, 'What a question again! I don't know how to deal with my own business and you ask me what I would do with the radio house' (*ibid.*, p. 161). It was not this particular group of social scientists (though it might well have been) who approached the head man of a Turkish village with the assurance, 'We are not from the government', to be greeted with the reply, 'Then why shouldn't we kill you?'

38 W. A. Mullins, 'On the concept of ideology in political science', *American Political Science Review*, 66:2 (June 1972), p. 504.

39 K. R. Popper, *Unended Quest*, p. 115.

40 J.-J. Rousseau, *Julie ou la nouvelle Héloïse*, part 2, letter 17.

41 On pre-Columbian Ayti see the classical work of E. Nau, *Histoire des caciques d'Haïti*; more recently J. Roumain, *Contribution à l'étude de l'ethnobotanique précolombienne des Grandes Antilles*, J. Fouchard, *Langue et littérature des aborigènes d'Ayti*; and H. M. Krieger, *The Aborigines of the Ancient Island of Hispaniola*.

42 Cox, p. 334 n. cf. also S. Bagù, *Economía de la sociedad colonial, passim*. Rudolfo Stavenhagen has, of course, developed this position — cf. 'Seven Fallacies about Latin America', in J. Petras and M. Zeitlin (eds.), *Latin America: Reform or Revolution?*, pp. 13ff; as has A. G. Frank, *Capitalism and Underdevelopment in Latin America* and *Latin America: Underdevelopment or Revolution*.

43 There is considerable disagreement among contemporary sources about these statistics; Hilliard d'Auberteuil gives a population of 300,000 slaves, 15,000 *affranchis* and 25,000 whites in the 1770s, in *Considérations sur l'état présent de la colonie française de Saint Domingue*, I, p. 69 and II, p. 40. Cf. also M. L. E. Moreau de Saint Méry, *Description . . . de l'île Saint-Domingue*, I, p. 119, II, p. 722, III, pp. 1164–5; also P. J. Laborie, *The Coffee Planter of Saint Domingo*, p. 57. For a later estimate see H. L. Castonnet des Fosses, *La perte d'une colonie: la révolution de Saint-Domingue*, pp. 7–8, where he gives the figures at the time of the French revolution as 500,000 slaves, 38,000 *affranchis* and 42,000 whites. There are recent estimates in C. Frostin, *Les révoltes blanches à Saint-Domingue aux XVIIe et XVIIIe siècles*, p. 28. Statistics on the number of plantations also vary. For Moreau's estimates, see *Description*, I, p. 111.

44 The *Code Noir* was an edict of the government of Louis XIV regulating the treatment of slaves and of other non-European subjects. It is reprinted in L. Peytraud, *L'esclavage aux Antilles françaises avant 1789*, pp. 158f. Article 59 of the *Code* granted full citizenship and rights to the *affranchis*.

45 On Moreau de Saint Méry see A. L. Elicona, *Un colonial sous la révolution en France et en Amérique: Moreau de Saint Méry*, and E. Taillemite,

'Biographie', in Moreau de Saint Méry, *Description*, I, pp. xff. Julien Raimond (sometimes spelled Raymond) insisted on referring to him as 'Moreau dit Saint Méry', to indicate his questionable heredity. For another hostile mulatto impression see B. Ardouin, *Etudes sur l'histoire d'Haïti suivies de la vie du général J. -M. Borgella*, I, p. 19.

46   There is a clear and perceptive account of the caste, class and colour divisions of Saint Domingue in Manigat, *Ethnicité, nationalisme et politique*, pp. 11ff. Cf. also David Nicholls, 'Caste, class and colour in Haiti', in Colin Clarke (ed.), *Caribbean Social Relations*, pp. 4ff.

47   Bryan Edwards, *An Historical Survey of the French Colony in the Island of St. Domingo*, p. 3, and Ardouin, *Etudes*, I, p. 7.

48   Quoted in Peytraud, pp. 193–4.

49   Gaston Martin, 'La doctrine coloniale de la France en 1789', *Cahiers de la Révolution française*, 3 (1935), p. 18; cf. also Jean Tarrade, *Le commerce colonial de la France à la fin de l'ancien régime*, and F. Thésée, *Négotiants bordelais et colons de Saint-Domingue*.

50   *Mémoire sur le commerce étranger avec les colonies françaises de l'Amérique*, p. 4, and M. R. Hilliard d'Auberteuil, *Du commerce des colonies, ses principes et ses lois*, p. 9; cf. also G. T. Raynal, *Essai sur l'administration de Saint Domingue*, p. 60.

51   Charles Esmangart, *Des colonies françaises et en particulier de l'île de Saint Domingue*, p. 6.

52   J. P. Garran-Coulon, *Rapport sur les troubles de Saint Domingue fait au nom de la Commission des Colonies, des Comités de Salut public, de Législation et de Marine réunis*, I, pp. 147–8. On the restlessness of the white population of Saint Domingue in the eighteenth century see G. Debien, *Esprit colon et esprit d'autonomie à Saint-Domingue au XVIIIe siècle*, and Frostin, *Les révoltes blanches*. Elsewhere I have stated that a large number of the white planters of Saint Domingue 'in no sense thought of themselves as belonging to Saint Domingue', and that there was on the part of the whites 'little conception of Saint-Domingue as having an interest of its own; they had interests as planters, not as Saint-Domingois' (*Economic Dependence*, p. 3). Leslie Manigat criticises me for saying this and cites as evidence against my contentions the 'powerful movement of autonomy' in the eighteenth century (*Caribbean Yearbook of International Relations*, 1975, p. 525), Charles Frostin, however, concludes his recent study of this movement, 'Saint-Domingue en effet n'était pas une patrie, seulement une terre de passage où l'on n'espérait séjourner que le temps d'une fortune rapide . . . Essentiellement composé de sentiments négatifs sans prise de conscience d'une nouvelle personnalité et exclusivement nourri de revendications d'intérêts, le mouvement colon, opposition larvée et révoltes ouvertes, ne pouvait donc déboucher sur rien', (Frostin, p. 387). Here Frostin clearly means individual interests, rather than the recognition of a common interest. Jean Tarrade comes to a similar conclusion (Tarrade, I, p. 155). For a contemporary witness see République de France, *Rapport fait par Dumas commissaire rapporteur de la commission chargée de présenter à l'Assemblée Nationale un plan d'organisation pour Saint-Domingue* (23 avril 1792).

53 Laborie, p. 47, L. J. Ragatz, *The Fall of the Planter Class in the British Caribbean*, pp. 126ff.

54 B. Maurel, 'Une société de pensée à Saint-Domingue: le "Cercle des Philadelphes" au Cap Français', *Franco-American Review*, 2:3 (1938), p. 147. On the Masonic movement in the colony see also P. de Vaissière, *Saint-Domingue: la société et la vie créole sous l'ancien régime*, p. 333, and A. Le Bihan, 'La franc-maçonnerie dans les colonies françaises du XVIIIe siècle', *Annales Historiques de la Révolution Française*, no. 215 (janvier–avril 1974), pp. 44ff. The powerful lodge Saint Jean de Jérusalem Ecossaise had been founded in Port-au-Prince in 1749; cf. G. Bord, *La franc-maçonnerie en France des origines à 1815*, I, p. 473.

55 On cultural life in the colony see J. Fouchard, *Plaisirs de Saint-Domingue*, R. Cornevin, *Le théâtre haïtien des origines à nos jours*, and F. Girod, *De la société créole*. On the journalism of the period see A. Cabon, 'Un siècle et demi de journalisme en Haïti', *Proceedings of the American Antiquarian Society*, N.S. 49 (1939), pp. 121ff.

56 De Vaissière, pp. 172ff; M. D. L. M. F. Y., *Mémoire sur l'esclavage des nègres*, pp. 54–5.

57 On the general conditions of the slaves in Saint Domingue see de Vaissière, pp. 166ff; Peytraud, *L'esclavage*; P. Trayer, *Etude historique de la condition légale des esclaves dans les colonies françaises*; A. Gisler, *L'esclavage aux Antilles françaises*; G. Debien, *Les esclaves aux Antilles françaises*.

58 'Amicus Mundi', *Defence of the Colonies*, p. xii n. Adam Smith, of course, shared the view that slaves were better treated in the French colonies than in the British but ascribed this to a difference in the form of government. 'The condition of a slave', he wrote, 'is better under an arbitrary government than under a free government', owing to the more effective protection which may be given them by magistrates who are responsible to the metropolitan government rather than to colonial assemblies (*The Nature and Causes of the Wealth of Nations*, 4:7).

59 'In all the French islands the general treatment of the slaves is neither much better nor much worse, as far as I could observe, than in those of Great Britain' (Bryan Edwards, p. 11). For the debate about whether there was any significant difference between slavery in the colonies of Latin countries and those of Anglo-Saxon countries, see G. Freyre, *The Masters and the Slaves* and *New World in the Tropics*; M. Harris, *Patterns of Race in the Americas*; W. D. Jordan, *White over Black: American Attitudes towards the Negro*; F. Tannebaum, *Slave and Citizen*; S. Elkins, *Slavery*; and the various writings of E. D. Genovese and H. Hoetink.

60 For the origin of the word *marron* see J. Fouchard, *Les marrons du syllabaire*, p. 1 n., and R. Price (ed.), *Maroon Societies*, p. 1 n. The French word was sometimes spelled *maron*.

61 Y. Debbasch, 'Le marronage: I. Le marron', *L'Année Sociologique*, 1961, p. 40.

62 Y. Debbasch, 'Le marronage: II. La société coloniale contre marronage', *L'Année Sociologique*, 1962, pp. 118ff.

63 Debbasch, 'Le marronage: I', p. 2 n. T. O. Ott also holds that 'There is no evidence that when the revolution erupted, these maroons came to the aid

of their fellow blacks' (*The Haitian Revolution 1789–1804*, p. 18); though he later states that Jean François, one of the leaders of the 1791 movement, 'had spent the last few years prior to 1791 as a maroon' (p. 47), and he notes the part played by 'the Suisse', who were possibly a band of *marrons* (p. 51). In denying the importance of the *marrons* in the revolution Ott is following T. L. Stoddard, *The French Revolution in San Domingo*, pp. 63ff.

64   G. Debien, 'Le marronage aux Antilles françaises au XVIIIe siècle', *Caribbean Studies*, 6:3 (1966), p. 41.

65   J. Fouchard, *Marrons de la liberté*, pp. 146ff. 'Nous pensons avoir prouvé que le marronage pouvait dépendre aussi d'une cause qui n'était autre que le refuse de l'esclavage et la volonté de Liberté' (*ibid.* p. 174). For Debien's criticism see 'Le marronage', p. 31.

66   Ardouin, *Etudes*, I, p. 17.

67   Moreau de Saint Méry, *Description*, I, p. 102; J. Raimond, *Observations sur l'origine et les progrès du préjugé des colons blancs contre les hommes de couleur*, p. 13. Raimond's figures are, however, somewhat suspect and are not even consistent. He stated that only 200 of the total *affranchi* population had not been born free, while in the following paragraph he estimated that something like 500 free blacks alone had been born in slavery. Perhaps his first figure should have been 2,000. On the role of the *affranchis* in the New World, see D. W. Cohen and J. P. Greene (eds.), *Neither Slave nor Free*.

68   Moreau de Saint Méry, *Description*, I, p. 110.

69   F. A. Stanislas, Baron de Wimpffen, *A Voyage to Saint-Domingo*, p. 62. 'Here . . . it is only necessary to have eyes, to be able to place every individual in the class to which he belongs' (*ibid.* p. 43).

70   *Ibid.*, p. 63. A Port-au-Prince businessman, giving an account of the 'three sorts of men' who lived in the colony, enumerated them by colour (G. Légal, *Dernier vœu de la justice de l'humanité et de la saine politique*, p. 12).

71   P. D. Curtin, *Two Jamaicas*, p. 47; A. C. Carmichael, *Domestic Manners and Social Conditions of the White, Coloured and Negro Population of the West Indies*, pp. 83 and 264.

72   Moreau de Saint Méry, *Description*, I, p. 96f. Barry Higman notes a similar categorisation of coloured people in Jamaica; again distinctions became more refined as the coloured person approached white. B. Higman, *Slave Population and Economy in Jamaica, 1807–1834*, chapter 7.

73   D. Bell, in N. Glazer and D. P. Moynihan (eds.), *Ethnicity: Theory and Experience*, p. 155. The Spanish clearly adopted race distinctions based upon blood in the seventeenth century; cf. H. de la Costa, 'The development of the native clergy in the Philippines', *Theological Studies*, 8 (June 1947).

74   B. Maurel, *Cahiers de doléances de la colonie de Saint-Domingue pour les états généraux de 1789*, p. 166.

75   Hilliard d'Auberteuil, *Considérations*, I, p. 130.

76   *Ibid.*, II, p. 73.

77   P.-E. B. de Boynes to P. G. comte de Nolivos, 14 mai 1771, AN, Col., B 138 fo. 103, quoted in Tarrade, I, p. 148.

78   Moreau de Saint Méry, *Considérations*, p. 44; cf. also *Description*, I, p. 102.
79   P. de Lacroix, *Mémoires pour servir à l'histoire de la révolution de Saint Domingue*, p. 15. In some parts of the South the *affranchis* had owned almost all the property; Moreau de Saint Méry, *Description*, III, p. 1400. It is possible that the *affranchis* owned a third of the *properties* (in general the smaller ones.)
80   J. Raimond, *Véritable origine des troubles de S. Domingue*, p. 4. But for the unreliability of Raimond cf. note 67 above. There is an article on Raimond by Mercer Cook in *Journal of Negro History*, April 1941.
81   De Fayet to Maurepas, 16 mai 1733, AN Col., C 9A, rec. 37; quoted in Frostin, p. 304. Moreau de Saint Méry, *Description*, I, p. 104.
82   Fouchard, *Marrons de la liberté*, p. 333.
83   Moreau de Saint Méry, *Description*, I, p. 110.
84   Of these *affranchis sans l'être*, Debbasch writes, 'le marron ne s'isole pas, il se fond dans la classe des affranchis en se prétendant libre, avec l'espoir – raisonable on le verra – qu'une possession d'état couvrira le défaut de titre' ('Le marronage: I', *L'Année Sociologique*, 1961, p. 21). But it is significant that of the few cases that he cites, two were mulattoes.
85   See p. 194 below.
86   Hilliard d'Auberteuil, *Considérations*, II, p. 162.
87   La Société des Amis des Noirs was founded by Brissot and others in 1788 in Paris; its members included Lafayette, Condorcet and Grégoire; see Claude Perroud, 'La société française des Amis des Noirs', *La Révolution Française*, 69 (1916), pp. 122ff; Léon Cahen, 'La Société des Amis des Noirs et Condorcet', *La Révolution Française*, 50 (1906) where the constitution of the society is printed on pp. 484ff; also S. T. McCloy, *The Humanitarian Movement in Eighteenth Century France*, pp. 102ff. The Saint Domingue planters founded a society in Paris to combat the Amis, called the Club Massiac; see G. Debien, *Les colons de Saint-Domingue et la révolution*.
88   C. S. Milscent, *Du régime colonial*, p. 7; Raimond, *Véritable origine*, p. 38.
89   Milscent, pp. 15ff.
90   Cf *Concordat* (of 19 october 1791, between *blancs* and *affranchis* of fourteen parishes in the Western province), p. 4.
91   With all its faults, particularly a somewhat uncritical reliance on secondary sources, this is still the best general book in English on the revolutionary period. James tends to underemphasise the importance of the colour question as a factor which influenced the course of events, wishing to explain developments in terms of economic interest (see especially p. 127). Racial and colour prejudice may indeed be explained as ultimately deriving from class antagonisms, but having developed they have a momentum of their own. In theory James recognises this: 'to neglect the racial factor', he wrote 'as merely incidental is an error only less grave than to make it fundamental' (p. 283). Anyone who knows James or is familiar with his writings will be astonished to see him described by T. O. Ott as a 'negro racist' (Ott, p. 199). James has indeed been a critic of colonialism, a prophet of Pan-Africanism, a Marxist and at times something of a romantic, but he has never been a racist in any conceivable sense of that term. His

interpretation of the Haitian revolution may properly be challenged, but this does not require resort to vulgar abuse.

92 On Toussaint, see Césaire, *Toussaint Louverture*; G. Laurent, *Toussaint Louverture à travers sa correspondance*; R. Korngold, *Citizen Toussaint: A Biography*.

93 For example Rotberg, pp. 54–5.

94 Laborie, p. 48.

95 Quadrupled if we accept the figures given by Charles Frostin (p. 28); doubled if we accept Hilliard's estimates of the picture in the mid-1770s rather than Frostin's.

96 Frostin, p. 29.

97 J. Leyburn, *The Haitian People*, p. 15. Some pages later, however, he states that 'If ever slaves had reason to rebel, the Negroes of Saint-Domingue did' (p. 22). But then we cannot expect blacks to behave reasonably!

98 Ott, *The Haitian Revolution*, pp. 42 and 188. Cf. T. L. Stoddard's view that Haiti 'owed its independence to a turn in European politics' in *The Rising Tide of Color against White World Supremacy*, p. 227, and Stoddard, *The French Revolution, passim*.

99 Ott, p. 13.

100 See O. Mennesson Rigaud, 'Le rôle du vaudou dans l'indépendance d'Haïti', *Présence Africaine*, février–mai 1958, p. 59; cf. also H. Trouillot, 'Introduction à une histoire du vodou', *Revue de la Société Haïtienne d'Histoire, de Géographie et de Géologie*, 34 (janvier–mars 1970), pp. 72ff.

101 De Lacroix, p. 103. It is likely that this statement was, like many similar statements, written by a European priest who was either sympathetic to the black cause, or who wrote under duress.

2. Fathers of national independence (1804–1825)

1 'Reproclaimed' would be more accurate, for there was a 'Proclamation' dated 29 November 1803, signed by Dessalines, Christophe and Clerveaux, which stated: 'L'indépendance de Saint Domingue est proclamée . . . ' (AAE, Mém. et Doc., Amérique 15, Saint Domingue, 1799–1825).

2 Article 20 of the 1805 constitution specified black and red as the national colours. However the flag used in January 1804 was blue and red. '. . . The use of the French flag is now prohibited – that which they now use is dark blue and red, the Blue uppermost . . . ' (Edward Corbet to George Nugent, 25 January 1804, PRO, CO 137/111). Corbet had just returned from a visit to Haiti, where he had held discussions with Dessalines earlier in the month about a commercial treaty. In May 1803 'the brigands' (as the indigenous army was called by the British and French) were displaying a flag which was 'half Blue half White, the Blue next the staff and vertically divided' (report of H.M.S. *Cumberland* to Rear-Admiral Sir I. T. Duckworth, 15 May 1803, PRO, CO 137/110). In November 1803 a French captain noted that the 'brigands' were displaying a white flag on one occasion and blue and white flags on another ('Journal du Capitaine de la Frégate l'Embuscade', 25 Brumaire, l'an XI (16 November 1803), AN, Marine, BB4:182).

3   On Goman see C. N. Céligni (*sic*) Ardouin, *Essais sur l'histoire d'Haïti*, pp. 106ff.
4   Ardouin, *Etudes*, VI, p. 17.
5   *Gazette Politique et Commerciale d'Haïti*, 30 mai 1805. Santo Domingo was at this time occupied by the French general Louis Ferrand.
6   Cf. the statement attributed to Stokeley Carmichael that Fidel Castro is 'one of the blackest men in the Americas', quoted in W. Rodney, *The Groundings with My Brothers*, p. 31. General George Nugent, governor of Jamaica, estimated that there were in mid-1803 about 500 Polish troops fighting with Dessalines (Nugent to Lord Hobart, 9 August 1803, PRO, CO 137/110). A number of Germans had deserted from the British army which occupied parts of Saint Domingue from 1793 to 1798. The Poles had deserted from Leclerc's army and had joined Dessalines. For further information on the part played by the Polish troops in Saint Domingue see 'Wiadomość o wyprawie części legionów polskich na wyspie San Domingo w r. 1803. Przez Gen. Kazimierza Małachowskiego', in Artur Oppman, *Na San Domingo*, pp. 59ff; also Gustaw Meinert, 'Legioniści Polscy na wyspie Santo Domingo', *Przewodnik Naukowy i Literacki*, 1886; this series of articles is in twelve parts and begins on p. 65.
7   Cf. F. Boisrond Tonnerre, *Mémoires pour servir à l'histoire d'Haïti*, p. x. Leyburn mistakenly asserts that Boisrond Tonnerre was black and practically illiterate (Leyburn, p. 213).
8   Ardouin, *Etudes*, VI, p. 8; and cf. M. Lubin, 'Les premiers rapports de la nation haïtienne avec l'étranger', *Journal of Interamerican Studies*, 10 (1968), p. 278.
9   Talleyrand to Turreau, 5 juillet 1805, AAE, Corr. Pol., Etats Unis, 58/188–9. For British fears, see Lord Hobart to General George Nugent, 18 November 1801, quoted in H. B. L. Hughes, 'British Policy Towards Haiti, 1801–1805', *Canadian Historical Review*, 25 (1944), pp. 397ff.
10   *Gazette Politique et Commerciale d'Haïti*, 17 octobre 1805. A correspondent challenged this view in a later issue of the *Gazette*: 'Je ne crois donc pas que nous ayons jamais aucune raison de suspecter ni la conduite ni les vues des américains, ni rien à appréhender de leur gouvernement' (*Gazette*, 14 novembre 1805).
11   Alain Turnier, *Les Etats-Unis et le marché haïtien*, p. 95.
12   Ardouin, *Etudes*, VI, p. 26.
13   *Gazette Politique et Commerciale d'Haïti*, 11 décembre 1805, and Ardouin, *Etudes*, VI, p. 61.
14   *Ibid.*, VI, pp. 45–6.
15   Leyburn, p. 32.
16   There has been considerable controversy on the question whether the term 'caste' can properly be used to describe social groups in post-colonial Haiti. The controversy springs from two causes: a different understanding of the term 'caste', and a different assessment of the Haitian situation. Cf. p. 94 below.
17   Beaubrun Ardouin, *Géographie de l'île d'Haïti*, p. 24, and Thomas Madiou, *Histoire d'Haïti*, III, p. 328; cf. also R. A. Saint-Louis, *La présociologie haïtienne*, p. 90.

18 P. David, *L'héritage colonial en Haïti*, p. 37; cf. pp. 21ff. above.
19 A. de Tocqueville, *L'ancien régime et le révolution*, note Z; and M. C. M. Simpson (ed.), *Correspondence and Conversations of Alexis de Tocqueville with N. W. Senior*, II, p. 103.
20 Leyburn, p. 32.
21 Speech at Cap, reported in *Gazette Politique et Commerciale d'Haïti*, 25 juillet 1805.
22 Baron de Vastey, one of Christophe's closest associates, stated that he was born in Grenada (*An Essay on the Causes of the Revolution and Civil Wars of Hayti*, p. 112). W. W. Harvey, who lived in Haiti during the last months of Christophe's reign, corroborated this statement (*Sketches of Hayti from the Expulsion of the French to the Death of Christophe*, p. 46); Joseph Saint-Rémy agreed, giving Christophe's date of birth as 6 October 1767 (*Essai sur Henri-Christophe, général haïtien*, p. 1). Leyburn, however, states that he was born on the island of St Christopher (St Kitts) (Leyburn, p. 42). This was a view current during Christophe's lifetime (cf. *Notice historique sur les désastres de Saint Domingue, par un officier français détenu par Dessalines*, p. 35). For further biographical details on Christophe see Hubert Cole, *Christophe: King of Haiti*.
23 Joseph Saint-Rémy, *Pétion et Haïti*, IV, p. 81.
24 Quoted in Ardouin, *Etudes*, VIII, p. 65.
25 F. D. Chanlatte, *Appel aux haytiens*, p. 4.
26 Comte de Rosiers, *Hayti reconnaissante en réponse à un écrit imprimé à Londres, et intitulé: l'Europe châtiée, et l'Afrique vengée*, pp. 5, 12, 22.
27 Juste Chanlatte, *Le cri de la nature*, p. 9; this work was substantially republished by A. J. B. Bouvet de Cressé, under the title *Histoire de la catastrophe de Saint-Domingue*. The French writer Mazères had written: 'The colour of the negro's skin already proclaims the darkness of his intelligence' (*De l'utilité des colonies, des causes de la perte de Saint-Domingue et des moyens d'en recouvrer la possession*, p. 61).
28 Bouvet de Cressé, p. 13.
29 E. L. Griggs and C. H. Prator (eds.), *Henry Christophe and Thomas Clarkson*, p. 135.
30 Prince Sanders (ed.), *Haytian Papers*, p. 211.
31 Chevalier de Prézeau, *Réfutation de la lettre du général français Dauxion Lavaysse*, p. 21. De Limonade also insisted upon racial equality; see *Le machiavélisme du cabinet français*, p. 18.
32 F. Darfour, 'Politique', *L'Eclaireur Haytien ou le Parfait Patriot*, 5 août 1818.
33 J. S. Milscent, 'Politique: suite et fin des réflexions sur quelques passages de la Genèse', *L'Abeille Haytienne*, 1 novembre 1818.
34 'Politique: suite des réflexions sur quelques passages de la Genèse', *L'Abeille Haytienne*, 16 octobre 1818.
35 'Politique: suite des réflexions sur quelques passages de la Genèse', *L'Abeille Haytienne*, 16 septembre 1818; see also 'La terre est peuplée d'hommes assortis aux divers climats; ils sont l'œuvre du même auteur: ils sont égaux devant lui' (Milscent, 'Politique', *L'Abeille Haytienne*, 1 août 1818).
36 Milscent, 'Politique: considérations sur l'île d'Haïti, I', *L'Abeille Haytienne*,

1 août 1817; see also article III in the same series, *L'Abeille Haytienne*, 16 août 1817.

37 Milscent, 'Politique', *L'Abeille Haytienne*, 1 septembre 1818.

38 Griggs and Prator, p. 106.

39 *Ibid.*, p. 245.

40 Darfour, 'Politique', *L'Eclaireur Haytien*, 20 août 1818.

41 Milscent, 'A M. Darfour', *L'Eclaireur Haytien*, 25 septembre 1818; Darfour, 'A M. Milscent', *L'Abeille Haytienne*, 16 septembre 1818.

42 See Oswald Durand, 'Tournée Littéraire', *Haïti Littéraire et Sociale*, 20 septembre 1905, p. 404; see also de Vastey to Clarkson, 29 novembre 1819, in Griggs and Prator, pp. 181–2.

43 Harvey, p. 223; cf. Ardouin's similar assessment of de Vastey: 'C'était un homme instruit, mais d'une corruption que sa méchanceté seule égalait' (*Etudes*, VI, p. 21).

44 De Vastey, *Réflexions sur une lettre de Mazères, ex-colon français* (cited hereafter as *Mazères*), pp. 11–12 and 86.

45 *Ibid.*, p. 54.

46 *Ibid.*, p. 22.

47 *Ibid.*, p. 82.

48 De Vastey, *Political Remarks on Some French Works and Newspapers Concerning Hayti*, p. 9.

49 *Ibid.*, p. 74; cf. also *Mazères*, p. 12.

50 De Vastey, *Political Remarks*, p. 19.

51 De Vastey, *Mazères*, p. 32.

52 *Ibid.*, pp. 35–6.

53 De Vastey, *Le système colonial dévoilé*, pp. 19–20.

54 *Ibid.*, p. 25.

55 Hegel, *Philosophy of Mind*, p. 43 (*Zusatz* to section 393).

56 De Vastey, *Notes à M. le baron de V. P. Malouet*, p. 20.

57 De Vastey, *Le système*, p. vi, and *Political Remarks*, p. 74 n.

58 *Le système*, p. 18.

59 De Vastey, *Mazères*, p. 14.

60 Griggs and Prator, p. 128. On Bolívar and Pétion see Paul Verna, *Robert Sutherland, un amigo de Bolívar en Haití*, Paul Verna. *Pétion y Bolívar*, and F. Dalencour, *Pétion devant l'humanité: Alexandre Pétion et Simon Bolívar*.

61 Griggs and Prator, p. 98.

62 *Ibid.*, p. 99: 'It would be unjust to confuse that part of the island, where disorder still reigns, with this Government, and to attribute to us actions which are contrary to our principles.'

63 *Ibid.*, p. 99.

64 De Vastey, *Political Remarks*, p. 20.

65 De Vastey, *An Essay*, pp. 208–9.

66 Prince Sanders, p. 182. A copy of the instructions given to the three French agents by the French government can be found in AN, Col., CC 9A 48.

67 'Adresse: Au Roi', issued by the Council of State in *Liberté et indépendance: Royaume d'Hayti*, p. 16; and Royaume d'Hayti, *Plan général de*

defense du Royaume, p. 2; cf. also 'A ma voix, Hayti s'est transformée en un vaste camp de soldats' (speech of the king, *Gazette Royale d'Hayti*, 19 juillet 1815).

68   Ardouin, *Etudes*, VIII, p. 27.

69   Quoted in de Vastey, *An Essay*, pp. xcii—xcv.

70   *Ibid*., p. lxxxiv.

71   De Limonade (Julien Prévost), *Relation des glorieux événements qui ont porté Leurs Majestés Royales sur le Trône d'Hayti*, p. xxiii.

72   'C'est à Pétion, haytiens, à qui nous devons cette insolence des ex-colons; c'est lui qui a eu la lâcheté de fléchir les genoux devant eux; c'est lui qui a nourri dans le cœur des ex-colons l'espoir de pouvoir nous rendre encore esclaves ou de nous exterminer!' (De Vastey in Royaume d'Hayti, *Communication officielle de trois lettres de Catineau Laroche, ex-colon, agent de Pétion*, p. 31). Cf. also de Vastey, *Cri de la patrie*, p. 3; *Cri de la conscience*, p. 55; and *Réflexions adressées aux haytiens de la partie de l'Ouest et du Sud, sur l'horrible assassinat du général Delvare*, p. 18. See also 'Coup d'œil politique sur la situation actuelle du Royaume d'Hayti' (anon.), in *Relation de la fête de S. M. la Reine d'Hayti*, p. 69.

73   L. F. Manigat, *Le délicat problème de la critique historique*, pp. 15 and 25—6. For a discussion of Boyer's position see pp. 64ff. below.

74   *Ibid*., p. 28.

75   *Ibid*., p. 30

76   *Ibid*., p. 27. Of course, this general statement needs qualification. People can often get away with inaccuracy and deception in private correspondence which would be impossible in published work.

77   Dauxion Lavaysse to S. E. le Ministre de la Marine, 10 septembre 1814, AN, Col., CC 9A 48. This recognition of French sovereignty would have been conditional on France's agreeing not to send a garrison within a specified period. According to Dauxion Lavaysse, Pétion also spoke of Haiti becoming 'une Colonie libre française' (*ibid*.).

78   *Ibid*.

79   Esmangart and Fontanges, 'Rapport', 27 janvier 1817, AN, Col., CC 9A 50. With respect to their proposals that there should be a restoration of French sovereignty with guaranteed local autonomy, Esmangart and Fontanges wrote, 'Pethion [*sic*] parut sentir que ces propositions seraient réellement plus avantageuses à St. Domingue que l'indépendance absolue; mais n'était plus libre de les accepter, après tout ce qu'il avait fait pour persuader au peuple soumis à son gouvernement que l'indépendance n'avait pas de défenseur plus zêlé que lui' ('Note sur Saint Domingue', 5 février 1821, AAE, Corr. Pol., Haïti 2/71—2). There is even the possibility that in 1810 Pétion was thinking of agreeing to some form of British sovereignty. This is referred to in Langlade to Doran, 21 septembre 1810 (PRO, WO 1/76).

80   'Note sur Saint Domingue', AAE, Corr. Pol., Haïti 2/52. See also 'En déclarant son indépendance le peuple d'Hayti l'a fait à l'univers entier et non à la France en particulier, rien ne pourra jamais le faire rétrograder de cette inébranlable résolution . . . Le peuple d'Hayti veut être libre et indépendant, je le veux avec lui' (Pétion to Esmangart and Fontanges, 10 novembre 1816, AN, Col., CC 9A 50). General Ferrand, in Santo

Domingo, had earlier speculated on Pétion's intentions but concluded that there was a real danger that, having defeated Christophe, he might turn on the eastern part of the island, whose inhabitants would be more likely to support a mulatto leader than a black (L'Armée de Saint-Domingue: Correspondance avec le Ministre, 1807–8; 1 avril 1808, AN, Col., CC 9A 43).

81 Cf. p. 229 below.

82 J.-B. G. Wallez. *Précis historique des négotiations entre la France et Saint-Domingue*, p. 169.

83 De Limonade to Clarkson, 20 novembre 1819, in Griggs and Prator, p. 176.

84 De Vastey, *Political Remarks*, p. 30.

85 Ardouin, *Etudes*, VI, p. 94; this pronouncement of Christophe was reprinted in London, but mistakenly dated 24 October, instead of 24 November. See *Adresse du gouvernement d'Haïti au commerce des nations neutres.*

86 *Gazette Officielle de l'Etat d'Haïti*, IV, 28 janvier 1808, p. 16.

87 *Relation des glorieux événements*, pp. xxv–xxvi.

88 De Vastey, *Political Remarks*, pp. 53–4.

89 *Ibid.*, p. 26.

90 Bouvet de Cressé, p. 89.

91 'La culture de la littérature Anglaise dans nos écoles, dans nos collèges, fera prédominer enfin, je l'espère, la langue Anglaise sur la Française; c'est le seul moyen de conserver notre indépendance, que de n'avoir absolument rien de commun avec une nation dont nous avons tant à nous plaindre, et dont les projets ne tendent qu'à notre destruction' (King Henry to William Wilberforce, 18 novembre 1816, in R. I. and S. Wilberforce, (eds.), *The Correspondence of William Wilberforce*, I, pp. 359–60).

92 Griggs and Prator, p. 146.

93 De Vastey, *An Essay*, p. 207.

94 Hérard Dumesle, *Réflexions politiques sur la mission des commissaires du roi de France*, quoted in Ardouin, *Etudes*, VIII, p. 57 n.

95 E. Bonnet, *Souvenirs historiques de G.-J. Bonnet*, pp. 334–5; cf also J. S. Milscent, 'Politique: suite des considérations sur l'île d'Haïti', *L'Abeille Haytienne*, 16 octobre 1817.

96 Ardouin. *Etudes*, VII, p. 14. Schiller Thébaud discusses Christophe's land policy, but appears to ignore this early decree: see 'L'évolution de la structure agraire d'Haïti (Thesis, University of Paris, Fac. de Droit, 1967), pp. 71ff.

97 Ardouin, *Etudes,* II, pp. 48ff.

98 P. Moral, *Le paysan haïtien*, p. 31.

99 Griggs and Prator, p. 107.

100 Charles Mackenzie to G. Canning, 9 September 1826, PRO, FO 35/4.

101 L. F. Manigat, *La politique agraire du gouvernement d'Alexandre Pétion*, pp. 46ff; cf. also J. Price Mars, *De la préhistoire d'Afrique à l'histoire d'Haïti*, pp. 170ff, Thébaud, 'L'évolution de la structure agraire', p. 83 and earlier, Lepelletier de Saint-Rémy, *Saint Domingue*, II, p. 169. A writer in *Le Progrès* (1 février 1844) declared that the policy had made 'civil war impossible' by giving the 'totality of the citizens' a vested interest in public order and tranquillity.

102 Ardouin, *Etudes*, VII, p. 9; J. S. Milscent, 'Politique: suite des considérations sur l'île d'Haïti', *L'Abeille Haytienne*, 1 septembre 1817.

103 Ardouin, *Etudes*, VII, p. 66.

104 For such a discussion cf. A. Thoby, *La question agraire en Haïti*, Manigat,
La politique agraire and Thébaud, 'L'évolution de la structure agraire'.
There is a more recent consideration of the subject by R. K. Lacerte,
'The First Land Reform in Latin America', *Inter-American Economic
Affairs*, 28:4 (1975). The author, however, relies heavily on secondary
sources.

105 'To say that the intermittent civil war between Christophe's kingdom of
the North and Pétion's republic of the South was a struggle between blacks
and colored people would not do great violence to the essential truth'
(Leyburn, p. 48). Leyburn also mistakenly asserts that Pétion drew up the
1806 constitution 'with his fellow mulattoes' (*ibid.*, p. 239).

106 Griggs and Prator, p. 184.

107 Cf. Y. Debbasch, *Couleur et liberté*, p. 257; 'Colombus', *Réponse à l'écrit
de M. H. Henry*, p. 1; and Harvey, *Sketches*, p. 395. Max Bissainthe
(*Dictionnaire*, p. 72) suggests that 'Colombus' may have been the *nom
de plume* of J.-B. Dupuy; this is unlikely, as 'Colombus' wrote 'Je suis
Etranger à l'île d'Hayti . . . ' (*Réponse*, p. 1). This pamphlet was clearly
by a republican sympathiser and was published in Port-au-Prince. Dupuy
was a minister in Christophe's kingdom and his *Deuxième lettre à M. H.
Henry* was published in Cap Henry.

108 De Vastey, *A mes concitoyens*, p. 6; cf. p. 17.

109 *Proclamation au peuple et à l'armée*, 14 janvier 1807; there is a copy of
this document in PRO, WO 1/29. Also Ardouin, *Etudes*, VIII, p. 29.

110 De Vastey, *An Essay*, pp. 91 and 94.

111 De Vastey, *Cri de la conscience*, p. 103; *Réflexions adressées aux haytiens*,
p. 20; *Cri de la patrie*, p. 5.

112 De Prézeau, *Lettre à ses concitoyens de partie de L'Ouest et du Sud.*

113 De Limonade, *Le machiavélisme du cabinet français*, p. 16.

114 'Colombus', p. 6.

115 'Christophe, cependant, atteste le ciel qu'il n'en veut point aux nuances
de l'épiderme; mais s'il n'en conservait les préjugés, oserait-il en parler?
L'Ouest et le Sud ignorent aujourd'hui ces absurdes préjugés; on n'y
connaît que des frères' (statement of the senate, 1807, in Saint-Rémy,
Pétion, IV, p. 104).

116 N. Colombel, *Examen d'un pamphlet ayant pour titre: 'Essai sur les causes
de la révolution et des guerres civiles d'Haïti, etc.'*, p. 14.

117 'En combattant le préjugé ridicule des couleurs, nous ne nous attendions
pas de trouver, parmi quelques-uns de nos Concitoyens, des partisans de
ce même préjugé' (F. Darfour, 'Littérature', *L'Eclaireur Haytien*, 27
août 1818).

118 Cf. *L'Avertisseur Haytien*, 23 janvier 1819.

119 Saint-Rémy actually suggested that the constitution of 1806 was directed
against Christophe (*Pétion*, IV, p. 86). The twentieth-century editor of
this work, Dr François Dalencour, rebukes Saint-Rémy (whose honesty,
at this point, got the better of his strong republican sympathies!) for this

departure from the strict mulatto interpretation of the past. For a further discussion of Dalencour see pp. 205 below.

120 'Colombus', pp. 5–6. For Pétion's statement see *Lettre du général Prévost adressée au président d'Hayti, et proclamation au peuple et à l'armée*, p. 8. See also *Le peuple de la république d'Haïti à messieurs Vastey et Limonade* (anon.).

121 Dumesle, 'Economie politique', *L'Observateur*, 15 juillet 1819; 'Economie politique', *L'Observateur*, 1 juin 1819; 'Résumé politique', *L'Observateur*, 15 octobre 1819.

122 *Adresse de la Chambre des Représentants des Communes aux citoyens de la République*, 21 juillet 1817; *Arrête de l'Assemblée Départementale du Sud*, 9 janvier 1811, and *Le Peuple du Département du Sud*, 3 novembre 1810.

123 Milscent, 'Politique', *L'Abeille Haytienne*, 1 août to 30 novembre 1819.

124 De Vastey, *An Essay*, p. 109.

125 De Vastey, *Cri de la conscience*, p. 82, and *An Essay*, p. 239.

126 De Vastey, *Political Remarks*, p. 20, and *An Essay*, p. 106.

127 *Political Remarks*, p. 18; see also de Limonade, 'Coup d'œil politique', in *Relation de la fête de S. M. la Reine d'Hayti*, pp. 57ff, where the author lays emphasis upon the importance of leadership. He also had an almost Rousseauite conception of the role of the legislator: 'L'on vit chaque législateur donner des institutions et des lois, qui, par leurs formes et leurs contextures, tenaient à la nature de leur génie' (*ibid.*).

128 Harvey, pp. 120–1.

129 *Ibid.*, p. 282; but cf. a different impression given by Karl Ritter in *Naturhistorische Reise*, as quoted in *Foreign Quarterly Review*, (October 1837), p. 81, where he wrote of 'a certain cold etiquette and distance' being preserved by the black nobility. On this and other matters Ritter's account conflicts with that of other authors, and he may not be entirely reliable.

130 'Rapport du Capitaine Montfert, du Brick la Bergère', 7 octobre 1819, AAE Corr. Pol., Haïti 2/16. J. Candler, *Brief Notices of Hayti*, p. 37; cf. also C. Mackenzie, *Notes on Haiti, Made during a Residence in that Republic*, I, p. 148.

131 G. Soriano (ed.), *Simón Bolívar: escritos políticos*, p. 131.

132 De Vastey wrote, 'les rois ne sont que les pères des peuples' (*Cri de la patrie*, p. 26). Pétion declared, 'Nous vivons tous en famille, votre chef est votre père . . . ' ('Au peuple et à l'armée', in *Lettre du général Prévost adressée au président d'Hayti*, p. 2). For Dessalines's paternalism see his speech at Cap, printed in *Gazette Politique et Commerciale d'Hayti*, 25 juillet 1805.

133 Mackenzie to Canning, 9 September 1826, PRO, FO 35/4.

134 Madiou, *Histoire*, III, p. 386.

135 Ardouin, *Etudes*, VI, p. 106.

136 William Wilson to Mrs T. Clarkson, 12 November 1821, in Griggs and Prator, p. 236.

137 *Correspondence Relative to the Emigration to Hayti of the Free People of Color in the United States*, p. 10.

138 *Ibid.*, p. 15.
139 *Ibid.*, p. 11.
140 Z. Macaulay, *Haïti ou renseignements authentiques sur l'abolition de l'esclavage*, p. 1.
141 V. Schoelcher, *Colonies étrangères et Haïti, passim.*
142 J. Franklin, *The Present State of Hayti*, p. vii.
143 *Ibid.*, p. 364.
144 *The Rural Code of Haiti*, p. iii.
145 'Particulars of which Mr. Consul Mackenzie should procure information as to the enforcement of agricultural labour in Hayti', PRO, FO 35/1.
146 Canning to Mackenzie, 27 March 1826, PRO, FO 35/2.
147 Mackenzie to Canning, 2 June 1826, PRO, FO 35/3.
148 Granville to Canning, 13 January 1825, PRO, FO 27/329.
149 'Mémoire sur Haïti', 9 février 1820, AAE, Corr. Pol., Haïti 2/20–1. For an interesting discussion of French relations with Haiti during the first half of the nineteenth century, see Benoît Joachim, 'Décolonisation ou néocolonialisme?', unpublished thesis of the University of Paris, 1969 (in Bibliothèque Nationale, Paris, Microfiche, m 398); also Joachim, 'Le néocolonialisme à l'essai', *La Pensée*, 156 (1971), pp. 35ff.
150 Esmangart to Pasquier, 'Projet de lettre au général Boyer', 2 janvier 1821, AAE, Corr. Pol., Haïti 2; quoted in W. S. Robertson, *France and Latin American Independence*, p. 451.
151 De Vastey, *An Essay*, p. 236.
152 Ardouin, *Etudes*, IX, p. 55; cf. Boyer to Lafayette: 'Le *préjugé de l'épiderme* est evidemment le seul motif de ce silence injurieux, puisque notre République offre au monde toutes les garanties qu'on peut désirer par la stabilité de ses institutions et de son gouvernement' (quoted in Ardouin, *Etudes*, IX, p. 75 n.).
153 V. Lecuna, *Simón Bolívar: un pensamiento sobre el congreso de Panama*, quoted in G. A. Belaunde, *Bolívar and the Political Thought of the Spanish-American Revolution*, p. 265.
154 J. B. Inginac, *Mémoires*, p. 93.
155 Mackenzie to Canning, 9 September 1826, PRO, FO 35/4.
156 F. J. Franco Pichado, *Los negros, los mulatos y la nación Dominicana*. See also F. Moya Pons, 'La invasión de Boyer', *Renovación*, 15 febrero 1972. On the period of Haitian rule see M. de J. Troncoso de la Concha, *La ocupación de Santo Domingo por Haití*, and for a recent and more balanced view, F. Moya Pons, *La dominación haitiana, 1822–1844*.
157 *Gazette de France*, 19 janvier 1825, quoted in Robertson, *France*, p. 460. For British views see Stuart to Canning, 26 July 1824, PRO, FO 27/312.
158 Quoted from the Archives Coloniales by L. F. Manigat, *Le délicat problème de la critique historique*, p. 32.
159 Esmangart to Portal, 9 juillet 1818, AN, Col., CC 9A 51. A French captain reported in 1819 that 'toutes les personnes de couleur étaient très jalouses de leur liberté et indépendance' (Report of Capitaine F. G. Laugier, AN, Col., CC 9A 51).
160 See p. 139 below. Though in the case of Salomon it was, of course, black supremacy which he wished to maintain.

161 Ardouin, *Etudes*, IX, p. 77. French recognition was, however, limited to the western part of the island; the royal ordinance does not recognise Haiti's claim to the former Spanish colony.

3. Pride and prejudice (1820–1867)

1 Brown, II, p. 259.
2 *Ibid.*, pp. 267–8.
3 Candler, p. 90.
4 Mackenzie to Canning, 9 September 1826, PRO, FO 35/4.
5 *Ibid.* See also Mackenzie, II, pp. 201ff. In addition to the regular army, Mackenzie estimated a national guard of perhaps 40,000. In 1822 Boyer had marched into the east with 12,000 men; see E. Rodríguez Demorizi, *Invasiones haitianas, 1801, 1805 y 1822*, p. 279. By 1860 the regular army numbered about 40,000, 'probably the largest standing army in the world, in proportion to the population' (B. S. Hunt, *Remarks on Hayti as a Place of Settlement for Afric-Americans; and on the Mulatto as a Race for the Tropics*, p. 19). De Delva, however, gave a figure of 7,826 officers and men for 1867 (*Considérations sur l'armée haïtienne*, pp. 32ff.) It is inconceivable that Geffrard reduced the size of the army to this extent. St John gave the more realistic figure of 20,000 for 1867 (S. St John, *Hayti: or the Black Republic*, p. 310).
   For population figures see Robert Bazile, 'Quelques aspects de la démographie en Haïti', in R. P. Schaedel (ed.), *Papers of the Conference on Research and Resources of Haiti*, pp. 38ff.
6 See S. W. Hanna, *Notes of a Visit to Some Parts of Haiti: Jan.–Feb. 1835*, p. 76; also Candler, p. 19. A French diplomat noted the same imbalance, Ragueneau de la Chainaye to Baron le Damas, 8 août 1826, AAE, Corr. Pol., Haïti 2/187.
7 Brown, II, p. 285.
8 *Ibid.*, pp. 269–70.
9 Leyburn, p. 66.
10 I have dealt with this matter in more detail in *Economic Dependence*, p. 12.
11 Franklin, *The Present State*, pp. 344–5.
12 'Memorandum of Information received from James Franklin Esq. respecting Hayti', 14 October 1826, PRO, FO 35/1.
13 Franklin, *The Present State*, p. 240.
14 Ardouin, *Etudes*, IX, p. 58.
15 For recent estimates of exports at this time see Moya Pons, appendix, and Rotberg, pp. 386ff.
16 Brown II, p. 280; see also Mackenzie, II, p. 124 and Hunt, *Remarks on Hayti*, p. 19.
17 Commander R. Sharpe to Commodore Byng, 13 March 1843, PRO, FO 35/27.
18 Brown II, p. 281 and Hunt, pp. 8–9.
19 Franklin, *The Present State*, p. 306; cf. also Hanna, p. 41.
20 Candler, p. 44.

21 Schoelcher, I, pp. 292–3; see also A. Cabon, *Notes sur l'histoire réligieuse d'Haïti de la révolution au concordat (1789–1860)*, p. 199.

22 Inginac, p. 88.

23 Bonnet, pp. 311–12.

24 Ardouin, *Etudes*, IX, p. 23 n.

25 There was a significant movement of mulattoes out of farming into commerce during this period, though many of them retained ownership of their estates; see B. Joachim, 'La structure sociale en Haïti et le mouvement d'indépendance au dix-neuvième siècle', *Journal of World History*, 1970, p. 456. Cf. C. C. Griffin, 'Economic and social aspects of the era of Spanish-American independence', *Hispanic American Review*, 29 (1949), p. 186.

26 Lepelletier de Saint-Rémy, 'La république d'Haïti', *Revue des Deux Mondes*, 15:4 (novembre 1845), p. 681.

27 *Le Temps*, 2 février 1843.

28 Alexandre Bonneau counted thirty-one such journals in the period from 1804 to 1856, 'Les noirs, les jaunes et la littérature française en Haïti', *Revue Contemporaine*, 29 (décembre 1856), p. 133. Typical of such journals would be *L'Opinion Nationale*, edited by E. Heurtelou, with 777 subscribers, 278 of whom came from the capital, with 26 from overseas; see *L'Opinion Nationale*, 2 mars 1861. On bookshops see Mackenzie, I, p. 43.

29 J.-P. Boyer to J. Bentham, undated letter in University College, London, Bentham MSS, 60:95.

30 'It is evident that Boyer is very much prejudiced against the blacks, as well as many of them to him' (Sanders to Clarkson, 14 July 1821, in Griggs and Prator, p. 227). Cf. also Harvey, pp. 85–6.

31 Franklin, *The Present State*, pp. 10–11; also p. 399.

32 Brown, II, p. 232.

33 *Ibid.*, II, pp. 259 and 283.

34 *Ibid.*, II, 284.

35 Candler, pp. 55–6.

36 A. L. Ragueneau de la Chainaye to Baron le Damas, 26 avril 1826, AAE, Corr. Pol., Haïti 2/162, and Ragueneau to Damas, 15 septembre 1827, AAE, Corr. Pol., Haïti 2/340.

37 Mackenzie to Canning, 9 September 1826, PRO, FO 35/4. Later, however, in a published work, Mackenzie suggested that there were many instances in which blacks were entrusted with important positions, and that it was an oversimplification to maintain that the mulattoes formed an aristocracy (Mackenzie, I, p. 29).

38 For an account of the whole incident from the government's side, see Ardouin, *Etudes*, IX, pp. 42ff. Boyer denounced Darfour as one of those who had determined to 'lancer parmi eux [haïtiens] les brandons de la discorde' (*Proclamation au peuple et à l'armée*, 9 septembre 1822).

39 Inginac, p. 66; and B. Ardouin, *Réponse du Sénateur B. Ardouin à une lettre de M. Isambert*.

40 Salomon *et al.*, 'Exposé aux délégués du gouvernement provisoire', 17 juillet 1843, quoted in L. E. L. F. Salomon *jeune, Une défense*, p. 27.

41 Ardouin, *Etudes*, IX, pp. 36–7; cf. p. 25 above. On the system of land-

holding in the Dominican Republic, see M. R. Ruiz Tejada, *Estudio sobre la propiedad inmobiliaria en la República Dominicana*.

42 The Amis des Noirs had attacked Moreau de Saint Méry, '*dont les traits du visage et la couleur de la peau font soupçonner une double trahison*: celle des droits de l'homme et de *ses frères* proprement dits . . .' (Ardouin, *Etudes*, I, p. 19n).

43 There was a tradition of resistance and of guerrilla warfare in the South, particularly in the region of La Grand'Anse; Goman had led a resistance to Pétion's government in this region. The British consul, Mackenzie, referred to the likelihood of armed resistance to the Rural Code of 1826 from southern peasants, this time in the region of Jacmel (Mackenzie to Canning, 25 November 1826, PRO, FO 35/4).

44 See Dumesle's speech in the Chambre des Communes, in *L'Union*, 19 juillet 1838. For his earlier expressions of liberalism, see p. 58 above.

45 For this aspect of their thought see pp. 90ff. below.

46 I have discussed this in *Economic Dependence*, pp. 11ff.

47 'Philosophie sociale', *Le Républicain*, 15 août 1836.

48 Emile Nau, in *Le Républicain*, 1 octobre 1836.

49 Anon., 'Littérature', *L'Union*, 27 juillet 1837; E. N., 'Littérature', *L'Union*, 16 novembre 1837.

50 See anon., 'De la nationalité', *L'Union*, 28 décembre 1837, and further articles in *L'Union*, 11 and 25 janvier 1838.

51 *L'Union*, 8 juin 1837.

52 B. Lespinasse, *Histoire des affranchis de Saint-Domingue*, p. 19.

53 Cf. *L'Union*, 3 janvier 1839.

54 M. S. Faubert *jeune*, in *L'Union*, 31 janvier 1839.

55 *Le Républicain*, 15 octobre 1836.

56 See pp. 158f. below.

57 Anon., 'De l'exclusion des étrangers du droit de propriété à Haïti', *Le Manifeste*, 19 décembre 1841. There was, however, disagreement on this issue; cf. J. H. Fresnel, in *Le Manifeste*, 9 juillet 1843.

58 *Le Manifeste*, 19 décembre 1841.

59 *Ibid.*

60 D. Lespinasse, in *Le Manifeste*, 12 décembre 1841.

61 Lespinasse in *Le Manifeste*, 30 janvier 1842.

62 *Le Manifeste*, 6 février 1842.

63 Ardouin, *Etudes*, XI, p. 55.

64 Guerrier *et al.* to Guizot, 2 juillet 1843, AAE, Corr. Pol., Haïti 11/14. A report of this letter was printed in the French newspaper *Le Globe*, 30 août 1843, and later in the Haitian journal *La Sentinelle de la Liberté*, 7 décembre 1843, which however, denounced it as a forgery. The journal stated, in a manner which was typical of the mulatto ideologists, that colour conflict could not exist in Haiti: 'La désunion des nègres et des mulâtres est impossible, croyez à nos paroles; les deux castes n'en sont qu'une seule.' For further evidence of southern discontent see Ussher to Aberdeen, 12 May 1843, PRO, FO 35/26, also 'en fin Exmo. Señor que los negros están enteramente decididos a no someterse de ningun modo a los mulatos' (D. Juan del Castillo to Capitán General O'Donnell, 5 junio

1844, quoted in J. L. Franco y Ferrán, *Revoluciones y conflictos internacionales en el Caribe, 1789–1854*, p. 214); and, for an earlier period, Ragueneau de la Chainaye to Damas, 15 septembre 1827, AAE, Corr. Pol., Haïti 2/340.

65 There is a copy of this letter in 'Haitian Papers', in the New York Public Library (*KF+PV 97).

66 *Le Manifeste*, 5 août 1843.

67 *Le Manifeste*, 20 août 1843; also *Proclamation*, 10 septembre 1843.

68 T. Madiou, *Histoire d'Haïti: années 1843–1846*, p. 148; Ardouin, *Etudes*, I, p. 24 n. On Acaau see also P. L. Jeannot, 'Louis Jean-Jacques Acaau', *Courrier du Sud*, 3, 10 and 17 août 1961. Leslie Manigat correctly describes *piquetisme* as 'fruit de la conjonction d'intérêts entre grands et moyens propriétaires noirs et petits paysans parcellaires également noirs' (*La révolution de 1843*, p. 25).

69 Madiou, *Histoire . . . 1843–1846*, p. 156; also Ussher to Lord Aberdeen, 7 April 1844, PRO, FO 35/28, and Thompson to Aberdeen, 23 July 1844, PRO, FO 35/28. Black hostility towards mulattoes was also noted at this time by a British resident in Jérémie: 'The black part of the rural population of the South from Tiburon to Léogane have risen 'en masse' crying vengeance and death to the brown people'. (P. Bridgeman to Sir C. Adams, 23 April 1844 PRO, FO 35/29). Hérard ascribed his own fall to the colour factor and to French encouragement of the blacks: 'Les noirs visent à rayer entièrement les hommes de couleur de la liste d'Haïti' (Charles Hérard to Aberdeen, n.d., PRO, FO 35/29).

70 'Proclamation', 1 avril 1844, in *Le Manifeste*, 26 mai 1844; Acaau had two mulattoes as his secretaries, cf. Madiou, *Histoire . . . 1843–1846*, p. 152.

71 J.-J. Acaau to Commodore Sharpe, 4 mai 1844, PRO, FO 35/29.

72 Madiou, *Histoire . . . 1843–1846*, pp. 67–8; cf. pp. 234ff below.

73 *Ibid.*, p. 159.

74 J.-J. Acaau, *Adresse*, 10 mai 1844.

75 Law of 4 November, in Madiou, *Histoire . . . 1843–1846*, p. 375.

76 Capitain Lartigue to Baron Mackau, 8 mai 1846, AAE, Corr. Pol., Haïti 14/244.

77 See pp. 63f. above; also J. Price Mars, *La República de Haití y la República Dominicana*, I, pp. 113ff. This book has been denounced by some Dominicans as partisan; see S. Nolasco, *Comentarios a la Historia de J. Price-Mars*.

78 These are collected in E. Rodríguez Demorizi, *Guerra Dominico-Haitiana*. On this whole period see Moya Pons, *La dominación haitiana*.

79 'Españoles, todos, todos, de cualquiera color que sean, somos hermanos y libres, y la República Dominicana no hace distinción de los hombres por el color, sino por sus virtudes' (J. M. Imbert, 'Pronunciamiento', 5 marzo 1844, in Rodríguez Demorizi, *Guerra*, p. 54).

80 J. S. Heneken to Viscount Palmerston, 20 March 1848, PRO, FO 23/1, and B. E. Green to J. M. Clayton, 27 September 1849, in W. R. Manning (ed.), *Diplomatic Correspondence of the United States: Inter-American Affairs, 1831–60*, VI, p. 50.

81 'I am a negro, but a white negro'; 'although I have a black skin, my heart

is white' (Green to Clayton, 24 October 1849, in Manning, VI, p. 59).
Charles Mackenzie had earlier noted a similar attitude on the part of those
living in the former Spanish colony towards their western neighbours
(Mackenzie, I, p. 215).

82   Heneken to Palmerston, 20 March 1848, PRO FO 23/1; Victor Place to
Guizot, 22 décembre 1847, AAE, Corr. Pol., Santo Domingo 2/382.

83   Levasseur to Guizot, 7 juillet 1844, AAE, Corr. Pol., Haïti 13/13. There
was much talk at this time of a French protectorate over the new republic.
Some of this correspondence has been published in a Spanish translation
in *Correspondencia de Levasseur y de otros agentes de Francia relativa a
la proclamación de la República Dominicana, 1843–1844*.

84   J. H. Fresnel, 'Du protectorat et de l'immigration en Haïti', MS in AAE,

85   Fresnel to Levasseur, 18 décembre 1845, AAE, Corr. Pol., Haïti 14/184–5.

86   J. H. Fresnel, 'Du protectorat et de l'immigration en Haïti', MS in AAE,
Mém. et Doc., Haïti 2/452. Fresnel also predicted that the island would
later be engulfed by the United States, which after invading Cuba and
Puerto Rico would occupy Hispaniola. Prophetic words!

87   *Ibid.*, 2/462.

88   'Les hommes des races jaune et noire de l'Amérique septentrionale qui
font restés à Haïti ont beaucoup contribué au perfectionnement et à
l'extension de l'industrie. Commerçants, cultivateurs, ouvriers, ils ont
tous été actifs, laborieux, intelligents' (*ibid.*, 2/463).

89   A. de Moges to Baron Mackau, 12 octobre 1843, AAE, Corr. Pol., Haïti
11/105; 'Saint Domingue' (juin 1852), AAE, Mém. et Doc., Haïti 2/370.

90   J. M. Caminero to J. C. Calhoun, 22 February 1845, in Manning, VI,
p. 32. It is doubtful, however, whether many Haitian mulattoes of this
period would have adopted quite this position with respect to slavery.
On relations between Cuba, Haiti and the Dominican Republic at this
time see Franco y Ferrán, pp. 178ff.

91   'Proclamation', 4 novembre 1845.

92   Pierrot, quoted in *Le Manifeste*, 28 décembre 1845.

93   Levasseur to Guizot, 9 mars 1846, AAE, Corr. Pol., Haïti 14/221.

94   Ussher to Palmerston, 23 October 1850, PRO, FO 35/38.

95   B. Ardouin to Lord J. Russell, 3 mai 1861, PRO, FO 35/55. Ardouin
described the Dominicans as 'une population qui tire aussi son origine de
la race noire' (Ardouin to Thouvenel, 3 mai 1861, AAE, Corr. Pol.,
Haïti 24/68).

96   Ardouin to Ussher, 17 septembre 1849, PRO, FO 35/36.

97   Roche Grellier, *Haïti: son passé, son avenir*, p. 70.

98   On the Masonic influence in Haiti at this time see *Feuille de Commerce*,
3 mai 1856, also Père Pascal, quoted in Paul Robert, *L'église et la
première république noire*, p. 235. It appears that the Jews played an
important role in the Port-au-Prince lodges; see I. S. and S. A. Emmanuel,
History of the Jews of the Netherlands Antilles, II, p. 830. For further
notes on Freemasonry in Haiti see p. 288 below. Some of Abbé Moussa's
pronouncements can be found in *Feuille de Commerce*, 29 avril 1854,
17 juin 1854 and 1 septembre 1855. The government's declared intention
to encourage an indigenous ministry can be seen in a report to the house

of representatives, quoted in *Feuille de Commerce*, 6 octobre 1855. Geffrard's ministers also voiced the same intention (*Feuille de Commerce*, 2 novembre 1861).

99   See Justin Bouzon, *Etudes historiques sur la présidence de Faustin Soulouque*, and G. d'Alaux, *L'empereur Soulouque et son empire*; for more recent discussions of Soulouque in English see J. E. Bauer, 'Faustin Soulouque, Emperor of Haiti: his character and his reign', *The Americas*, VI (1949–50), pp. 131ff, and M. J. MacLeod, 'The Soulouque regime in Haiti, 1847–1859', *Caribbean Studies*, 10:3 (1970), pp. 35ff.

100   Byron to Salisbury, 24 August 1872, PRO, FO 35/107; cf. also Byron to Malmesbury, 26 Feburary 1859, PRO, FO 35/53, where Salomon is referred to as 'a very quiet and inoffensive person'.

101   St John, p. 97.

102   James Leyburn adopted a rather unfair view of the emperor; see Leyburn, pp. 91ff. For a fairer assessment cf. Macleod, 'The Soulouque regime in Haiti'.

103   R. S. E. Hepburn, *Haiti As It Is*, pp. 5ff.

104   *British and Foreign State Papers*, 1862–3, 53, p. 619. On becoming president, Geffrard declared, 'Noirs, jaunes ou blancs, nous sommes tous les enfants du même Dieu, nous sommes tous de la même race, de la même famille' (*Le Moniteur Haïtien*, 12 février 1859).

105   E. Heurtelou, in *Le Progrès*, 11 août 1860.

106   De Moges to Guizot, 3 juin 1843, AAE, Corr. Pol., Haïti 10/390.

107   Holly had paid a preliminary visit to Haiti some years before, and had published in 1857 a tract entitled *A Vindication of the Capacity of the Negro Race for Self-Government and Civilized Progress as Demonstrated by Historical Events of the Haytian Revolution; and the Subsequent Acts of that People since their National Independence;* this has been reprinted in H. H. Bell, *Black Separatism and the Caribbean, 1860*. Holly was born in 1829 of Roman Catholic parents in Washington D.C., and died in 1911. There is an article by Holly on Christianity in Haiti in *Anglo-African Magazine*, I (1859). He adopted the French forms, Jacques Théodore, for his Christian names.

108   James Redpath (ed.), *A Guide to Hayti*, p. 5.

109   Geffrard was described as 'a great favorite amongst the coloured or mulatto population of whom he is considered the head' (Ussher to Ward, 22 January 1859, PRO, FO 35/53); cf. also J. A. Firmin, *Monsieur Roosevelt, président des Etats Unis, et la république d'Haïti*, p. 373.

110   Hepburn,, p. 68; and St John, p. 140.

111   Hector *cadet*, *Le Progrès*, 11 février 1860, and E. H., *Le Progrès*, 14 avril 1860; also J. E. Bauer, 'The presidency of Nicolas Geffrard of Haiti', *The Americas*, X (1953–4), p. 438.

112   *Le Moniteur Haïtien*, 3 mars 1866. The British vice-consul stated that Geffrard had agreed to lease Ile La Vache to the Germans, and was nego-tiating to lease La Tortue to the French (Byron to Russell, 8 November 1862, PRO, FO 35/56). Byron, however, had married a Haitian who was hostile to Geffrard; cf. St John to Stanley, 23 May 1867, PRO, FO 35/69. There is no evidence in the French diplomatic archives that Geffrard was negotiating with France for the lease of La Tortue at this time.

113 St John to Clarendon, 6 June 1866, PRO, FO 35/66. For further details see R. W. Logan, *The Diplomatic Relations of the United States with Haiti, 1776–1891*, p. 321. The text of Salnave's letter to the United States government offering the naval base is reprinted in A. Turnier, *Les Etats-Unis et le marché haïtien*, p. 200.

114 Charles Hérard, *Proclamation*, 21 août 1843. For a somewhat similar assessment see his *Proclamation au peuple et à l'armée*, 4 janvier 1844: 'Il appartenait au général Dessalines, à ce vengeur de la race africaine . . . de donner à Haïti, par la puissance de ses armes et par son instinct civilisateur, un rang parmi les nations; son gouvernement fondé par la force conserva ce caractère farouche, ombrageux et belliqeux [*sic*] que l'opprimé acquiert après s'être fait justice de ses tyrans. – La force avait péri par la force . . .'

115 Salomon *jeune*, 'Discours', *Procès Verbal*, pp. 6ff. He went on to criticise Ogé and Chavannes for having betrayed their mandate in fighting only for the rights of the *affranchis* and not also for those of the slaves.

116 *Le Progrès*, 8 décembre 1860. The controversy is discussed by Salomon in *Une défense*, p. 89 n. The French consul summarised his discussion with Geffrard in the following words: 'Le général Geffrard me dit qu'il m'avait prévenu en faisant des sévères remonstrances à Mr. Heurtelou qui accord le patronage de sa feuille à ce projet; puis, par un de ces revirements, ou une de ces contradictions qui caractèrisent l'esprit noir, il ajoutai, certes je veux que la mémoire de mon père soit honorée, mais pour cela je n'ai besoin de personne; comme citoyen je contribuerai volontiers à l'érection d'un monument' à Dessalines, mais le Gouvernement ne doit y prendre aucune part' (L. Levraud to L. Thouvenel, 23 décembre 1860, AAE, Corr. Pol., Haïti 23/383).

117 M. Dorvelas Dorval, 'Allocution', *Feuille de Commerce*, 23 janvier 1858, and 'Historique de l'éducation publique en Haïti jusqu'en 1858', *Feuille de Commerce*, 20 avril 1861.

118 Salomon *jeune*, pp. 10 and 87–8.

119 A fourth volume dealing with the years 1843–46 was published posthumously in 1904.

120 For details of Madiou's life see A. Lescouflair, *Thomas Madiou*, C. Pressoir *et al.*, *Historiographie d'Haïti*, and Placide David, 'Thomas Madiou *fils*', *Reflets d'Haïti*, 4, 11 and 25 février 1956.

121 Madiou, *Histoire*, I, p. i.

122 Madiou, in *Feuille de Commerce*, 10 juin 1849.

123 Madiou, *Histoire*, I, pp. iv and v.

124 Madiou, *Histoire . . . 1843–1846*, p. 166.

125 Madiou, 'La Crête à Pierrot', *L'Union*, 13 décembre 1838; cf. p. 39 above.

126 A. Bonneau, 'Les noirs, les jaunes, et la littérature française en Haïti', *Revue Contemporaine*, 29, (décembre 1856), p. 144.

127 Saint-Rémy, *Pétion*, I p. 8.

128 According to Michael Oakeshott a legend is 'a drama from which all that is casual, secondary and unresolved has been excluded; it has a clear outline, a unity of feeling and in it everything is exact except place and time' (*Rationalism in Politics*, p. 166); the last condition, however, is not

fulfilled in the case of the writers we are considering here; they locate the events in time and space.

129 *Ibid.*, pp. 137ff.
130 H. Butterfield, *The Whig Interpretation of History*, p. 11.
131 J. R. Seeley, *The Expansion of England*, pp. 196–7.
132 'The study of history has never been a mere curiosity, a withdrawal into the past for the sake of the past . . . Historical science has been and remains an arena of sharp ideological struggle; it has been and remains a class, party history' (editorial in *Voprosy istorii*, VIII (1960); quoted in N.W. Heer, *Politics and History in the Soviet Union*, p. 1).
133 M. Khaldiev emphasised this aspect of history as part of the general responsibility of society for educating the younger generation who 'did not see with their own eyes the great labor victory of their fathers and mothers, the first people in the world to build a socialist society' (*Pravda*, 28 November 1965; quoted in Heer, p. 14).
134 Quoted in *ibid.*, p. 11. A practical approach to the past has been defended, with respect to the post-colonial situation, by C. A. Diop, *L'unité culturelle de l'Afrique noire*, p. 9, and 'Apports et perspectives culturels de l'Afrique', *Présence Africaine*, N. S. 8–10 (juin–novembre 1956), p. 342.
135 For biographical details on Ardouin see F. Dalencour's introduction to the 1958 edition of Ardouin's *Etudes*; also Pressoir *et al.*, *Historiographie*.
136 For biographical details on Saint-Rémy, see F. Dalencour's introduction to the 1956 edition of *Pétion et Haïti*.
137 Ardouin, *Etudes*, I, pp. 3 and 5.
138 Writing of the generation of Haitians who fought in the revolutionary wars, Ardouin stated, 'La génération qui a hérité de ses travaux doit à sa mémoire de recueillir ses hauts faits pour les transmettre à la postérité: elle serait coupable de ne pas remplir ce devoir sacré' (*ibid.*, I, p. 5).
139 *Ibid.*, V, p. 103.
140 Lespinasse, p. 10.
141 Saint-Rémy, *Pétion*, I, p. 10.
142 Alibée Féry, *Essais littéraires*, p. 336; Pierre Faubert, *Ogé, ou le préjugé de couleur*, p. 41.
143 Nau, *Histoire des caciques*, I, p. 12.
144 Ardouin, *Etudes*, I, p. 3. Cf. Eric Williams, prime minister of Trinidad and Tobago, who writes history in order to 'get out of his system some of the poison which is perhaps unnecessarily imbibed in political activity in countries which have learned only too well the lessons of colonialism' (*History of the People of Trinidad and Tobago*, p. viii).
145 Saint-Rémy, introduction to *Mémoires du général Toussaint L'Ouverture écrits par lui-même*.
146 Lespinasse, p. 5.
147 Ardouin, *Etudes*, I, p. 5.
148 *Ibid.*, XI, p. 75.
149 *Ibid.*, V, p. 103.
150 Saint-Rémy, *Pétion*, I, p. 10.
151 Saint-Rémy, introduction to *Mémoires du général Toussaint L'Ouverture*, pp. 8 and 15.

152 Lespinasse, p. 19.

153 Ardouin, *Etudes*, I, p. 17.

154 S. Linstant (de Pradine), *Essai sur les moyens d'extirper les préjugés des blancs contre le couleur des Africains et des sang-mêlés*, p. 60. Cf. also 'Le préjugé colonial descend en droite ligne de la distinction qui existait en France entre les diverses classes de la société' (*ibid.*, p. 33). The author became a baron under Soulouque and adopted the name Linstant de Pradine.

155 *Ibid.*, pp. 7–8 and 60.

156 *Ibid.*, pp. 69ff.

157 *Ibid.*, pp. 96ff.

158 Quoted in Ardouin, *Etudes*, VI, p. 51.

159 *Ibid.*, VI, p. 51.

160 *Ibid.*, VI, p. 52; cf. also *Réponse du Sénateur B. Ardouin*, p. 74.

161 Linstant, *Essai*, p. viii.

162 Saint-Rémy, introduction to Boisrond Tonnerre, *Mémoires*, p. xix. Nevertheless, his urging of his own generation to secure the extinction of all animosity of caste or race suggests that at least on some occasions he recognised the existence of significant colour divisions in the country. Cf. Saint-Rémy, *Pétion*, V, p. 3.

163 Cf. pp. 113 below.

164 Schoelcher, II; also Saint-Rémy, 'Lettres à M. Victor Schoelcher relativement à son livre sur Haïti', *La Sentinelle de la Liberté*, 9 novembre and 14 décembre 1843; also letter by Laforestrie in C. A. Bissette, *Réfutation du livre de M. V. Schoelcher sur Haïti*, p. 138.

165 Ardouin, *Etudes*, I, p. 7.

166 *Ibid.*, I, p. 7.

167 In his more polemical writings Ardouin was dogmatic on this issue: 'dans la révolution de Saint-Domingue, les hommes de couleur n'ont pas séparé leur cause de celle des noirs'; *Réponse du Sénateur B. Ardouin*, p. 17.

168 Saint-Rémy, *Pétion*, I, p. 17.

169 *Ibid.*, I, p. 23.

170 Lespinasse, p. 5.

171 Bonnet, p. 68.

172 H. A. Brouard, 'Histoire: Affaire du Fonds Parisien', *L'Union*, 24 août 1837. See also E. Nau, *Réclamation par les affranchis des droits civils et politiques: Ogé et Chavannes*, *passim*.

173 See F. E. Dubois, *Précis historique de la révolution haïtienne de 1843*, p. 37; also Nau, *Réclamation par les affranchis*, p. 46. In the 'Manifeste' of 1842, signed by Charles Hérard, Hérard Dumesle and others, the nine 'illustrious founders of our liberty and of our independence' who were mentioned included only one black, David Troy.

174 Lespinasse, p. 15.

175 Saint-Rémy, *Pétion*, III, p. 34ff.

176 Ardouin, *Etudes*, V, p. 102; cf. also Céligny Ardouin on Toussaint: 'il se montra tout entier le servile instrument des doctrines machiavéliques de nos oppresseurs' ('Siège de Jacmel', *L'Union*, 1 mars 1838).

177 Ardouin, *Etudes*, V. p. 50.

178 Saint-Rémy, introduction to *Mémoires du général Toussaint l'Ouverture*, pp. 17ff.

179 *Ibid.*, p. 19. Saint-Rémy bestowed on Boisrond Tonnerre the distinction of having cast into Haiti the germs of class and race antagonism; see introduction to Tonnerre, *Mémoires*, p. xix.

180 Saint-Rémy, *Pétion*, II, p. 3.

181 Saint-Rémy, 'Lettres à M. Victor Schoelcher', *La Sentinelle de la Liberté*, 28 décembre 1843.

182 Bonnet, p. 75; cf. also H. Dumesle, *Voyage dans le nord d'Haïti*, p. 335.

183 Lespinasse, pp. 9–10.

184 Ardouin, *Etudes*, VI, pp. 84–5, and Lespinasse, pp. 8–9; cf. also MS by Covin *aîné*, 'Examen de la géographie d'Haïti', in the copy of Ardouin's 1832 book sent by Covin to Victor Schoelcher and now in the Bibliothèque Nationale, Paris, at 8° Pu 279. Dessalines is here both 'le libérateur d'Haïti' and 'l'homme de l'indépendance africaine', on the one hand, and 'intrépide despote' on the other.

185 Saint-Rémy, *Pétion*, IV, p. 58, and *Essai sur Henri-Christophe*, p. 13.

186 Bonnet, p. 136.

187 Ardouin, *Etudes*, I, p. 24.

188 Ardouin, *Géographie*, p. 91.

189 Ardouin, *Etudes*, VI, p. 106 and I, p. 24.

190 See p. 60 above.

191 Ardouin, *Etudes*, VIII, pp. 4 and 111.

192 Ardouin, *Géographie*, pp. 26–7.

193 Ardouin, *Etudes*, VII, pp. 10 and 66.

194 *Ibid.*, I, p. 24 n.

195 *Ibid.*, VIII, p. 44.

196 *Ibid.*, VIII, p. 25.

197 Ardouin to Ussher 17 septembre 1849, PRO, FO 35/36.

198 Saint-Rémy, *Essai sur Henri-Christophe*, p. 1.

199 *Ibid.*, p. 16; cf. also Alibée Féry, who called Christophe 'le farouche désolateur du Nord' (Féry, p. 200); and Covin *aîné*, who had nothing good to say of Christophe ('Examen', p. 6). Continuous propaganda against Christophe was maintained. See 'Une Caprice du roi Christophe', *Le Progrès*, 15 février 1844; 'Une Récréation du roi Christophe', *Le Progrès*, 29 février 1844.

200 Though Saint-Rémy also criticised Pétion for the tone of his letter to Christophe of 24 December 1806; *Pétion*, IV, p. 76.

201 *Ibid.*, IV, pp. 86–7.

202 *Ibid.*, V, p. 127.

203 *Ibid.*, I, p. 7; cf. also Saladin Lamour: 'Pétion n'était pas seulement homme; il était un demi-dieu' (*Réfutation de faits controuvés et d'appréciations contradictoires que contient l'œuvre intitulée: Souvenirs historiques de Guy-Joseph Bonnet*, p. 82.

204 Saint-Rémy, introduction to Tonnerre, *Mémoires*, pp. xix–xx. Ardouin, as we have seen, later changed his views on this matter, and was prepared to accept foreign ownership.

205 Ardouin, *Etudes*, VII, pp. 100 and 123.

206 Saint-Rémy, *Pétion*, V, pp. 127 and 131.
207 Ardouin, *Géographie*, p. 27.
208 Ardouin, *Etudes*, I, p. 25, and *Géographie*, p. 29.
209 D. Trouillot in *Feuille de Commerce*, 15 septembre 1860.
210 Ardouin, *Etudes*, VII, p. 9.
211 Beaubrun Ardouin pointed with approval to Boyer's supposed attempt to combat the supremacy of the military over the civil in politics (*Etudes*, XI, p. 75). Thomas Ussher, the British consul, noted that 'the democratic party in Hayti have made great intentions to substitute civil for military form of government', though he did not entertain much hope for its success (Ussher to Aberdeen, 5 January 1844, PRO, FO 35/28). Salomon and the blacks, however, were concerned to maintain the position of the army, 'cette sauvegarde de l'ordre public, ce palladium de notre nationalité' (report to house of representatives, in *Feuille de Commerce*, 16 septembre 1854).
212 Saint-Rémy, *Pétion*, IV, p. ii.
213 Ardouin, *Etudes*, VIII, p. 16.
214 *Ibid.*, IV, p. 34.
215 See p. 110 below. Wisely he did not actually take part in the invasion.
216 *See Le Droit*, 24 juin 1893; Placide David, 'Edmond Paul', *Cahiers d'Haïti*, mars 1945. On Jean Paul, see Rulx Léon, *Propos d'histoire d'Haïti*, II.
217 Hepburn, p. 15. cf. also 'Un Haïtien', *Aux hommes impartiaux*, pp. 8–12.
218 *De la gérontocratie en Haïti*, pp. 87–8.
219 E. Paul, *Questions politico-économiques*, II, p. 59.
220 *Ibid.*, II, p. 70.
221 *Ibid.*, II, p. 67.
222 *Le Civilisateur*, 16 mars 1870.
223 Paul, *Questions*, II, p. 57. On Chevalier, see J. Walch, *Michel Chevalier: économiste saint-simonien*.
224 *Ibid.*, II, p. 56.
225 *Ibid.*, II, p. 51.
226 *Ibid.*, I, p. 37 and II, p. 50. On the importance of capital accumulation for growth, see M. Chevalier, *The Labour Question*, p. 15.
227 Paul, *Questions.*, I, p. 30.
228 *Ibid.*, I, p. 31.
229 *Ibid.*, II, p. 79; this view is echoed by Cheik Anta Diop in our own day, in *Nations nègres et culture*, p. 10.
230 E. Paul, *De l'impôt sur les cafés et lois du commerce intérieur*, p. 136.
231 E. Paul, *Les causes de nos malheurs*, p. 225.
232 *De l'impôt*, p. 1.
233 Paul, *Questions*, II, p. 79.
234 E. Paul, *Haïti au soleil de 1880*, p. 62.
235 *Questions*, I, pp. 13–14.
236 *De l'impôt*, pp. 137–8.
237 *Les causes*, p. 34.
238 *Questions*, I, p. 14.
239 E. Paul, 'Le despotisme éclairé', *Le Civilisateur*, 18 octobre 1871.
240 *Les causes*, p. 5.

241 *Questions*, I, pp. 20–1.
242 Cf. the discussion of Saint-Simon in E. Durkheim, *Socialism*, especially chapters 7 and 8.
243 *Questions*, II, p. 3.
244 *Les causes*, p. 238.
245 'Le despotisme éclairé'.

4. Liberals and Nationals (1867–1910)

1 Cf. Firmin, *M. Roosevelt*, p. 388. Also M. Domingue, 'Aux citoyens trompés par Salnave', in *La Voix du Peuple*, 8 octobre 1868; the accusation was repeated in the following year, cf. *La Voix du Peuple*, 18 mars 1869.
2 D. Delorme, *La reconnaissance du général Salnave*, *passim*.
3 The term *cacos* denotes peasant irregulars, usually from the North, who from time to time took up arms against the government of the day. The word is probably derived from *taco*, a rather fierce little bird found in Haiti. Père Cabon, however, states that the word is derived from *caraco*, a garment worn by peasants, *Monsignor A.-J. M. Guilloux*, p. 122 n.
4 'Protestation', quoted in F. D. Légitime, 'Souvenirs historiques (1867–1870)', *Revue de la Société de Législation*, octobre 1907, p. 103. *Créole* songs like the following reflected Salnave's popular support:

> Bon Guié ban moin Salnave
> La Vièrge ban moin Delorme,
> Cacos vlé ouété li (*bis*)
>   N'a ba yo cannon
>   N'a ba yo boulet.

> ('Gèdè [a powerful Voodoo spirit] give me Salnave,
> Virgin give me Delorme,
> The *cacos* want to remove them;
>   We shall give them cannon,
>   We shall give them bullet.')

(Quoted by Légitime, 'Souvenirs historiques (1867–1870)', *Revue de la Société de Législation*, novembre 1907, p. 119.)
5 A. Thoby, 'Nos constitutions républicaines', *Revue de la Société de Législation* août 1899, p. 8; F. D. Légitime, 'Souvenirs historiques (1867–1870)', *Revue de la Société de Législation*, décembre 1907, p. 138.
6 Légitime, who was himself engaged in the *cacos* war of 1867–9, wrote: 'Nègres et mulâtres formant les cadres de ce qu'on nomme chez nous la *classe intermédiaire* constituaient dans l'Ouest et surtout dans le Sud, la masse du parti des Cacos', *ibid*. I believe those writers to be mistaken who assert that the *cacos* bands relied for support principally upon the rural sub-proletariat; cf. M. de Young, 'Class parameters in Haitian society', *Journal of Interamerican Studies*, I (1959), p. 450; J. Casimir, 'Aperçu sur la structure sociale d'Haïti', *América Latina*, VIII (julho–setembro 1965), p. 48; Juan Bosch, *De Cristóbal Colón a Fidel Castro*, p. 656.
7 See *Che Guevara Speaks*, p. 29.
8 E. R. Wolf, 'Peasant Rebellion and Revolution', in N. Miller and R. Aya (eds.), *National Liberation*, p. 55.

9 Cf. J. Price Mars, *Jean-Pierre Boyer Bazelais et le drame de Miragoâne*, *passim*.

10 *L'Avant-Garde*, 15 juin 1882. Marcelin, with his monocle and waxed moustache, was generally disliked by his fellow mulattoes, who regarded him as a traitor; cf. E. Mathon, *M. Frédéric Marcelin, ou l'homme de la petite dime*, *passim*.

11 Firmin, *M. Roosevelt*, p. 426.

12 Hunt to Granville, 8 May 1882, PRO, FO 35/115.

13 E. Mathon, *Documents pour l'histoire d'Haïti: révolution de 1888–9*, p. 8; cf. also 'Verax' (H. Price), *The Haytian Question*, p. 80.

14 See p. 86 above.

15 Byron to Salisbury, 24 August 1879, PRO, FO 35/107.

16 *Le Peuple*, 3 janvier 1880.

17 *L'Avant-Garde*, 7 mai 1883; cf. also 'Les nègres ne peuvent rien faire sans le mulâtre, et les mulâtres ne sont rien sans les nègres' (Salomon in *l'Œil*, 9 juin 1883).

18 Salomon, *A l'armée*, 16 février 1884.

19 Cf. '. . . de même que le parti libéral n'était pas mort avec M. Boyer Bazelais, le parti national survécut à la chute de leur chef' (*Le Pays*, 5 février 1890). Tribonien Saint-Justé claimed that his National Progressive Party, the group which had been led by Firmin until his death, was the successor to the National Party. Yet Firmin had, of course, been a leading opponent of the National Party in its heyday. This is what leads some writers to talk of Firmin's conversion from the Liberal to the National cause: E.g. Saint-Justé, *La mort de l'illustre M. Anténor Firmin*. Other writers, however, denied that it was meaningful to talk of Liberal and National parties after the death of Boyer Bazelais and Salomon; e.g. *La Voie*, 30 novembre 1889.

20 E. Edouard, *Essai sur la politique intérieure d'Haïti*, p. 28.

21 Cf. Solon Ménos, *L'affaire Lüders*, *passim*.

22 G. Séjourné, *Haïti: un siècle d'indépendance*, p. 20, and *Monsieur le général François-Guillaume Saint-Sérin Manigat*, p. 9.

23 P. F. Frédérique in *L'Impartial*, 14 avril 1909; A. Charmant, *Haïti: vivra t elle?*, pp. 259 and 266.

24 E. Edouard, *Essai*, pp. 50ff. Frédéric Marcelin also traced the hostility between black and mulatto to the colonial era, in *Nos douanes (Haïti)*, pp. 24–5.

25 Edouard, pp. 67ff. and 87. See also Roche Grellier, *Haïti: la politique à suivre*, p. 79, and *Haïti: son passé, son avenir*, p. 22.

26 Edouard, p. 77.

27 *Ibid.*, p. 26.

28 J. Justin, *Les relations extérieures d'Haïti*, p. 133.

29 J. Justin, *Etude sur les institutions haïtiennes*, I, p. 40, and *La question du Môle Saint-Nicolas*, p. 9.

30 J. B. Dorsainvil, in *Le Nouvelliste*, 4 mars 1909.

31 See pp. 120 below.

32 For later black views of these presidents cf. J. A. Firmin, *M. Roosevelt*, p. 410 on Boisrond Canal; and 'Nissage était griffe; il détestait foncière-ment le noir, bien qu'il fût le produit du noir et du jaune, et s'était voué

corps et âme à la cause des hommes de couleur' ('Un sacristan au pouvoir',
L'Avant-Garde, 15 juin 1882).

33 'Ah Jacot!', *L'Avant-Garde*, 16 février 1882.
34 F. Marcelin, *La politique*, pp. 134–5, and 176.
35 A. Thoby, *Questions politiques d'Haïti*, pp. 9–10.
36 A. Michel, *Salomon jeune et l'affaire Louis Tanis*, p. vii.
37 For *piquets*, see p. 77 above.
38 See pp. 229ff below.
39 L. J. Janvier, *Les antinationaux*, pp. 22, 26.
40 L. J. Janvier, *L'égalité des races*, p. 11 and *Les affaires d'Haïti, 1883–84*, pp. 189ff.
41 L. J. Janvier, *Les constitutions d'Haïti*, p. 225 and *Le vieux piquet*, p. 9. But cf. *La république d'Haïti et ses visiteurs*, where Janvier stated that Dessalines had a 'conception aristocratique' of society (p. 585).
42 *Les constitutions*, p. 145.
43 *La république d'Haïti*, p. 585, *Les constitutions*, pp. 149ff; cf. also *Les affaires*, pp. 45 and 68ff.
44 *Les constitutions*, p. 232.
45 *Les affaires*, p. 194; see also *Les antinationaux*, p. 49.
46 *Les affaires*, p. 68.
47 *Le vieux piquet*, p. 4.
48 *Les affaires*, p. 58, and *Les constitutions*, p. 227.
49 *Le vieux piquet*, p. 28.
50 Janvier, in J. Auguste *et al.*, *Les détracteurs de la race noire et de la république d'Haïti*, p. 49.
51 *La république d'Haïti*, p. 283.
52 *Ibid.*, pp. 155ff; cf. also Janvier, *Du gouvernement civile en Haïti*, where the author discussed the conflicts between Liberals and Nationals without referring to the colour question (pp. 73ff).
53 *Les affaires*, pp. 208–9.
54 *Les antinationaux*, p. 24; cf. also *Les affaires*, where Janvier wrote of the mulattoes, 'Ce sont eux, ce sont leurs chefs qui ont des préjugés de couleur contre les noirs d'Haïti' (p. 247).
55 In addition to the writings of Antoine Michel, cited in this chapter, cf. the writings of Leslie Manigat on Pétion, p. 268 below.
56 Michel Oreste wrote of Charmant, 'il a un pied chez les libéraux, il veut placer l'autre chez les nationaux' (*Le Pays*, 9 avril 1890); cf. also another article attacking Charmant in the same issue of *Le Pays* under the title 'Le mannequin de Jacmel'. Charmant's journalistic enterprises included *Le Conservateur*, *Gazette Parlementaire* and *L'Intransigeant*.
57 Charmant, *Haiti: vivra-t-elle?* pp. 179–80.
58 *Ibid.*, pp. xxi and 260.
59 Quoted in S. Vincent, *En posant les jalons*, I, p. 17; cf. also the poem 'Le Passé' by Oswald Durant in *Haïti Littéraire et Sociale*, 20 février 1905.
60 'Hier et aujourd'hui', *L'Avant-Garde*, 26 janvier 1882; 'Liberaux et Nationaux', *L'Avant-Garde*, 22 juin 1882. Cf. also François Manigat in E. Edouard, *Le panthéon haïtien*, p. 23.

61 E. Kernizan, *L'avenir politique*, pp. 22–3; cf. also Antoine Pierre Paul, *Henri Christophe, passim.*

62 Cf. speech by Dr Aubry, *La Voie*, 14 décembre 1889.

63 J. Duclervil, 'Le préjugé de couleur et nos partie politiques', *L'Impartial*, 28 février 1910; J. B. Dorsainvil, 'Du développement de la constitution d'Haïti', *L'Impartial*, 3 février 1910; cf. also J. B. Dorsainvil, 'Hommage à Dessalines', *Haïti Littéraire et Sociale*, 20 octobre 1906, and 'L'histoire nous révèle que le bel Alexandre se montra absolument faible et incapable comme chef d'état . . . Henri, son farouche et redoutable ennemi, lui fut – incontestablement – de beaucoup supérieur' (A. C. (probably Alfred Chatelain), 'Les erreurs du Président Pétion', *L'Artibonite*, 15 mai 1909).

64 Michel, 'En marge de l'histoire d'Haïti de M. Auguste Magloire', *L'Impartial*, 10 février 1910.

65 See p. 133 below.

66 'N'est-ce-pas révoltant que nous soyons obligés d'avoir des maîtres chez nous, après que nos pères se soient sacrifiés pour nous léguer une patrie, et fait d'Haïti un état libre et indépendant? Franchement, les agissements de ces Messieurs du clergé nous vexent et nous humilient' ('La question du jour', *L'Avant-Garde*, 16 février 1882).

67 'Mgr. Guilloux et le clergé national haïtien', *L'Avant-Garde*, 28 septembre 1882.

68 'Le songe d'Alexis Guilloux', *L'Avant-Garde*, 15 juin 1882.

69 'Le clergé et l'éducation sociale en Haïti', *L'Œil*, 4 mars 1882. Cf. also '*Le bulletin religieux d'Haïti*, no. 12', *L'Avant-Garde*, 12 janvier 1882.

70 'Les derniers mots de Salnave', *L'Avant-Garde*, 27 avril 1882. Salnave had attempted to dismiss the archbishop of Port-au-Prince, Mgr Testard du Cosquer, in 1869 (*Le Moniteur*, 3 juillet 1869); for further details see S. St John to Lord Clarendon, 25 October 1869, PRO FO 35/78.

71 'Dénoncez le Concordat', *L'Œil*, 18 juin 1881.

72 'Mgr. Guilloux et le clergé national haïtien', *L'Avant-Garde*, 5 octobre 1882.

73 Janvier, *Les affaires*, p. 297 and *La république d'Haiti*, pp. 372ff.

74 *Les constitutions*, p. 277 and *La république d'Haïti*, p. 375.

75 *Les affaires*, p. 303.

76 *Les constitutions*, p. 286; cf. also 'Les papes et les conciles l'avaient permis en déclarant que le noir *n'avait pas d'âme*' (*La république d'Haïti*, p. 373).

77 L. J. Janvier, *Haïti aux haïtiens*, p. 36; and Janvier in J. Auguste *et al.*, p. 43; cf. also *Les constitutions*, p. 286. The Puerto Rican nationalist Hostos also insisted that Protestantism was 'más adelantado en la evolución religiosa que el catolicismo' (E. M. de Hostos, *Moral Social*, p. 178) Anténor Firmin later echoed this view, pointing to the England of Queen Elizabeth I as an illustration of the connection between Protestantism and progress (*M. Roosevelt*, p. 30). It was in the same year that Max Weber published *The Protestant Ethic and the Spirit of Capitalism*. The French statesman Guizot had made a similar case for Protestantism in his *Histoire de la civilisation en Europe*, as had Ernest Renan, and the Belgian economist Emile de Laveleye in 'Le protestantisme et le catholicisme dans leurs rapports avec la liberté et la prosperité des peuples', *Revue de Belgique*, 1875.

78   Janvier, *La république d'Haïti*, pp. 95 and 372.

79   'Au Sénégal, à Sierra Leone, à Libéria, chez les Cafres et les Bassoutos, les missionnaires anglais sont eux-mêmes étonnés de la facilité avec laquelle les nègres acceptent les croyances évangéliques, et, avec elles, le levain de la culture occidentale' (Janvier, *L'égalité des races*, p. 29).

80   Janvier described 'haïtianisme' as 'une espèce de religion où, à l'imitation de l'ancien gallicanisme, le clergé soit entièrement dans la main du gouvernement temporel, même au point de vue des doctrines; il faut que les dogmes enseignés et pratiqués ne soient pas en désaccord avec cette donnée, à savoir que: *L'Etat haïtien est tout, l'Eglise n'est rien que par l'Etat auquel elle doit obéissance absolue*' (*La république d'Haïti*, pp. 374–5).

81   Schoelcher, II, p. 271; St. John, p. 285. For Freemasonry in colonial Saint Domingue see p. 23 above. B. L. (probably Beauvais Lespinasse) reminded the youth of his day that 'c'est surtout dans les sociétés maçonniques que nos pères se sont formées' ('Des sociétés maçonniques en Haïti', *Le Républicain*, 15 décembre 1836, p. 8); cf. also 'Mes explications', *Feuille de Commerce*, 4 avril 1856, where the author stated that the Masonic movement strengthens national sentiment. Some of Soulouque's principal ministers were Freemasons (see *Feuille de Commerce*, 3 mai 1856). For the continued influence of Freemasonry in the later nineteenth century see 'Un mot en passant', *Le Peuple*, 19 septembre 1880, and Janvier, *La république d'Haïti*, pp. 94ff. There is a somewhat hostile account of the Masonic movement in Haiti in Jules Caplain, *La France en Haïti*, pp. 71ff. This book was in fact published by 'Un groupe d'anti-maçons du 16ᵉ arrondissement de Paris' in the early years of the present century. For further information on the Masonic movement in this period see the files of *La Fraternité*, a Masonic newspaper, not to be confused with the journal of the same name edited by Bénito Sylvain. The Masonic movement appears to have suffered a decline in the nineteenth century. Paul Vibert wrote in 1895, 'La Franc-Maçonnerie . . . est malheureusement bien endormie en Haïti' (*La république d'Haïti: son présent, son avenir économique*, p. 273). For Freemasonry in the Dominican Republic see H. Hoetink, *El pueblo dominicano 1850–1900*, pp. 246ff; and for Cuba, see F. J. Ponte Dominguez, *El delito de francmasonería en Cuba*, and R. Fernandez Callejas, *Historia de la franc-masonería en Cuba*.

82   *L'Œil*, 17 mai 1884.

83   'A Monsieur Alexis Guilloux', *L'Œil*, 6 décembre 1884.

84   *La Fraternité*, 1 octobre 1889, p. 6.

85   Letter of 23 janvier 1880, in Cabon, *Monsignor A. J. M. Guilloux*, p. 378.

86   *Exposé général de la situation de la République d'Haïti: 1882*, p. 66. Cf. also Salomon, in *Exposé général: 1885*, p. 75.

87   L. Laroche, *Haïti, une page d'histoire*, p. 82.

88   A. Bowler, *Une conférence sur Haïti*, pp. 27–8.

89   J. N. Léger, *Haïti: son histoire et ses détracteurs*, p. 290. J. Dévot, 'Bibliographie: à propos du livre de M. H. Price', *Revue de la Société de Législation*, août 1901, pp. 78ff; and L. Audin, 'Le culte de la vie en Haïti', *Revue de la Société de Législation*, juin 1904, p. 116.

90 A. Thoby, 'Nos constitutions républicaines', *Revue de la Société de Législation*, février 1894, p. 205.
91 A. Thoby, *De la capacité présidentielle sous le régime parlementaire*, p.1.
92 A. Thoby, *La question agraire*, p. 1.
93 Thoby, *La question agraire*, pp. 31ff.
94 Thoby, *De la capacité*, p. 6.
95 H. Price, *Pourquoi cette guerre?*, p. 5, and the section on Toussaint and Rigaud in Price, *De la réhabilitation de la race noire par la république d'Haïti*, pp. 229ff.
96 L. Laroche, pp. 79 and 72.
97 *Ibid.*, pp. 88, 92 and 85.
98 Cf. *L'Œil*, 6 décembre 1884 (Price's letter is dated 2 novembre 1884). He went on: 'Je ne m'occupe ni de vous, ni des misérables qui se gorgent à votre table de la sueur du sang de mes compatriotes, de mes frères.' Price regarded the overthrow of Salomon in 1888 as not merely the defeat of a government or a party, but as 'l'écrasement d'une bête immonde' (*Pourquoi cette guerre?*, p. 15).
99 L. Laroche, p. 91. This of course, is a quite misleading statement of the position of the National Party; cf. p. 114 above and p. 229 below.
100 *Ibid.*, p. 81. For the term *griffe* see p. 25 above. Laroche failed to mention Christophe in this context, who was said by Firmin to have been a *griffe* (*M. Roosevelt*, p. 316).
101 L. Audin, 'Le culte de la vie en Haïti', *Revue de la Société de Législation*, juin 1904, p. 116.
102 L. Laroche, pp. 98–9.
103 G. Luperón, *Notas autobiográficas y apuntes históricas*, I, pp. 27 and 35; cf. H. Hoetink in M. Mörner (ed.), *Race and Class in Latin America*, pp. 96ff.
104 'Faut-il désespérer de l'avenir?', *Le Civilisateur*, 16 juin 1870.
105 Quoted in *L'Avant-Garde*, 12 avril 1883. Duraciné Vaval in a later generation reiterated the need for an intellectual aristocracy in any successful democracy ('L'aristocratie intellectuelle', *Haïti Littéraire et Sociale*, 5 mai 1907).
106 Cf. F. D. Légitime, *L'armée haïtienne: sa necessité, son rôle*, pp. 25ff. The army performed a similar social function in the neighbouring Dominican Republic; see Hoetink in Mörner, pp. 119ff.
107 'De l'armée', *Le Civilisateur*, 7 avril 1870; cf. also A. Thoby, 'L'armée indigène', in D. Bellegarde (ed.), *Ecrivains haïtiens*, pp. 115ff. Frédéric Marcelin agreed that militarism was a plague in Haiti which weighed upon the poor peasant in particular ('Choses d'Haïti', *La Fraternité*, semaine 4, mars 1892). On this issue Hannibal Price was in accord with his political opponent (*De la réhabilitation*, p. 45).
108 *Le Messager du Nord*, 14 septembre 1878; Firmin, *M. Roosevelt*, p. 294.
109 L. J. Marcelin, *Haïti: ses guerres civiles*, p. 40.
110 L. J. Marcelin, *La lutte pour la vie*.
111 J. Dévot, *Considérations sur l'état mental de la société haïtienne*, pp. 10 and 48. On Dévot, see François Mathon, 'Justin Dévot', *Cahiers d'Haïti*, mai 1945, pp. 29ff.

112   L. J. Marcelin, *Haïti*, p. v.; and J. Dévot, *Considérations*, p. 62.
113   *Le Travail*, 18 mars 1892.
114   M. Morpeau, *Pro patria*, p. 21.
115   *Le Travail*, 18 janvier 1893.
116   S. Vincent, *Discours*, p. 8; cf. also Vincent, 'Un bilan', *L'Effort*, 1 avril 1902.
117   J. B. Dorsainvil, *Essai sur l'histoire de l'établissement des institutions et des mœurs de Saint-Domingue*, I, p. viii.
118   See pp. 152 and 210 below.
119   *Revue de la Société de Législation*, 2 avril 1892.
120   E. Vilaire, 'Notice autobiographique', quoted in R. Gaillard, *Etzer Vilaire: témoin de nos malheurs*, p. 47.
121   *La Ronde*, 5 mai 1898; on Marcelin, Lhérisson and Hibbert, see Y. Gindine, 'Satire and the Birth of Haitian Fiction', *Caribbean Quarterly*, September 1975.
122   Justin, *Etude*, p. 9.
123   Justin, *Les relations*, p. 140; cf. also Emmanuel Morpeau, *Haïti au point de vue critique*.
124   On Firmin cf. S. Pradel, 'Anténor Firmin', *Le Temps*, 15 septembre 1934; H. P. Sannon, 'Anténor Firmin', *Le Temps*, 17 août 1938; L. Viaud, 'La personnalité de Joseph-Anténor Firmin', *Revue de la Société Haïtienne d'Histoire et de Géographie*, janvier 1948; C. Moise, 'Anténor Firmin', *Conjonction*, no. 117 (décembre 1971).
125   Firmin, *M. Roosevelt*, pp. 318 and 345. On Boyer see also J. A. Firmin, *Haïti au point de vue politique, administratif et économique*, pp. 22–3.
126   *M. Roosevelt*, pp. 388 and 410.
127   *Ibid.*, p. 394.
128   Cf. particularly *ibid.*, pp. 316 and 345.
129   Cf. F. Marcelin, *Le passé*, pp. 18ff.
130   He was called 'le doyen du Tribunal de Commerce' (*Le Peuple*, 13 janvier 1881).
131   Marcelin, *La politique*, p. 359.
132   F. Marcelin, *Haïti et l'indemnité française*, p. 55.
133   H. Price, 'Medite cives', reprinted in *L'Action*, 23 décembre 1908. Marcelin denied having said this; cf. *L'Œil*, 15 juillet 1882.
134   F. Marcelin, *Autour de deux romans*, p. 120.
135   J. A. de Gobineau, *The Inequality of the Human Races*, pp. 50, 133, and 205.
136   R. Knox, *The Races of Man*, p. 5.
137   *Journal of the Anthropological Society of London*, IV (1866), p. lxxviii.
138   *Memoires read before the Anthropological Society of London*, I (1863–4), p. 53; quoted in J. W. Burrow, *Evolution and Society*, p. 121 n. Cf. also C. Bolt, *Victorian Attitudes to Race*.
139   J. Michelet's preface of 1869 to *L'histoire de France, Œuvres complètes*, I, p. iv.
140   J. E. Renan, *Réforme intellectuelle et morale de la France*, p. 93.
141   See W. B. Cohen, 'Literature and race: nineteenth century French fiction, blacks and Africa, 1800–1880', *Race and Class*, 16:2 (October 1974); and L. F. Hoffmann, *Le nègre romantique*.

142 L. de Saussure, *Psychologie de la colonisation française*; also G. le Bon, *Les lois psychologiques de l'évolution des peuples.*

143 De Gobineau, pp. 46ff, and L. Quesnel, in *Revue politique et littéraire*, 4 février 1882.

144 St John, pp. 123 and 134–5.

145 *Ibid.*, p. xi. Nevertheless St John was able to write: 'I have dwelt above forty years among coloured people of various races, and am sensible of no prejudice against them' (*ibid.*, p. x).

146 Janvier, *La république d'Haïti*, p. 57.

147 J. N. Léger, *Haïti et la revision*, pp. 31–2; Edouard, *Le panthéon haïtien*, p. 7.

148 Both quoted by Sténio Vincent (*En posant les jalons*, I, p. 17); see T. Guilbaud, 'Le Drapeau', *Patrie*, pp. 121ff.

149 *Le Justicier*, 5 décembre 1903.

150 *L'Œil*, 10 novembre 1883.

151 Séjourné, *Haïti: un siècle d'indépendance*, p. 23.

152 J. A. Firmin, *De l'égalité des races humaines*, p. 653.

153 *Ibid.*, p. 662.

154 *Ibid.*, pp. 660–1.

155 'J'affirme que la race noire est capable, autant que les autres, de tous les progrès moraux et matériels, et qu'il ne lui a manqué jusqu'ici que les conditions propres à favoriser son développement dans tous les sens' (Roche Grellier, *Etudes économiques sur Haïti*, p. 29). Cf. also Justin, *Les relations*, p. 79, Justin, *Etude*, p. 9, Charmant, p. 13.

156 Price, *De la réhabilitation*, pp. 29 and 120.

157 *Ibid.*, p. 509.

158 *Ibid.*, p. 531.

159 *Ibid.*, p. 150.

160 Charmant, pp. 9ff. See above, p. 25.

161 Firmin, *De l'égalité*, p. 334. Cf. also 'De l'avenir de la race noire', *L'Œil*, 19 août 1882.

162 *De l'égalité*, p. 341.

163 *Ibid.*, pp. 351–2.

164 A. Casseus, *Du rôle civilisateur de la race noire*, pp. 35ff.

165 M. Morpeau, *Simples considérations patriotiques*, p. 7.

166 Jérémie, in his preface to E. Chancy, *L'indépendance nationale d'Haïti.*

167 L. Laroche, pp. 62ff. Cf. also D'Ussol, 'Pouvons-nous avoir une littérature nationale?', *Haïti Littéraire et Sociale*, 5 février 1905.

168 J. Dévot, *Cours élémentaire d'instruction civique et d'éducation patriotique*, p. 172; and J. Dévot, in Auguste *et al.*, p. 88. B. Sylvain also insisted that 'all Haitians are French at heart' ('France et Haïti', *La Fraternité*, semaine 4, février 1892).

169 E. Vilaire, 'A Junie', *Années tendres*, p. 70.

170 Price, *De la réhabilitation*, p. 206.

171 *L'Essor*, 20 août 1912, reprinted in C. Delienne, *Souvenirs d'épopée*, p. 100.

172 L. Audin, *Le mal d'Haïti*, pp. 50–1.

173 'Bientôt, nous en avons l'espoir et la sincère intention, il s'élèvera sur les ruines que nous déplaçons, un ordre de choses régulier et nouveau, sur le

modèle des civilisations qui se poursuivent en Europe' (Delorme to Salomon, 4 juillet 1867, PRO, FO 35/71). See also J. Price Mars, *Ainsi parla l'oncle*, pp. 190–1.

174 L. J. Janvier in Auguste *et al.*, p. 37. It is true that he stated that Haitians had also to struggle against the turbulence of the blood of the early French adventurers who peopled Saint Domingue.

175 *Ibid.*, p. 27; see also Janvier, *L'égalité des races*, pp. 25–6.

176 L. J. Janvier, *Humble adresse aux électeurs de la commune de Port-au-Prince*, p. 54. See also 'Nos aïeux . . . se berçaient surtout du noble espoir de nous faire imiter la France et l'Angleterre' (Janvier, 'Notre République', *Haïti Littéraire et Sociale*, 5 janvier 1907).

177 Firmin, *Haïti au point de vue politique*, pp. 46–7. Leslie Manigat criticises me for not having recognised that Firmin 'experienced a personal evolution in his ideas from liberalism to nationalism' (*Caribbean Yearbook of International Relations*, 1975, p. 523). Firmin certainly changed his ideas about the foreign ownership of land, from opposition to advocacy, but this is hard to reconcile with what Manigat himself says about the National Party; cf. p. 136 and note 205 of this chapter.

178 Charmant, p. 8.

179 F. D. Légitime, 'Some General Considerations on the People and the Government of Haiti', in G. Spiller (ed.), *Papers on Inter-Racial Problems Communicated to the First Universal Races Congress*, p. 183. The Congress included such functions as 'Opening reception to members at the Fishmongers' Hall, London Bridge, E.C., by kind invitation of the Worshipful Company of Fishmongers, Mlle. Jamotha, Court Pianist to the German Emperor, has kindly offered to give a short Concert during the evening. Evening Dress optional', and 'Visit of members to Warwick Castle, by kind invitation of the Countess of Warwick, who will entertain the visitors at Luncheon and Tea'.

180 Janvier, *Les constitutions*, p. 281, and *La république*, p. 94.

181 B. Sylvain, 'La Lanterne et le vaudoux', *La Fraternité*, 7 octobre 1890, and J. N. Léger, *Haïti: son histoire*, p. 357. 'The truth is that voodoo and cannibalism do not exist any more in Hayti than the "night doctor" in Washington' (J. N. Léger, 'The Truth about Hayti', *North American Review*, no. 177 (1903), p. 48). Other Haitian writers pointed to the existence of superstitions in many European countries; see A. Bowler, in Auguste *et al.*, p. 143.

182 F. M. Kersuzan, *Conférence populaire sur le vaudoux*, pp. 3, 7 and 21.

183 'Vaudou et Vaudouilleurs', *L'Œil*, 23 juillet 1881.

184 'Le diabolisme et le vaudoux', *L'Impartial*, 10 septembre 1896.

185 J. F. T. Manigat, *Conférence sur le vaudoux*, p. 1. Alcius Charmant also referred to Voodoo as 'coutume païenne encore pratiquée clandestinement en Haïti par quelques esprits grossiers, malgré les efforts du clergé' (Charmant, p. 266).

186 Léon Audin, 'Le culte de la vie en Haïti', *Revue de la Société de Législation*, juin 1904, p. 112.

187 F. Marcelin, *Haïti et l'indemnité*, p. 7.

188 B. Sylvain, 'Le partage d'Afrique', *La Fraternité*, avril, semaine 2, 1892. Not all Haitians accepted this position. A writer in *L'Œil*, for example, attacked colonialism: 'Ce n'est pas le bien que l'étranger désire au pays, mais la convoitise d'y posséder, à l'occasion, des points stratégiques et commerciaux . . . Tel est le fond réel du système de toute colonisation' ('L'avenir de la race noire en Haïti', *L'Œil*, 4 novembre 1882). Engels had, of course, taken a more benevolent view of colonial expansion when he had written in 1848: 'The conquest of Algeria is an important and fortunate fact for the progress of civilisation' (*The Northern Star*, no. 535 (22 January 1848), in Marx and Engels, *Collected Works*, VI, p. 471).

189 Quoted in M. A. Lubin, 'Un chapitre des relations haïtiano-éthiopiennes', *Le Nouvelliste*, 22 avril 1966.

190 B. Sylvain, *Du sort des indigènes dans les colonies d'exploitation*, pp. 254 and 327.

191 *Ibid.*, p. 523.

192 *Ibid.*, pp. 511 and 513.

193 *L'Etoile Africaine*, janvier 1906, p. 46. On the Pan-African movement in general see Imanuel Geiss, *The Pan-African Movement, passim*; he says nothing, however, about L'Œuvre.

194 *La Revue Haïtienne*, mars–avril 1906.

195 Janvier, *Les affaires*, p. 223 n.

196 A. Rameau, *Idées et opinions*, p. 60. 'Amicus', *Réflexions sur la crise agricole, commerciale et financière d'Haïti*, p. 15.

197 Reprinted in *L'Impartial*, 15–16 mars 1910.

198 A. Innocent, *Mimola*, p. xiv. Cf J. Price Mars, 'Antoine Innocent, Ethnographe', in *Conjonction*, no. 48 (décembre 1953).

199 See pp. 152ff below.

200 C. Desmangles, *Des étrangers en Haïti*, p. 15.

201 *L'Œil*, 2 décembre 1882; see also Jérémie, 'L'Afrique endormie s'est réveillée en Haïti', *L'Effort*, p. 347.

202 Justin, *Les relations*, pp. 79ff.

203 Nicholls, *Economic Dependence*, pp. 14ff, where full documentation can be found to support the assertions made in this paragraph.

204 Hunt to Granville, 13 December 1882, PRO, FO 35/115, and Burdel to Challemel-Lacour, 5 mars 1883, AAE, Corr. Pol., Haïti 33/54. I discuss this in more detail in 'The Wisdom of Salomon: myth or reality?', *Journal of Interamerican Studies*, 20 (November 1978), pp. 377ff.

205 J. A. Firmin, in *Messager du Nord*, 26 janvier 1878; and J. A. Firmin, *Lettres de Saint Thomas*, pp. 4–5.

206 Janvier, *Haïti aux haïtiens*, pp. 10ff; Edouard, *Solution de la crise industrielle française*, p. 35.

207 Linstant de Pradine, *Nos fils, ou de la néotocratie en Haïti*, p. v; Edouard, *Solution de la crise*, p. 25. Laroche wrote: 'Aujourd'hui, l'action des Allemands s'étend jusque dans les cercles gouvernementaux. Cette action est d'autant plus funeste, qu'elle est occulte et invisible. Nous sommes dupes de leur politique, victimes de leurs intrigues, esclaves de leur capitaux' (L. Laroche, p. 59).

208 'La conception latine du travail'. *Le Matin*, 4 juin 1907, and 'La conception

anglo-saxonne du travail', *Le Matin*, 5 juin 1907. An earlier example of the pro-Anglo-Saxon position may be found in E. M., *Haïti et Cuba, conséquences de la guerre américano-espagnole*, pp. 16ff.

209   *Le Matin*, 7 mars 1908.

210   D. Laroche, *Coup de clairon*, pp. 16 and 23.

211   'Les mouvements ouvriers', *Le Matin*, 15 juin 1907; 'Ce qu'il faut lire', *Le Matin*, 27 juillet 1907.

212   L. Audin, p. 29.

213   'Race et éducation', *Le Matin*. 1 juillet 1907.

214   *Le Matin*, 4 mars 1908.

215   *Le Trait d'Union*, 7 mars 1908.

216   L. F. Manigat, 'La substitution de la prépondérance américaine à la prépondérance française en Haïti au début du XXe siècle: la conjonction de 1910–11', *Revue d'Histoire Moderne et Contemporaine*, 14 (1967), p. 335n. Manigat is misleading in suggesting that the 'anglo-saxonnistes' were 'réalistes communautaires'; most of them, in fact, argued strongly for 'particularisme' rather than collectivism.

217   See Logan, p. 330.

218   For a copy of the reputed offer see *Le Moniteur*, 30 janvier 1915.

219   Langston to Frelinghuysen, 30 May 1883, USNA-DS, Diplomatic Dispatches, Haiti 16; see Logan, p. 374.

220   Cf. Logan, p. 376.

221   Burdel to Challemel-Lacour, 5 octobre 1883, AAE, Corr. Pol., Haïti 33/107.

222   Quoted in *L'Avant-Garde*, 12 avril 1883. See also the statement by Edmond Paul on the question of the national bank, above, p. 105.

223   Salomon to F. Manigat, 24 juin 1884, PRO, FO 35/125. The Maunder claim was for compensation in connection with the expropriation of the Maunder family in the isle of La Tortue. For an account of the extended dispute see J. B. W. Maunder to Earl Granville, 9 January 1885, PRO, FO 35/125. and République d'Haïti, *Documents diplomatiques, relations extérieures, affaire Maunder*.

224   F. Douglass to J. Blaine, 7 May 1891, USNA-DS, Diplomatic Dispatches, Haiti 25. Firmin, however, told Douglass that he was personally in favour of the lease of the Môle to the Americans; see Douglass to Blaine, 29 January 1891, USNA-DS, Diplomatic Dispatches, Haiti 25.

225   This *créole* chant is quoted in 'Chants populaires et littérature créole', *Le Phare*, 15 novembre 1902.

226   Firmin had unsuccessfully attempted to deal with the problem when he was minister in Hyppolite's government. For details see Nicholls, *Economic Dependence*, p. 19. Jules Auguste wrote: 'Cette question des étrangers en Haïti est des plus graves et mérite plus que toute autre, avant toute autre, qu'on s'en occupe sérieusement une bonne fois' (*Quelques vérités à propos des récents événements de la République d'Haïti*, p. 33).

227   'C'est l'indépendance, c'est l'avenir de mon pays, que je sauvegarde . . . ' ('Proclamation', in *Le Trait d'Union*, 21 mars 1908). On the Syrio-Lebanese question see Nicholls, *Economic Dependence*, pp. 25ff; A. Poujol, 'La question des Syriens en Haïti', *Revue Général de Droit International Public*, juillet–août 1905; and Turnier, pp. 161ff.

228 Sténio Vincent, 'Contre les révolutionnaires', *Le Matin*, 4 mai 1908.
229 See p. 112 above.
230 E. Héraux to P. Carteron, 9 mars 1909, quoted in Turnier, pp. 217–8.
231 L. F. Manigat, 'La substitution', *Revue d'Histoire Moderne et Contemporaine*, 14 (1967), pp. 321ff. G. Pierre-Charles, *L'économie haïtienne et sa voie de développement*, p. 44.

5. Occupied Haiti (1911–1934)

1 Saint-Justé, introduction.
2 H. Schmidt, *The United States Occupation of Haiti*, pp. 34–5.
3 D. G. Munro, *Intervention and Dollar Diplomacy in the Caribbean, 1900–1921*, p. 326 n.
4 Tribonien Saint-Justé to E. Grey, 20 August 1914, PRO, FO 371/2002.
5 *Ibid.*
6 L. F. Manigat, 'La substitution', *Revue d'Histoire Moderne et Contemporaine*, 14 (1967), pp. 321ff; and J. Chatelain, *La banque nationale*.
7 J. Pyke to E. Grey, 30 April 1912, PRO, FO 371/1382.
8 A. Murray to E. Grey, 30 November 1911, PRO, FO 371/1132.
9 Reporting a conversation with the United States commandant of Guantánamo, the British diplomat Stephen Leech wrote, 'He informed me that in his opinion the naval station at Guantánamo was from its position of no real service to the United States and that he had reported in that sense to Washington, and that most naval officers held the same view' (S. Leech to E. Grey, 20 January 1914, PRO, FO 371/2001).
10 W. A. MacCorckle, *The Monroe Doctrine in its Relation to the Republic of Haiti*, preface and p. 28.
11 A. Murray to E. Grey, 30 April 1911, PRO, FO 371/1132.
12 Schmidt, p. 54; some writers have over-emphasised the narrowly economic factor, cf. G. Pierre-Charles, *L'économie haïtienne*, pp. 138–9, and S. Castor, *La ocupación norteamericana de Haití y sus consecuencias (1915–1934)*, pp. 20ff.
13 Munro, *Intervention, passim*. The idea of dollar diplomacy was well summarised by President Taft: 'It is therefore essential that the countries within that sphere [i.e. the Caribbean] shall be removed from the jeopardy involved by heavy foreign debt and chaotic national finances and from the ever-present danger of international complications due to disorder at home. Hence the United States has been glad to encourage and support American bankers who were willing to lend a hand to the financial rehabilitation of such countries' (*Congressional Record*, 62nd Congress, 3rd Session, p. 9).
14 L. F. Manigat, 'La substitution', *Revue d'Histoire Moderne et Contemporaine*, pp. 341ff.
15 A. K. Weinberg, *Manifest Destiny. A study of Nationalist Expansionism in American History*.
16 E. E. Morison (ed.), *The Letters of Theodore Roosevelt*, IV, p. 724.

17   Quoted in R. Gaillard, *Les blancs débarquent, 1914–1915: les cent-jours de Rosalvo Bobo*, p. 243. See also R. Bobo, *Voies de réforme*, pp. 8ff.
18   J. Price Mars, *Vilbrun Guillaume Sam: ce méconnu*, p. 171: cf. also Gaillard, *Les blancs débarquent, passim.*
19   C. Moravia, in *La Plume*, 25 août 1915.
20   E. Depestre, *La faillité d'une démocratie 1889–1915*, avertissement.
21   Quoted in Schmidt, p. 72.
22   M. Morpeau, *L'inconstitutionnalité de la convention américano-haïtienne*, p. 1; also *Haïti Intégrale*, 21 août 1915.
23   Cf. Schmidt, pp. 73–4.
24   Cf. Gaillard, *Les blancs débarquent*, pp. 209ff.
25   Christophe's constitutions of 1807 and 1811, however, had allowed foreign ownership; cf. p. 53 above.
26   Quoted in Schmidt, p. 118.
27   There is some controversy about the exact area of land acquired by American companies at this time; cf. Nicholls, *Economic Development*, p. 29 n. Leslie Manigat has accused me of taking 'a malicious pleasure' in pointing out inaccuracies in Suzy Castor's figures (L. F. Manigat in Manigat (ed.), *The Caribbean Yearbook of International Relations*, 1975, p. 525). Only critics who believe themselves to be endowed with psychic powers can ascribe malice to their colleagues. Readers of my monograph can judge for themselves. It was in fact on the editor's suggestion that I added the footnote to give details substantiating the general claim which I made in the text. Incidentally Manigat does not deny the truth of my assertions.
28   Quoted in Schmidt, p. 184.
29   A. C. Millspaugh, *Haiti under American Control, 1915–1930*, p. 163; *Report of the President's Commission for the Study and Review of Conditions in the Republic of Haiti*, p. 19. On the subject of technical schools, the American high commissioner wrote: 'This wise policy on the part of the Haitian government will rapidly develop a middle class that will become the backbone of the country and go far to assure stability of government' (*Report of the American High Commission*, 1928, p. 7).
30   J. J. Johnson, *Political Change in Latin America: The Emergence of the Middle Sectors*; J. P. Gillin, 'Cultura emergente', in J. L. Arriola (ed.), *Integración social en Guatemala*; and 'Some Signposts for Policy', in R. N. Adams *et al.*, *Social Change in Latin America Today*.
31   Millspaugh, p. 2.
32   Schmidt, p. 234; in the light of evidence produced by Schmidt, the statement by Sidney Mintz that the occupation was 'relatively unexploitative' needs to be regarded with caution; Mintz in Leyburn, p. xi. For U.S. policy in the neighbouring Dominican Republic see M. M. Knight, *Los Americanos en Santo Domingo*, and C. A. Herrera, *Les finanzas de la República Dominicana*. For a comparative study see Suzy Castor, 'El impacto de la ocupación norteamericana en Haití (1915–1934) y en la República Dominicana (1916–1924), in G. Pierre-Charles (ed.), *Política y sociología*, pp. 42ff.
33   There was a brief resistance in the early months led by General Pierre

Benoît Rameau, who had been minister of war in Bobo's revolutionary government; he was imprisoned by the Americans from 1915 to 1926.
34 R. Gaillard, in *Conjonction*, no. 115 (1971), pp. 100–1, and Schmidt, pp. 100ff. Estimates of the number of peasant guerrillas ranged from 2,000 to 40,000.
35 Reprinted in *Conjonction*, no. 115 (1971), p. 102.
36 There is an English translation of this book (misleadingly called a 'Voodoo Book') in the library of St Louis de Gonzague. It is a curious combination of Christian prayers and various magic charms to deal with such things as toothache, and to be worked on fighting cocks, horses etc. It includes a prayer against bullets, and a 'Revolutionary Prayer to our Saviour Jesus'. There is also a prayer to be said over a strangled beast:

> God who was born,
> God who died,
> God who came to life again,
> God who was crucified,
> God who was hanged.

The emphasis upon 'the crucified God' is interesting; cf. J. Moltmann, *The Crucified God*, especially chapter 8.
37 Cf. G. S. Jean Baptiste, 'L'attitude de la presse port-au-princienne, 1915–26', unpublished thesis, Faculty of Ethnology, Université d'Etat, Haiti, 1968.
38 *Le Courrier Haïtien*, 1 décembre 1921; also G. Sylvain, *Dix années du lutte pour la liberté: 1915–25*.
39 H. P. Sannon *et al.*, *Memoir of the Political, Economic and Financial Conditions existing in the Republic of Haiti under the American Occupation*.
40 L'Union Nationaliste, *Dépossessions*, pp. v and x.
41 *Ibid.*, p. 15, and F. Dalencour, *Le sauvetage national par le retour à la terre*, p. 15.
42 A. Ruhl, 'What America is doing for Haiti', *Current History*, 22 August 1925, p. 734.
43 This is well-documented by Schmidt, pp. 137ff.
44 S. G. Inman, *Trailing the Conquistadors*, p. 131.
45 D. Bellegarde, *La résistance haïtienne*, p. 86; for a criticism of Bellegarde's account of his activities at this time see J. Blanchet, *Peint par lui-même, ou la résistance de Mr. Dantès Bellegarde*.
46 J. F. Brierre in preface to R. Lataillade, *L'urne close*, p. iv. There is a discussion of these literary reactions to the occupation in J. Michael Dash's unpublished PhD thesis at the University of the West Indies, Mona, Jamaica (1972), entitled 'Nationalism in Haitian Poetry, 1915–1946'.
47 F. García Calderón, *Latin America: its Rise and Progress*, p. 392.
48 C. Pressoir, 'Psychological Aspects of the Application of Point Four', *Revue de la Société Haïtienne d'Histoire, de Géographie et de Géologie*, juillet 1951, pp. 59ff.
49 *Le Courrier du Soir*, 23 mai 1921 and 14 avril 1921.

50   Duval Duvalier, 'Pages de mon carnet', *Le Courrier du Soir*, 20 juin 1921.

51   Cf. Duval Duvalier, 'Sociologie pratique', *Le Courrier du Soir*, 25 mai 1921 and following numbers.

52   Louis Borno, message to the Council of State, quoted in *Seventh Annual Report of the American High Commissioner*, 3 January 1929, p. 4.

53   *Ibid.*, p. 1.

54   There is a chapter dealing with the United States withdrawal from Haiti in D. G. Munro, *The United States and the Caribbean Republics, 1921–1933*, pp. 309ff.

55   H. P. Sannon, in *Bulletin de la Société d'Histoire et de Géographie d'Haïti*, 1 mai 1925, p. 2.

56   J. C. Dorsainvil, *Militarisme et hygène sociale*, p. 38. Later, in 1934, he reiterated his criticism of the elite, whom he described as lacking in initiative, egoistic and having no conception of social solidarity; they depend too much on the state and lack self-confidence (*Quelques vues politiques et morales*, p. 23).

57   Dorsainvil, 'Des idées collectives, II', *Le Matin*, 8 janvier 1908.

58   Dorsainvil, 'L'éducation dans la race, I', *Le Matin*, 7 décembre 1907.

59   Dorsainvil, 'L'éducation dans la race, III', *Le Matin*, 10 décembre 1907.

60   'Nous aurions dû nous orienter vers une méthode d'éducation plus conforme à notre état mental' ('Evolution et mentalité, II', *Le Matin*, 28 avril 1908); cf. also 'Evolution sociale, II', *Le Matin*, 2 juin 1908.

61   'Un mot sur la psychologie du peuple haïtien', *Le Nouvelliste*, 17 octobre 1907.

62   Dorsainvil, *Vôdou et névrose*, first published in *Haïti Médicale*, 1913.

63   *Quelques vues*, p. 88.

64   *Ibid.*, pp. 73 and 84.

65   *Organisons nos partis politiques*, p. 62.

66   *Vôdou et névrose*, p. 28; cf. also 'Nous affirmons que le vôdouisme répond à un habitus nerveux racial stabilisé par la croyance, des pratiques séculaires, chez de nombreuses familles haïtiennes' (*ibid.*, p. 48).

67   *Quelques vues*, pp. 88 and 111.

68   *Vôdou et névrose*, pp. 33 and 139; cf. also Dorsainvil, *Vôdou et magie*, pp. 23ff.

69   *L'échec d'hier et l'effort pour l'avenir*, p. 19.

70   *Ibid.*, pp. 10ff.

71   *Quelques vues*, pp. 22ff. and 35; cf. also *La Presse*, 31 mars 1930.

72   See p. 84 above.

73   A. Holly, *Rapport entre l'instruction, la psychologie et l'état social*, pp. 5–6.

74   A. Holly ('Her-Ra-Me-El'). *Dra-Po: étude ésoterique de Egregore africain, traditionnel, social et national d'Haïti*, p. 11.

75   *Rapport*, p. 19.

76   *Dra-Po*, pp. i and vii.

77   *Rapport*, pp. 17ff.

78   *Dra-Po*, p. 367; also A. Holly, *Les daïmons du culte voudo*, p. ii.

79   *Dra-Po*, p. 31.

80   L. S. Senghor *et al.*, *Témoignages sur la vie et l'œuvre du Dr. Jean Price Mars*; H. Trouillot, 'La pensée du Docteur Jean Price-Mars,' *Revue de la*

Société Haïtienne d'Histoire, de Géographie et de Géologie, juillet–août 1956; there is also some autobiographical material in J. Price Mars, *Lettre ouverte au Dr. René Piquion*, where Price Mars corrects some of the information given by Piquion in his *Manuel de négritude*.

81   J. Price Mars, 'La réforme de l'enseignement primaire', *Haïti Littéraire et Scientifique*, juillet 1912; 'L'éducation technique', *Haïti Littéraire et Scientifique*, octobre 1912; 'A propos des écoles du soir', *L'Essor*, 4–5 juin 1917.

82   'La réforme de l'enseignement primaire, II', *Haïti Littéraire et Scientifique*, septembre 1912.

83   *Ibid.*

84   J. Price Mars, *La vocation de l'élite*, pp. 60, 81 and 97.

85   Price Mars, *Ainsi parla l'oncle*, p. 220.

86   M. Delafosse, *The Negroes of Africa*, p. 150.

87   *Ainsi parla l'oncle*, p. iii.

88   J. Price Mars, *Une étape de l'évolution haïtienne*, pp. 128–9. This type of religious belief was called 'naturism' by Durkheim; cf. *Elementary Forms of the Religious Life*, I, chapters 2 and 3.

89   *Une étape*, p. 150.

90   *Ainsi parla l'oncle*, p. 32; cf. Price Mars, 'Le sentiment et le phénomène religieux chez les nègres de Saint Domingue', *Bulletin de la Société d'Histoire et de Géographie d'Haïti*, mai 1925, p. 43.

91   J. Price Mars, 'La diplomatie haïtienne et l'indépendance dominicaine', *Revue de la Société d'Histoire et de Géographie d'Haïti* (janvier 1939), p. 2; and preface to Jacques Roumain, *La montagne ensorcelée*.

92   cf. H. S. Reiss (ed), *The Political Thought of the German Romantics,* and G. Ipsen, *Das Landvolk: ein soziologischer Versuch.*

93   *Ainsi parla l'oncle*, pp. 17 and 190ff.

94   *Casa de las Américas*, No. 49, (1968), pp. 137ff; translated in *Savacou*, 5 (June 1971), pp. 71ff. On the movement of black students in Paris centred on the journal *Légitime Défense* see L. Kesteloot, *Les écrivains noirs de langue française: naissance d'une littérature*, pp. 25ff, and L. Kesteloot, *Négritude et situation coloniale*; cf. also T. Melone, *De la négritude*.

95   A. Carpentier, *Ecué-Yamba-O*, p. 66; quoted in G. R. Coulthard, *Race and Colour in Caribbean Literature*, p. 30.

96   Quoted in Coulthard, p. 34.

97   Suzanne Césaire, 'Léo Frobenius et le problème des civilisations', *Tropiques*, 1 (avril 1941). Delafosse's works included *Haut-Sénégal-Niger*, *Les frontières de la Côte d'Ivoire, de la Côte d'Or et du Soudan*, and *Les noirs d'Afrique*.

98   Lorimer Denis and François Duvalier mention the influence which this novel had on the thinking of Louis Diaquoi and the early *Griots* writers, in J. Oriol *et al., Le mouvement folklorique en Haïti*, p. 13. L. Kesteloot discusses the wider influence of this novel upon black intellectuals of the twenties and thirties in *Les écrivains noirs*, chapter 6.

99   Georges Hardy, 'L'art nègre, son inspiration, ses apports à l'occident', *La Revue du Monde Noir*, 2 (mars 1932).

100   See poems of Langston Hughes translated by Piquion in *La Relève*, juin

1933, septembre 1933, mars 1934, etc.; and J. Price Mars, 'A propos de la "renaissance nègre" aux Etats Unis', *La Relève*, juillet, août, septembre 1932. For a fuller discussion of the influence of these movements on Haitian literature in this period see N. Garrett, *The Renaissance of Haitian Poetry*, pp. 68ff. Cf. also Ulrich Fleischmann, *Ideologie und Wirklichkeit in der Literatur Haitis*, pp. 55ff. (There is a summary of this work in Fleischmann, *Ecrivain et société en Haïti*.) Other works on Haitian literature of this period include A. Viatte, *Histoire littéraire de l'Amérique française, des origines à 1950*, and G. Gouraige, *Histoire de la littérature haïtienne*. In English there is an excellent introduction to this literature in Coulthard, chapters 3, 4 and 5.

101   A. Vieux and P. Thoby-Marcelin, 'La littérature d'hier et celle de demain', *La Nouvelle Ronde*, juillet 1925; in the following decade see also *La Nouvelle Haïti*, founded in March 1934. Cf. Garrett, pp. 65ff.

102   Normil Sylvain, 'Un rêve de Georges Sylvain', *La Revue Indigène*, juillet 1927, p. 5.

103   See his letter from Zurich to the director of *Le Courrier Haïtien*, 15 janvier 1925, quoted in Georges Sylvain, *Dix années*, II: pp. 134–5.

104   J. Roumain, in *Le Petit Impartial*, 2 juin 1928; G. Petit and J. Roumain, in *Le Petit Impartial*, 4 avril 1928.

105   Translated in Coulthard, p. 75.

106   L. Laleau, *Musique nègre*, p. 15.

107   Carl Brouard, 'Le livre de Mr. Price Mars', *Le Petit Impartial*, 13 octobre 1928.

108   Cf. C. Brouard, 'Inayat Khan, messager de soufisme', *La Revue Indigène*, 2 (août 1927), and 'Hâfiz', *La Revue Indigène*, 3 (septembre 1927). On the life and work of Brouard see R. Gaillard, *La destinée de Carl Brouard*.

109   Reprinted in C. Brouard, *Pages retrouvées*, pp. 23–4.

110   Translated in Coulthard, p. 72.

111   Brouard, 'Pour Normil G. Sylvain', *Le Petit Impartial*, 9 février 1929.

112   J. Roumain and G. Petit, in *Le Petit Impartial*, 13 décembre 1928; cf. also J. Roumain, 'Un prêtre a le droit d'être un soldat quand sa patrie est en danger', *Le Petit Impartial*, 20 juin 1928. On Jacques Roumain see R. Gaillard, *L'univers romanesque de Jacques Roumain*, and M. Dash, 'The Marxist Counterpoint – Jacques Roumain', *Black Images*, 2:1 (1973), pp. 25ff.

113   *La Revue Indigène* 2 (août 1927); reprinted in Brouard, pp. 19–21.

114   'Nous préconisons par-dessus tout l'union. Le terme qui resplendit au fronton des associations fascistes: Le Faiseau et qui fait tant d'honneur au Duce, nous le ferons connaître' (*La Trouée*, 1, (1927)).

115   N. Sylvain, 'Un rêve de Georges Sylvain', *La Revue Indigène*, 1 (juillet 1927).

116   M. Hudicourt, 'Coup d'œil sur la démocratie', *La Nouvelle Ronde*, janvier 1926, pp. 150–1.

117   E. Charlier, 'Gouvernants et gouvernés', *La Nouvelle Ronde*, novembre 1925, p. 106.

118   W. E. B. Dubois, *Darkwater: Voices from Within the Veil*, p. 3.

119   There is an excellent account of Blyden's life and thought in Hollis R. Lynch, *Edward Wilmot Blyden: Pan-Negro Patriot, 1832–1912*.

6. Literature and dogma (1930–1945)

1 L. Denis, 'Ma génération', *L'Action Nationale*, 23 juin 1932.
2 C. Brouard, 'Hommage', *L'Assaut*, 4–6 mars 1935, and editorial in *L'Assaut*, 30 octobre 1935.
3 *Cahiers d'Haïti*, septembre 1943.
4 On the racial aspects of Haitian–Dominican relations see M. Acosta and A. Corten in M. Acosta *et al.*, *Imperialismo y clases sociales en el Caribe*, and F. J. Franco in G. Pierre-Charles *et al.*, *Problemas dominico-haitianos y del Caribe*.
5 There is a series of articles on Diaquoi by Hébert Magloire in *Circuit Artibonite*, 9 mars 1958, and following numbers.
6 Cf. M. Delafosse, *The Negroes of Africa*, p. 268, and H. Trouillot, 'L'école des griots', *Les Griots*, 29 juillet 1949.
7 L. Diaquoi, 'L'art et la science au service de l'action: le Dr. Price Mars', *L'Action Nationale*, 29 avril 1932. On the influence of Price Mars on this group see also R. Piquion, 'La flamme sacrée', *L'Action Nationale*, 18 mai 1932; C. Brouard in *La Bataille*, 5 mars 1932; and K. Georges Jacob, *L'ethnie haïtienne*, pp. 158–9.
8 L. Diaquoi, in *L'Action Nationale*, 12 mai 1932.
9 'Considérations sur nos origines historiques', *Les Griots*, octobre–décembre 1939, pp. 623ff.
10 'Les sanglots d'un exile', reprinted in F. Duvalier, *Hommage au martyr de la non-violence*, pp. 76ff.
11 L. Denis and F. Duvalier, 'L'ethnie haïtienne', *Le Nouvelliste*, 11 septembre 1936.
12 Denis and Duvalier, 'Question d'anthropo-sociologie: le déterminisme racial', *Les Griots*, 3 (1939), pp. 303ff.
13 Duvalier, 'La civilisation haïtienne – notre mentalité, est-elle africaine ou gallo-latine?', *Revue de la Société d'Histoire et de Géographie d'Haïti*, mai 1936, p. 12. On the racial theories of the *Griots* group, see David Nicholls, 'Biology and Politics in Haiti', *Race*, 13:2 (1971), pp. 203ff.
14 *Le Nouvelliste*, 30 décembre 1935 to 3 janvier 1936.
15 Denis and Duvalier, 'Les civilisations négro-africaines et le problème haïtien', *Revue de la Société d'Histoire et de Géographie d'Haïti*, janvier–avril 1936, reprinted in F. Duvalier, *Œuvres essentielles*, (3rd edn.), I, pp. 71–2.
16 K. Georges Jacob, *Contribution à l'étude de l'homme haïtien*, pp. 23 and 42 n. 'Il importe de tenir compte des données historico-culturelles qui forment de substrat à la physionomie particulière des peuples' (*ibid.*, p. 9).
17 Georges Jacob, *L'ethnie haïtienne*, p. xiv.
18 R. Piquion, 'Africa mater', *L'Action Nationale*, 22 décembre 1932.
19 Denis and Duvalier, 'Psychologie ethnique et historique', *Les Griots*, 4 (1939), p. 501.
20 'L'évolution stadiale du voudou', in Duvalier, *Œuvres*, I (3rd edn), p. 177.
21 Diaquoi, 'Satan conduit le bal, II' *Le Petit Impartial*, 11 décembre 1930.

22 Diaquoi, 'Satan conduit le bal, XI', *Le Petit Impartial*, 22 janvier 1931.

23 Georges Jacob, *L'ethnie haïtienne*, p. vii.

24 'Le social et le politique', *L'Action Nationale*, 19 juillet 1934, reprinted in F. Duvalier ('Abderrahman'), *Médaillons*, pp. 125ff.

25 Duvalier and Denis, 'Considérations sur nos origines historiques', *Les Griots*, octobre–décembre 1939, p. 621; cf. also Denis and Duvalier, 'Tribus mandingue?', *Le Nouvelliste*, 26 octobre 1936.

26 Duvalier, *Œuvres*, I, (3rd edn), p. 420; Karl Lévêque, 'L'interpellation mystique dans le discours duvaliérien', *Nouvelle Optique*, 4 (décembre 1971), pp. 5ff.

27 L. Diaquoi, 'La place au soleil', *L'Action Nationale*, 18 avril 1932.

28 *L'Action Nationale*, 4 juin 1932.

29 Georges Jacob, *L'ethnie haïtienne*, p. 65. 'Mensonge est tout cet étalage démocratique' (*ibid.*).

30 R. Piquion, 'Force ou dictature', *La Relève*, avril 1934, p. 13.

31 Piquion, 'Le salut par la force', *La Relève*, mars 1934, p. 9.

32 Piquion, 'Force ou dictature', p. 13. Cf. the words of Marcel Gouraige, 'Le peuple haïtien, dans ses propres intérêts ne doit être gouverné que par la *dictature*' ('La dictature, forme moderne de gouvernement', *L'Action Nationale*, 24 janvier 1935).

33 Georges Jacob, 'L'enseignement en Haïti', *Les Griots*, 4 (1939), p. 549, and 'Question de l'ordre du jour', *Pangloss*, 5 juillet 1940, p. 2.

34 Georges Jacob, 'Nécessité d'un redressement, ou d'une éducation adéquate au milieu', *Pangloss*, 28 juin 1940, p. 2.

35 Duvalier, in *L'Action Nationale*, 11 juillet 1934, reprinted in *Médaillons*, pp. 113ff; Georges Jacob, *L'ethnie haïtienne*, p. 35, and *Contribution*, pp. 59 and 69.

36 Magloire Saint Aude, 'La plus belle race du monde', *L'Assaut*, 5 août 1935.

37 J. Roumain, 'L'écroulement du mythe nationaliste', in *Analyse schématique, 32–34*, pp. ii–iv.

38 Roumain, 'Préjugé de couleur et lutte de classes', in *Analyse*, p. v; see also Roumain in Cardinal J.-P. Verdier *et al.*, *L'homme de couleur*, p. 112.

39 Roumain, 'Réplique finale au R. P. Foisset, VII', *Le Nouvelliste*, 13 juillet 1942.

40 J. Stalin, *Works*, IV, p. 170. See also V. I. Lenin, *On the National and Colonial Questions*, *passim*.

41 W. Record, *The Negro and the Communist Party*; also R. Wright, in R. Crossman (ed.), *The God that Failed*; G. Padmore, *Panafricanism or Communism*.

42 Particularly J. C. Mariátegui, *Siete ensayos de interpretación de le realidad peruana*.

43 J. Roumain, *Bois d'ébène*.

44 J. Roumain, *Gouverneurs de la rosée*, p. 212. On Haitian immigration into Cuba at this time, see J. Pérez de la Riva, 'La inmigración antillana en Cuba durante el primer tercio del siglo XX', *Revista de la Biblioteca Nacional José Martí*, mayo–agosto 1975, pp. 75ff.

45 Roumain, 'La poésie comme arme', *Cahiers d'Haïti*, novembre 1944, p. 37. Of poetry he wrote elsewhere, 'elle reflétait ce qu'on appelle communément

une époque, c'est à dire la complexité dialectique des relations sociales, des contradictions et des antagonismes de la structure économique et politique à une période définie de l'histoire' ('Réplique finale au R. P. Foisset, VII', *Le Nouvelliste*, 13 juillet 1942).

46   Roumain, preface to Edris Saint-Amand, *Essai d'explication de 'Dialogue de mes lampes'*, p. 10.

47   R. Michels, *Political Parties*, p. 230.

48   J. F. Brierre, *Nous garderons le dieu*.

49   Cf. pp. 102 ff above.

50   J. Blanchet, 'L'évolution économique', *La Relève*, juin 1935, p. 2, and 'L'Etat et la production', *L'Action Nationale*, 23 décembre 1935. See also J. Blanchet and R. Piquion, *Essais sur la culture*, pp. 5–6.

51   Blanchet, 'Classes sociales et syndicalisme', *La Relève*, avril 1935, pp. 1ff, and 'La primauté de l'économique', *La Relève*, février 1935, pp. 1ff.

52   Blanchet, 'Tendences nouvelles', *La Relève*, septembre 1935, pp. 2–3.

53   Blanchet, 'Idéologies nouvelles', *Maintenant*, 15 février 1936.

54   Blanchet, 'Cadres de techniciens et état technique', *La Relève*, août 1937, pp. 4ff.

55   Blanchet, 'La primauté de l'ésprit', *La Relève*, janvier 1935, p. 21.

56   Blanchet, 'L'enquête de Réveil', *Le Réveil*, 3 février 1940.

57   H. de Saint-Simon, *L'industrie*, III, p. 23.

58   J. Blanchet, 'Horizons', *Le Nouvelliste*, 18 décembre 1945.

59   F. Dalencour, *Essai d'une synthèse de sociologie économique*.

60   Dalencour, *Précis méthodique d'histoire d'Haïti*, p. 155.

61   Dalencour, *Le sauvetage national*, pp. 35–6 and 48–9.

62   G. Séjourné, 'Haïti et la petite propriété', *Revue de la Société d'Histoire et de Géographie d'Haïti*, octobre 1939.

63   F. Dalencour, *Précis méthodique*, p. 151 n., and *La croisée des chemins*, pp. 34ff and 44ff.

64   *Précis méthodique*, p. 138.

65   *La croisée*, p. 21.

66   D. Bellegarde, 'Mentalité mystique et superstitieuse', *La Phalange*, 3 juin 1939. For Sténio Vincent's criticism of Voodoo see his *Efforts et résultats*, p. 257.

67   Bellegarde, 'La science et l'église contre le racisme', *La Phalange*, 8 avril 1939, and 'La race n'existe pas', *La Phalange*, 1 avril 1939.

68   Bellegarde, 'La culture haïtienne', *La Phalange*, 29 avril 1939.

69   Bellegarde, 'Vaudou et civilisation chrétienne', *La Phalange*, 27 mai 1939.

70   F. Dalencour, *Principes d'éducation nationale*, p. 33. See also p. 58 and *La croisée*, p. 18.

71   S. Vincent, *En posant les jalons*, I, pp. 4 and 14.

72   *Ibid.*, pp. 38 and 41.

73   *Ibid.*, p. 153.

74   Dalencour, *Essai d'une synthèse*, p. 98. Cf. S. M. Lipset, *Political Man*, pp. 27ff.

75   Dalencour, *La croisée*, pp. 31ff.

76   Bellegarde, 'La nation haïtienne', *La Phalange*, 22 avril 1939; 'La société haïtienne', *La Phalange*, 10 juin 1939.

77   Vincent, *Efforts et résultats*, pp. 277ff; *En posant les jalons*, I, p. 342;

here he used the phrase 'une cloison étanche' to characterise the situation. Cf. Bellegarde, 'Notre société . . . ne présente point de compartements séparés par des cloisons étanches' ('La société haïtienne', *La Phalange*, 10 juin 1939).

78 *En posant les jalons*, IV, p. 202; *Efforts et résultats*, p. 289.
79 *En posant les jalons*, IV, p. 202.
80 'Eloge de la discipline', *En posant les jalons*, V, p. 153.
81 J. Magloire, in *Maintenant*, 31 octobre 1936.
82 J. Magloire, in *Maintenant*, 19 septembre 1936.
83 J. Magloire, in *Maintenant*, 1 mai 1937.
84 F. Mirambeau, 'Les blancs et les rouges', *Maintenant*, 22 août 1936.
85 M. Bissainthe, in *Maintenant*, 12 septembre 1936. In 1937 this journal changed its name to *Psyche*.
86 G. de Catalogne, 'Salut à Franco', *La Phalange*, 20 février 1940.
87 De Catalogne, 'Le libéralisme contre la liberté', *La Phalange*, 3 octobre 1940.
88 Cf. G. de Catalogne, *Notre révolution* and *Haïti devant son destin*; this latter book was divided into three parts: 'Eléments d'une doctrine', 'Une nation en marche' and 'Les théories au pouvoir', from which the titles of Duvalier's *Œuvres essentielles* were taken; de Catalogne wrote an introduction to the first volume of this collection.
89 J. Magloire, in *Le Matin*, 31 août 1945.
90 C. Magloire, 'Ethiopie menacée', *L'Assaut*, 17 juillet 1935; R. Piquion, 'Pour Hailé Selassie', *L'Assaut*, 13 mars 1935; also Piquion, 'Pour une mobilisation de la race', *L'Action Nationale*, 11 mars 1935.
91 C. Magloire, 'L'enthousiasme raciale', *L'Assaut*, 31 juillet 1935. See also C. Magloire, 'Le racisme nègre', *L'Action Nationale*, 13 août 1935.
92 Denis and Duvalier, 'La race éthiopienne: est-elle nègre?', *Le Nouvelliste*, 22 juillet 1935.
93 C. Brouard, 'A propos d'Ethiopie', *L'Assaut*, 22 juillet 1935.
94 *Le Temps*, 20 juillet 1935.
95 League of Nations, *Records of the 16th Ordinary Session of the Assembly*, Plenary Meeting, Text of Debates, 10 October 1935, pp. 107–8.
96 Cf. S. K. B. Asante, 'The Afro-American and the Italo-Ethiopian Crisis', *Race*, 15 (February 1973), pp. 167ff.
97 P. Robert, *La Phalange*, 8 avril 1941.
98 Lescot, quoted by J. Foisset in *La Phalange*, 14 mai 1941.
99 *La Phalange*, 12 septembre 1941. For the text of the oath, see Alfred Métraux, *Le vaudou haïtien*, pp. 302–3.
100 Métraux, *Le vaudou haïtien*, p. 299.
101 See Rémy Augustin, *Cantiques pour la campagne anti-superstitieuse*.
102 *La Phalange*, 26 janvier 1942.
103 See Georges Jacob, *L'ethnie haïtienne*, pp. 71ff.
104 See preface to C. E. Peters, *Lumière sur l'humfort*, p. 4.
105 G. de Catalogne, 'Graves incidents à Delmas', *Le Soir*, 23 février 1942; see also 'Clairvoyance du temporel', *Le Soir*, 26 février 1942.
106 J. Roumain, 'Réplique finale au R. P. Foisset, VIII', *Le Nouvelliste*, 30 juillet 1942.

107   Roumain, *A propos de la campagne 'anti-superstitieuse'*, p. 11.
108   'Réplique finale au R. P. Foisset, VI', *Le Nouvelliste*, 10 juillet 1942. See also Edris Saint-Amand, 'Pour l'ethnologie', *Le Nouvelliste*, 11 décembre 1942.
109   Roumain, *A propos*, p. 13.
110   *Listin Diario*, 24 febrero 1942.
111   On Breton's visit, see P. Laraque, 'André Breton en Haïti', *Nouvelle Optique*, 2–3 (mai 1971), pp. 126ff; also *Présence Haïtienne*, 3 (octobre 1975), pp. 5ff. For some reflections on the controversies of 1946 by one who was involved in them, see Roger Dorsainville, '1946 ou le délire opportuniste', *Nouvelle Optique*, 6 (septembre 1972), pp. 117ff.
112   'Lescot, you have left without saying a word to me.'
113   E. Charlier, in *Le Nouvelliste*, 18 janvier 1946; Jules Blanchet also wrote of the constitutions of Vincent and Lescot as 'fasciste' (*Demain*, 8 février 1946).
114   E. Charlier, 'Politique', *La Nation*, 13 juillet 1950.
115   *L'Action Nationale*, Bulletin 29, 22 mars 1946.
116   *Ibid.*, Bulletin 30, 23 mars 1946.
117   *Ibid.*, Bulletin 41, 6–7 avril 1946.
118   *Ibid.*, Bulletin 60, 13 mai 1946.
119   *Ibid.*, Bulletin 57, 6 mai 1946.
120   See D. P. Calixte, *Haïti: le calvaire d'un soldat*.
121   *Flambeau*, 9 juin 1946.
122   *Le Nouvelliste*, 14 août 1946.
123   'Le gouvernement et le PSP', *Chantiers*, 28 juin 1947.
124   *L'Artibonite Journal*, 7 février 1946.
125   On Estimé see L. Daumec in *Ultime hommage au président Dumarsais Estimé*, and J. Magloire, *Dumarsais Estimé: esquisse de sa vie politique*.
126   E. Brutus, 'Peu de mots', *Demain*, 30 janvier 1946.
127   Gérard Martelly, in *La Ruche*, 3 août 1946.
128   *Le Nouvelliste*, 28 janvier 1946.
129   'Politique', *La Nation*, 26 juillet 1950. Cf. also Max Ménard of the PCH: 'Pour nous, Marxistes, la question de couleur ne conduit pas, malgré toutes les apparences du contraires, au cœur des problèmes sociaux en Haïti . . . La plus grande partie de la classe privilégiée se trouve couverte par l'élément mulâtre. Sur notre problème de classe vient se greffer la question de couleur . . . [mais] le bourgeois n'a pas de couleur propre . . . Que le fils du proletariat comprenne donc que le bourgeois noir n'est pas plus son frère que le bourgeois mulâtre' ('A propos de la question de couleur', *La Ruche*, 26 janvier 1946).
130   M. Vaval, 'Max Hudicourt au pilori', *La République*, 28 mai 1946.
131   R. Dorsainville, 'Racisme', *La République*, 4 juin 1946.
132   *Demain*, 28 juin 1946. On Rigaud see p. 29 above.
133   See J. J. Doubout and U. Joly, *Notes sur le développement du mouvement syndical en Haïti*.
134   D. P. Calixte, in *La République*, 20 août 1946.
135   O. David, 'Le Parti Communiste et le gouvernement actuel', *Combat*, 28 novembre 1946.

136   R. Depestre, 'Notre combat', *Flambeau*, 19 octobre 1946.

137   Leyburn, *The Haitian People*; J. Lobb, 'Caste and Class in Haiti', *American Journal of Sociology*, 46 (1940) pp. 23ff; G. E. Simpson, 'Haiti's Social Structure', *American Sociological Review*, 6 (1941), pp. 640ff.

138   R. Wingfield and V. J. Parenton, 'Class Structure and Class Conflict in Haitian Society', *Social Forces*, 43 (1964–5), p. 343.

139   Reprinted in J. Price Mars, *De la préhistoire d'Afrique à l'histoire d'Haïti*, p. 210. In 1936 Dantès Bellegarde referred to 'a middle class which is very numerous', ('Haiti and her Problems', *The University of Puerto Rico Bulletin*, 7:1 (September 1936), p. 15); cf. also note 29 to chapter 5 above.

140   Leyburn, p. 101.

7.   Authentics and their adversaries (1946–1957)

1   'Ainsi Lescot faisait pratiquement de la discrimination raciale, vous en faites, vous pratiquement et théoretiquement' (*Le Justicier*, 7 mars 1947).

2   *La Nation*, 4 juillet 1950.

3   Speech on 23 July 1950 at Les Cayes, quoted in C. Bonhomme, *Révolution et contre-révolution en Haïti*, p. 73.

4   Cf. T. Draper, 'Haiti: the return of the elite', *Reporter*, 2 October 1951.

5   'Discours prononcé par Son Ex. Mgr. Robert', *La Phalange*, 7 novembre 1950; Lélio Jeannot, 'Contre les pratiques et rites superstitieux', *La Phalange*, 20 and 21 août 1950.

6   *Construction*, 20 août 1952. For Fignolé's account of these years, see his *Mon mandat*.

7   *Le Nouvelliste*, 14 janvier 1954.

8   Doubout and Joly, p. 26.

9   *Chantiers*, juin 1946.

10   Reprinted in Duvalier, *Œuvres*, I, p. 287.

11   The situation with respect to Pétion was later remedied by Leslie Manigat! See p. 54 above.

12   Duvalier, *Œuvres*, I, p. 297.

13   Duvalier, in *Les Griots*, 16 avril 1948, reprinted in *Médaillons*, pp. 187ff.

14   Duvalier, *Œuvres*, II, pp. 23 and 152.

15   M. Vaval, 'Mis au point', *Flambeau*, 31 octobre 1946.

16   Duvalier, *Œuvres*, I, pp. 303, 309 and 312.

17   *Ibid.*, p. 310.

18   *Ibid.*, pp. 312–3.

19   Duvalier and Denis, 'Le drame social haïtien', *Flambeau*, 27 janvier 1946.

20   See p. 230 below.

21   Duvalier and Denis, 'Masques d'hier et d'aujourd'hui', *Les Griots*, 19 mars 1948, reprinted from *L'Action Nationale*, 2 juillet 1934.

22   René Malary, 'Nation et tradition', *Les Griots*, 7 mai 1948; cf. also *Les Griots*, 6 février 1948, and K. Georges Jacob, 'Reflexions', *Les Griots*, 27 août 1948.

23   'Pour une plus fière Haïti', *Les Griots*, 13 février 1948.

24   'L'éducation qu'il nous faut', *Flambeau*, 7 décembre 1946; cf. also M. Aubourg and L. Viaud, 'Considérations sur la mentalité haïtienne', *Flambeau*, 6 février 1947.

25 Cf. 'Table rond: le créole et la loi', *Optique*, juillet 1954; also E. C. Paul, *Culture, langue, littérature*, pp. 11ff. This emphasis upon the importance of *créole* was not restricted to *noiriste* writers; see F. Morisseau Leroy, 'La littérature haïtienne d'expression créole: son avenir', *Présence Africaine*, décembre 1957–janvier 1958, p. 55. Also C. F. Pressoir, *Débats sur le créole et le folklore*, passim.

26 Duvalier and Denis, 'Culturologie', *Les Griots*, 25 juin 1948, reprinted in Duvalier, *Œuvres*, I, pp. 56ff.

27 *Ibid.*, p. 63.

28 Gérard Gayot, *Clergé indigène*, pp. 61–2.

29 M. Cadet, in *Les Griots*, 31 décembre 1948.

30 J. Foisset, 'Il faut lutter ouvertement contre la magie homicide', *La Phalange*, 30 décembre 1948.

31 J. Foisset, 'Le folklore', *La Phalange*, 17 mars 1949.

32 Duvalier and Denis, 'L'avenir du pays et l'action néfaste de M. Foisset', *Les Griots*, 25 mars 1949.

33 J. Foisset, 'L'assaut contre le Christ', *La Phalange*, 30 mars 1949.

34 P. Robert, *Texte du rapport sur la superstition*, p. 1.

35 P. Robert, *Problèmes et recherches*; this monograph, together with others, is reprinted in Paul Robert, *Catholicisme et vaudou*.

36 P. Robert, *Difficultés et ressources*, pp. 1, 4, 19, 20.

37 P. Robert, *Positions et propositions*, pp. 3, 9, 21.

38 'La nationalisation des clergés; obligation de l'état', *Le Mercure*, 18 septembre 1946; *Lumière*, 12 juillet 1947; *Construction*, 20 avril 1952.

39 Percival Thoby, 'Le vaudou et la morale', *L'Action*, 23 avril 1951.

40 *L'Action*, 1 février 1951.

41 Gayot, preface.

42 Marc Pierre, 'Tempête sur l'église épiscopale', *La Nation*, 31 août 1950.

43 D. Morisseau, 'L'Eglise Episcopale d'Haïti attaquée', *Les Griots*, 15 and 22 avril 1949.

44 See p. 118 above.

45 Duvalier and Denis, 'Société haïtienne: révolution ou évolution', *Les Griots*, 30 janvier 1948.

46 République d'Haïti, Département du Travail, *Actes du premier congrès national du travail*, p. 385.

47 *Ibid.*, pp. 567–8. See also 'il existe le déterminisme social. La sociologie enseigne que les peuples évoluent selon des lois qui semblent emprunter parfois la rigueur des lois de la physique . . .' (Duvalier and Denis, 'Société haïtienne', *Les Griots*, 30 janvier 1948).

48 Duvalier and Denis, 'Climat politique', *Les Griots*, 14 mai 1948.

49 *Les Griots*, 30 janvier 1948.

50 See Duvalier and Denis, *Le problème des classes*, in Duvalier, *Œuvres*, I, pp. 313 and 317.

51 J. D. Baguidy, *Esquisse de sociologie haïtienne*, pp. 13–14.

52 Hervé Boyer, 'L'institut haïtien de crédit agricole et industriel', *Optique*, juin 1954, pp. 22–3.

53 J. L. Déjean, 'Conscience et lutte de classe dans l'histoire d'Haïti', *Flambeau*, 27 février 1947.

54 E. Charlier, 'Politique', *La Nation*, 26 juillet 1950.

55 Charlier, 'Politique', *La Nation*, 23 août 1950; also 29 juillet 1950.
56 Charlier, 'Politique', *La Nation*, 15 and 19 juillet 1950.
57 Charlier, 'Politique', *La Nation*, 21 juillet and 3 août 1950.
58 'A Saint-Domingue et en Haïti, c'est la couleur qui est l'élément désignatif de classe. Mais scientifiquement, ce qui détermine la classe, c'est la statut économique et ce qui forme le contenu de classe, c'est encore le facteur économique et la représentation collective qu'on s'en fait' (E. C. Paul, *Questions d'histoire*, pp. 23–4).
59 *Ibid.*, p. 34.
60 E. Charlier, *En marge de notre 'Aperçu'*, pp. 24 and 39.
61 *Ibid.*, p. 37.
62 *Le Nouvelliste*, 5 janvier 1955.
63 Charlier, *En marge*, pp. 14–15.
64 *Ibid.*, p. 36.
65 R. Depestre, 'Notre Combat', *Flambeau*, 19 octobre 1946.
66 R. Depestre, *Gerb de sang*, p. 49.
67 J. S. Alexis, 'La belle amour humaine, 1957', in *Europe*, janvier 1971, p. 21. This edition of *Europe* contains a number of articles on Alexis.
68 J. S. Alexis, *Compère général Soleil*, p. 34.
69 J. S. Alexis, *Les arbres musiciens*, p. 209.
70 Alexis, 'Debate sobre el folklore', *Casa de las Américas*, 53 (1969), pp. 113ff (originally written in 1956), and 'Of the Marvellous Realism of the Haitians', *Présence Africaine* (English edition), June–November 1956, p. 260; also Alexis, 'Lettre à R. P. Salgado', *Le Nouvelliste*, 6 janvier 1958.
71 Alexis, 'Restons dans le sujet', *Reflets d'Haïti*, 4 février 1956.
72 Alexis, 'Of the Marvellous Realism', p. 271; R. Depestre, 'Introduction à un art poétique haïtien', *Optique*, février 1956, p. 10. For his later views on *négritude* cf. p. 231 below; also Frantz Fanon, *Toward the African Revolution*, p. 17.
73 Alexis, 'Lettre à Jacques Lenoir', *Reflets d'Haïti*, 12 novembre 1955, and Alexis, 'La belle amour', *Europe*, janvier 1971, p. 22.
74 J. Michael Dash, 'Marvellous Realism – the way out of négritude', *Caribbean Studies*, 13:4 (1974), p. 68. On Alexis see also J. M. Dash, *Jacques Stéphen Alexis*. Dash, however, exaggerates the change in Alexis's position between 1946 and 1956, when he writes of a *volte-face* (p. 46). Even in 1946 Alexis was by no means an orthodox Marxist, as Dash himself acknowledges when he refers to his 'violent and anarchistic' position at this time (p. 10).
75 Pp. 88 above.
76 F. Dalencour, *Projet de constitution conforme à la destinée glorieuse du peuple haïtien*, p. 10. Geffrard and Saget were, of course *griffes*, but were very much associated with the mulatto party; see pp. 83ff and 109 above.
77 Dalencour, introduction to Ardouin, *Etudes*, I, p. ii.
78 *Ibid.*, p. i.
79 Dalencour, *Projet*, p. 7.
80 A. Viau, *Toussaint L'Ouverture, considéré à la lumière de ses actes et attitudes*, pp. xi–xiii.

81 *Ibid.*, p. 56. But earlier in this book, as I have noted in the text, Viau listed Dessalines as a follower of Toussaint.

82 A. Viau, *Noirs, mulâtres, blancs, ou rien que du sang*, pp. 19 and 22; yet the author denounced colour prejudice as the cause of all the country's evils and as the pest which devours Haiti, *ibid.*, p. 11.

83 *Ibid.*, pp. 30–1.

84 'Discours', *La Phalange*, 8 novembre 1950; 'Discours', *La Phalange*, 10 novembre 1950.

85 F. E. Roy, 'Christianisme et résignation', *L'Action Social*, 15 décembre 1946.

86 *Indépendance*, 27 avril 1957.

87 *Cohésion*, 12 juillet 1957.

88 For further information on the election campaign of 1956–7 see Clément Célestin, *Compilations pour l'histoire*, I and II; also Bonhomme, pp. 91ff.

89 Duvalier, 'Débats sur la culture,' *Les Griots*, 2 juillet 1948.

90 Duvalier, 'Discours aux Verrettes', *Œuvres*, II, p. 91.

91 Duvalier, 'Discours du Cap', *Œuvres*, II, p. 63; and 'Le discours de Jacmel', *Œuvres*, II, p. 44.

92 Duvalier, 'Le discours de Port-de-Paix, *Œuvres*, II, p. 132, 'Le Dr. Duvalier nous a dit', Duvalier, *Œuvres*, II, p. 230.

93 'Le Dr. Duvalier parle', Duvalier, *Œuvres*, II, p. 115.

94 Cf. Brumaire Louis, who denounced the Roman Catholic church as 'le rideau derrière lequel se perpétue la colonie française de St. Domingue' (*Cohésion*, 17 août 1957); cf. also: 'L'église s'est alliée à la réaction pour faire de Paul Magloire un Chef d'Etat constitutionnel' ('Lettre ouverte à Msgr. Poirier', *Cohésion*, 6 septembre 1957).

95 Duvalier, 'Message à la ville des Gonaïves', *Œuvres*, II, p. 206.

96 Duvalier, 'A Ouanaminthe', *Œuvres*, II, p. 69.

97 Duvalier, 'Message adressé aux populations des arrondissements des Cayes et des Coteaux', *Œuvres*, II, pp. 153ff.

98 Duvalier, 'Message à la nation', *Œuvres*, II, p. 22.

99 Duvalier, 'Le grand discours de la Grand'Anse', *Œuvres*, II, p. 140.

100 Duvalier, 'Dernier discours du Cap-Haïtien', *Œuvres*, II, p. 214.

101 Duvalier, 'Discours de Léogane', *Œuvres*, II, p. 112; cf. also pp. 51 and 207.

102 Duvalier, 'Message du jour de l'an', *Œuvres*, II, p. 51; cf. also pp. 61, 76, 193, 196.

103 'Déclaration de principe', *Panorama*, 27 juillet 1957.

104 Duvalier, 'Discours du Cap', *Œuvres*, II, p. 61; see also p. 200.

105 Duvalier, 'Discours du Limbé', *Œuvres*, II, p. 59.

106 Duvalier, 'Le grand discours de la Grand'Anse,' *Œuvres*, II, p. 137.

107 Duvalier, 'A Fort Liberté', *Œuvres*, II, pp. 67–8.

108 M. Aubourg, 'Bases idéologiques du Parti Unité National', *Panorama*, 20 juillet 1957.

109 J. D. Baguidy, 'Le drame de la bourgeoisie haïtienne', *Panorama*, 14 août 1957; cf. Duvalier, *Œuvres*, II, p. 200.

110 Duvalier, 'Adresse à l'armée d'Haïti,' *Œuvres*, II, p. 49; cf. also pp. 18 and 98.

8. Culture and tyranny (1957–1971)

1 D. Nicholls, 'Embryo-Politics in Haiti', *Government and Opposition*, 6:1 (1971), pp. 75ff; and Nicholls in *Social and Economic Studies*, 22:3 (1973), pp. 303ff.

2 L. F. Manigat, *Haiti of the Sixties, Object of International Concern*, p. 24. R. W. Logan and M. C. Needler (in M. C. Needler (ed.), *Political Systems of Latin America*, p. 159) mistakenly suggest that Haiti under Duvalier became 'as much of a totalitarian state as the under-developed technology at his disposal made possible'.

3 See A. Singham, *The Hero and the Crowd*; T. Munroe, *The Politics of Constitutional Decolonization: Jamaica, 1944–62*; and S. D. Ryan, *Race and Nationalism in Trinidad and Tobago*. René Depestre writes: 'Haití, en efecto, a la hora de Duvalier, es un laboratorio en el que los países recientemente decolonizados pueden estudiar en detalle hasta qué punto nuestras sociedades también son capaces de fabricar barbaridades y monstruos autóctonos . . .' ('Los fundamentos socioculturales de nuestra identidad', *Casa de las Américas*, 58 (1970), pp. 29–30).

4 S. E. Finer, *Comparative Government*, pp. 539–40. Elsewhere Finer recognises that Haiti under Duvalier was not, strictly speaking, a military regime; *ibid.*, pp. 56 and 575, and *The Man on Horseback*, pp. 120–1.

5 For a detailed account of this incident see Célestin, IV.

6 See J. K. Galbraith, *How to Control the Military*, and David Nicholls, 'On Controlling the Colonels', *Hemisphere Report* (Trinidad), July 1970. E. Lieuwen is therefore quite wrong when he suggests that Duvalier's government was an out-and-out military dictatorship, listing Haiti as a country where the armed forces are dominant (*Arms and Politics in Latin America*, p. 290), and where 'civilian elements do not have the power potential to compete seriously with them' (*Generals vs Presidents, Neo-militarism in Latin America*, p. 8). I. L. Horowitz makes the same mistake, when he assumes that Haiti has 'a political military', in S. M. Lipset and A. Solari (eds.), *Elites in Latin America*, p. 148.

7 Duvalier, *Œuvres*, IV, p. 221.

8 *Les Griots*, 3 février 1968.

9 Duvalier, *Mémoires d'un leader du tiers monde*, p. 86.

10 In 1892 Jérémie wrote, 'Chez nous, le mot grève est encore inconnu, les ouvriers ne savent même pas ce que c'est que l'association pour la lutte' (*Haïti indépendant*). Léon Audin wrote twelve years later: 'les grèves sont inconnues. La première, celle des bouchers de Port-au-Prince, qui a duré deux jours et s'est résolue d'elle-même, date de cette année' ('Le culte de la vie en Haïti', *Revue de la Société de Législation*, juin 1904, p. 115).

11 See Doubout and Joly, *Notes sur le développement*, *passim*; J. B. Brutus, 'Aperçu historique du mouvement syndical en Haïti', and M. Brisson, 'Jalons de notre législation ouvrier de 1946 à 1961', both in *Rond Point*, 7 (mai 1963).

12 P. Déjean, 'Panorama actuel de syndicalisme haïtien', *Rond Point*, 7 (mai 1963), p. 25.

13 M. C. Needler, *Political Development in Latin America*, p. 96; cf also Victor Alba, *Politics and the Labor Movement in Latin America*.

14 *New York Times*, 23 October 1957.

15 Duvalier, *Œuvres*, III, pp. 238ff.

16 'Un faux exemple: celui de Porto Rico', *Panorama*, 24 septembre 1962.

17 For details see Manigat, 'La crise Haïtiano-Dominicaine de 1963–4', *Revue Française de Science Politique*, 15 (1965); and R. D. Tomasek, 'The Haitian–Dominican Republic controversy of 1963 and the OAS', *Orbis*, 12 (1968), pp. 294ff.

18 Léonce Viaud, 'A l'occasion du 22 septembre', *Panorama*, 23 septembre 1963.

19 *An address by the President . . . on 31 October 1969*, p. 8.

20 See p. 196 above.

21 See p. 118 above. This was, of course, a familiar argument in European countries as well, employed by Gladstone, Bismarck and others. See David Nicholls, 'Newman, Gladstone and the politics of pluralism', in J. Bastable (ed.), *Newman and Gladstone: Centennial Essays*.

22 *La Phalange*, 15–16 août 1959; this section of the chapter is based on my article 'Politics and Religion in Haiti', *Canadian Journal of Political Science*, 3 (1970), pp. 400ff.

23 *Haïti Journal*, 25 août 1959.

24 P. Blanchet, in *La Phalange*, 25 août 1959.

25 M. Cadet, in *Les Griots*, 31 décembre 1948.

26 F. Poirier, in *La Phalange*, 18 août 1959.

27 P. Halaby, in *La Phalange*, 29 août 1959.

28 *New York Times*, 1 December 1960.

29 *New York Times*, 17 November 1962.

30 Duvalier, *Mémoires*, pp. 53–6.

31 Duvalier, 'Allocution', *Œuvres*, IV, p. 152.

32 Duvalier, *Mémoires*, p. 59.

33 *Ad gentes*, chapter 1.

34 *New York Times*, 25 June 1966 and 28 November 1966.

35 *Caribbean Monthly Bulletin*, May 1967. For further statements of a similar kind from the new hierarchy see 'The Catholic Church in Haiti', *Idoc International*, 6 (1970), pp. 35ff.

36 Duvalier, *Mémoires*, p. 280.

37 Blanchet, *Panorama*, 18, 19 and 21 juin 1969.

38 See Duvalier, 'Message adressé à la nation', *Œuvres*, III, p. 76.

39 République d'Haïti, *Programme révisé et plan d'études de l'enseignement secondaire* (1963).

40 G. Bissainthe, 'Catholicisme et indigénisme', in A. Abble *et al.*, *Des prêtres noirs s'interrogent*, pp. 111ff; but cf. J. Parisot, 'Vodou et christianisme', in the same volume, where the author shows little appreciation of the positive value of Voodoo. The same might be said of J. M. Salgado, *Le culte africain de vaudou et les baptisés en Haïti, passim*.

41 C. Souffrant, 'Un catholicisme de résignation', *Social Compass*, 17 (1970), pp. 425ff. See also Souffrant, 'La foi en Haïti', *Parole et Mission*, 55 (mars 1971). Whether it is proper to write in unqualified terms of the

'fatalism of the Haitian peasant' is doubtful. As our earlier chapters have shown, the peasants have in the past played a vital role in the politics of Haiti, from Goman, Acaau and Salomon, through the *piquets* and *cacos*, to the resistance of Péralte and Batraville. Serge Gilles has recently criticised Père Riou for having referred in his book *Adieu La Tortue* to Haitian peasants as 'resignés'; see Gilles, 'Le phénomène migratoire haïtien', *Haïti Par Etapes*, 3–4 (1975), p. 25.

42   Souffrant, 'Catholicisme et négritude à l'heure du black power', *Présence Africaine*, N.S. 75 (1970), p. 139. Souffrant also insists that the racial factor in Haiti cannot be reduced to other factors but must be accepted *sui generis*: 'Le facteur racial ne se laisse donc pas réduire au facteur social et culturel. Le promotion du Noir, en tant que noir, est un problème spécifique qui requiert des dispositions et des dispositifs particuliers' (*ibid.*, p. 137).

43   L. Hurbon, *Dieu dans le vaudou haïtien, passim*, and also 'Incidence culturelle et politique de christianisme dans les masses haïtiennes', *Présence Africaine*, N.S. 74 (1970), p. 99.

44   Bastien, in H. Courlander and R. Bastien, *Religion and Politics in Haiti*, p. 48; though perhaps the refusal of *houngans* to climb on to the international development bandwagon may not be an entirely bad thing. For Price Mars see p. 155 above.

45   D. Bébel-Gisler and L. Hurbon, *Cultures et pouvoir dans la Caraïbe*, Cf F. Fanon, *A Dying Colonialism*, chapter 1. On Ryo see J.-M. Paré, 'Dimension politique du fait religieux en Haïti', *Nouvelle Optique*, nos. 6–7 (1972), pp. 5ff.

46   Ulrich Saint Louis, Speaker of the House of Representatives, *Ouverture solennelle de la 6ème et dernière session de la 39ème législature*, pp. 16 and 33.

47   Duvalier, *Œuvres*, IV, p. 243.

48   Duvalier, *Hommage au marron inconnu*, pp. 23–4.

49   See pp. 49ff., 54 and 64f.

50   Manigat, *Un fait historique: l'avènement à la présidence d'Haïti du général Salomon*, pp. 30 and 33. In his remarkable review of my monograph on *Economic Dependence* Manigat's legendary position emerges clearly. He actually counts the number of lines which I devoted to the Liberal Edmond Paul and compares it with the number devoted to the National L. J. Janvier. The reason for giving more space to Paul than to Janvier is simply that Paul was a more original and systematic thinker in the field with which I was dealing. My reference to Paul as 'the Lord Snow of nineteenth century Haiti' was by no means intended as a 'flattering epithet' but rather refers to his barbaric attempt to oppose literary to technical education. Manigat's review is printed in *The Caribbean Yearbook of International Relations*, 1975, pp. 521ff.

51   'Le Parti National préconise: Rattachement d'Haïti à une Civilisation noire, en d'autres termes, le retour d'Haïti à l'Afrique' (Saint-Louis, *La présociologie haïtienne*, p. 108). For an extended discussion of this issue see David Nicholls, 'The Wisdom of Salomon: myth or reality?', *Journal of Interamerican Studies*, 20:4 (1978).

52   See pp. 131ff.

53   Antoine, *Lysius Salomon jeune: martyr volontaire de sa classe*, p. xli.

54   *Ibid.*, p. 64.

55   J. Price Mars, *Lettre ouverte au Dr. René Piquion, passim*; Piquion, *Manuel de négritude*, p. 168.

56   Figaro, 'Contrition', *Le Jour*, 19–20 mai 1967.

57   For the original see Duvalier, 'Le grand discours de la Grand'Anse', *Œuvres*, II, p. 137. The reprinted passage, omitting reference to Price Mars, is in *Le docteur François Duvalier le dernier marron . . . s'adresse à la jeunesse de son pays*, pp. 13–14.

58   R. Piquion, *Masques et portraits*, pp. 22ff.

59   R. Depestre, 'Une tâche de sang intellectuelle', *Le Nouvelliste*, 5 mars and 7 mars 1958.

60   J. S. Alexis, 'A propos de la première réunion de la S.A.C.', *Le Nouvelliste*, 26 février 1958.

61   Alexis, 'La main dans le "S.A.C."', *Le Nouvelliste*, 14 mars 1958.

62   *Ibid.*

63   Alexis, 'Va-t'en guerre, en déroute . . . ', *Le Nouvelliste*, 22 mars 1958.

64   Depestre, 'Jean Price Mars et le mythe de l'Orphée noir', *L'Homme et la Société*, 7 (1968), p. 171.

65   *Ibid.*, pp. 173–4.

66   Depestre, 'Les métamorphoses de la négritude en Amérique', *Présence Africaine*: N.S. 75 (1970), pp. 22ff; also Depestre, 'Problemas de la identidad del hombre negro en la literatura antillana', *Casa de las Américas*, 53 (1969), p. 21: 'Este cimarronaje cultural es forma original de rebelión que se ha manifestado en los campos de la religión, del folklore, del arte y, singularmente, en el de las letras antillanas.'

67   R. Depestre, *Un arc-en-ciel pour l'occident chrétien.*

68   Depestre, 'Carta', *Casa de las Américas*, 45 (1967), p. 39.

69   Depestre, 'Lo que pasa en Haití', *Casa de las Américas*, 17–18 (1963), p. 100; also Depestre, 'Jean Price Mars', *L'Homme et la Société*, 7 (1968), p. 176.

70   'Cuba enseña que es posible unificar las fuerzas étnicas de un mismo país en torno a una programa de liberación nacional' (Depestre, 'Carta de Cuba sobre el imperialismo de la mala fé', *Casa de las Américas*, 34 (1966), p. 53).

71   A. G. Petit, *Incidences ethniques de la lutte des classes.* This author has, however, followed a Maoist line, and has attacked Cuban leaders; see Petit, *Castro, Debray contre le marxisme-léninisme.* The Haitian exile journal *Manchette*, published in Belgium, has adopted a similarly pro-Chinese position.

72   Duvalier, 'Message à la Chambre Législative', *Œuvres*, IV, p. 355.

73   Duvalier, *Speech on the Delivery of the Hebrew Translation of 'The Class Problem in the History of Haiti'* (12 janvier 1967), p. 65.

74   G. de Catalogne, *Haïti à l'heure du tiers monde*, p. 52; also de Catalogne, introduction to Duvalier, *Œuvres*, I, pp. 24ff.

75   An example of his political opportunism may be seen in R. Piquion, *L'actualité de Paul E. Magloire.*

76 R. Piquion, *La tactique du double visage, passim*; also Piquion, 'Le mouve-
    ment des Griots', *Nouveau Monde*, 7 juin 1971; 'Entre le négritude et le
    pouvoir noir', *Nouveau Monde*, 11 juin 1971; 'Une rencontre suggestive',
    Nouveau Monde, 18 juin 1973.

77 K. Lévêque, 'L'interpellation mystique dans le discours duvaliérien',
    Nouvelle Optique, 4 (1971), pp. 5ff.

78 Duvalier, 'Important Adresse', *Œuvres*, IV, p. 132; also Duvalier, 'Message',
    Œuvres, III, p. 176; 'Message à la Nation', *Œuvres*, II, p. 200; *Mémoires*,
    p. 313.

79 Duvalier, 'Adresse', *Œuvres*, IV, p. 136; also Duvalier, 'Adresse', *Œuvres*,
    II, p. 172, cf. 'en la personalidad de Trujillo y en el sentido de su obra
    la acumulación de fuerzas transcendentales, casi cósmicas, destinadas
    a satisfacer mandatos ineluctables de la conciencia nacional' (Peña Batlle
    in A. R. Nanita, *Era de Trujillo*, p. 58).

80 R. M. Jean Louis, *Duvalier: sauveur d'Haïti*, pp. 33ff; Préval, 'En guise
    de préface', in Duvalier, *Médaillons*, p. 14.

81 De Catalogne, in Duvalier, *Œuvres*, I, p. 19.

82 Cf. the claim by an early Chaldean king: 'I have mastered the secrets of
    the rivers for the benefit of man . . . I have led the waters of the rivers
    into the wilderness', quoted in G. V. Plekhanov, *Fundamental Problems of
    Marxism*, p. 118 n.

83 J. M. Fourcand, *Catéchisme de la révolution*, pp. 17 and 32.

84 *Ibid.*, p. 37; cf. also the confession of 'Camoquins' (i.e. opponents of
    Duvalier): 'Je confesse à Doc Tout-Puissant, à la charitable Simone
    toujours Bonne, à la Milice Civile, à l'armée populaire, aux cohortes et à
    Vous Duvaliéristes, que j'ai beaucoup péché par pensée, par propagandes
    et par actions clandestines. C'est ma faute! C'est ma faute, c'est ma très
    grande faute! C'est pourquoi je supplie la police du Gouvernement, les
    Tontons-Macoutes, les fillettes Lalo, les Duvaliéristes de prier pour moi
    le Dr. Duvalier Chef de la révolution . . . ' (*ibid.*, p. 38).

85 See Rudolf Rocker, *Nationalism and Culture*, pp. 250ff.

86 H. J. Rosenbaum and P. C. Dederberg, 'The occult and political develop-
    ment', *Comparative Politics*, 4 (1971), pp. 561ff. In certain respects
    General de Gaulle exemplified this tendency.

87 Alex Jean-Paul, *Ode pour célébrer le 60ème anniversaire d'un glorieux
    leader, Dr François Duvalier.*

88 B. Diederich and A. Burt, *Papa Doc: Haiti and Its Dictator*, pp. 354ff.

89 The *noiriste* Janvier, for example, assumed that it was Christophe who
    first adopted the black and red, and he showed little interest in returning
    to this flag ('Le drapeau haïtien', *Haïti littéraire et Sociale*, 20 mai 1907,
    pp. 1397ff).

90 A. Holly ('Her-Ra-Me-El'), *Dra-Po*, pp. 31ff. For more on Holly see p. 154
    above.

91 Aubourg, 'Le drapeau dessalinien', *Revue de la Société Haïtienne d'Histoire,
    de Géographie et de Géologie*, 104 (1957), pp. 7ff. For a note on the colour
    of the first Haitian flag cf. chapter 2, note 2, p. 264.

92 Report of Debate on 12 December 1957, in *Revue de la Société Haïtienne*,
    104 (1957), p. 30.

93 Duvalier, 'Message', *Œuvres*, III, p. 67.
94 Duvalier, in *Ultime hommage au président Dumarsais Estimé*.
95 Duvalier, *Hommage au marron inconnu*, p. 56.
96 *Ibid.*, p. 52.
97 Cf. Duvalier, *Œuvres*, IV, pp. 307ff.
98 Duvalier, *Speech on the Delivery of the Hebrew Translation*, p. 64; cf. also *Les Griots*, 3 février 1968: 'Je suis venu non point comme un politicien . . .'
99 U. Pierre-Louis, *La révolution duvaliériste*, pp. 26 and 33.
100 H. L. Charles, *La révolution duvaliériste et la compréhension des masses*, pp. 26–7.
101 *Panorama*, 30–31 mars 1962; cf. also Duvalier, 'Message', *Œuvres*, III, p. 167.
102 Duvalier, 'Nouvelle Proclamation', *Œuvres*, III, p. 88.
103 See p. 109 above.
104 It is not entirely accurate to see Duvalier and his collaborator Denis as the spokesmen of the old northern black elite, as Rémy Anselme does, 'Le phénomène Duvalier: sa signification', *Acoma*, nos. 4–5 (avril 1973), p. 137. This is, however, a generally perceptive and balanced account of Duvalierism.

9. Conclusion

1 See David Nicholls ('An Observer'), 'Dynastic republicanism in Haiti', *The Political Quarterly*, 44:1 (1973), pp. 77ff, and David Nicholls, 'Poorest nation of the western world', *The Geographical Magazine*, 50:1 (October 1977), pp. 47ff.
2 For Haitian migrants in the U.S.A. see Claude Souffrant, 'Les haïtiens aux Etats-Unis', *Population*, mars 1974, pp. 133ff, and 'La situation dramatique de quelques haïtiens à New York', *Présence Haïtienne*, 1 (août 1975), pp. 38ff. Also there are a number of journals concerned with Haitian exiles in the U.S.A., including *Haïti Observateur, Sel, Lakansiel*. For Haitians in Canada see Emerson Douyon, 'Les immigrants haïtiens à Montréal', 'Migration Symposium' in *Proceedings of the 34th Annual Meeting of the Society for Applied Anthropology*, Amsterdam, 1975. For Haitians in France see R. Bastide *et al., Les haïtiens en France*, and for Martinique see 'Expulsion d'haïtiennes en Martinique', *Présence Haïtienne*, 1 (août 1975), p. 33. For Haitians in the Bahamas see Dawn Marshall, 'The Haitian Problem' (MSc thesis, Geography Faculty, University of the West Indies, Jamaica, 1974). For Haitians in the Dominican Republic see Frank Marino Hernández, *La inmigración haitiana*, Isis Duarte *et al., Inmigración haitiana y producción azucarera en la República Dominicana*, and A. Díaz Santana, 'The role of Haitian *braceros* in Dominican sugar production', *Latin American Perspectives*, 8 (winter 1976), pp. 120ff. More generally, see Serge Gilles, 'Le phénomène migratoire haïtien', *Haïti par Etapes*, 3–4 (1975), pp. 24ff.
3 Institut Haïtien de Statistique, *Guide économique de la République d'Haïti*, décembre 1971.

4 See David Nicholls, 'Caste, Class and Colour in Haiti', in Clarke, pp. 10ff.

5 Mesmin Gabriel, *Conscience de soi du nègre dans la culture*, for Holly see p. 154 above.

6 J. Lamartinière, *Le noirisme*, pp. 23 and 26.

7 See particularly Franck Etienne, *Ultravocal* and *Dézafi*, and J.-C. Fignolé, *Pour une poésie de l'authentique et du solidaire*.

8 C. Souffrant, 'La religion du paysan haïtien', *Social Compass*, 19:4 (1972), pp. 585ff, and 'Une catholicisme de resignation', *Social Compass*, 17:3 (1970), pp. 425ff; Hurbon, *Dieu dans le vaudou haïtien*, and Bébel-Gisler and Hurbon, *Cultures et pouvoir*.

9 Bébel-Gisler and Hurbon, pp. 29 and 112–5.

10 P. Laraque, 'Politique et culture', *Présence Haïtienne*, 2 (septembre 1975), p. 37.

11 J.-J. Honorat, *Enquête sur le développement*, p. 223.

12 Ryan, p. 422.

13 Honorat, p. 151.

14 See for example W. G. Demas, *Change and Renewal in the Caribbean*, pp. 1ff. The idea is, of course, present also in the writings of Che Guevara: 'To build communism a new man must be created' (*Socialism and Man in Cuba and Other Works*, p. 9). See also F. Fanon, *The Wretched of the Earth*, p. 30.

15 C. Manigat *et al.*, *Haïti: quel développement?*, chapters 3 and 4.

16 Leslie Manigat refers proudly to his uncle and to his grandfather in a recent political manifesto, though he fails to mention François Manigat, one of the black generals who sided with Pétion against Christophe in 1806! ('Interview-Radioscopie', *Présence Haïtienne*, 4 (novembre–decembre 1975), p. 6).

17 I am thinking in this paragraph particularly of Gérard Pierre-Charles, Jean Luc and the writers associated with the now-defunct journal *Nouvelle Optique*.

18 G. Pierre-Charles, *Radiografía de una dictadura*, p. 103.

19 Fanon, *The Wretched of the Earth*, pp. 31ff.

20 Cf. J. S. Furnivall, *Colonial Policy and Practice*, and M. G. Smith, *The Plural Society in the British West Indies*; I have discussed the concept of a plural society in David Nicholls, *Three Varieties of Pluralism*, chapter 4.

21 There are, however, a number of occasions when national pride or misguided altruism have led to such acquisitions.

22 For recent considerations of such dependent economies see C. Y. Thomas, *Dependence and Transformation*, and J. R. Mandle, *The Plantation Economy, Population and Economic Change in Guyana 1838–1960*.

23 David Nicholls, 'Caste, Class and Colour in Haiti', in Colin Clarke, p. 11; and David Nicholls ('An Observer'), 'Dynastic Republicanism in Haiti', *The Political Quarterly*, 44:1 (1973), pp. 77ff.

24 Examples of such work are to be found in the region of Laborde, directed by Père Ryo, and in the region of Chardonniers and Les Anglais, sponsored by the Oblates of Mary. For a rather hostile critique of Ryo's work, see Jean-Michel Paré, 'Dimension politique de fait religieux en Haïti', *Nouvelle Optique*, nos. 6–7 (avril–septembre 1972)), pp. 5ff.

25 See David Nicholls, *The Pluralist State*, pp. 119ff.

26 A. W. Singham (ed.), *The Commonwealth Caribbean into the Seventies*, pp. xiff. For Stone see 'Urban Social Movements in Post-War Jamaica', in *ibid.*, pp. 71ff, and C. Stone, *Electoral Behaviour and Public Opinion in Jamaica*, pp. 34ff.

27 Fanon, *The Wretched of the Earth*, p. 123. This cult became totally laughable one year in Trinidad when the victor in the People's National Movement 'Buy Local' Carnival Queen competition was 'Miss Texaco'!

28 For example Munroe, pp. 185ff, and L. Lindsay, *The Myth of Independence: Middle Class Politics and Non-mobilization in Jamaica*, pp. 5ff.

29 Fanon, *The Wretched of the Earth*, pp. 67 and 73.

30 *Ibid.*, pp. 73 and 117.

31 *Ibid.*, p. 73.

32 *Ibid.*, pp. 74 and 117. See also Fanon, *Toward the African Revolution* and *A Dying Colonialism*.

33 F. Engels, *On Authority* (1874), in Marx and Engels, *Selected Works*, I. p. 578.

34 Firmin, *Monsieur Roosevelt*, p. 294.

35 M. B. Bird, *The Black Man, or Haytian Independence Deduced from Historical Notes*, p. 406.

36 See especially F. Barth (ed.), *Ethnic Groups and Boundaries: The Social Organisation of Cultural Difference*; and N. Glazer and D. P. Moynihan (eds.), *Ethnicity: Theory and Experience*. The theoretical section of Orlando Patterson's contribution to the latter volume (pp. 305ff), for example, is a tissue of confusion. He defines ethnicity as a condition in which 'certain members of a society' emphasise as 'their most meaningful basis of primary extrafamilial identity certain cultural, national or somatic traits' (p. 308). This implies that if, in a particular context, an East Boston Italian construction worker considers his economic class as the most meaningful primary allegiance, ethnicity is totally absent from the situation; but this is clearly not always so (as Patterson realises, p. 311). Ethnicity may well be a *secondary* but important factor influencing the man's actions. On p. 307 Patterson states that a Jamaican while in Jamaica is 'not a member of any ethnic group', because he is an elite member of the dominant group, while on p. 309 n. he suggests that a Frenchman in France (presumably even an elite Frenchman) should be thought of as belonging both to the French nation (he presumably means state) and to the French ethnic group, even though this is the largest ethnic group in France. (Patterson in fact states that, in the case of France, ethnic group coincides with nation, which is bad news for the Bretons and Basques.) If by a 'nation' he means something other than a state – a legally defined entity – it is not clear what he does mean. His reference to 'the view that a nation is or should be a community of people sharing a common history and "blood"' (p. 309) only adds to the confusion. Does he mean 'is' or 'should be'? If the former, then we have simply a definition of the nation in terms of ethnicity; but in calling this 'view' 'a peculiar product of modern political thought' he appears to be referring to the nationalist dogma that state boundaries should follow national (i.e. ethnic) boundaries. In which case 'nation' clearly means 'state'.

37   M. Hechter, 'The Political Economy of Ethnic Change', *American Journal of Sociology*, 79:5 (1974), pp. 1154ff.

38   The words are taken from Hechter, who does not, however, make precisely the assertion which I am criticising in the text. He rightly insists that we ought not to equate ethnic solidarity with such primordial sentiment, but fails to consider what role this sentiment plays in the development of ethnic solidarity (Hechter, 'The Political Economy of Ethnic Change', p. 1177).

39   Sidney Mintz is right when he writes: 'color . . . is not salient in Haiti in the way it is in a truly racist society like the United States' (*Caribbean Transformations*, p. 283). Colour is, however, *more salient* in Haiti among non-whites than it is among negroes in the United States.

Bibliography

Note: The following bibliography does not purport to be a full list of books on Haiti or by Haitians, but lists the works quoted or referred to in this book. I give the date of the edition which I have used, and where significant the date of the first edition. The fullest bibliography of Haitian works is that of Max Bissainthe, *Dictionnaire de bibliographie haïtienne* (Washington D.C., 1951), with an appendix published in Washington D.C. in 1973. This work contains a comprehensive list of Haitian periodicals with details of the dates of publication. Reference should also be made to Ulrich Duvivier, *Bibliographie générale et méthodique d'Haïti* (Port-au-Prince, 1941). There is a useful (though incomplete) running bibliography in *Caribbean Studies*. The libraries which I have used are:

Bibliothèque St Louis de Gonzague, Port-au-Prince
Bibliothèque Edmond Mangonès, Pétionville
Bibliothèque Jean Price Mars, Delmas
Bibliothèque de l'Etat Major, Port-au-Prince
The British Library, London
Foreign and Commonwealth Office Library, London
Bodleian Library, Oxford
Bibliothèque Nationale, Paris
New York Public Library, including Schomburg Collection
Boston Public Library
Harvard University Library, Cambridge, Mass.

Abble, A., *et al.*, *Des prêtres noirs s'interrogent*, Paris, 1957
Acosta, Mercedes, *et al.*, *Imperialismo y clases sociales en el Caribe*, Buenos Aires, 1973
Acton, J. E. E. D., *The History of Freedom*, London, 1907
Adams, R. N., *et al.*, *Social Change in Latin America Today*, New York, 1960
Adresse du gouvernement d'Haïti au commerce des nations neutres, London, 1806
Alaux, G. d', *L'empereur Soulouque et son empire*, Paris, 1856
Alba, Victor (Pedro Pages), *Politics and the Labor Movement in Latin America*, Stanford, 1968
Alexis, Jacques Stéphen, *Les arbres musiciens*, Paris, 1957
    Compère général Soleil, Paris, 1955
Alexis, Stéphen, *Le nègre masqué*, Port-au-Prince, 1933
Althusser, Louis, *Lenin and Philosophy and Other Essays*, English translation by Ben Brewster; London, 1971
'Amicus', *Réflexions sur la crise agricole, commerciale et financière d'Haïti*, Paris, 1882

'Amicus Mundi', *Defence of the Colonies*, London, 1816

Antoine, Max A., *Lysius Salomon jeune: martyr volontaire de sa classe*, Port-au-Prince, 1968

Ardouin, (Alexis) Beaubrun, *Etudes sur l'histoire d'Haïti suivies de la vie du général J.-M. Borgella*, Port-au-Prince, 1958; first published in Paris, 1853–60

Géographie de l'île d'Haïti, Port-au-Prince, 1832

Réponse du Sénateur B. Ardouin à une lettre de M. Isambert, Port-au-Prince, 1842

Ardouin, C. N. Céligni, *Essais sur l'histoire d'Haïti*, Port-au-Prince, 1865

Arriola, J. L. (ed.), *Integración social en Guatemala*, Guatemala City, 1956

Audin, Léon, *Le mal d'Haïti*, Port-au-Prince, 1908

Auguste, Jules, *Quelques vérités à propos des récents événements de la République d'Haïti*, Paris, 1891

Auguste, Jules, *et al.*, *Les détracteurs de la race noire et de la république d'Haïti*, Paris, 1882

Augustin, Rémy, *Cantiques pour la campagne anti-superstitieuse*, Port-au-Prince, 1942

Bagú, S., *Economía de la sociedad colonial: ensayo de la historia comparada de América Latina*, Buenos Aires, 1949

Baguidy, Joseph D., *Esquisse de sociologie haïtienne*, Port-au-Prince, n.d.

Barth, F. (ed.), *Ethnic Groups and Boundaries: The Social Organisation of Cultural Difference*, Bergen and Oslo, 1969

Bastable, J. (ed.), *Newman and Gladstone: Centennial Essays*, Dublin, 1978

Bastide, Roger, Morin, F., and Raveau, F., *Les haïtiens en France*, The Hague, 1974

Bébel-Gisler, Dany, and Hurbon, Laënnec, *Cultures et pouvoir dans la Caraïbe*, Paris, 1975

Belaunde, V. A., *Bolivar and the Political Thought of the Spanish-American Revolution*, New York, 1967

Bell, H. H. (ed.), *Black Separatism and the Caribbean, 1860*, Ann Arbor, 1970. This volume contains tracts by J. T. Holly and J. D. Harris

Bellegarde, Dantès, *Ecrivains haïtiens*, Port-au-Prince, 1950

Un haïtien parle, Port-au-Prince, 1934

La résistance haïtienne, Montreal, 1937

Bird, Mark B., *The Black Man, or Haytian Independence Deduced from Historical Notes*, New York, 1869

Bissette, C. A., *Réfutation du livre de M. V. Schoelcher sur Haïti*, Paris, 1844

Blanchet, Jules, *Peint par lui-même, ou la résistance de Mr. Dantès Bellegarde*, Port-au-Prince, 1936

Blanchet, Jules, and Piquion, René, *Essais sur la culture*, Port-au-Prince, n.d. (c. 1936)

Bobo, Rosalvo, *Voies de réforme*, Cap Haïtien, 1910

Bolt, Christine, *Victorian Attitudes to Race*, London, 1971

Bonhomme, Colbert, *Révolution et contre-révolution en Haïti*, Port-au-Prince, 1957

Bonnet, Edmond, *Souvenirs historiques de G.-J. Bonnet*, Paris, 1864

Bord, G., *La franc-maçonnerie en France des origines à 1815*, Paris, 1908

Bosch, Juan, *De Cristóbal Colón a Fidel Castro*, Madrid, 1970

Bouvet de Cressé, A. J. B., *Histoire de la catastrophe de Saint-Domingue*, Paris, 1824

Bouzon, Justin, *Etudes historiques sur la présidence de Faustin Soulouque*, Port-au-Prince and Paris, 1894

Bowler, Arthur, *Une conférence sur Haïti*, Paris, 1888

Boyer, Jean-Pierre, *Proclamation au peuple et à l'armée*, Port-au-Prince, 1822

Bradley, F. H., *Collected Essays*, Oxford, 1935

Brierre, Jean F., *Nous garderons le dieu*, Port-au-Prince, 1945

British and Foreign State Papers, 1862–3 (vol. 53), London, 1868

Brouard, Carl, *Pages retrouvées*, Port-au-Prince, 1963

Brown, Jonathan, *The History and Present Condition of St. Domingo*, Philadelphia, 1837

Burrow, John W., *Evolution and Society*, Cambridge, 1966

Butterfield, Herbert, *The Whig Interpretation of History*, London, 1931

Cabon, A., *Monsignor A.-J. M. Guilloux*, Port-au-Prince, 1929

Notes sur l'histoire religieuse d'Haïti de la révolution au concordat (1789–1860), Port-au-Prince, 1933

Calixte, Démosthènes Pétrus, *Haïti: le calvaire d'un soldat*, New York, 1939

Campagne anti-superstitieuse: documentation, Cap Haïtien, 1941

Candler, J., *Brief Notices of Hayti*, London, 1842

Caplain, Jules, *La France en Haïti*, Paris, 1905

Carmichael, A. C., *Domestic Manners and Social Condition of the White, Coloured and Negro Population of the West Indies*, London 1833

Carpentier, Alejo, *Ecué-Yamba-O*, Madrid, 1933

Casseus, A., *Du rôle civilisateur de la race noire*, Paris, 1911

Castonnet des Fosses, H. L., *La perte d'une colonie: la révolution de Saint-Domingue*, Paris, 1893

Castor, Suzy, *La ocupación norteamericana de Haití y sus consecuencias (1915–1934)*, Madrid and Buenos Aires, 1971

Catalogne, Gérard de, *Haïti à l'heure du tiers monde*, Port-au-Prince, 1964

Haïti devant son destin, Port-au-Prince, n.d.

Notre révolution, Montreal, 1943–5

Célestin, Clément, *Compilations pour l'histoire*, 4 vols., Port-au-Prince, 1958–60

Césaire, Aimé, *Toussaint Louverture*, Paris, 1962

Chancy, Emmanuel, *L'indépendance nationale d'Haïti*, Paris, 1884

Chanlatte, F. D., *Appel aux haytiens, ou riposte à l'attaque impreuve de la cour royale de Bordeaux et de Mr. Martignac, avocat*, Port-au-Prince, 1817

Chanlatte, Juste, *Le cri de la nature*, Cap Haïtien, 1810

Charles, H. L., *La révolution duvaliériste et la compréhension des masses*, Port-au-Prince, 1962

Charlier, Etienne, *Aperçu sur la formation historique de la nation haïtienne*, Port-au-Prince, 1954

En marge de notre 'Aperçu', Port-au-Prince, 1955

Charmant, Alcius, *Haïti: vivra-t-elle?* Le Havre, 1905

Chatelain, Joseph, *La banque nationale*, Port-au-Prince, 1954

Chevalier, Michel, *The Labour Question*, London, 1848

Clarke, Colin (ed.), *Caribbean Social Relations*, Liverpool, 1978
Cohen, David W., and Greene, J. P., (eds.), *Neither Slave nor Free: The Freedmen of African Descent in the Slave Societies of the New World*, Baltimore and London, 1972
Cole, Hubert, *Christophe: King of Haiti*, London, 1967
Coleridge, Samuel Taylor, *On the Constitution of the Church and State According to the Idea of Each*, edited by John Barrell, London, 1972
Colombel, Noel, *Examen d'un pamphlet ayant pour titre: 'Essai sur les causes de la révolution et des guerres civiles d'Haïti, etc.'*, Port-au-Prince, 1819
Réflexions sur quelques faits relatifs à notre existence politique, Port-au-Prince, 1818
'Colombus', *Réponse à l'écrit de M. H. Henry*, Port-au-Prince, 1814
Cornevin, Robert, *Le théâtre haïtien des origines à nos jours*, Montreal, 1973
Correspondence Relative to the Emigration to Hayti of the Free People of Color in the United States, New York, 1824
Correspondencia de Levasseur y de otros agentes de Francia relativa a la proclamación de la República Dominicana, 1843–1844, Ciudad Trujillo, D.R., 1944
Coulthard, G. R., *Race and Colour in Caribbean Literature*, London, 1962
Courlander, Harold, and Bastien, R., *Religion and Politics in Haiti*, Washington D.C., 1966
Cox, Oliver C., *Caste, Class and Race*, New York, 1970; first published 1948
Crossman, Richard (ed.), *The God that Failed*, New York, 1950
Curtin, Philip D., *Two Jamaicas*, New York, 1970
Dalencour, François, *La croisée des chemins*, Port-au-Prince, 1926
Essai d'une synthèse de sociologie économique, Paris, 1937
Pétion devant l'humanité: Alexandre Pétion et Simon Bolivar, Port-au-Prince, n.d.
Philosophie de la liberté, Paris, 1953
Précis méthodique d'histoire d'Haïti, Port-au-Prince, 1935
Principes d'éducation nationale, Port-au-Prince, 1925
Projet de constitution conforme à la destinée glorieuse du peuple haïtien, Port-au-Prince, 1946
Le sauvetage national par le retour à la terre, Port-au-Prince, 1923
David, Placide, *L'héritage colonial en Haïti*, Madrid, 1959
Dash, J. Michael, *Jacques Stéphen Alexis*, Toronto, 1975
Debbasch, Yvan, *Couleur et liberté, vol. I: l'affranchi dans les possessions françaises de la Caraïbe*, Paris, 1967
Debien, Gabriel, *Les colons de Saint-Domingue et la révolution: essai sur le Club Massiac (août 1789–août 1792)*, Paris, 1953
Les esclaves aux Antilles françaises, Basse-Terre, Guadeloupe, 1974
Esprit colon et esprit d'autonomie à Saint-Domingue au XVIIIᵉ siècle, Paris, 1954
Delafosse, Maurice, *Les frontières de la Côte d'Ivoire, de la Côte d'Or et du Soudan*, Paris, 1908
Haut-Sénégal-Niger, Paris, 1912
The Negroes of Africa, Port Washington, N.Y., 1968; English translation of *Les noirs d'Afrique*, Paris, 1922

Delienne, Castera, *Souvenirs d'épopée*, Port-au-Prince, 1935
Delorme, Demesvar, *La misère au sein des richesses: réflexions divers sur Haïti*, Paris, 1873
    La reconnaissance du général Salnave, Paris, 1868
    La voie, no publication details and published anonymously
Delva, A. de, *Considérations sur l'armée haïtienne*, Paris, 1867
Demas, W. G., *Change and Renewal in the Caribbean*, Barbados, 1975
Depestre, Edouard, *La faillité d'une démocratie 1889–1915*, Port-au-Prince, 1916
Depestre, René, *Un arc-en-ciel pour l'occident chrétien*, Paris, 1967
    Etincelles, Port-au-Prince, 1945
    Gerb de sang, Port-au-Prince, n.d.
Desmangles, C., *Des étrangers en Haïti*, Port-au-Prince, 1841
Dévot, Justin, *Considérations sur l'état mental de la société haïtienne*, Paris, 1901
    Cours élémentaire d'instruction civique et d'éducation patriotique, Paris, 1894
Diederich, Bernard, and Burt, A., *Papa Doc: Haiti and its Dictator*, London, 1969
Diop, Cheik Anta, *L'unité culturelle de l'Afrique noire*, Paris, 1959
    Nations nègres et culture, Paris, 1954
Dorsainvil, J. B., *De la démocratie représentative: histoire et principes*, Port-au-Prince, 1900
    Essai sur l'histoire de l'établissement des institutions et des mœurs de Saint-Domingue, Port-au-Prince, 1892
    Précis d'histoire d'Haïti, Port-au-Prince, 1894
Dorsainvil, Justin Chrysostome, *L'échec d'hier et l'effort pour l'avenir*, Port-au-Prince, 1915
    Militarisme et hygène sociale, Port-au-Prince, 1909
    Organisons nos partis politiques, Port-au-Prince, 1925
    Quelques vues politiques et morales, Port-au-Prince, 1934
    Vôdou et magie, Port-au-Prince, 1937
    Vôdou et névrose, Port-au-Prince, 1931; first published in *Haïti Médicale*, 1913
Doubout, J. J., and Joly, U., *Notes sur le développement du mouvement syndical en Haïti*, n.p., 1974
Duarte, Isis, *et al.*, *Inmigración haitiana y producción azucarera en la República Dominicana*, Santo Domingo, D. R., 1976
Dubois, F. E., *Précis historique de la révolution haïtienne de 1843*, Paris, 1866.
Dubois, W. E. B., *Darkwater: Voices from within the Veil*, New York, 1969
Dumesle, Hérard, *Voyage dans le nord d'Haïti*, Port-au-Prince, 1824
Dupuy, J.-B., *Deuxième lettre à M. H. Henry*, Cap Henry, 1814
Durkheim, Emile, *Elementary Forms of the Religious Life*, New York, 1965
    Socialism, New York, 1962
Duvalier, François, *Hommage au martyr de la non-violence*, Port-au-Prince, 1968
    Hommage au marron inconnu, Port-au-Prince, 1969
    Le docteur François Duvalier le dernier marron, président à vie de la république, s'adresse à la jeunesse de son pays, Port-au-Prince, 1967
    Médaillons, Port-au-Prince, 1968 (written under the pseudonym 'Abderrahman')
    Mémoires d'un leader du tiers monde, Paris, 1969
    Œuvres essentielles, 4 vols., Port-au-Prince; vol. I, 1966 (3rd edition 1968), vol. II, 1966, vol. III, 1967, vol. IV, 1967

Speech on the Delivery of the Hebrew Translation of 'The Class Problem in the History of Haiti' (12 janvier 1967), Port-au-Prince, 1967

E.M., *Haïti et Cuba, conséquences de la guerre américano-espagnole*, Port-au-Prince, 1898

Edouard, Emmanuel, *Essai sur la politique intérieure d'Haïti*, Paris, 1890
Le panthéon haïtien, Paris, 1885
Solution de la crise industrielle française, Paris, 1884

Edwards, Bryan, *An Historical Survey of the French Colony in the Island of St. Domingo*, London, 1797

Elicona, A. L., *Un colonial sous la révolution en France et en Amérique, Moreau de Saint-Méry*, Paris, 1934

Elkins, Stanley, *Slavery*, Chicago, 1959

Emmanuel, I. S. and S. A., *History of the Jews of the Netherlands Antilles*, Cincinnati, 1970

Esmangart, Charles, *Des colonies françaises et en particulier de l'île de Saint Domingue*, Paris, l'an X (1801–2)

Etienne, Franck, *Dézafi*, Port-au-Prince, 1975
Ultravocal, Port-au-Prince, 1972

Fanon, Frantz, *A Dying Colonialism*, New York, 1967
Toward the African Revolution, New York, 1967
The Wretched of the Earth, New York, 1963

Faubert, Pierre, *Ogé, ou le préjugé de couleur*, Paris, 1856

Fernandez Callejas, R., *Historia de la franc-masonería en Cuba*, Havana, 1944

Féry, Alibée, *Essais littéraires*, Port-au-Prince, 1876

Fignolé, Daniel, *Mon mandat*, Port-au-Prince, 1954

Fignolé, Jean-Claude, *Pour une poésie de l'authentique et du solidaire*, Port-au-Prince, 1974

Finer, S. E., *Comparative Government*, Harmondsworth, 1974; first published 1970
The Man on Horseback, Harmondsworth, 1975

Finot, J., *Préjugé de race*, Paris, 1905

Firmin, (Joseph) Anténor, *De l'égalité des races humaines*, Paris, 1885
Haïti au point de vue politique, administratif et économique, Paris, 1891
Lettre ouverte aux membres de la Société de Législation, Basse-Terre, Guadeloupe, 1904
Lettres de Saint Thomas, Paris, 1910
Monsieur Roosevelt, président des Etats Unis, et la république d'Haïti, New York and Paris, 1905

Fleischmann, Ulrich, *Ecrivain et société en Haïti*, Fonds St Jacques, Martinique, 1976
Ideologie und Wirklichkeit in der Literatur Haitis, Berlin 1969

Foner, L., and Genovese, E. (eds.), *Slavery in the New World: a Reader in Comparative History*, Englewood Cliffs, N.J., 1969

Fordham, Monroe, *Major Themes in Northern Black Religious Thought, 1800–1860*, Hicksville, N.Y., 1975

Fouchard, Jean, *Langue et littérature des aborigènes d'Ayti*, Paris, 1972
Marrons de la liberté, Paris, 1972
Les marrons du syllabaire, Port-au-Prince, 1953

Plaisirs de Saint-Domingue, Port-au-Prince, 1955

Fourcand, Jean M., *Catéchisme de la révolution*, Port-au-Prince, 1964

Franco Pichado, F. J., *Los negros, los mulatos y la nación dominicana*, Santo Domingo, D. R. 1969

Franco y Ferrán, J. L., *Revoluciones y conflictos internacionales en el Caribe, 1789--1854*, Havana, 1965

Frank, A. G., *Capitalism and Underdevelopment in Latin America*, Harmondsworth, 1971

Latin America: Underdevelopment or Revolution, New York, 1969

Franklin, James, *The Present State of Hayti*, London, 1828

Franklin, John H. (ed.), *Color and Race*, New York, 1968

Freyre, G., *The Masters and the Slaves*, New York, 1946

New World in the Tropics, New York, 1963

Frostin, Charles, *Les révoltes blanches à Saint-Domingue aux XVIIe et XVIIIe siècles*, Paris, 1975

Furnivall, J. S., *Colonial Policy and Practice*, Cambridge, 1948

Gabriel, Mesmin, *Conscience de soi du nègre dans la culture*, Port-au-Prince, 1973

Gaillard, Roger, *Les blancs débarquent, 1914–1915: les cent-jours de Rosalvo Bobo*, Port-au-Prince, 1973

La destinée de Carl Brouard, Port-au-Prince, 1966

Etzer Vilaire: témoin de nos malheurs, Port-au-Prince, 1972

L'univers romanesque de Jacques Roumain, Port-au-Prince, 1965

Galbraith, John K., *How to Control the Military*, New York, 1969

García Calderón, F., *Latin America: Its Rise and Progress*, London, 1907

Garran-Coulon, J. P., *Rapport sur les troubles de Saint-Domingue fait au nom de la Commission des Colonies, des Comités de Salut public, de Législation et de Marine réunis*, Paris, l'an IV–l'an V (1796).

Garrett, Naomi, *The Renaissance of Haitian Poetry*, Paris, 1963

Garrido, Victor, *Política de Francia en Santo Domingo, 1844–1846*, Santo Domingo, D.R., 1962

Gayot, Gérard, *Clergé indigène*, Port-au-Prince, 1956

Geiss, Imanuel, *The Pan-African Movement*, London, 1974; English translation by A. E. Kemp of *Panafricanismus. Zur Geschichte der Dekolonisation*, Frankfurt, 1968

Genovese, E. D., *In Red and Black*, New York, 1972

Georges Jacob, Kléber, *Contribution à l'étude de l'homme haïtien*, Port-au-Prince, 1946

L'ethnie haïtienne, Port-au-Prince, 1941

De la gérontocratie en Haïti, Paris, 1860

Girod, François, *De la société créole (Saint Domingue au 18e siècle)*, Paris, 1972

Gisler, A., *L'esclavage aux Antilles françaises*, Fribourg, 1965

Glazer, Nathan, and Moynihan, D. P. (eds.), *Ethnicity: Theory and Experience*, Cambridge, Mass., 1975

Gobineau, J. A. de, *The Inequality of the Human Races*, London, 1915; English translation by A. Collins of *Essai sur l'inégalité des races humaines*, Paris, 1853–5

Gouraige, Ghislain, *La diaspora d'Haïti et l'Afrique*, Ottawa, 1974

Histoire de la littérature haïtienne, Port-au-Prince, 1961
Gramsci, Antonio, *Selections from the Prison Notebooks*, English translation by
    Q. Hoare and G. Nowell-Smith; London, 1971
Grellier, Roche, *Abrège de l'histoire d'Haïti à l'usage des écoles primaires*, Paris,
    1893
    Etudes économiques sur Haïti, Paris, 1891
    Haïti: la politique à suivre, Paris, 1892
    Haïti: son passé, son avenir, Paris, 1891
    Histoire d'Haïti à l'usage des écoles, vol. I, Paris, 1893
Griggs, E. L., and Prator, C. H. (eds.), *Henry Christophe and Thomas Clarkson*,
    New York, 1968
Guevara, Ernesto Che, *Che Guevara Speaks*, New York, 1968
    Socialism and Man in Cuba and Other Works, London, 1968
Guizot, F. P. G., *Histoire de la civilisation en Europe depuis la chute de l'empire
    romain jusqu'en 1789*, Paris, 1829–32
Hanna, S. W., *Notes of a Visit to Some Parts of Haiti: Jan.–Feb. 1835*. London,
    1836
Harris, Marvin, *Patterns of Race in the Americas*, New York, 1964
Harvey, W. W., *Sketches of Hayti from the Expulsion of the French to the Death
    of Christophe*, London, 1827
Heer, N. W., *Politics and History in the Soviet Union*, Cambridge, Mass., 1971
Hegel, Georg Wilhelm Friedrich, *Philosophy of Mind*, English translation by W.
    Wallace and A. V. Miller; Oxford, 1971
    Philosophy of Right, English translation by T. M. Knox; Oxford, 1942
    Political Writings, English translation by T. M. Knox; Oxford, 1964
Hepburn, R. S. E., *Haiti as it is*, Kingston, Jamaica, 1861
Hérard, Charles, *Proclamation*, Port-au-Prince, 1843
    Proclamation au peuple et à l'armée, Port-au-Prince, 1844
Herrera, César A., *Las finanzas de la República Dominicana*, Ciudad Trujillo,
    D. R., 1955
Higman, Barry, *Slave Population and Economy in Jamaica 1807–1834*, Cambridge,
    1977
Hilliard d'Auberteuil, M. R., *Considérations sur l'état présent de la colonie française
    de Saint Domingue*, Paris, 1776–7
    Du commerce des colonies, ses principes et ses lois, n.p., 1785
Hoetink, H., *El pueblo dominicano 1850–1900*, Santiago, D.R., 1972
    Slavery and Race Relations in the Americas, New York, 1973
    Caribbean Race Relations: a Study of Two Variants, London, 1967
Hoffmann, L. F., *Le nègre romantique*, Paris, 1973
Holly, Arthur, *Les daïmons du culte voudo*, Port-au-Prince, 1918–19
    *Dra-Po: étude ésotérique de Egregore africain, traditionnel, social et national
    d'Haïti*, Port-au-Prince, 1928 (written under the pseudonym 'Her-Ra-
    Me-El')
    Rapport entre l'instruction, la psychologie et l'état social, Port-au-Prince,
    1921
Honorat, Jean-Jacques, *Enquête sur le développement*, Port-au-Prince, 1974
Hostos, E. M. de, *Moral social*, Santo Domingo, D.R., 1968; first published
    in 1888

Hunt, Benjamin S., *Remarks on Hayti as a Place of Settlement for Afric-Americans; and on the Mulatto as a Race for the Tropics*, Philadelphia, 1860

Hurbon, Laënnec, *Dieu dans le vaudou haïtien*, Paris, 1972

Inginac, J. B., *Mémoires*, Kingston, Jamaica, 1843

Inman, S. G., *Trailing the Conquistadors*, New York, 1930

Innocent, Antoine, *Mimola*, Port-au-Prince, 1906

Ipsen, Gunther, *Das Landvolk: ein soziologischer Versuch*, Hamburg, 1933

James, C. L. R., *The Black Jacobins*, New York, 1963; first published in 1938

Janvier, Louis Joseph, *Les affaires d'Haïti, 1883–84*, Paris, 1885

  Les antinationaux, Paris, 1884

  Les constitutions d'Haïti, Paris, 1886

  L'égalité des races, Paris, 1884

  Du gouvernement civile en Haïti, Lille, 1905

  Haïti aux haïtiens, Paris, 1884

  Humble adresse aux électeurs de la commune de Port-au-Prince, Port-au-Prince, 1907

  La république d'Haïti et ses visiteurs, 1840–1882, Paris, 1883

  Le vieux piquet, Paris, 1884

Jean Louis, R. M., *Duvalier: sauveur d'Haïti*, Port-au-Prince, 1965

Jean-Paul, Alex, *Ode pour célébrer le 60ème anniversaire d'un glorieux leader, Dr François Duvalier*, Port-au-Prince, 1967

Jérémie, C., *Haïti indépendant*, Port-au-Prince, 1892

  L'effort, Port-au-Prince, 1905

Johnson, J. J., *Political Change in Latin America: The Emergence of the Middle Sectors*, Stanford, 1958

Jordan, Winthrop D., *White over Black: American Attitudes Towards the Negro*, Chapel Hill, N.C., 1968

Justin, Joseph, *Etude sur les institutions haïtiennes*, Paris, 1894–5

  La question du Môle Saint-Nicolas, Paris, 1891

  Les relations extérieures d'Haïti, Paris, 1895

Kautsky, Karl, *Foundations of Christianity*, New York, 1925; first published in 1908

Kernizan, E., *L'avenir politique*, Port-au-Prince, 1895

Kersuzan, F. M., *Conférence populaire sur le vaudoux*, Port-au-Prince, 1896

Kesteloot, Lilyan, *Les écrivains noirs de langue française: naissance d'une littérature*, Brussels, 1965

  Négritude et situation coloniale, Yaoundé, Cameroun, 1970

Knight, Melvyn M., *Los Americanos en Santo Domingo*, Santo Domingo, D.R., 1939; Spanish translation of *The Americans in Santo Domingo*, New York, 1928

Knox, R., *The Races of Man*, London, 1850

Korngold, R., *Citizen Toussaint: A Biography*, New York, 1944

Kreiger, H. M., *The Aborigines of the Ancient Island of Hispaniola*, Washington D.C., 1929

Laborie, P. J., *The Coffee Planter of Saint Domingo*, London, 1798

Lacroix, P. de, *Mémoires pour servir à l'histoire de la révolution de Saint Domingue*, Paris, 1819

Laleau, Léon, *Musique nègre*, Port-au-Prince, 1931

Lamartinière, Jacqueline, *Le noirisme*, Paris, 1976

Lamour, Saladin, *Réfutation de faits controuvés et d'appréciations contradictoires que contient l'œuvre intitulée: 'Souvenirs historiques de Guy-Joseph Bonnet'*, Port-au-Prince, n.d.

Laroche, Déjoie, *Coup de clairon*, Cap Haïtien, 1908

Laroche, Léon, *Haïti, une page d'histoire*, Paris, 1885

Lataillade, R., *L'urne close*, Port-au-Prince, 1933

Laurent, G., *Toussaint Louverture à travers sa correspondance*, Port-au-Prince, 1953

Le Bon, G., *Les lois psychologiques de l'évolution des peuples*, Paris, 1900

Légal, G., *Dernier vœu de la justice, de l'humanité et de la saine politique*, Paris, 1797

Léger, A. N., *Histoire diplomatique d'Haïti*, Port-au-Prince, 1930

Léger, J. N., *Haïti et la revision*, Paris, 1885

Haïti: son histoire et ses détracteurs, New York, 1907

Légitime, F. D., *L'armée haïtienne: sa nécessité, son rôle*, Paris and Port-au-Prince, 1879

Lenin, V. I., *On the National and Colonial Questions*, Peking, 1967

Léon, Rulx, *Propos d'histoire d'Haïti*, Port-au-Prince, 1974

Lepelletier de Saint-Rémy, M. R., *Saint Domingue*, Paris, 1846

Lerner, D., *The Passing of Traditional Societies*, New York, 1964

Lescouflair, A., *Thomas Madiou*, Port-au-Prince, 1950

Lespinasse, Beauvais, *Histoire des affranchis de Saint-Domingue*, Paris, 1882

Lettre du général Prévost adressée au président d'Hayti, et proclamation au peuple et à l'armée, Port-au-Prince, 1816

Leyburn, James, *The Haitian People*, New Haven, Conn., 1966; first published in 1941

Liberté et indépendance: Royaume d'Hayti, Cap Henry, n.d.

Lieuwen, Edwin, *Arms and Politics in Latin America*, New York, 1961

Generals vs Presidents, Neomilitarism in Latin America, London, 1964

Limonade, Comte de (Julien Prévost), *Le machiavélisme du cabinet français*, Cap Henry, n.d.

Relation des glorieux événements qui ont porté Leurs Majestés Royales sur le Trône d'Hayti, Cap Henry, 1811

Lindsay, Louis, *The Myth of Independence: Middle Class Politics and Non-mobilization in Jamaica*, Kingston, Jamaica, 1975

Linstant (de Pradine), S., *Essai sur les moyens d'extirper les préjugés des blancs contre le couleur des Africains et des sang-mêlés*, Paris, 1841

Nos fils, ou de la néotocratie en Haïti, Paris, 1876

Lipset, S. M., *Political Man*, Garden City, N.Y., 1963

Lipset, S. M., and Solari, A., eds., *Elites in Latin America*, New York, 1967

Logan, R. W., *The Diplomatic Relations of the United States with Haiti, 1776–1891*, Chapel Hill, N.C., 1941

Louis-Charles, Hermann, *La révolution duvaliériste et la compréhension des masses*, Port-au-Prince, 1962

Lubin, Maurice, *L'Afrique dans la poésie haïtienne*, Port-au-Prince, 1965

Luc, Jean, *Structures économiques et lutte nationale populaire en Haiti*, Montreal, 1976

Luperón, G., *Notas autobiográficas y apuntes históricos*, Santiago, D.R., 1939

Lynch, Hollis R., *Edward Wilmot Blyden: Pan-Negro Patriot, 1832–1912*, London, 1967

M. D. L. M. F. Y., *Mémoire sur l'esclavage des nègres*, Paris, 1790

Macaulay, Zachary, *Haïti ou renseignements authentiques sur l'abolition de l'esclavage*, Paris, 1835

McCloy, Shelby T., *The Humanitarian Movement in Eighteenth Century France*, Kentucky, 1957

MacCorckle, W. A., *The Monroe Doctrine in its Relation to the Republic of Haiti*, New York, 1915

Macleod, Duncan, *Slavery, Race and the American Revolution*, Cambridge, 1977

Mackenzie, Charles, *Notes on Haiti, Made during a Residence in that Republic*, London, 1830

Madiou, Thomas, *Histoire d'Haïti*, 3 vols., Port-au-Prince, 1847–8.

Histoire d'Haïti: années 1843–1846, Port-au-Prince, 1904

Magloire, Jean, *Dumarsais Estimé: esquisse de sa vie politique*, Port-au-Prince, 1950

Mandle, Jay R., *The Plantation Economy, Population and Economic Change in Guyana 1838–1960*, Philadelphia, 1973

Manigat, Charles, Moïse, C., and Olivier, E., *Haïti: quel développement?*, Montreal, 1975

Manigat, J. F. T., *Conférence sur le vaudoux*, Cap Haïtien, 1897

Manigat, L. F., *L'Amérique latine au XXe siècle, 1889–1929*, Paris, 1973

Le délicat problème de la critique historique, Port-au-Prince, 1954

Ethnicité, nationalisme et politique: le cas d'Haïti, New York, 1975

Un fait historique: l'avènement à la présidence d'Haïti du général Salomon, Port-au-Prince, 1957

Haiti of the Sixties, Object of International Concern, Washington D.C., 1964

Maîtriser la conjoncture, New York, 1975

La politique agraire du gouvernement d'Alexandre Pétion, Port-au-Prince, 1962

La révolution de 1843, Port-au-Prince, n.d.

Statu quo en Haïti?, Paris, 1971

Manning, W. R. (ed.), *Diplomatic Correspondence of the United States: Inter-American Affairs, 1831–60*, Washington, D.C., 1932

Marcelin, Frédéric, *Autour de deux romans*, Paris, 1903

Choses haïtiennes, Paris, 1896

Le passé, Paris, 1902

Haïti, et l'indemnité française, Paris, 1897

Nos douanes (Haïti), Paris, 1897

Une évolution nécessaire, Paris, 1899

La politique, Paris, 1887

Questions haïtiennes, Paris, 1891

Marcelin, L. J., *Haïti: ses guerres civiles*, Paris, 1892

La lutte pour la vie: lois d'agrégation, de développement et de désagrégation dans l'univers connu; études de sciences physiques et naturelles, morales et politiques, Paris, 1896

Mariátegui, José Carlos, *Siete ensayos de interpretación de la realidad peruana*, Lima, 1971; first published 1928

Marino Hernández, Frank, *La inmigración haitiana*, Santo Domingo, D.R., 1973

Marx, Karl, *The Poverty of Philosophy*, Moscow, n.d.; first published 1847

Marx, K. and Engels, F. *Collected Works*, London, vols. I–VI, 1975–6

    Selected Works, Moscow, 1950

Mathon, Etienne, *Documents pour l'histoire d'Haïti: révolution de 1888–9*, Paris, 1890

M. Frédéric Marcelin, ou l'homme de la petite dime, Port-au-Prince, 1895

Maurel, B., *Cahiers de doléances de la colonie de Saint-Domingue pour les états généraux de 1789*, Paris, 1933

Mazères, F., *De l'utilité des colonies, des causes de la perte de Saint-Domingue et des moyens d'en recouvrer la possession*, Paris, 1814

Melone, Thomas, *De la négritude*, Paris, 1962

Memoire sur le commerce étranger avec les colonies françaises de l'Amérique, Cap Français, 1794

Ménos, Solon, *L'affaire Lüders*, Port-au-Prince, 1898

Métraux, Alfred, *Le vaudou haïtien*, Paris, 1958

Michel, Antoine, *Salomon jeune et l'affaire Louis Tanis*, Port-au-Prince, 1913

Michelet, Jules, *Œuvres complètes*, Paris, 1893–99

Michels, Robert, *Political Parties*, New York, 1962; first published in 1911

Miller, N., and Aya, R. (eds.), *National Liberation*, New York, 1971

Millspaugh, Arthur C., *Haiti under American Control, 1915–1930*. Boston, 1931

Milscent, C. S., *Du régime colonial*, Paris, 1792

Mintz, Sidney W., *Caribbean Transformations*, Chicago, 1974

Moltmann, Jürgen, *The Crucified God*, London, 1974

Montague, Ludwell L., *Haiti and the United States, 1714–1938*, Durham, N.C. 1940

Moral, Paul, *Le paysan haïtien*, Paris, 1961

Moreau de Saint Méry, M. L. E., *Considérations présentés aux vrais amis du repos et du bonheur de la France*, Paris, 1791

    Description topographique, physique, civile, politique et historique de la partie française de l'île Saint-Domingue, Paris, 1958; first published Philadelphia, 1798

Morison, E. E. (ed.), *The Letters of Theodore Roosevelt*, Cambridge, Mass., 1951–4

Mörner, M. (ed.), *Race and Class in Latin America*, New York, 1970

Morpeau, Emmanuel, *Haïti au point de vue critique*, Port-au-Prince, 1915

Morpeau, Moravia, *L'inconstitutionnalité de la convention américano-haïtienne*, Port-au-Prince, 1915

    Pro patria, Port-au-Prince, 1908; first published in 1889

    Simples considérations patriotiques, no publication details, (c. 1906)

Moya Pons, F., *La dominación haitiana, 1822–1844*, Santiago, D.R., 1972

Munro, Dana G., *Intervention and Dollar Diplomacy in the Caribbean, 1900–1921*, Princeton, 1964

    The United States and the Caribbean Republics, 1921–1933, Princeton, 1974

Munroe, Trevor, *The Politics of Constitutional Decolonization: Jamaica, 1944–62*, Kingston, Jamaica, 1972

Nanita, A. R., *Era de Trujillo*, Ciudad Trujillo, D. R., 1955

Nau, Emile, *Histoire des caciques d'Haïti*, Port-au-Prince, 1963, first published in 1854

Réclamations par les affranchis des droits civils et politiques: Ogé et Chavannes, Port-au-Prince, 1840

Needler, Martin C., *Political Development in Latin America: Instability, Violence and Evolutionary Change*, New York, 1968

Needler, Martin C. (ed.), *Political Systems of Latin America*, Princeton, 1964

Nicholls, David, *Economic Dependence and Political Autonomy: The Haitian Experience*, Montreal, 1974

The Pluralist State, London, 1975

Three Varieties of Pluralism, London, 1974

Nolasco, S., *Comentarios a la Historia de J. Price-Mars*, Ciudad Trujillo, D.R., 1955

Notice historique sur les désastres de Saint Domingue, par un officier français détenu par Dessalines, Paris, n.d.

Oakeshott, Michael, *Experience and its Modes*, Cambridge, 1933

Rationalism in Politics, London, 1962

Oppman, Artur, *Na San Domingo*, Warsaw, 1917

Oriol, J., *et al.*, *Le mouvement folklorique en Haïti*, Port-au-Prince, n.d.

Ott, T. O., *The Haitian Revolution, 1789–1804*, Knoxville, 1973

Padmore, George (Malcolm Nurse), *Panafricanism or Communism*, Garden City, N.Y., 1972; first published 1956

Paul, Edmond, *Les causes de nos malheurs*, Kingston, Jamaica, 1882

De l'impôt sur les cafés et lois de commerce intérieur, Kingston, Jamaica, 1876

Haïti au soleil de 1880, Kingston, Jamaica, 1880

Questions politico-économiques, vol. I: *Instruction publique*, Paris, 1861; vol. II: *Formation de la richesse nationale*, Paris, 1863

Paul, Emmanuel C., *Culture, langue, littérature*, Port-au-Prince, 1954

Questions d'histoire, Port-au-Prince, 1955

Payne, D. A., *History of the African Methodist Episcopal Church*, Nashville, Tenn., 1891

Peters, C. E., *Lumière sur l'humfort*, Port-au-Prince, 1941

Petit, Antoine G., *Castro, Debray contre le marxisme-léninisme*, Paris, 1968

Incidences ethniques de la lutte des classes, no publication details

Petras, J., and Zeitlin, M. (eds.), *Latin America: Reform or Revolution?*, Greenwich, Conn., 1967

Le peuple de la république d'Haïti à messieurs Vastey et Limonade, Port-au-Prince, n.d.

Peytraud, L., *L'esclavage aux Antilles françaises avant 1789*, Paris, 1897

Pierre-Charles, Gérard, *L'économie haïtienne et sa voie de développement*, Paris, 1967

Radiografía de una dictadura, Mexico, 1969

Pierre-Charles, Gérard (ed.), *Política y sociología en Haití y la República Dominicana*, Mexico, 1974

Pierre-Charles, Gérard, *et al.*, *Problemas dominico-haitianos y del Caribe*, Mexico, 1973

Pierre-Louis, U. *La révolution duvaliériste*, Port-au-Prince, 1965

Pierre Paul, Antoine, *Henri Christophe*, Port-au-Prince, 1911

Piquion, René, *L'actualité de Paul E. Magloire*, Port-au-Prince, 1950

Manuel de négritude, Port-au-Prince, n.d.

Masques et portraits, Port-au-Prince, 1967
La tactique du double visage, Port-au-Prince, 1968
Plekhanov, G. V., *Fundamental Problems of Marxism*, translated by Julius Katzer, New York, 1969
Ponte Dominguez, F. J., *El delito de francmasonería en Cuba*, Mexico, 1951
Popper, K. R., *Unended Quest*, London, 1976
Pressoir, C. F., *Débats sur le créole et le folklore*, Port-au-Prince, 1947
Pressoir, C., Trouillot, E., and Trouillot, H., *Historiographie d'Haïti*, Mexico, 1953
Prézeau, Chevalier de, *Lettre à ses concitoyens de partie de l'Ouest et du Sud*, Sans Souci, 1815
    Réfutation de la lettre du général français Dauxion Lavaysse, Cap Henry, 1814
Price, Hannibal, *The Haytian Question*, New York, 1891 (written under the pseudonym 'Verax')
Price, Hannibal, *De la réhabilitation de la race noire par la république d'Haïti*, Port-au-Prince, 1900
    Pourquoi cette guerre?, Panama, 1889
Price, Richard (ed.), *Maroon Societies*, Garden City, N.Y., 1973
Price Mars, Jean, *Ainsi parla l'oncle*, New York, 1954; first published 1928
    Une étape de l'évolution haïtienne, Port-au-Prince, 1929
    Jean-Pierre Boyer Bazelais et le drame de Miragoâne, Port-au-Prince, 1948
    Lettre ouverte au Dr. René Piquion: le préjugé de couleur, est-il la question sociale?, Port-au-Prince, 1967
    De la préhistoire d'Afrique à l'histoire d'Haïti, Port-au-Prince, 1962
    La República de Haití y la República Dominicana, Port-au-Prince, 1953; Spanish translation of *La Republique d'Haïti et la République Dominicaine*, Port-au-Prince, 1953
    Vilbrun Guillaume Sam: ce méconnu, Port-au-Prince, 1961
    La vocation de l'élite, Port-au-Prince, 1918
Ragatz, L. J., *The Fall of the Planter Class in the British Caribbean*, New York, 1928
Raimond (also spelled 'Raymond'), Julien, *Observations sur l'origine et les progrès du préjugé des colons blancs contre les hommes de couleur*, Paris, 1791
    Véritable origine des troubles de S. Domingue, Paris, 1792
Rainsford, M., *An Historical Account of the Black Empire of Hayti*, London, 1805
Rameau, Auguste, *Idées et opinions*, Paris, 1894
Raventós de Marin, N., *Haití a horcajadas de su independencia en la visión de Alejo Carpentier*, Ciudad Universitaria, Costa Rica, 1973
Raynal, G. T., *Essai sur l'administration de Saint Domingue*, n.p., 1785
Record, W., *The Negro and the Communist Party*, Chapel Hill, N.C., 1951
Redpath, James (ed.), *A Guide to Hayti*, Boston, 1861
Reiss, H. S. (ed.), *The Political Thought of the German Romantics*, Oxford, 1955
Relation de la fête de S. M. la Reine d'Hayti, Cap Henry, n.d.
Renan, Joseph Ernest, *Réforme intellectuelle et morale de la France*, Paris, 1871
République de France, *Rapport fait par Dumas, commissaire rapporteur de la commission chargée de présenter à l'Assemblée Nationale un plan d'organisation pour Saint-Domingue*, Paris, 1792

République d'Haïti, *Actes du premier congrès national du travail*, Port-au-
 Prince, 1949
Documents diplomatiques, relations extérieures, affaire Maunder, Paris,
 1882
Programme révisé et plan d'études de l'enseignement secondaire, Port-au-
 Prince, 1963
Riou, Roger, *Adieu La Tortue*, Paris, 1974
Ritter, Karl, *Naturhistorische Reise nach der westindischen Insel Hayti*, Stuttgart,
 1836
Robert, Paul, *Catholicisme et vaudou* (CIDOC, Sonedos no. 82), Cuernavaca,
 Mexico, 1971
Difficultés et ressources, Gonaïves, 1952
L'église et la première république noire, Rennes, 1964
Positions et propositions, Gonaïves, 1955
Problèmes et récherches, Port-de-Paix, 1951
Rapport sur la superstition, Port-au-Prince, 1947
Robertson, W. S., *France and Latin American Independence*, Baltimore, 1939
Rocker, Rudolf, *Nationalism and Culture*, Los Angeles, 1937
Rodney, Walter, *The Groundings with my Brothers*, London, 1969
Rodríguez Demorizi, E., *Invasiones haitianas, 1801, 1805 y 1822*, Ciudad
 Trujillo, D. R., 1955
Guerra Dominico-Haitiana, Ciudad Trujillo, D.R., 1944
Rodríguez Demorizi, E. (ed.), *Papeles de Pedro F. Bonó*, Santo Domingo, D.R.,
 1964
Rosiers, Comte de, *Hayti reconnaissante en réponse à un écrit, imprimé à Londres,
 et intitulé: l'Europe châtiée, et l'Afrique vengée*, Sans Souci, 1819
Rotberg, Robert, *Haiti: The Politics of Squalor*, Boston, 1971
Roumain, Jacques, *A propos de la campagne 'anti-superstitieuse'*, Port-au-Prince,
 1942
Analyse schématique 32–34, Port-au-Prince, 1934
Bois d'ébène, Port-au-Prince, 1946
*Contribution à l'étude de l'ethnobotanique précolombienne des Grandes
 Antilles*, Port-au-Prince, 1942
Gouverneurs de la rosée, Paris, 1946; first published 1944
La montagne ensorcelée, Port-au-Prince, 1931
Rousseau, Jean-Jacques, *Julie ou la nouvelle Héloise*, Paris, 1817; first published
 1761
Royaume d'Hayti, *Communication officielle de trois lettres de Catineau Laroche,
 ex-colon, agent de Pétion*, Cap Henry, 1816
Plan général de défense du Royaume, Cap Henry, 1814
Ruiz Tejada, M. R., *Estudio sobre la propiedad inmobiliaria en la República
 Dominicana*, Ciudad Trujillo, R. D., 1952
The Rural Code of Haiti, London, 1827
Ryan, Selwyn D., *Race and Nationalism in Trinidad and Tobago*, Toronto, 1972
Saint-Amand, Edris, *Essai d'explication de 'Dialogue de mes lampes'*, Port-
 au-Prince, 1975; first published 1942
St John, Spencer, *Hayti: or the Black Republic*, London, 1889
Saint-Justé, Tribonien, *La mort de l'illustre M. Anténor Firmin*, Saint Thomas,
 n.d. (c. 1911)

Saint-Louis, R. A., *La présociologie haïtienne*, Ottawa, 1970
Saint-Rémy, Joseph, *Essai sur Henri-Christophe, général haïtien*, Paris, 1839
      Pétion et Haïti, Port-au-Prince and Paris, 1956; first published in Paris, 1854–7
      Vie de Toussaint L'Ouverture, Paris, 1850
Saint-Rémy, Joseph (ed.), *Mémoires du général Toussaint L'Ouverture écrits
      par lui-même*, Paris, 1853
Saint-Simon, Henri de, *L'industrie*, Paris, 1817
Salgado, J. M., *Le culte africain du vaudou et les baptisés en Haïti*, Rome, 1962
Salomon, Louis E. L. F. (Salomon *jeune*), *A l'armée*, Port-au-Prince, 1884
      Procès verbal, Les Cayes, 1845
      Une défense, Brussels, 1861
Sanders (also spelled 'Saunders'), Prince (ed.), *Haytian Papers*, London, 1816
Sannon, H. Pauléus, *et al.*, *Memoir of the Political, Economic and Financial
      Conditions existing in the Republic of Haiti under the American Oc-
      cupation*, n.p., 1921
Saussure, L. de, *Psychologie de la colonisation française*, Paris, 1899
Schaedel, Richard P. (ed.), *Papers of the Conference on Research and Resources
      of Haiti*, New York, 1969
Schmidt, Hans, *The United States Occupation of Haiti, 1915–1934*, New
      Brunswick, N.J., 1971
Schoelcher, Victor, *Colonies étrangères et Haïti*, Paris, 1843
Seeley, J. R., *The Expansion of England*, London, 1902
Séjourné, Georges, *Haïti: un siècle d'indépendance*, Anvers, 1903
      Monsieur le général François-Guillaume Saint-Sérin Manigat, Paris, 1898
Senghor, Léopold S., *et al.*, *Témoignages sur la vie et l'œuvre du Dr. Jean Price
      Mars*, Port-au-Prince, 1956
Simpson, M.C.M. (ed.), *Correspondence and Conversations of de Tocqueville with
      N.W. Senior*, London, 1872
Singham, A. W., *The Hero and the Crowd*, New Haven, Conn., 1968
Singham, A. W. (ed.), *The Commonwealth Caribbean into the Seventies*, Montreal,
      1975
Smith, Adam, *The Nature and Causes of the Wealth of Nations*, in *Works of Adam
      Smith*, vol. III, London, 1811
Smith, Michael G., *The Plural Society in the British West Indies*, Berkeley and
      Los Angeles, 1965
Soriano, G. (ed.), *Símon Bolívar: escritos políticos*, Madrid, 1969
Spiller, G. (ed.), *Papers on Inter-Racial Problems Communicated to the First
      Universal Races Congress*, London, 1911
Stalin, Joseph, *Works*, Moscow, 1953
Stavenhagen, Rudolfo, *Les classes sociales dans les sociétés agraires*, Paris, 1969
Stoddard, T. L., *The French Revolution in San Domingo*, Boston, 1914
      The Rising Tide of Color against White World Supremacy, London, 1920
Stone, Carl, *Electoral Behaviour and Public Opinion in Jamaica*, Kingston, Jamaica,
      1974
Sylvain, Bénito, *Du sort des indigènes dans les colonies d'exploitation*, Paris,
      1901
Sylvain, Georges, *Dix années de lutte pour la liberté, 1915–25*, Port-au-Prince,
      n.d. (c. 1925)

Tannebaum, F., *Slave and Citizen*, New York, 1947

Tarrade, Jean, *Le commerce colonial de la France à la fin de l'ancien régime.*
Evolution du régime de l'exclusif de 1763 à 1789, Paris, 1972

Tempels, Placide, *La philosophie bantoue*, Elizabethville, Belgian Congo, 1945

Thésée, Françoise, *Négotiants bordelais et colons de Saint-Domingue: Liaisons*
d'habitations. La maison Henry Romberg, Bapst et Cie, 1783–1793,
Paris, 1972

Thoby, Armand, *De la capacité presidentielle sous le régime parlementaire*, Port-
au-Prince, n.d.
La question agraire en Haïti, Port-au-Prince, 1888
Questions politiques d'Haïti, Paris, 1883

Thomas, Clive Y., *Dependence and Transformation*, New York and London, 1974

Tocqueville, Alexis de, *L'ancien régime et la révolution*, Paris, 1856

Tonnerre, F. Boisrond, *Mémoires pour servir à l'histoire d'Haïti*, Paris, 1851

Trayer, P., *Etude historique de la condition légale des esclaves dans les colonies*
françaises, Paris, 1887

Troeltsch, E., *Gesammelte Schriften*, Tübingen, 1913
Protestantism and Progress, London, 1912; English translation by W. Mont-
gomery of *Die Bedeutung des Protestantismus für die Entstehung der*
modernen Welt, Leipzig, 1911

Troncoso de la Concha, M. de J., *La ocupación de Santo Domingo por Haití*,
Ciudad Trujillo, D.R., 1942

Turnier, Alain, *Les Etats-Unis et le marché haïtien*, Washington D.C., 1955

Ultime hommage au président Dumarsais Estimé, Port-au-Prince, 1968

'Un Haïtien', *Aux hommes impartiaux*, Paris, 1850

L'Union Nationaliste, *Dépossessions*, Port-au-Prince, 1930

United States, Department of State, *Report of the President's Commission for*
the Study and Review of Conditions in the Republic of Haiti, Washington
D.C., 1930

Vaissière, P. de, *Saint-Domingue: la société et la vie créole sous l'ancien régime*,
Paris, 1909

Vastey, Pompée Valentin, Baron de, *A mes concitoyens*, Cap Henry, 1815
Cri de la conscience, ou réponse à un écrit imprimé au Port au Prince intitulé
'Le peuple de la République d'Hayti à Messieurs Vastey et Limonade',
Cap Henry, 1815
Le cri de la patrie, ou les intérêts de tous haytiens, Cap Henry, n.d.
An Essay on the Causes of the Revolution and Civil Wars of Hayti, Exeter,
1823; English translation of *Essai sur les causes de la révolution et des*
guerres civiles d'Hayti, Sans Souci, 1819
Notes à M. le baron de V. P. Malouet, Cap Henry, 1814
Political Remarks on Some French Works and Newspapers Concerning Hayti,
London, 1818; English translation of *Réflexions politiques*, Sans Souci,
1817
Réflexions adressées aux haytiens de partie de l'Ouest et du Sud, sur l'horrible
assassinat du général Delvare, Cap Henry, n.d.
Réflexions sur une lettre de Mazères, ex-colon français, Cap Henry, 1816
Le système colonial dévoilé, Cap Henry, 1814

Verdier, Jean-Pierre, Cardinal, *et al.*, *L'homme de couleur*, Paris, 1939

Verna, Paul, *Pétion y Bolívar: cuarenta años (1790–1830) de relaciones haitiano-venezolanas y su aporte a la emancipación de Hispanoamerica*, Caracas, 1969

Robert Sutherland, un amigo de Bolívar en Haití, Caracas, 1966

Viatte, A., *Histoire littéraire de l'Amérique française, des origines à 1950*, Quebec and Paris, 1954

Viau, Alfred, *Noirs, mulâtres, blancs, ou rien que du sang*, Ciudad Trujillo, D.R., 1956

Toussaint L'Ouverture, considéré à la lumière de ses actes et attitudes, Ciudad Trujillo, D.R., 1958

Vibert, Paul, *La république d'Haïti: son présent, son avenir économique*, Paris and Nancy, 1895

Vilaire, Etzer, *Années tendres*, Paris, 1907

Vincent, Sténio, *Discours*, Port-au-Prince, 1904

Efforts et résultats, Port-au-Prince, n.d. (c. 1938)

En posant les jalons, Port-au-Prince, 1939–1945

Walch, Jean, *Michel Chevalier: économiste saint-simonien*, Lille, (Service de Reproduction des Thèses), 1974

Wallez, J.-B. G., *Précis historique des négotiations entre la France et Saint-Domingue*, Paris, 1826

Weber, Max, *The Protestant Ethic and the Spirit of Capitalism*, New York, 1958; first published 1904–5

Weinberg, A. K., *Manifest Destiny. A Study of Nationalist Expansionism in American History*, Baltimore, 1935

Wells, Sumner, *Naboth's Vineyard*, New York, 1928

Wilberforce, R. I. and S. (eds.), *The Correspondence of William Wilberforce*, London, 1840

William, J., *Le bouc émissaire*, Port-au-Prince, 1931

Williams, Eric, *History of the People of Trinidad and Tobago*, Port of Spain, Trinidad, 1962

Wimpffen, F. A. Stanislas, Baron de, *A Voyage to Saint-Domingo*, London, 1817: English translation of work first published in French in 1797

Index

CAMBRIDGE LATIN AMERICAN STUDIES

Cambridge Latin American Studies